Desert Lawmen

DESERT LAWMEN

THE HIGH SHERIFFS OF NEW MEXICO AND ARIZONA 1846–1912

LARRY D. BALL

UNIVERSITY OF NEW MEXICO PRESS
ALBUQUERQUE

Library of Congress Cataloging-in-Publication Data

Ball, Larry D., 1940-
Desert lawmen : the high sheriffs of New Mexico and Arizona
1846-1912 / Larry D. Ball.—1st ed.
    p. cm.
Includes bibliographical references and index.
ISBN 0-8263-1346-9 0-8263-1700-6 (pbk.)
    1. Sheriffs—New Mexico—History.
    2. Sheriffs—Arizona—History.
    3. Criminal justice, Administration of—New Mexico—
      History.
    4. Criminal justice, Administration of—Arizona—History.
    I. Title
HV8145.N6B33   1992
363.2'82'09789—dc20   92-7610
                                  CIP

Contents

Maps and Illustrations

MAPS

ILLUSTRATIONS

Preface

On 15 July 1881, a New Mexico sheriff informed the governor that he had shot and killed a notorious badman in Fort Sumner on the previous evening. The confrontation had taken place in the bedroom of rancher Pete Maxwell when the fugitive unwittingly walked in upon the two men. The lawman explained that he had visited Maxwell in search of information about the movements of the outlaw:

> I . . . had just commenced talking to him [Maxwell] about the object of my visit at such an unusual hour, when a man entered the room in stockinged feet, with a pistol in one hand, [and] a knife in the other. He came and placed his hand on the bed just beside me, and [said] in a low whisper [to Maxwell], 'who is it?. . . .
>
> I at once recognized the man. . . . and reached behind me for my pistol, feeling almost certain of receiving a ball from his [weapon] at the moment of doing so, as I felt sure he had now recognized me, but fortunately he drew back from the bed at noticing my movement, and, although he had his pistol pointed at my breast, he delayed to fire, and asked in Spanish, 'Quien es, Quien es?' [Who is it, Who is it?] This gave me time to bring mine [revolver] to bear on him, and the moment I did so I pulled the trigger and he received his death wound. . . .*

In this fleeting moment, Sheriff Patrick Floyd Garrett took the life of outlaw Billy the Kid and created a story central to American

---

*Patrick F. Garrett to W. G. Ritch, Acting Governor, 15 July 1881, quoted in, William A. Keleher, *Violence in Lincoln County, 1869–1881: A New Mexico Item (Albuquerque: University of New Mexico, 1957), pp. 342–43.

frontier history and lore. Not only did this incident launch the lawman's victim, Billy the Kid, into legend, but it also connected his death forever with the officer—a county sheriff—who freed society from this desperado. It is unfortunate that in the corpus of stories that surrounds this duo of outlaw and lawman, the former is accorded a primary place. The sheriff receives secondary, even sinister, recognition for ending the career of a man who participated in the assassination of one sheriff and personally and singlehandedly murdered two deputy sheriffs. Nonetheless, Garrett's deed had the immediate effect of restoring the respectability of the Lincoln County shrievalty and of increasing the stature of this important office across the Southwestern frontier. The word *sheriff* joined that of *marshal* to become synonymous with *lawman*.

In this volume, I make an effort to go behind such incidental activities as Sheriff Garrett's killing of a notorious outlaw and uncover the various and many-sided activities of the hundreds of men who held this county office in New Mexico and Arizona territories. It is my hope that this work will serve as a companion to a previous book, *The United States Marshals of New Mexico and Arizona Territories, 1846–1912* (Albuquerque: University of New Mexico, 1978). Taken together, these two studies provide a clear and balanced picture of frontier peacekeeping. In spite of popular writing about the violent "wild west" aspects of western law enforcement, the role of the county sheriffs in the territories remains only imperfectly known.

In the face of overwhelming data and sources, I selected a few themes to write about in discussing the affairs of the frontier shrievalty. My goal has been to lay the groundwork for a better understanding of this subject so fundamental to the stability of frontier society. It is hoped that the list of sheriffs in the appendices will also be useful. I realize that some objections will be raised to the omission of additional analytical chapters. In the absence of a volume devoted alone to this frontier county lawman, some basic "nuts and bolts" work is necessary. Perhaps this book will prompt others to produce more specialized works.

Larry D. Ball
Jonesboro, Arkansas
March 1991

Acknowledgments

The author desires to recognize the many acts of kindness that made this book possible.

Among the institutions that provided assistance were the National Archives and the Library of Congress, Washington, D.C.; the Special Collections Department, Zimmerman Library, University of New Mexico Albuquerque; the Museum of New Mexico Historical Library and the State Library and Archives, Santa Fe; the Rio Grande Collection and the Rare Books Department, New Mexico State University, Las Cruces; the Chaves County Historical Society, Roswell; the Arizona Historical Society and the Special Collections Department, University of Arizona, Tucson; the Special Collections Department and the Arizona Historical Foundation, in the Hayden Library, Arizona State University, Tempe; the Phoenix Public Library; the Special Collections Department, Northern Arizona University, Flagstaff; the Sharlot Hall Museum, Prescott; the Nita Stewart Haley Library, Midland, Texas; the Special Collections Department, University of Texas at El Paso; the El Paso Public Library; and the Indiana Historical Society, Indianapolis.

Many individuals have provided very valuable aid. John P. and Cheryl Wilson of Las Cruces, New Mexico, deserve special mention. Not only did the hospitality of their home ease the tedium of long research stints but their knowledge of people and sources for this book was very valuable. Jack took time away from his personal work to make available copies of numerous documents that otherwise would have been missed, and he graciously guided this writer on a firsthand tour of historic Lincoln, New Mexico. As rare book librarian at New Mexico State University, Cheryl's knowledge of the literature of the Southwest was especially informative. Many other persons also deserve recognition. They include, Bruce Dinges, editor of the *Journal of Arizona History*, Blaise Gagliano, archivist (retired) of the Arizona State Library and Archives; Bonnie Greer of Flagstaff; Melba M. McCaskill, a descendant of Deputy Sheriff William Voris of Gila County, Arizona; and Barbara J. Judge, a member of the Maricopa County Sheriff's Office, in Phoenix. John Grassham, now of the Southwest Research Institute at the University of New Mexico, provided translations of records pertaining to the earliest Taos County sheriffs. Dennis Rousey, a colleague in the Department of History, Arkansas State University, generously provided data about lawmen gleaned from New Mexico territorial censuses.

Some material from this book appeared in the following journals: "Frontier Sheriffs at Work," *Journal of Arizona History* 27 (Autumn 1986): 283–96; "The Frontier Sheriff's Role in Law and Order," *Western Legal History* 4 (Winter/Spring 1991): 13–25.

My thanks also go to the staff of the Dean B. Ellis Library, Arkansas State University, for many courtesies over the years. Margaret Daniels and her assistants in the interlibrary loan department demonstrated much patience and the willingness to go to the extra step to obtain hard-to-find works that facilitated my research.

And finally, my appreciation goes out to Ruth, my wife, and Dur, my son. Ruth not only read and reread chapters but patiently shared her dining room table with piles of notes for months on end. Dur, who is a doctoral candidate at the University of New Mexico, made many useful suggestions and provided encouragement when this task appeared beyond fulfillment. To the many persons whose names I have failed to mention, thanks to you all.

Desert Lawmen

1

The Origins of
the Sheriff's Office
in New Mexico
and Arizona Territories

 The office of sheriff originated in ninth-century Anglo-Saxon England as a representative of the Crown in local government. The sheriff (shire-reeve) exercised many duties, including peacekeeping, holding court, collecting taxes, and commanding the militia. For some time under the Norman kings of the eleventh and twelfth centuries, the sheriff exercised extraordinary powers as a viceroy of the king. In subsequent centuries, the Crown and Parliament removed the power to preside over courts, but the sheriff continued to exercise law enforcement functions and generally represented the gentry class. When the English began to colonize the east coast of North America in the seventeenth century, the office of sheriff became a standard feature of the colonial judiciary. These colonial sheriffs—also from the wealthier class—served the process of county court and district courts, maintained the peace, kept the jail, and collected taxes. This latter task was not strictly a chore of the sheriff, but an ex officio duty. When the founders of the American Revolutionary era set the judiciary of the American Republic in motion in the late eighteenth century, the sheriff remained an essential component. As the frontiersmen took up lands in the West, this county lawman became a permanent fixture. Each new territory, beginning with the Northwest Territory in 1787, legislated this law enforcement post into existence and provided basic rules of operation.[1]

Just as the military victory of the American Revolutionaries over the British Empire paved the way for the installation of the shrievalty in the Mississippi Valley, the march of the victorious Army of the West made possible the planting of this ancient county office in the Mexican Cession in 1846. When General Stephen Watts Kearny occupied Santa Fe in August of that year, he quickly established a temporary provisional government. Kearny appointed a governor—Charles Bent—three district judges, and other officials at the territorial level. Bent was the recognized leader of "The American Party," a colony of Missouri merchants who had long engaged in trade with this Mexican province. Kearny proclaimed a code of laws on 22 September. Although a composite of the laws of Missouri, Texas, and the Republic of Mexico, this code included a proviso for sheriffs and other local officials common to Anglo-American county government. In turn, Governor Bent set this new regime in motion and made the first appointments.[2]

Kearny divided his new conquest into three judicial circuits (districts): northern, central, and southeastern. A superior court served each district. Kearny divided the settled portion of New Mexico into counties, which became the homes of the first sheriffs. These counties, the boundaries of which were not clearly known, were clustered along the upper Rio Grande. Valencia and Bernalillo counties made up the Southeastern Circuit; Santa Ana, Santa Fe, and San Miguel, the Central; and Rio Arriba and Taos, the Northern. Of these seven counties in 1846, Valencia presented the first incumbent with the greatest difficulty. This county had no clear southern boundary and the eastern and western borders trailed off into the wastelands.[3]

The first New Mexico sheriffs performed the tasks long associated with their office. They served warrants, subpoenas, and other writs—collectively called "process"—of probate and district courts within their counties. As the Kearny Code declared, the sheriffs served "all process issued" to them. In addition, they conserved the peace by suppressing "assaults and batteries." The code charged them with "the custody, rule . . . and charge of the jail" within their counties. Should the sheriffs encounter forces beyond their control, they were empowered to summon the *posse comitatus,* or Power of the County, which consisted of all able-bodied adult males in their counties. The Kearny Code also followed tradition by assigning the sheriff the duty of tax collector.[4]

The Kearny Code prescribed only minimal rules for the conduct of the shrievalty. The sheriff served a two-year term. He filed two bonds, one for the shrievalty and the other as tax collector. Bonding was standard procedure for all officials who collected or disbursed public monies. As the Kearny Code read, the bonds insured "the faithful discharge of his duties." In 1847 Donaciano Vigil, acting governor, drafted instructions for sheriffs. These guidelines provided that the sheriffs receive a $200 annual salary plus a percentage

Map 1. New Mexico County Boundaries, 1850

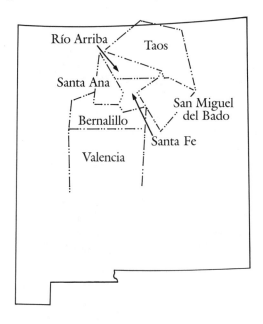

Source: Warren A. Back and Ynez D. Haase, *Historical Atlas of New Mexico* (Norman: University of Oklahoma Press, 1969), no. 41

of fees collected. The county was required to provide office space. Vigil also created the position of county auditor to examine the accounts of the sheriffs and other public servants. These written instructions went into effect on 1 January 1848. In an ironic turn of events, Donaciano Vigil, a person of Spanish heritage, found himself facing the task of defining a law enforcement position derived from another culture.[5]

Governor Charles Bent appointed the first county lawmen. Bent, who had a longtime association with this former Mexican province, selected James Lawrence Hubbell as sheriff of Valencia County. Hubbell arrived in this region in 1844 and married into the prominent Gutierrez family. He joined the American Army during the war with Mexico and served briefly as collector of customs at Ponge's Station, present-day El Paso, Texas. Don Santiago, as the local residents called Hubbell, became prominent in the Santa Fe Trade and, in the 1850s, in freighting across the Southwest. Don Santiago sired a large family. Two of his sons later became noted territorial sheriffs. Don Santiago Hubbell served two years as Valencia County sheriff, from September 1846 to September 1848, when he became probate judge.[6]

Stephen Louis Lee became first sheriff of Taos County in December 1846. In 1828, when sixteen years of age, he settled in this northern trading community to represent his family's mercantile house, then headquartered in St. Louis, Missouri. He became a naturalized Mexican citizen and married a Taoseña. Like his colleague in the Valencia County shrievalty, Stephen Lee hispanicized his name to Don Estevan. While Lee attempted to become an accepted member of the community, he earned a reputation in business circles as a fractious individual. Among the persons with whom Lee quarreled was another Taos merchant, Charles Bent. As the new governor of New Mexico, Bent ignored these strained relations and issued the sheriff's commission to Stephen Lee. The reason for Bent's decision is unclear. Perhaps, the new executive bowed to the influence of the Lee family in the Santa Fe Trade. The fact that Lee was a member of that small group of Americans in New Mexico—merchants, miners, and fur trappers—upon whom the new Anglo regime relied for support might account for Governor Bent's decision.[7]

Francis (Frank) Redman received the appointment as sheriff of Santa Fe County, although the date is not clear. However, he served the process of the first session of court in the capital, in December 1846. Redman's background is also obscure, although he engaged in the Santa Fe Trade. Redman later participated in freighting ventures between Santa Fe and Utah.[8]

Governor Bent filled the remaining shrievalties with Hispanos. These Spanish-speaking inhabitants, perhaps some 60,000 persons, presented the conquerors with a dilemma. While many of the wealthy, landed aristocracy were well educated and fully capable of serving in the new territorial government, Bent had some reason to doubt their loyalty. In December 1846, the governor began to receive reports of conspiracies against the American regime. However, Bent had longtime associations with many New Mexicans and had sufficient confidence in some to risk appointing them to the shrievalty, as well as other offices. Among the Hispanos to receive sheriff's badges were Salvador Lopez in Rio Arriba County, Romualdo Archiveques in Santa Ana, Santiago Trujillo in San Miguel, and Antonio Aragon in Bernalillo. Not much is known about these appointees, although the 1850 census listed Antonio Aragon as forty-six years of age, unmarried, with property worth $1,200. Salvador Lopez, age forty, farmed and possessed property valued at $460.[9]

The Kearny Code retained many aspects of the preceding regime. The Mexican judiciary had consisted of two layers, federal and state, with supreme, circuit, and district courts. However, many persons were exempted from the jurisdiction of these tribunals. For instance, military personnel and Catholic Church officials were subject to their own codes. Litigation was very expensive and only the well-to-do had access to higher courts. Appeals were very difficult to implement and were directed to distant Chihuahua. The people preferred *arbitratos,* or arbitration by third parties. Nuevo Mexico was divided into three districts, with a prefect over each. *Alcaldes mayores* administered *partidos,* lesser subdivisions. *Alcaldes ordinarios* served as judges in smaller (precinct) areas. These latter officials were also called *juez de paz,* or justices of the peace. The Americans did not introduce this title. The enforcement arm of these Mexican courts included *alguacils,* or bailiffs. *The alguacil mayor* (also called *alguacil primero*) served the higher alcalde courts (*el consejos*). The *soto-alguacil* (lower bailiff) served the minor courts. The *baton de juste,* a long wooden staff, served as a symbol of judicial authority. These officials often combined judicial and law enforcement duties, a practice that Americans regarded as ultimately corrupting and very objectionable.[10]

American visitors in the early 1840s were surprised at the power of Mexican alcaldes. The common people—*los pobres,* the poor ones, or peons—showed them great deference. The "fiat of the Alcalde is law," said one observer. The procedures of this judge were somewhat mystifying. The alcalde kept few written records, ignored the jury system (for the most part), maintained few jails, and inflicted corporal punishment liberally. Since the American traveler failed to see the entire native judicial system at work, he spoke very contemptuously of his host's system of justice. Instead, the conquerors introduced their more costly, litigious system. While the Mexican Cession was by no means court-free, the inhabitants hardly possessed the money or the inclination to settle all disputes in court.[11]

In spite of these differences, the American and Mexican judicial systems resembled each other in some ways. These similarities enabled General Kearny to graft some of the American judicial apparatus onto the native system, which allowed the Hispanic population to better accommodate these foreign impositions. Kearny's three judicial circuits were the three districts of the Mexican province, and his seven counties were identical to the seven *partidos* of the former regime. He even retained the prefect, the officer in charge of the district, and the alcalde, although with lesser powers. Since the American and Mexican judicial systems possessed similarities, the Hispanos concluded that some law enforcement positions were interchangeable. In their adaptation to this foreign system, the *alcalde ordinario* became the American justice of the peace, the *soto-alguacil* became the constable, and the *alguacil mayor* became the sheriff. In counties where the Hispanos predominated, this latter title remained current into this century. The Americans resigned themselves to this predilection for the more familiar Mexican nomenclature.[12]

Of these Mexican holdovers, the prefect remained very important to the sheriffs. The prefect supervised roads and *acequias* (irrigation canals). He presided over the county probate court in Kearny's Code and performed many other functions of county supervisor. As Governor Abraham Rencher observed a few years later, this post was "among the most sacred and important" and affected "the interests both of the living and the dead." The sheriff served the process of the prefect (probate) court, but otherwise was technically independent of this official. Since considerations of class dominated Hispanic society, the occupant of the prefect's office often ranked higher socially than the sheriff. This latter official probably bowed to the former's whims.[13]

Within each county, the Americans established the traditional precinct system with its justices of the peace and constables. Precincts or townships were the building blocks of the county. While Kearny used the titles of alcalde and justice of the peace interchangeably, he curtailed the powers of this once powerful Mexican office. Yet, the justice of the peace remained the most influential official in the precinct, and this office soon became the subject of much lore and legend. The justice of the peace presided over the justice court. While this minor bench tried only lesser cases, the "judge" wielded considerable influence. He was empowered to try minor cases, usually involving $100 or less. He held hearings to determine if a crime had been committed and bound the accused person over to action of the next grand jury at the district court. The justice of the peace, or alcalde, continued to wield much influence among the Hispanos, who remembered the prestige of this official under the Mexican regime. The Kearny Code authorized only four justices of the peace in a county, although many more precincts existed in each unit of government. A constable served the process of the justice of the peace court, although a sheriff could serve this minor bench as well. The constable was the precinct counterpart of the county sheriff and held powers equal to the sheriff, but only within his narrower jurisdiction. The constable often held a concurrent commission of deputy sheriff, if the chief county lawman had confidence in this lesser officer.[14]

The sheriff earned an income primarily from fees rather than salary. This was the usual method of payment of public officials in the Anglo-American tradition. The Kearny Code prescribed a fee for each service of the sheriff. A few examples are included in this itemized list:

Serving a writ of execution in a criminal case (warrant)	$ 1.00
Levying an execution in a civil case (writ of attachment)	1.00
Summoning a jury (serving a venire)	.50
Summoning witnesses (each)	.50
Attendance at court (daily)	1.50
Calling each witness (in court)	.05
Summoning the grand jury	5.00
Committing a prisoner to jail	1.00
Furnishing a prisoner with board (daily)	.25
Execution of death warrant (hanging)	15.00
Travel (per mile)	.05

This fee bill also authorized "reasonable" expenses for services not specified. The assembly also passed special relief laws for out-of-the-ordinary expenses of sheriffs. The lawman's workload was seasonal to some degree. He and his staff worked intensely around the spring and fall sessions of district court. Tax collection duties were also seasonal. Jail duty and peacekeeping took place the year round.[15]

Some notions about the conditions in which these pioneer sheriffs labored can be gathered from the 1850 census, which enumerated 61,525 persons in New Mexico. Some 58,415 of these persons were natives. The Indians—not counted—were estimated at an additional 80,000.

County	Population	Square Miles
Bernalillo	7,749	2,089
Rio Arriba	10,667	26,237
San Miguel	7,070	10,895
Santa Ana	4,644	1,961
Santa Fe	7,699	1,961
Socorro	5,706	(part of Valencia)
Taos	9,507	30,371
Valencia	14,189	125,508

Socorro County had just recently been added to the original seven units of local government. While these population statistics do not appear especially burdensome, the sheriffs were often constrained to travel great distances to enforce the laws.[16]

These first county sheriffs enforced the laws in a provisional military government that pleased few persons. Its four-year lifespan provoked outcries of military despotism and usurpation of civil law. In October 1847, a Santa Fe County grand jury complained about the "illy" defined limits of military and civil authorities, while the local newspaper complained that the men in uniform "doubted and denied" the jurisdiction of the superior courts. Congress expressed concern about this makeshift government, but for reasons other than the objections of the handful of Americans in New Mexico. The national lawmakers concluded that General Kearny lacked the power to create a republican government. Furthermore, the lands of the Mexican Cession did not become American territory until the conclusion of the Treaty of Guadalupe Hidalgo in 1848. Only then could the United States Government introduce its republican institutions. In recognition of this nettlesome problem, Congress abolished some civilian posts in New Mexico in February 1848, including the United States marshal and district attorney. The military commander also assumed the duties of civilian governor. The lesser civilian positions, including the sheriff, continued to function. Apparently Congress did not regard minor positions as an embarrassment, and local government was essential to stability.[17]

In a very real sense, the sheriff's office of New Mexico (and Arizona) began on 9 September 1850, when Congress created the Territory of New Mexico. A presidential appointee stepped into the governor's office and instituted a civilian regime. The fears of the constitutionalists about the legality of the provisional government were allayed. This territorial law imposed the full complement of American officials at all levels of government, and the native population experienced the full weight of this foreign regime for the first time. At the county level, Congress provided for a sheriff and other officials common to the Anglo-American tradition. While some of Kearny's accommodation to Mexican institutions continued, this new territorial government desired to acclimate the Hispanos more quickly to American institutions and to achieve statehood as soon as possible. Some new arrivals in the territory believed this coveted status in the Union would come very soon, for New Mexico already possessed the necessary 60,000 settled population.[18]

James S. Calhoun, who became the first governor under the new civilian government, made a clean break with the preceding military regime. In February 1851, he removed some incumbent public servants and appointed new ones. To officials not removed, Calhoun issued new commissions. He applied this policy to the sheriffs as well. These new appointees served only to September, when general elections were held for probate judges (who continued as prefects), sheriffs, constables and justices of the peace. Sheriffs and probate judges would serve two-year terms, while the latter two officials served one-year terms.[19]

The first sessions of the new assembly in 1851 and 1852 began to reshape the counties of New Mexico Territory and thus influenced the duties of the future sheriffs. Under military government, counties were clustered along the Rio Grande, while vast arid stretches to the east and west of the river were unorganized. Native New Mexicans claimed these regions, but the Spanish and Mexican governments had failed to adequately occupy them. Texas also claimed all lands to the east bank of the Rio Grande, while much of the western expanse to the Colorado River and Sierra Madre Mountains remained effectively the domain of the Indians. The Lone Star State went so far as to send a delegation, including a sheriff, to take possession of eastern New Mexico and form a new county in December 1848. However, Congress reduced the Texas claim in 1850 and accorded New Mexico Territory a new boundary on the edge of the grassland called the Llano Estacado (Staked Plain). The new Territory of New Mexico sprawled across the Southwest from the western border of Texas to the Colorado River and beyond.[20]

The new government briefly retained the counties of General Kearny in 1850–51, the exception being a new county—Socorro—carved from southern Valencia County. The date of creation is also uncertain, but it may have been in the making under the provisional government. The border with the Republic of Mexico had been troublesome since the conquest in 1846. Don Santiago Hubbell, the first sheriff of Valencia County, squabbled with the Mexican alcalde in Mesilla, who insisted that this town was within his nation's borders. A county seat with accompanying sheriff near this nettlesome problem could prove useful. On 21 April 1851, Governor Calhoun appointed the first officers for Socorro County, among them Esquipula Vigil as sheriff.[21]

On 6 January 1852, lawmakers met in Santa Fe to draw up new county boundaries and incorporate the land acquired under the

Compromise of 1850. This revision resulted in nine counties, although the results were not very satisfactory. Some counties were giant, elongated monstrosities that sprawled across the territory. Three counties—Taos, Santa Fe, and San Miguel—remained more modest in size. Sheriffs of these new creations must have breathed sighs of relief. But Rio Arriba, Santa Ana, and Bernalillo counties stretched from the Rio Grande to the Sierra Madre in present-day California. Two southern counties—Valencia and Socorro—extended farther, some 800 miles from Texas to the Colorado River. The responsibility for such giants must have daunted the early sheriffs, as mining camps began to spring up on the Colorado River. These lawmakers with spread-eagle vision also created the new county of Doña Ana in the south. Doña Ana became the southernmost unit of local government. Colonel Edwin V. Sumner, acting for an absent Governor Calhoun, issued a proclamation for the election of a sheriff and three justices of the peace to take place on 25 July 1852. John Jones became the first sheriff of Doña Ana County. While Jones's county was smaller than his northern neighbors' responsibilities, he inherited jurisdictional quarrels with Mexico. (This Jones should not be confused with John G. Jones, who held the shrievalty of Santa Fe County.)[22]

The territorial assembly set about redefining the boundaries of the judicial districts, which also directly affected the work of the sheriffs. In June 1851, the first legislative session numbered the judicial districts: First, Santa Fe, San Miguel, and Santa Ana counties; Second, Bernalillo, Valencia, and any new counties added in the south; Third, Taos and Rio Arriba. In 1860, the lawmakers rearranged the judicial districts, so that First included Santa Fe, Santa Ana, San Miguel, Mora, Taos, and Rio Arriba. The Second District contained the counties of Bernalillo, Valencia, and Socorro, while Doña Ana County (created in 1852) and its progeny formed the Third District.[23]

Even as the new Doña Ana County sheriff adjusted to his duties, Congress was in the process of enlarging his responsibilities. In 1853, the United States purchased a vast, 20,000 square mile tract on the southern border of Doña Ana County. This Gadsden Purchase included the Gila River Valley in the far west and made Doña Ana equal in size, and perhaps larger, than Socorro County. Mexico transferred this new acquisition in increments. Sheriff Samuel G. Bean, who had succeeded John Jones, attended the formal transfer of the eastern segment in 1854. The more westerly portion, called Arizona, was added two years later. Bean recalled the awesomeness of his new responsibility. "My jurisdiction was not as large as the Czar of Russia . . . ," he remarked humorously, but "it extended from Texas to California," roughly 300 by 800 miles.[24]

The remote "Arizona" section of Doña Ana County often perplexed Sheriff Bean. Tucson and Tubac, in the San Pedro Valley, lay 300 miles to the west of Mesilla, the county seat and Bean's place of residence. Fort Buchanan and a few mining companies provided the only order. At the western tip of Doña Ana County lay Arizona City (later Yuma), Gila City, and a few prospecting centers up the Colorado River. In 1859, the army established Fort Mohave to protect these advanced elements. As late as 1860, the census registered only 2,000 sedentary persons in this distant region. Samuel Bean noted that the vast majority of his citizen body were nomadic. He had 10,000 more Indians "in my county than I had [settled] constituents." To add to his troubles, desperadoes and other troublemakers began to swarm into Doña Ana County. In Bean's words, the Gadsden Purchase "had a charm about it" for outlaws.[25]

The chief lawman of this exaggerated county was representative of the handful of Americans in New Mexico in the 1850s. Born about 1819, Samuel G. Bean hailed from Kentucky. His father, Peter Bean, raised a large family but failed to prosper, and the family relocated to Carthage, Missouri. The sons soon earned roughneck, even lawless, reputations. O. W. Williams, who resided in Carthage at this time and renewed an acquaintance with Samuel, and brother Roy Bean, in New Mexico, recalled that two Bean brothers served prison terms in Missouri for theft. At least three Bean brothers—Samuel, Roy, and Joshua—trekked westward on the Santa Fe Trail before the Mexican War. While Joshua became somewhat prominent in California, Roy and Samuel settled briefly in Chihuahua after the war with Mexico. Roy reportedly killed a citizen of this sister republic and fled for his life. In March 1849, Samuel married Petra, daughter of the infamous scalphunter James (Santiago) Kirker, and opened a hotel and saloon in Las Cruces. He later owned a trading firm in Mesilla and—with brother Roy— opened a branch in the mining camp of Pinos Altos (near present-day Silver City, New Mexico). Samuel Cozzens, who was acquainted with Samuel Bean at this time, described the sheriff as a

large, powerfully-built man, about forty years old; his long black hair hung low upon his broad and massive shoulders; a full, brown beard, keen, black eyes, and open, generous countenance, were the distinguishing characteristics of his features. . . ."

Samuel Bean's biographer regards him as "perhaps the brightest of the Bean brothers," but admits that even this able sheriff could not police all of Doña Ana County. Evildoers plied their lawless trades in distant regions without interference. Bean sometimes neglected to even carry a weapon. Although election records are incomplete for Doña Ana County, it appears that Bean was elected sheriff on 4 September 1854. He later claimed to have served for eight years, or until the outbreak of the Civil War, but this cannot be verified.[26]

The settlements that made up Doña Ana County complained regularly about the absence of consideration in distant Santa Fe. The dreadful desert—the Jornado del Muerto (Journey of Death)—separated these southern hamlets from the north. Communications with the territorial capital were fitful and unreliable. The inhabitants of "Arizona" felt even more isolated and unprotected. The *Arizonian,* the first newspaper in that remote region, regularly reminded the territorial officials of the need for judicial protection. "A couple of deputy sheriffs, two deputy U.S. marshals, and a constable for each settlement," said this journal in 1857, would be helpful. These distant Doña Anans desired a separate "Fourth" judicial district, a demand that only the United States Congress could grant. The national lawmakers considered and refused this request. As a half-way measure, the New Mexico Assembly authorized a probate judge, constables, and justices of the peace in 1856, shortly after the Mexican army evacuated Tucson and Tubac. Sheriff Samuel Bean appointed a deputy, George Matterson, who became the first representative of the shrievalty in Arizona. These efforts to bring the far western precincts into the fold of New Mexico Territory were half-hearted, and the Arizonans began to agitate for separate territorial status. This separatist movement soon engulfed all of Doña Ana County. By 1860 the southern region refused to recognize the authority of Santa Fe. When these angry inhabitants created an extralegal Territory of Arizona, Samuel G. Bean accepted the position of marshal of this new creation. His term as sheriff had apparently ended in the previous September. Although the New Mexico assembly created an Arizona County from western Doña Ana, this lame effort failed to satisfy the southerners.[27]

The Civil War intervened to prevent the new county from becoming effectual and temporarily disrupted the judicial districts in the upper Rio Grande Valley of New Mexico. Colonel John R. Baylor's Rebel army, which consisted of Texans—traditional enemies of the New Mexicans—occupied Doña Ana County in the summer of 1861. On 1 August 1861, Baylor proclaimed a Confederate Territory of Arizona, to include all of Doña Ana County to the Colorado River. On the next day, this Rebel officer appointed officials. John A. Roberts became sheriff. Baylor divided the new territory into four counties and granted "Arizona" a separate judicial district, something the isolated pioneers had long demanded. However, these Confederate creations did not endure long enough to become effective. General H. H. Sibley, who succeeded Baylor, singled out the sheriffs for attention as he marched upriver. He seized the tax receipts of Sheriff and Collector Lorenzo Montano in Albuquerque and presumably did the same in other counties. As the invader approached Santa Fe, Kirby Benedict, Unionist judge, administered the loyalty oath to all sheriffs, except in Doña Ana County. In March 1862, the Confederates occupied the territorial capital, and Benedict was forced to admit to his superior in Washington that "My judicial district [the First] . . . was overrun by Texans." This alien regime was shortlived and beat a hasty retreat in the following month.[28]

The Rebel retreat did not remove the Confederate menace completely. Colonel E. R. S. Canby, Union commander in New Mexico, suspended the writ of habeas corpus. General James Henry Carleton, successor to Canby in 1862, proclaimed martial law outright. Military commissions usurped many judicial functions and tried civilians, while provost marshals carried out some duties formerly performed by sheriffs and the United States marshal. As Carleton's conquering army—the California Column—entered Arizona from the West Coast, he separated this region from New Mexico. Carleton drew Arizona a new eastern boundary which ran north-south (in the vicinity of the present border), rather than adhere to the Confederacy's east-west line. Carleton gave a military commission absolute judicial powers in this area, which he found devoid of any civil lawmen. The general responded to Rebel confiscations with much more thorough sequestrations of the property of Confederates and suspected sympathizers. Among his victims in southern New Mexico was Samuel G. Bean, former sheriff and Confederate.[29]

Doña Ana County presented more difficult problems for both military and civilian authorities on the Union side. When Carleton arrived in Mesilla, according to the *Santa Fe Weekly Gazette,* "there were no civil officers who recognized the . . . United States." Indeed, Acting Governor W. F. M. Arny informed the Secretary of State in May 1863 that these fractious inhabitants of the south had refused to elect officers under New Mexico law since 1859. The *Gazette* charged that the Doña Ana County sheriff-collectors had failed to turn in revenues to Santa Fe officials since April of the previous year. Arny added that they were not all Rebels or sympathizers; many merely desired a separate territory under Union sponsorship. However, General Carleton took no chances and imposed martial law "in all the rigors of the system," said one journalist. On 29 January 1863, the New Mexico Assembly restored the two southernmost counties, Doña Ana and Arizona. (The latter county had never become operative.) Governor Arny decided not to hold elections in Arizona County since Congress was then considering a bill to form a separate territory. As sheriff of the rejuvenated Doña Ana County, Arny appointed Frederick Beckner (Burckner), a loyal Unionist. Beckner also carried a deputy United States marshal's badge. Although the new sheriff's relations with the military governor were not always congenial, the office of county lawman became permanent and continuous for the remainder of the territorial era. Its status, as well as that of Doña Ana County in general, had been uncertain since the American conquest in 1846. General Carleton lifted martial law throughout New Mexico on 4 July 1865. The sheriff of Doña Ana County, as well as his colleagues in all the counties, suddenly emerged from the restrictions of the four-year military emergency.[30]

The creation of Arizona Territory on 20 February 1863 represented a giant step forward in the delivery of county and federal law enforcement to the remote precincts formerly a part of New Mexico. When new shrievalties were set up in Arizona, they divested their counterparts in the Rio Grande Valley of this impossible responsibility. Those giant and improbable counties created in 1852 were suddenly lopped off at 109 degrees of latitude. After a brief ceremony of creation at Navajo Springs, in late 1863, Governor John C. Goodwin made a more permanent capital at Prescott in January of the following year. He divided the territory into three judicial districts and appointed a sheriff and other officials for each. To assign a sheriff to a judicial district rather than a county was perhaps not unprecedented, but very unusual. For the First Judicial District (seat at Tucson), Goodwin appointed Hill Barry DeArmitt on 9 April 1864; Isaac C. Bradshaw for the Second (Yuma) on 1 June; and Van Ness C. Smith for the Third District (Prescott) on 15 June.[31]

In September 1864, the first session of the Arizona Assembly gathered in Prescott. While the lawmakers retained the three judicial districts, they created four new counties and assigned the sheriffs to them. Very little boundary shuffling was required. Pima

Map 2. Judicial Districts of Arizona, 1864

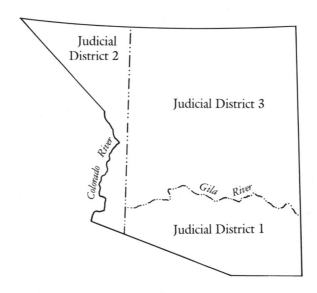

Source: Henry P. Walker and Don Bufkin, *Historical Atlas of Arizona*
(Norman: University of Oklahoma Press, 1979), no. 30

County became synonymous with the First Judicial District, Yava-pai County with the Third, while Yuma and Mohave counties com-prised the Second Judicial District. Governor Goodwin chose Milton G. Moore as the first sheriff of Mohave on 15 December 1864. Very little is known about the first four chief county lawmen of Arizona, although they were probably associated with mining. Van Ness Smith had served as recorder for the extralegal mining dis-trict of Yavapai which preceded the territorial government.[32]

Although officials held high hopes for the future of Arizona and New Mexico in the postwar years, they were generally disappointed. Economic and population growth was sluggish. Statehood was far off. However, some salutary changes took place at the local level, alterations that impinged directly upon the sheriffs. In an address to the New Mexico Assembly in December 1871, Governor Marsh Giddings observed that the time had come to create boards of county commissioners to govern each county. This reform would remove the burden of managing the counties from the probate judges (prefects). While Giddings did not elaborate, the Americans resented this one-man local government as a vestige of the Mexican regime. The territorial lawmakers did not comply with Giddings's request until 1876, some time after his departure from the governorship. The new boards consisted of three persons, which allowed for much more democracy in local government. The probate judge continued to perform judicial duties. While the effects of this change upon the sheriffs is unclear, it probably resulted in the elevation of the chief lawman's position. Whereas the prefects were involved in many day-to-day chores for the counties, the new boards met only infrequently to examine the conduct of officials and make policy. The public tended to look to the sheriffs as the officials who got things done.[33]

While the Anglos desired to remove all reminders of previous governments from New Mexico, the Hispanos continued to dominate many counties and to exercise much influence in the capital. The sheriff's office was no exception. Of 153 men who held this office from 1846 through 1880, 113 were Hispanos. Only in recently created Grant and Colfax Counties did Anglos monopolize the office. This exercise of power nettled new arrivals. In November 1888, an Arizonan expressed disgust that Spanish prevailed in New Mexico courts even though English was the official language. Not only did courts open and close in Spanish but, even more disconcerting, Anglos held office in most counties only at the "suffrance of Mexicans." Even voting was done in this foreign language—*boleto* was used for ballot—and successful Anglo candidates changed their names to the Spanish equivalent in order to win coveted votes. Perhaps this unknown observer had been a victim of this peculiar situation in New Mexico. One scholar has noted that the Anglos quickly learned to circumvent some of this native control. Recent immigrants often created new counties on the periphery of Hispanic areas, in order to be free to control local government.[34]

The Hispanos exercised no such control in Arizona, which, except for Indians, contained only a few settlers clustered in the Gila and Colorado Valleys. The modest intrusion of outsiders after 1846 consisted largely of American miners and, after the Civil War, some ex-Confederates. Of the thirty-eight men who occupied the sheriff's office through 1880, only one was a Hispano. Governor John C. Fremont appointed Alejandro Peralta as the first sheriff of newly created Apache County in 1879. At that time, the Hispanic sheep ranching and mercantile interests, which intruded from New Mexico after the Civil War, controlled the Little Colorado Valley. Otherwise, outsiders from the eastern states and California prevailed. Nor did this new territory contain a noticeable number of persons of mixed ancestry—as in New Mexico—to ease the transition after the conquest in 1846.[35]

The rather moribund condition of New Mexico and Arizona in the immediate post-Civil War era was revealed in the censuses. From a population of 80,567 in 1860, New Mexico grew to 90,573 in 1870, and to 109,793 ten years later. Of this last figure, 92,271 were born in New Mexico, while only 9,471 were born in other parts of the United States. Migration into New Mexico had been minuscule. This meager increase did lead to the creation of new counties, a fact of immense importance to the growth of the shrievalty. New Mexico created only four permanent counties in the decade of the 1860s: Mora, Grant, Colfax, and Lincoln. Colfax and Grant Counties resulted from Anglo advances into mining regions. Lincoln arose in a cooperative venture between Don Saturnino Baca, a Socorro politician, and Thomas B. Catron, a lawyer, land speculator, and political kingpin in Santa Fe. New Mexico actually lost one established county—Santa Ana—which the assembly added to Bernalillo County in 1876. The Santa Ana's sheriff's office was dissolved. Only twelve sheriffs served the entire territory in 1880, whereas thirteen policed New Mexico ten years earlier.[36]

In 1880 this mere handful of sheriffs was responsible for monumental geographic areas, but few people:

County	Population	Area (sq. miles)
Bernalillo	17,225	6,500
Colfax	3,398	7,000
Doña Ana	7,612	6,700
Grant	4,539	7,000
Lincoln	2,513	20,000
Mora	9,751	3,700
Rio Arriba	11,023	12,500
San Miguel	20,638	10,600
Santa Fe	10,867	1,250
Socorro	7,875	12,000
Taos	11,029	1,400
Valencia	13,095	7,500

The creation of Arizona Territory had reduced the land area of New Mexico, and, hence, of some counties.[37]

The county lawmen in Arizona labored under similar handicaps. The division of Arizona into four counties hardly eased their burden and continued to perpetuate the ludicrous assumption that the meager resources of the sheriffs could adequately service these areas. At best these new shrievalties introduced only a modicum of law enforcement to an otherwise forgotten wilderness. Like New Mexico, Arizona grew at a snail's pace in the years before 1880. The population at the first territorial census in 1866 was a mere 5,526. Hostile Indians far outnumbered settlers who, in 1870, had increased to 9,658, and to 40,440 ten years later. In the 1870s, the assembly felt compelled to add only three new counties: Apache, Maricopa, and Pinal. While some New Mexico sheriffs were fortunate enough to preside over counties with more tightly clustered populations, their Arizona counterparts faced widely scattered constituencies.[38]

In spite of the many obstacles to the enforcement of the laws in New Mexico and Arizona Territories, the county sheriffs persevered in the three decades after the American conquest. This era served as a seedbed in which the Anglo-American judicial and law enforcement system took root in the Mexican Cession. The process of acclimatization would take many years, but both conquerors and conquered demonstrated the ability to compromise and accommodate. While the Americans withheld the United States marshalcy—the chief federal lawman—from Hispanos until 1885, the conquerors opened the office of sheriff—the chief county lawman—to them in 1846. One student of this subject concluded that many of the Hispano officeholders probably continued to think in terms of the Mexican predecessor office—*alguacil*—although occupying the sheriff's office. District courts functioned as well under Hispano as under Anglo process servers. Perhaps it was actually a boon for the sheriffs that hostile Indians occupied much of New Mexico and Arizona Territories. The existence of those regions labeled "Indian Country" confined the sheriffs to smaller areas while they learned their tasks. The presence of the military forces of the United States and, briefly, of the Confederacy also reduced the responsibilities of the sheriffs. At the same time, the army assisted the sheriffs measurably as a constabulary when necessary. These thirty-five years represented a time of testing that the sheriff's office weathered satisfactorily.[39]

Organization of
the Sheriff's Office

To set up and maintain a regime in the sheriff's office in frontier New Mexico or Arizona required considerable effort. The period between election and entry into the office was filled with intense activity. In addition to obtaining qualified bondsmen, the sheriff-elect had to select deputies from among a sometimes inadequate constituency. The fact that the new lawman was ex officio tax collector complicated the appointment process, since his subordinates would serve in this area as well. In addition, the territorial governments and boards of county commissioners did not always provide the sheriffs with clearcut and effective guidance. One of the most controversial aspects of the shrievalty was the income of office, which the incumbents regarded as inadequate and the public as excessive.

The newly elected sheriff began the process of claiming his office soon after receiving formal notice of election or appointment. The county clerk issued a commission, the wording of which probably derived from one of several handbooks for sheriffs that circulated in the territories. Sheriff William Sanders Oury of Pima County, Arizona, received his commission on 31 December 1872.

> I, O[scar] Buckalew Clerk of the District Court of the 1st Judicial [District of] Arizona do hereby certify that Wm. G. [sic] Oury having been duly eleted to the office of sheriff of the county of Pima and haveing [sic] been so elected has duly qualified and given the bonds required by law. . . .

The oath also followed a prescribed wording. On 25 November 1854, Samuel G. Bean took the oath as sheriff of Doña Ana County:

I, Samuel G. Bean, sheriff and collector of the county of Doña Ana and Territory of New Mexico do solemnly swear before Almighty God that I will discharge my duties as sheriff and collector of said county and that I will support the Constitution of the United States, so help me God.

The date of swearing-in varied according to the time of election or appointment. Eventually, both Arizona and New Mexico designated midnight 31 December.[1]

The transition from one regime to another could be a delicate matter. New Mexico law provided for an itemized list of county property that "The [incumbent] sheriff shall deliver to his successor. . . ." They paid especial attention to jail property and the number and condition of county prisoners. Other items included "All process, orders, rules, commitments, and all other papers or documents." This statute also required that "the former sheriff shall execute an instrument [inventory], reciting the property, process, documents, and prisoners delivered. . . ." The outgoing sheriff was also required to turn over all court process that he had endorsed as served, as well as any goods or real estate that he had attached by court order. The completed inventory was filed with the county board, since this document provided an official record of the incoming lawman's official liabilities.[2]

The risk of inadvertently incurring financial responsibilities of the former sheriff or of stumbling into the clutches of political enemies persuaded the incoming lawman to be extremely careful. Such occasions could occur during contested elections, when accusations of voting fraud were freely exchanged. The races for Pima County sheriff were hotly contested in the 1880s and each incumbent took pains to ensure that all county property was accurately inventoried. When Robert H. Paul contested the 1880 election of Charles A. Shibell in this Arizona county, the courts did not authorize the transition of office until spring of the following year. The inventory, dated 1 May 1881, averred that "The following is a true and correct statement of all property [in the sheriff's office] including office fixtures, account books and jail property received by me [Robert H. Paul]. . . ." Rumors fired by political animosity often ballooned such transfers out of proportion. A Las Cruces journal noted the circulation of "Puerile reports" that incumbent Martin Lohman had refused to turn over the Doña Ana County shrievalty to his successor, Guadalupe Ascarate, in January 1895. "The transfer was peacefully made, . . ." said this writer, who attributed this irresponsible claim to Ascarate's enemies.[3]

An especially spectacular controversy arose in Bernalillo County, New Mexico, when Sheriff Thomas S. Hubbell stubbornly refused to relinquish his official quarters in Albuquerque. On 31 August 1905, Governor Miguel A. Otero had removed Hubbell and other county officials from their posts after a hearing on alleged wrongdoings. When Perfecto Armijo, the new appointee, arrived at the sheriff's office, Hubbell physically obstructed his entry. Captain John F. Fullerton of the newly created Mounted Police informed a colleague on 12 September 1905 that Hubbell and his subordinates "still insist in holding their offices." Problems could result, he added, since the courts and county board no longer recognized the former sheriff. "I understand that the County Commissioners will not pay any of the jail expense," added Fullerton, "from the time Profecto [sic] Armijo was sworn in. . . ." "Tom Hubbell will have quite a bill to pay in keeping up the jail," observed the mounted policeman. While the aggrieved former lawman was angry, Fullerton still concluded that "I don't expect we [Mounted Police] will have a call to settle matters there." Thomas Hubbell eventually vacated, although he never forgot this humiliation. Otero's abrupt dismissal of the longtime Bernalillo County sheriff was not only a personal insult but a slight of a distinguished family that had produced two generations of sheriffs.[4]

The newly elected sheriff faced a real test of his influence in the search for sureties on his bonds. Many candidates probably obtained commitments from political friends prior to the election. The early sheriffs of New Mexico and Arizona filed only one bond to cover any liabilities that they incurred in the performance of law enforcement duties and tax collections. Eventually, the sheriffs in both territories filed separate bonds, one for each task. The amount of the sheriff's bond was pegged to the amount of monies that passed through his office. In 1871, the Arizona Assembly required a $10,000 bond of each sheriff, supported by three sureties whose total wealth exceeded this amount. The bond as tax collector was tied to the value of assessed, taxable property in a county. Andrew J. Moore, Sheriff of Yavapai County in the late 1860s, posted a $30,000 bond as ex officio collector. The tendency was always toward higher amounts as property values in both territories appreciated. In 1903, Sheriff Andrew Laird of Grant County, New Mexico, was required to post a $100,000 bond. George Curry posted the same amount in Lincoln County. He was pleasantly surprised when the man whom he had just defeated in the 1892 elections signed his bond. This was a truly unusual and chivalric gesture in an era of sometimes morbidly partisan politics.[5]

To acquire the necessary sureties at the beginning of a term did not guarantee the sheriff's security throughout his term. Bondsmen sometimes suffered financial reverses and withdrew their commitment to the lawman. Others lost confidence in the sheriff for various reasons. If any surety suffered bankruptcy, the district judge—the reviewing officer—ordered the sheriff to obtain a replacement. If a substitute was not forthcoming, the county board or governor could remove the peace officer. Even the failure to complete the bonding process by the appointed day—usually 20 January—could result in removal. Governor Samuel Axtell used this latter failure as justification for the removal of John N. Copeland in Lincoln County in 1878, when political enemies accused Copeland of political partisanship in a bloody feud.[6]

The sheriff sported a badge as a symbol of his newly acquired public office. This shield was apparently a holdover from the era of knighthood and heraldry in medieval Europe. Whatever the origin, this small metal object became a cherished item of apparel on the frontier. Drummers peddled badges from town to town. Each salesman offered a variety of shapes and sizes. When a sheriff or other lawman selected a badge, the salesman hand-stamped the title of office on the spot. In the absence of this formal source, the sheriff fashioned a temporary symbol from a tin can. This expediency prompted the expression "tin star," a term which became synonymous with lawman. This shiny object differed radically from the symbol of authority of the sheriff's Mexican predecessor, the *alguacil*, who carried a long staff called the *batón de juste*.[7]

Some sheriffs' badges were owned by the county and were passed on within an office. In Yavapai County, Arizona, the sheriffs passed on a noted shield, the Hassayampa Gold Badge. Carl Hayden of adjoining Maricopa County was pleasantly surprised when a prisoner made a silver badge for his captor. This shield consisted of six points with a bulb on each. In January 1897, Navajo County Sheriff Frank Wattron purchased badges for himself and his undersheriff from a San Francisco company. The Holbrook *Argus* described Wattron's new possession as "very handsome." It "is a five pointed star, [of] solid gold, set with a magnificent diamond in the center," this writer continued. It carried the inscription 'Sheriff of Navajo County' in black enamel. In turn, Wattron presented Undersheriff Joseph Bargman with "an elegant" star.[8]

A shiny new star hardly compensated for the very humble official quarters that frontier counties were able to provide. In 1899, George Curry, first chief lawman of Otero County, New Mexico, set up business in "a small frame building." The jail was an even shakier structure nearby. Lincoln County neglected to provide office space for the first decade of its existence. Sheriff Ham Mills evidently used his own residence. Only in 1881 did the county purchase a vacant store building formerly belonging to Lawrence G. Murphy. Similar difficulties beset Thomas Murphy (evidently of no relation), who initiated county law enforcement in Sierra County five years later. Murphy used personal funds to furnish his Hillsboro office with lamps, stove, and a safe. Some months passed before the county board admitted that the situation was "deroggatory [sic] to the honor and credit of our County . . ." and reimbursed him.[9]

The official surroundings of Arizona sheriffs were no better. John H. Behan, first sheriff of Cochise County, rented a small room in back of a tobacco shop. When Coconino County failed to provide the necessary quarters, Sheriff Jerome J. (Sandy) Donahue set up an office in his Senate Saloon in Flagstaff. Donahue and his office deputy, Merrill Ashurst, were very conspicuous to saloon patrons, since only a large plate glass separated the officers from the bar. Ashurst's mother, who was very proud of her son, expressed dismay at the location of his office. "She never could have believed that she would live to see a son of her's [sic] behind the bar . . .[!]," said this chagrined mother.[10]

As counties grew in wealth, they sometimes furnished not only office space but quarters for the sheriff's family. Such quarters enabled incumbents who resided far from the county seat to pay closer attention to official duties; this also permitted the voters to keep him under closer scrutiny. Official housing also reduced the possibility of absenteeism. The *St. Johns Herald* referred to this problem in November 1895, when James Scott, newly elected sheriff, promised to reside in town. The *Herald* remarked that the preceding occupant, meaning W. R. Campbell, had been "very conspicuous by his absence from the county seat for the last two years." An Arizona law of 1871 required the sheriff to keep his office open during court sessions and to "keep the same open during the usual [public] business hours each day, Sunday excepted." The assembly later revised this statute to require the lawman to remain open for business every day of the year between the hours of nine and five o'clock, except holidays.[11]

When Marion Littrell took up his duties in Springer, New Mexico, in January 1895, his wife and children settled into rooms on the second floor of the court building. Offices and jail were on the lower floor. Daughter Ollie recalled the excitement among her friends as the family moved in. The impressionable playmates looked up to the sheriff's daughter now that she resided in such a prestigious location. For Littrell's wife, this change of residence brought additional responsibilities. She cooked for prisoners and helped clean her husband's office. Other counties provided chief lawmen with similar residences.[12]

The selection of efficient and trustworthy subordinates was key to a successful administration. Official personnel normally included a chief deputy, office deputy, active field deputies, and a jailor. In counties of lesser means, the sheriff combined the functions of several subordinates into one man. A clerk or cashier was sometimes necessary if much money flowed through the office. The sheriff also commissioned trusted individuals as special deputies to serve intermittently. The Arizona shrievalty included an undersheriff rather than a chief deputy. The undersheriff was empowered to operate the office if the sheriff died or became incapacitated. Such an eventuality took place in Tucson in September 1887. When Sheriff Eugene O. Shaw resigned due to ill health, Undersheriff Charles Shibell (a former sheriff himself) maintained the office until a new appointee took the oath. In day-to-day administration of the office, the duties of chief deputy and undersheriff did not differ very much.[13]

The absence of this critical subordinate, the undersheriff, from the New Mexico shrievalty caused some problems. The chief deputy could not legally keep the office open if his superior died or was removed. The commissions of the entire staff became invalid. When lawyer Alexander McSween accused Lincoln County Deputy Sheriff George Peppin of illegally making arrests after the assassination of Sheriff William Brady in April 1878, this attorney knew his law. The *Rio Grande Republican* called attention to a similar case in Las Cruces in October 1892. Although Sheriff Mariano Barela had passed away in the previous month, his replacement, Martin Lohman, permitted the old staff members to continue in their positions. This was a violation of the law, since their commissions terminated with the death of their superior. This journalist advised Lohman to "check the law books" and issue new commissions.[14]

The chief deputy or undersheriff administered the daily routine of office, and the sheriff selected him—the "chief"—with care. When Sheriff-elect James Lowry designated H. H. Cartter (correct spelling) as undersheriff in December 1890, a Prescott journalist expressed delight. Cartter possessed the right credentials. He was a lawyer and a twenty-year resident of Prescott. He was also married and therefore "settled," according to this writer. A Tombstone newspaper congratulated Sheriff Jerome L. Ward for his choice of lawyer A. O. Wallace as undersheriff in November 1882. "Wallace's knowledge of law, his integrity, and his popularity makes [sic] the selection one highly to be commended," said this writer. Sheriff Eugene Van Patten of Doña Ana County, New Mexico, won applause when he employed as chief deputy Alexander L. Morrison, Jr. The latter had served as deputy to his father, United States Marshal Alexander L. Morrison, Sr. The *Daily New Mexican* noted that the junior Morrison was "an accomplished accountant, [and] hence his father's books as U.S. marshal were [always] in . . . excellent order. . . ."[15]

Some sheriffs regarded the office as an onerous duty and selected seconds-in-command with a view to delegating many responsibilities. Numa Reymond, sheriff of Doña Ana County in 1894, had "no time or liking" for official duties, according to one observer. Reymond, a Swiss immigrant and wealthy entrepreneur, assigned the duties of office to Chief Deputy Ben Williams. Williams continued in this position under Pat Garrett, Reymond's successor. Navajo County's chief executive, Frank Wattron, followed suit when he hired Joseph Bargman as undersheriff. C. O. Pease, who settled in Holbrook in 1899, soon concluded that Bargman "was the real sheriff" and performed "all the outside work." Wattron played the part of the "high" sheriff and operated his nearby store. Tom Talle, the last sheriff of McKinley County, New Mexico, in the territorial era, likewise permitted Chief Deputy Patrick J. Dugan to run the office. One resident of Gallup characterized Dugan as "honest, efficient, and incorruptible." Talle spent much time on his ranch some 100 miles away.[16]

The educational background of sheriffs and deputies was very uneven. Some possessed the ability to read and write while others could barely sign their names. Several Hispanos who occupied New Mexico shrievalties received college training at Catholic institutions in Santa Fe or St. Louis, Missouri. Buckey O'Neill of Yavapai County, Arizona, was a trained court stenographer and newspaper editor. As historian Jeff C. Dykes has pointed out, three Lincoln County lawmen wrote, or at least contributed to, book-length works. Pat Garrett narrated several chapters of the biography of Billy the Kid, which bears the sheriff's name as author. Actually, Chief Deputy Ash Upson, a schoolteacher, composed this work. John W. Poe, also a deputy to Garrett, wrote his recollections of the death of Billy the Kid. George Curry, sheriff of this same county in

1893–94, wrote a substantial autobiography. Two relatives of Lincoln County sheriffs also wrote books that bear upon the conduct of these lawmen. Sophie Poe, wife of John, wrote recollections about her husband. James Brent, son of Sheriff James R. Brent also described some of his fathers law enforcement activities.[17]

Few sheriffs, if any, were abjectly illiterate. This was the century that prided itself upon basic literacy for the masses. Chief Deputy Orme-Johnson's observation that his superior in Lincoln, Jake Owen, "could barely sign his name" may be an exaggeration. Arizonans told a humorous story reflecting upon the literacy of R. N. Leatherwood, popular sheriff of Pima County. The sheriff had written Lindley Orme, his counterpart in Phoenix, on official business:

> The Maricopa County sheriff [the story goes] could not make out Bob's [Leatherwood's] letter so he sent it back to Bob without comment. After several attempts by Leatherwood to read the letter [not realizing it was his own] and failing he took it to Harry Trachman, a courthouse officer. 'Look ahere, Harry,' said Bob, 'What's this feller trying to say in this writin'. I can't make heads or tails of it.'[18]

The chief deputy or undersheriff could be the only fully literate staff member, and thus played an even more critical role. In 1876, Oliver Stratton, a well-educated new arrival in Florence, Arizona, walked right into the position of undersheriff of Pinal County, a brand new local government. Michael Rogers, the newly appointed sheriff, was desperately in need of an educated man to open the first set of record books. Stratton recalled that "clerical men were very scarce" in Florence, a boisterous mining camp with few educated citizens. Stratton also fulfilled the tasks of tax assessor and collector. W. Orme-Johnson's educational background in England appealed to Lincoln County Sheriff John W. "Jake" Owen for similar reasons. The son of an engineer, this transplanted Englishman became Lincoln County's chief deputy sheriff shortly after the turn of this century. Orme-Johnson recalled that Owen could hardly write his name and that as the chief deputy, his primary duty was the official paperwork. Among the more literate westerners, journalists were sought after for these positions in the shrievalty. Ashmun (Ash) Upson, a schoolteacher and journalist, served as chief deputy in Lincoln County, while Harry Woods, editor of the Tombstone *Daily Nugget,* held the post of undersheriff in Cochise County.[19]

The sheriff also paid close attention to applicants for all deputyships, since all acts of subordinates were ultimately the superior's responsibility. Arizona statutes declared that deputy sheriffs served at the pleasure of the sheriff, who "shall be in all respects responsible" for the conduct of the subordinate. The sheriff could also revoke all commissions "at his pleasure." Each deputy's commission was in writing, and each underling (like the sheriff) was forbidden to practice law or to have a partner who practiced law. New Mexico law forbade any person "under indictment or . . . known as a notorious bad character, or as a disturber of the peace . . ." from holding a deputyship. James East, a lawman in Tascosa, Texas, and Globe, Arizona, was very familiar with the personnel problems of southwestern sheriffs. He recalled that as a sheriff in Tascosa he was sensitive to the problems that reckless deputies could provoke. They "are not as responsible for what they do as [is] a sheriff," said East, and "They are usually without bond."[20]

The sheriff looked for certain qualifications in a deputy. The candidate for a deputyship had to be a person of known bravery, possess proficiency with guns, be able to ride horseback for long periods, and be familiar with the countryside. Sheriff Ben W. Crawford of Graham County, Arizona, characterized Deputy Ben Clark as a superior officer, "fearless . . . cool and level headed." Dan Williamson, who held the post of chief lawman in neighboring Gila County, recalled that "I picked my deputies with great care." One of his selections was Ben McKinney, a fearless man who had seen much action against badmen in the wilds of Arizona. When Governor Lew Wallace of New Mexico sought a reliable deputy sheriff for the turbulent San Juan region in western Rio Arriba County in March 1881, he demanded "a good man of sound judgment and dispassionate but brave and energetic—if such a one can be found." When Mariano J. Soto applied to United States Marshal Charles Overlock for a deputy marshalship in September 1909, he recalled his previous experience as a deputy sheriff. Soto was aged fifty and a merchant:

I am sober[,] do not drink[,] [am] not afraid to go forward and make arrests and [am] a very fair shot with rifle or pistol and heretofore always attended strictly to business.

If a man was especially desirous of an appointment as deputy sheriff, he circulated a petition. In January 1893, John Jones, a resident of Clayton, New Mexico, used this procedure to strengthen his application to Sheriff Oscar McCuiston.[21]

In the absence of an adequate manpower pool, the sheriffs were often frustrated in the search for competent deputies. In the late 1870s, Albert Franklin Banta lectured Sheriff Charles Shibell about the poor quality of the typical deputy sheriff. When Shibell offered Banta a deputy's commission, the latter replied:

> Look here Charles, my experience with the average deputy sheriff . . . is, they don't know [how] to pound sand into a rat hole; they can swagger around town, knock down some drunken man over the head with a gun, [and] drag him off to jail . . . , but put them out [in the field] where they have to use a little brains—which they haven't got—they are simply a bunch of bone-heads. . . .

Banta accepted the commission temporarily, but soon resettled to Apache County where he continued to hold local public office. While Banta's adverse criticism was probably exaggerated, he may have struck near some truth.[22]

The sheriff who possessed the funds to employ a separate clerk or cashier was very fortunate. George Curry, who was very alert to public criticism, took care to employ a cashier in the Lincoln County office in 1893. Matt DeVane had no sooner accepted the post of bookkeeper in the Yuma shrievalty in 1901 when he was tragically killed while attempting an arrest. In May 1877, Edward Bowers surprised the citizens of Prescott, Arizona, when he hired as a clerk a man with a criminal record. James S. Giles, a former postmaster, had absconded with postal receipts but was captured in Utah. Although Sheriff Bowers tried to reassure the public that Giles had made a private settlement with the Post Office Department and obtained his release, many residents of Yavapai County doubted that a man who had recently been a resident of the sheriff's jail could be so easily rehabilitated. Bowers persisted nonetheless. Good clerks were hard to find on the frontier.[23]

A written commission for each employee was filed with the county clerk. On 6 September 1878, Sheriff Charles Shibell of Pima County, Arizona, deputized Robert Kirker—probably the son of early-day scalp hunter James Kirker—for the Santa Rita Placers in the mountains of the same name near the Mexican border. "Know all men by these presents," read this document, "that I [Charles Shibell] . . . do hereby appoint Robert Kirker . . . a deputy sheriff. . . ." Kirker's oath followed:

> I, Robert Kirker do solemnly swear that I will support the Constitution of the United States and the laws of the Territory; that I will

[with] true faith and allegiance bear to the same, and defend them against all enemies whatsoever, and that I will faithfully and impartially discharge the duties of the office of Deputy Sheriff according to the best of my abilities, so held me God.

A few days later, Kirker was forced to kill a man who resisted arrest.[24]

To become a deputy sheriff required the conscious and formal act of the sheriff, in spite of legends about informal practices of appointing lawmen. One widely circulated myth persists that Elfego Baca, a young Socorran, made himself a "self-appointed" deputy to Sheriff Pedro A. Simpson in October 1884. Baca, who lived a long and eventful life, created and perpetuated this wild tale. In his reminiscences, Baca maintained that this fictitious status enabled him to arrest riotous Texas cowboys in San Francisco Plaza. Baca's efforts led to a spectacular shootout in which he killed one man. A second cowhand died when his horse fell on him. Baca claimed that the regular deputy was too frightened to enforce the law. Actually, Elfego Baca held a written commission from Simpson. It is dated 26 October 1884 and was admitted into evidence at Baca's trial for the deaths of the cowboys. Since Baca was on official business at San Francisco Plaza, the jury ruled that he acted in self-defense.[25]

The number of full-time staff members varied according to the size and population of the county, the degree of lawlessness, the workload of district court, and the efficiency of the sheriff. In 1864, the New Mexico Assembly limited the number of deputy sheriffs, permitting each sheriff only four full-time deputies. Just what prompted this "rule of four" is not clear. The *Daily New Mexican* viewed this law as a serious hindrance to the sheriff's efficiency, since four men could hardly patrol the larger counties. Writing from district court in Las Vegas, an anonymous member of the bar lamented that this restrictive legislation hampered the sheriff's ability to serve the court, especially when called upon to summon many witnesses from the remote parts of San Miguel County. This writer pleaded for "More liberal and enlightened legislation." Not until 1891 did the legislature amend this "rule of four" to permit five deputies for counties of fifteen precincts and one additional underling for every additional four precincts.[26]

Arizona and New Mexico also permitted the sheriff to appoint "any competent, respectable and orderly person" as a special deputy to perform one official act. On 15 April 1881, Sheriff James W. Southwick appointed Robert Olinger as a special deputy to escort

Billy the Kid—convicted for the murder of Sheriff William Brady—to Lincoln for hanging. The Kid had been tried in Mesilla; hence Southwick had the responsibility of transporting the youthful outlaw to the place of execution. Olinger's commission read:

> Be it known that I have this day appointed Robert Olinger a Deputy Sheriff in and for the County of Doña Ana. And he is hereby charged with the Special trust of taking William Bony [sic] alias The Kid alias Henry Antrim from the County seat of Doña Ana Co. and Delivering him to the Sheriff of Lincoln County. With full powers and authority to summons Possy [posse comitatus] or to do any and all things necissary [sic] for the safe Deliver [sic] of Said Prisner [sic] in the hands of the above named Authirty [sic].

Panhandle Sheriff Jim East recalled that he filled out his staff in the busy season by hiring "one or two men extra at district court time." The sheriff could issue commissions by letter, telegram, and later, by telephone.[27]

Sheriffs were occasionally driven to unusual extremes as they made appointments. Two or more sheriffs might deputize the same person during an emergency. This evidently explains Tom Horn's recollection that he held simultaneous deputyships in three Arizona counties—Gila, Yavapai, and Apache—in the late 1880s. If Horn can be trusted, the three sheriffs agreed to this irregular procedure as a means to muster posses against the feuding factions in the Pleasant Valley War. Sheriff E. S. Stover of Apache County took an unusual (and probably illegal) means to place a deputy in a key trouble spot in 1881. The thinly settled area along the New Mexico-Arizona border presented Stover with many problems. To monitor this lawless area, Stover deputized his nephew, E. S. Clark, who managed a trading post at Pueblo Springs, New Mexico. When the nephew reminded his uncle that he (Clark) was not a resident of Apache County, Stover replied: "Makes no difference. Folks that do things they shouldn't over here [in St. Johns] were [sic] likely to head over there [New Mexico], and [I] want you to take 'em, and bring 'em back. . . ."[28]

These frontier sheriffs were also compelled to deputize men with shadowy backgrounds or persons known to be associates of badmen. To fight fire with fire was a not uncommon tactic of other law enforcement agencies. Pat Garrett, Lincoln County sheriff, caused some raised eyebrows among the voters when he chose his deputies in 1881. He commissioned Barney Mason, who had ties with Billy the Kid. Critics humorously characterized Mason the outlaw's "first deputy." Mason went to prison for cattle theft later in the decade. Another Garrett deputy, Robert Olinger, also had a questionable reputation. Garrett defended this selection by saying, "It wasn't by choice." Garrett meant that he would rather have Olinger close and under the sheriff's eye than to let the troublemaker run loose. The sheriff may also have felt the need to placate United States Marshal John Sherman, Jr., who had already deputized Olinger. Elsewhere, in Cochise County, Arizona, Sheriff John Slaughter deputized Burt Alvord, whom many citizens regarded as a saloon bum. Slaughter may have desired an entre into the underworld that thrived in the local bars.[29]

One of the most notable instances of an outlaw turning deputy sheriff was that of Daniel "Red" Pipkin, a former train robber who had participated in the murder of three Valencia County lawmen in 1898. After serving a short prison term, Pipkin settled in Gallup, New Mexico. When Arizona rancher Prime T. Colman spied a deputy sheriff's badge on Pipkin's shirt, the cattleman exclaimed, "'What the hell are you doin' here?'" "'I'm a peace officer now, Prime,'" admitted the former train robber, "'and a d—n good one.'" Pipkin informed Colman over drinks that Tom Talle, the sheriff of McKinley County (1909–12), was a shrewd judge of circumstances. Not only did Pipkin know the outlaw element, but he was loyal to Talle, who had generously given the former outlaw a job. Pipkin reportedly committed suicide many years later.[30]

A wise personnel policy took into account minorities and other groups in the county. By deputizing representatives of these communities, the alert sheriff accorded these interests standing in the community. The lawman also recognized the importance of their votes. In many instances, the sheriff lacked the ability to speak other languages. Hence, deputies from these elements were essential. The sheriffs of Pima County, Arizona, were, with one exception, Anglo during the entire territorial era. Yet a sizeable Hispanic minority resided in Tucson, and the sheriffs generally employed at least one deputy from the Spanish-speaking population. When a Chinese community began to emerge in Tucson in the late 1880s, Sheriff Eugene O. Shaw hired an Oriental man to assist him in special cases. This office was also fortunate enough to employ Nathan Appel, a German immigrant who had resided in southern Arizona since the Gadsden Purchase. Appel spoke not only his native language but French, Spanish, and English. He also married a local Hispano woman, which gave him access to the inner circle of that community. Graham County Officers shrewdly recognized the large Italian community of mine workers in Morenci and Clifton at the turn of this century. Sheriff James V. Parks deputized Little Dave Arzatte, who, according to the lawman's sister, was brave and loyal. Arzatte's background enabled him to obtain "information which other [Anglo] officers were unable to get."[31]

Sheriffs from Hispanic communities experienced the reverse problem in choosing deputies—how to recognize the Anglo minority. When a fresh wave of outsiders followed the new railroad into New Mexico in 1879, Hispanic San Miguel County lawmen adroitly bowed to the often shrill demands of these interlopers. When the Anglos recommended Arthur F. Jilson for deputy sheriff, Sheriff Hilario Romero readily granted a commission. In Socorro County, Sheriff Pedro A. Simpson experienced an influx of Texas and foreign cattlemen about this same time. To satisfy the cattle-raising precincts, Simpson deputized Dan Bechdolt. As his subordinate in San Francisco Plaza, the sheriff selected Pedro Sarracino, a merchant. Each community also insisted upon justices of the peace from their own races. This delicate balance could be easily upset, as Deputy Sheriff Elfego Baca learned in October 1884. The efforts of Baca to arrest lawbreaking cowboys helped to set off a confrontation, "The Mexican War."[32]

When the sheriff found it impossible or inexpedient to commission a deputy for communities that desired one, a temporary alternative was possible in the form of a subscription deputy. Citizens contributed toward his salary by pledges. The sheriff might also contribute a percentage. In 1891, citizens of the new and boisterous cattle town of Clayton, in far eastern Colfax County, proposed a subscription deputy when Sheriff Matthias Stockton neglected to commission one. This adverse publicity apparently persuaded Stockton to provide a deputy. Sheriff Holm O. Bursum maintained at least two subscription deputies in the far western precincts of Socorro County. Deputy Cipriano Baca, who served the mining camp of Mogollon, received $100 per month from mining companies and $25 from the sheriff. However, paychecks were erratic. In August 1895, Baca complained that the businessmen had failed to pay him. When a second subscription deputy, C. H. Kirkpatrick, made the same complaint, the sheriff appealed to subscribers to "Kindly pay over . . . the amount of your subscription for the month of July, for services rendered as Deputy Sheriff, . . . an oblige![33]

That businesses, such as mining or cattle companies, desired resident deputy sheriffs was not uncommon. These organizations often lay in remote locales and kept large sums of money or valuable ores that enticed would-be bandits. Such companies offered to pay the wages of a deputy sheriff outright or requested that employees be commissioned, presumably at no extra pay. In 1882, the Raton Coal and Coking Company asked Sheriff Allen C. Wallace to deputize an employee, William A. Bergen, who worked in its Blossburg Camp, a few miles north of Raton. Thomas J. Bull, Sheriff of Doña Ana County, obliged the Sierra Mining Company in Lake Valley, in May 1882, after bandits attempted to rob the operation. Not only did the company employ six new guards but, said the *Daily New Mexican,* "Sheriff Bull has just appointed two of the [company] employees . . . [as] deputy sheriffs." This same arrangement also prevailed in Arizona. Harry Saxon, Sheriff of Santa Cruz County, in 1907, recalled that "The custom was that . . . mining companies [in the Santa Rita Mountains] would help pay deputies for the sheriff. . . ." This was necessary, said Saxon, because "the sheriff was on fees and had to pay his own deputies. . . ."[34]

Cattle companies were equally desirous of having deputies on their payroll. Tempers sometimes exploded over ownership of livestock during roundups. Cowboys quarreled. Fugitives sought food, sanctuary, or companionship on isolated ranches. The sheriffs of counties in which cattle ranges existed were eventually constrained to post deputies in those wilderness spots. Just when the county lawmen began to designate some subordinates as range deputies is not clear. However, in December 1914, a Pima County range deputy, James A. Mercer, was shot and killed by rustlers near Pantano. In the 1890s, the sheriff of Colfax County, New Mexico, deputized Tom Kane, a wagon boss for the great Bell Ranch. A boisterous Irishman, Kane had reportedly trained for the ministry. Cattleman Jack Culley concluded that Kane just "liked that kind of work" as a deputy.[35]

These frontier sheriffs subscribed to the adage "blood is thicker than water" and routinely deputized relatives. Some offices became "family affairs." Not only did the county lawmen desire to provide relatives with economic opportunities to better themselves, but the sheriffs feared political enemies were always trying to compromise their deputies. Deputies with family or marriage ties to the chief lawman provided additional bonds against such threats. Hispanos also practiced blatant nepotism. The dons apparently subscribed to the aristocratic notion that the privilege of officeholding accompanied class status. Family appointments probably took place in most county shrievalties, although some sheriffs were more enthusiastic about this than others. To give just one example, Cochise County sheriffs were very adept practitioners of nepotism. Sheriff Jerome L. Ward (1883–84) deputized two sons, one of whom was jailer. John Slaughter turned his office into a family enterprise, to include the deputization of three in-laws. Scott White, who served two terms as sheriff in the 1890s, deputized his brother, John.[36]

Another very common personnel practice of the sheriffs was cross-deputization. This happened frequently in a frontier environment where the population was sparse and earnings from fees very meager. To support a family on the minimal income of a deputy sheriff was very difficult, as Dee R. Harkey, a veteran New Mexico lawman recalled. But the combination of incomes from two or more government posts provided the prospects of more economic security. In September 1864, Governor John N. Goodwin gave formal encouragement to concurrent officeholding when he urged the Arizona Assembly to create only the minimum necessary offices and asked that the duties of two or more be combined. This expediency would promote economy and pay a dual office holder enough to encourage proper attention to duty. The lawmakers complied. The combination of sheriff with tax collector was only one of many expressions of this official jointure. New Mexicans practiced this same technique, although it does not appear the legislature made laws to this end.[37]

Perhaps the most common instances of cross-deputization took place between sheriffs and deputy United States marshals. These two officials worked closely since federal and territorial cases were tried at the same sessions. In July 1877, Marshal John E. Sherman, Jr., raised this subject with the Attorney General. Sherman observed that the men in New Mexico who were most capable of holding deputy marshal's commissions were the county sheriffs. It made sense for a sheriff or deputy sheriff to be vested with federal authority. When they rode into the hinterland to serve court process, they could serve federal as well as territorial court papers on the same route. Although Sherman went no further about cross-deputization, sheriffs of both territories bestowed deputyships upon city marshals and precinct constables.[38]

Bizarre cases of cross-deputization occasionally occurred. Dee R. Harkey of Eddy County, New Mexico, boasted that he held six jobs simultaneously in the 1890s: deputy sheriff, constable, city marshal, deputy United States marshal, cattle inspector for the Cattle Raisers' Association of Texas, and the same position for the Cattle Sanitary Board of New Mexico. A similar case in Nogales, Arizona, won notoriety. Pima County Deputy Sheriff T. F. Broderick held the concurrent positions of city marshal and constable. (The writer overlooked the fact that Broderick was also sergeant of militia.) While this penman expressed surprise that Broderick had time to tend to a private business, he added that "This concentration of responsibility is really a very common occurrence . . ." in Arizona. One commentator, who took note of this easterner's observations, concluded that Broderick could hold so many offices because there was "little to do in any of them."[39]

The combination of sheriff with tax collector complicated the lawman's duties and caused him to make special arrangements with subordinates to care for these tasks. Sheriff John D. Walker and Deputy Dee Harkey agreed at the outset of the superior's term that the latter would administer the law enforcement office while the former collected taxes. That the sheriff chose to collect taxes rather than perform the chores of policeman was not uncommon. Of the two very different jobs, tax collecting was obviously more politically sensitive and certainly more lucrative. If pressed to publicly choose between the two, the incumbent would almost certainly select the tax office. While it is impossible to judge from the perspective of today, this tendency to slight the very important tasks of the shrievalty may have harmed the overall efficiency of frontier law enforcement. The joint duties of tax collecting and "lawing"—in the parlance of that day—extended to deputy sheriffs, who often held simultaneous commissions as deputy tax collectors.[40]

Good working relations between sheriff (employer) and deputy (employee) were desirable but not always possible. John P. Meadows, deputy to Pat Garrett in Lincoln and later in Las Cruces, recalled that "We would differ once in a while . . . , but we could always settle it without any sharp words. . . ." "I never met . . . a man who was any more truthful, and more honorable," averred the former deputy, "or any better citizen than he. . . ." One young deputy of Sheriff James V. Parks in Solomonville, Arizona, regarded his superior as a good man, but too reticent. This underling resigned because he never knew where he stood with Parks. Peter Gabriel, the noted chief lawman of Pinal County, had a fiery temper. Mike Rice once observed Gabriel "spitting fire" at his undersheriff, George

Evans, for failing to arrest a troublemaker who "treed" the town. Gabriel stormed out of the office and promptly shot the rowdy to death.[41]

Although noted as a gunfighter-sheriff in Apache County, Arizona, Commodore Perry Owens failed in personnel relations. He was a temperamental and suspicious person. Owens abruptly dismissed his popular undersheriff, Joe T. McKinney, without any formality. McKinney learned about his termination while on the trail of jailbreakers. Owens used the absence of his deputy to blame him for the breakout. The sheriff was playing a dangerous game because McKinney possessed an explosive temper. "I was very much surprised," recalled McKinney, "as I figured that I had done well . . ." as undersheriff. In a furious state of mind, the deputy confronted his former boss in the sheriff's office in St. Johns. "I called him [Owens] every name . . . ," said the angry man, and charged that the sheriff "had neglected his duty and let those men get away." With a revolver conspicuously jutting from his waistband, McKinney declared that Owens's reputation as "a hard man" did not frighten him. Surprisingly, the sheriff apologized and replied that, "I am sorry I have [done you] as I have. . . ." "You will never hear it mentioned again . . . ," the sheriff promised. Whereupon, McKinney walked away. The board of county supervisors apparently found the sheriff's personnel practices questionable and awarded McKinney the position of constable at Winslow. Commodore Owens then hired Jefferson D. Milton, former Texas Ranger, to replace McKinney. This new appointee lasted only six days! "I didn't like the man," confessed Milton, who simply walked out.[42]

Turnover among deputies was commonplace, and the possibility of the creation of a professional body of such men was remote on the New Mexico-Arizona frontier. Men who possessed the education and temperament for deputyships were in big demand for better-paying positions. One study of Pima County Sheriff Charles Shibell found that he employed fifty-two men as deputies, jailers, and guards in a two-year period. Just how many were employed at any one time is not clear. Occasional examples of lengthy service in the shrievalty did occur. In June 1904, the *Arizona Republican* announced that William (Billy) Blankenship was celebrating his twenty-sixth year as a deputy sheriff in Arizona. Blankenship began as a deputy to George Mowry in Phoenix in 1878 and remained in this office until 1899. He transferred to the Yavapai County shrievalty for four years and then to Cochise County for three. He also served concurrently as city marshal of Phoenix for six years. This

veteran lawman boasted that he had never had to kill a man, although he suffered serious wounds in the line of duty.[43]

The modern reader of Wild West literature or patron of the
Hollywood screen is led to believe that the "office" of sheriff did not
exist on the frontier. Instead, the typical western story focuses on
one man, the sheriff, who stalks through the script and concludes
the adventure with a climactic gunfight. Such episodic popular
literature grossly distorts the truth. In fact, the pioneer sheriffalties
of Arizona and New Mexico territories followed the standard organization and procedures of such offices in the East. From the taking
of the oath of office and filing of bonds to the employment of office
staff, the southwestern sheriffs abided by time-honored prescrip-
tions. Far from managing the office alone, the sheriff maintained a
staff that practiced some—although limited—specialization. While
well-qualified men were hard to find, the sheriff demanded some
qualifications, to include not only bravery and dexterity with weapons but literacy when possible. The sheriff also had to be alert to the
political peculiarities of his constituency and see to it that his appointments took the voters into consideration. While it is impossible to generalize with much accuracy, the typical office included
the sheriff, chief deputy or undersheriff, and three or four deputies.
The more affluent offices might support an office deputy or cashier.
These men also doubled as deputy tax collectors.

3

The Sheriff and the Law Enforcement System

The county sheriff was only a part—though a critical part—of a large and very complex law enforcement and judicial system in New Mexico and Arizona territories. Although Congress refused to give these frontier districts all the judicial fineries of the East, the territories supported numerous agencies, from precinct justice of the peace to county probate court, district court, and territorial supreme court. The sheriffs worked with many law enforcers in this apparatus: from precinct constable, to town marshals, to United States marshals, and eventually, to territory-wide ranger or mounted police organizations. Cordial working relationships were not always possible, since jealousies were easily aroused. In such dilemmas, the county lawman had recourse to the territorial governors, who were expected to rise above political considerations that affected law enforcement questions. Outside this immediate precinct-to-capital framework, the sheriffs encountered many other law enforcement officials, both public and private. The proximity of the Republic of Mexico brought its representatives into official contact with the sheriffs. In spite of the remoteness of the Southwest, a vast network of independent, yet mutually dependent, agencies of justice thrived there. This system was much more complicated than met the eye, and the wonder was that it functioned so well. That the sheriffs managed to wend their way through this labyrinthine system was testimony to their alertness and agility.

The precinct justice of the peace, or *alcalde,* was at the ground-level of the Anglo-American justice system. Although the smallest unit, the precinct was a vital element in the law enforcement and judicial scheme. Several precincts made up the county. From heavily populated precincts, new counties sprang. The residents of each precinct elected one justice of the peace and one constable. This latter official served the process of the justice court. The JP, as he often was called, examined accused persons and held hearings to decide whether the evidence was sufficient to bind them over for action of the grand jury. He tried minor cases, usually involving $100 or less.[1]

John W. Wentworth, a justice of the peace in Globe, Arizona, heard a wide variety of cases, many of which arose on the streets. In the words of Wentworth's biographer, these cases included:

> Fighting, shooting pistols, being drunk and disorderly, [and] making loud and unusual noises were common lesser offenses, not to mention riding horses on the board sidewalks, . . . These violators usually drew a fine of five dollars, plus the cost of [court] action. . . .

Justices of the peace often held concurrent commissions as United States commissioners, the federal counterpart to this precinct official. The United States marshal brought violators of United States statutes to the commissioner, just as the sheriff and constable delivered persons who contravened territorial law to the justice of the peace. Easy access to the judicial system was a hallmark of the Anglo-American tradition. The sheriff and other lawmen were required to take prisoners immediately upon arrest to the nearest court, usually the justice of the peace.[2]

These frontier justices of the peace came from all walks of life. A Prescott journalist observed two justices of the peace "hobnobbing" in November 1899. One was an undertaker and the other a minister. The country storekeeper, the miner, the farmer all held this office, since no legal training was required. The *Daily New Mexican* of 14 December 1892 noted the recent enactment of an amended Justice of the Peace Law and reflected upon the importance of this hallowed office:

> Of all positions this is the one nearest the people. It has to do with the every-day affairs of life more than any other. For the business man it is particularly important, and the good conduct of a community largely depends upon the vigor with which this officer rules his court. . . .

This editor urged the public to take an active interest in elections to this post and believed that candidates should be "fair-minded," "progressive," and "earnest." In an address to the New Mexico Bar Association, in January 1889, attorney Benjamin M. Read criticized voters for electing unsuitable men to this position. He went on to observe that "In no other tribunal are the rights of the Territory and of its citizens tried as before the Courts of Justices of the Peace. . . ."[3]

These lowly judges came in for much criticism. In April 1859, a grand jury in Albuquerque chastised them for neglecting "to send up to [district] court the criminal causes presented before them" as well as other pertinent documents. Another panel in this same county complained later that the justices of the peace were "very ignorant as to the law" and neglected to keep the necessary records. A Las Cruces precinct judge "ought to be impeached," said the local paper, *Newman's Thirty-Four,* in February 1881. This unnamed official "is almost constantly under the influence of liquor," alleged this writer. When Socorro County rancher William French sought a JP in Cooney mining camp, the stockman discovered him sleeping off a binge "in a trench . . . dug for the foundation of a new mill." Justice of the Peace John B. Wilson received adverse public comment when he attempted to try a man twice for the same crime in Lincoln![4]

Hard men occasionally slipped into this critical position. Jim Burnett, a Cochise County justice, rendered decisions arbitrarily and without recourse to law books. He refused to report his fee collections to the board of supervisors. This bullyish man was later killed by mining magnate William Greene. Rather than place Greene in jail, Sheriff Scott White permitted him to remain at liberty until the next session of court. Hyman G. G. Brown, alias "Hoodoo," a Dodge City gambler and troublemaker, inexplicably became a justice of the peace in East Las Vegas, New Mexico, in 1879. Railroad construction gangs and bands of outlaws had descended upon this unfortunate community. Brown organized a robber band and used his official position to shield it from the law. Vigilantes eventually ran Brown and his henchmen out of town. In Arizona, Leonard Redfield followed Brown's unsavory example. Redfield presided over a JP court at Riverside, a stage stopover forty miles north of Tucson. When vigilantes learned that he aided and abetted stagecoach robbers, "Judge Lynch" put an end to the errant judge and his comrades. Even Newman H. "Old Man" Clanton, the lawless patriarch of a family of badmen in Cochise County, had the audacity to apply for this important precinct post. Evidently, he did not receive a commission.[5]

Many energetic and conscientious justices of the peace served the frontier communities of the Southwest. In the 1850s, Tucson was a distant outpost of civilization, and the justices of the peace represented the only judicial presence for hundreds of miles. Mark Aldrich and Charles H. Meyer, the local judges, were long remembered for their steadfastness. Meyer, a German immigrant, lacked any legal training, and friends noted with a smile that his "law" library consisted of copies of *Materia Medica* and *Fractured Bones*. Yet, he was "a man of conviction and loved justice." While Meyer's decisions might be delivered in "salty" language, they were so "vigorous and straightforward" that he set an oratorical example for trained members of the bar. The presence of such men as Aldrich and Meyer in these vital judgeships reflected the existence of a healthy sense of justice. One historian who studied the precinct justices in Washington Territory found their decisions "fair and consistent" and characterized by "reason, accessibility, celerity, and community acceptance." This same conclusion could no doubt be drawn for their Southwestern counterparts.[6]

These justices of the peace often became their own constables in the post-Civil War Southwest. Jack Swilling, a justice of the peace in Wickenburg, Arizona, was forced to kill a man who resisted arrest. Swilling admitted later that he should not have been so impatient and should have awaited the return of his constable. Charles Flake, who held this same post in Snowflake, was killed in an attempt to arrest a suspected bank robber in December 1892. The fact that Flake's brother shot the robber provided little comfort. Other acts of initiative were not so unfortunate but equally dangerous. In 1895, a Pima County precinct judge admitted to his board that he stretched his authority. He organized a posse and led it against thieves. "I did what I thought was the best thing to do," he explained, since "I had no constable here." A JP in Deming, New Mexico, took the same action against train robbers two years later. He admitted to Assemblyman Holm O. Bursum that "I may not have had jurisdiction in this case. . . .," but "I considered everything . . ." and took the initiative.[7]

Although a minor official, the justice of the peace sometimes loomed large in civil disturbances. During the Lincoln County War, rival factions sought the services of various judicial agencies. One group, the Murphy-Dolans, were believed to have the loyalty of Sheriff William Brady. The opposition, led by lawyer Alexander McSween, used Justice of the Peace John Wilson, whose precinct was the township of Lincoln. Wilson obliged McSween by appointing deputy constables from among the latter's followers. Thus the posses of the contending parties were cloaked with a veil of legality. The justices of the peace also played an important part in an explosive situation in western Socorro County, as large herds of cattle—many from Texas—began to take up the grasslands formerly occupied by the native Hispanic population. Each side insisted upon the protection of a justice of the peace, constable, and deputy sheriff from its own community. In October 1884, when a violent confrontation took place in San Francisco Plaza, the cattlemen descended upon the village, bringing in tow their own justice of the peace and deputy sheriff.[8]

As sheriffs' officers went about their routines, they sometimes encountered testy justices of the peace who guarded their precincts jealously. A quarrel between Colfax County deputy sheriffs and Raton Justice of the Peace Harvey Moulton led to unfortunate consequences in 1882. When the deputies arrested Gus Mentzer in the village for a double murder, Moulton demanded custody. A heated argument between the lawmen and Moulton led to a gunfight in which Moulton and one deputy were killed. A mob lynched Mentzer in the meantime, making the death toll five for the day. To add to the unforseen results of this violent episode, the surviving deputy sheriff, R. P. Dollman, resigned his commission, leaving Raton without a sheriff's representative. The uneasy citizens formally organized a vigilante committee. Justice of the Peace John Wentworth of Globe, Arizona, was also known for gruff behavior, in this case toward the Gila County sheriff. However, he went too far on one occasion. Sheriff Benjamin Pascoe was known as a hardworking officer. One night in the mid-1880s, Pascoe awakened Wentworth to ask for a hearing over two suspected stagecoach robbers. The precinct judge, apparently upset at this midnight call, angrily sent the sheriff away. Pascoe resented this abruptness, but consented to place the two prisoners in jail and await the morning. The two desperadoes escaped jail before dawn, burning the facility in the process. Justice of the Peace Wentworth wisely left town for a few days to permit tempers to cool.[9]

The constable constituted the first echelon of local peacekeeping at the precinct level and often worked closely with the county sheriff. While the constable served as the enforcement arm of the justice court, he also held powers within his precinct equivalent to the sheriff in the county. Yet the constable was not formally a subordinate of the sheriff. The two peace officers were separate and autonomous. The constable appointed a deputy constable and possessed the power to summon the *posse comitatus*. He earned a meager income from fees and normally maintained a full time private occupation. He possessed fewer resources—and less prestige—than the sheriff. Although the public often associated the constable with the "rougher element," the sheriffs sometimes deputized them. In this way, the county officer could exercise some control over these lesser lawmen.[10]

The constables often resented the encroachments of the more powerful county peace officer. Sheriff Hyler Ott encountered such a constable in Tucson in the early 1870s. This local lawman complained that Ott took away potential fee income when the sheriff made arrests within the town (precinct) limits. The constable asked Justice of the Peace Charles Meyer to grant an injunction against the sheriff, forbidding him from making arrests in town. Although Meyer refused, Ott agreed informally to avoid arrests in town when possible. A similar flareup between deputy sheriffs and constables in Las Vegas, New Mexico, had tragic results. Sheriff Lorenzo Lopez had made a sincere effort to assist a Hispano constable in keeping the peace during riots surrounding the American Railway Union strike in the summer of 1894. However, an ongoing tension between two of Lopez's deputies in East Las Vegas (the Anglo section) and the Hispanic community kept tempers boiling. The two deputies had recently killed a member of the Spanish-speaking community in an attempted arrest. When Constable Jose Martinez attempted to arrest the deputies, they fortified their residence and then killed one member of a posse, a Hispano deputy constable. Only United States troops, who were present in Las Vegas to suppress labor violence, prevented further bloodshed. The two deputy sheriffs were later ambushed and killed under mysterious circumstances.[11]

In 1901, Sheriff Gus Livingston was called upon to protect Constable Marion Alexander in Yuma, Arizona. Alexander and a posse had killed a woman while searching for fugitives. The woman defied the lawmen, shotgun in hand, and ordered them off her property. Although the details of this encounter were unclear, the family of the dead woman swore vengeance against Constable Alexander, the man in charge of the posse. This threat was very real, since Frank and Samuel King were brothers of the victim. They were tough men with strong family loyalties. The possibility of an outbreak of blood feud was very likely. Sheriff Livingston took measures to ensure Alexander's safety until the trial. In spite of these efforts, assassins killed the prisoner as he was being escorted to court. The murderers were never found.[12]

Among frontier officials, the coroners were most misunderstood. Territorial law specifically provided for them. In 1867, New Mexico law required the justices of the peace to serve as coroner and "to inquire into and investigate the cause of death of any human being . . . found dead in the precinct . . . , when it may appear that said death was caused by violence or any other illegal means." The JP was required to summon six persons as a coroner's jury. A subsequent law combined the coronership with the position of chief of police in such towns as Santa Fe. Some counties contracted with a physician for post mortem services. Dr. John Goodfellow surprised the Cochise County board of supervisors when he charged $100 for a post mortem. The board rejected his demand and paid half this amount.[13]

One of the prevailing images of the frontier concerns the impromptu burial of nameless dead in lonely unmarked graves. While many deceased persons were interred without the formality of a coroner's inquest, just as often concerned citizens made an effort to carry out the law and determine cause of death. On 15 July 1894, Jordan Rogers, a Grant County rancher, wrote Sheriff Andrew Laird:

> Dear Sir: I have this day killed James Huffman. I wish you would come over here and hold an inquest. There is no Justice of the peace here, and a number of men at the [Gila Hot] springs will answer for [coroner's] jurymen.

When V. H. Whitlock, with other cowboys, happened upon two dead men some distance from Roswell, New Mexico, he immediately informed the sheriff's office. A deputy soon arrived with a coroner and justice of the peace. These three men formed a coroner's jury and ruled that lightning was the cause of death. Whitlock ensured that the horses and other property of the deceased reached the proper parties.[14]

Frontiersmen were a rough-hewn lot, and some sheriffs were equally hard men. When a Yuma constable sent a posse of Indians after an unarmed jailbreaker, the pursuers brutally shot him to death. A dispatch to the Prescott *Weekly Miner* deplored the insensitivity of the officials who administered the coroner's inquest:

The body of [the] deceased was most inhumanely placed upon the dirt floor, in the office of the justice of the peace, and his person [genitalia] exposed; even at the coroner's inquest, the sheriff [James T. Dana] walked up and down the room in which the corpse was lying, almost striking its head with his foot, and would not even deputize one of the many persons present to wash and place the corpse in a more decent position. . . .

The townspeople were outraged at such callous conduct and finally cleansed the body and provided a covering. Some angry citizens proposed to lynch the constable and other officials for the brutal killing and "shameless" treatment of the dead man.[15]

The commendable efforts of Tucson Coroner W. M. Jacobs to identify a murder victim revealed the high ideals of one such official. When the body of this man was found on the road between Tucson and the Southern Belle Mine, Jacobs (who was also a justice of the peace) mailed letters "In all directions" in search of identifying information, according to the *Arizona Weekly Star*.

It goes to show that with a little alertness many cases that are pronounced impossible [to identify] are possible if placed in the right hands. Many men have met violent deaths in Arizona and have been buried and the usual headboard graced with the word 'unknown.' It would be well to investigate all cases of doubt of identity to a point that would establish a surety of the name.

Coroner Jacobs was at last able to identify the dead man as Pablo Cervantes, although the coroner's jury could only conclude that he was "murdered by parties unknown."[16]

In addition to the coroner, the sheriffs of Arizona and New Mexico territories worked closely with town police forces. While urbanization proceeded very slowly, towns of one or two thousand did flourish and required a policeman in addition to the precinct constable. An early New Mexico law authorized the justice of the peace to appoint a policeman for each plaza in counties with a population of 2,000 or more. However, communities were not permitted a separate marshal until the territorial legislature granted articles of incorporation. When the village of Santa Fe received this coveted status in 1851, lawmakers authorized a marshal who "shall have and exercise the powers and duties of a constable within the jurisdiction of the mayor." Evidently, this marshal functioned much as a precinct constable, since Santa Fe did not adopt a code of police ordinances to govern his conduct until five years later. Policing in the capital reached a new plateau in 1866 when the village was authorized a police force of up to ten men. The chief of police (also serving concurrently as coroner) received sixty dollars per month. This same statute authorized Las Vegas a four-man police department. Albuquerque drafted police ordinances in 1863 and permitted a police magistrate (judge) with power to appoint a marshal. In spite of the seeming independence of these early towns to police themselves, the legislature was reluctant to set them completely free. The 1866 law which permitted the Santa Fe police force included a blanket proviso that the sheriff of each county appoint the policemen in all incorporated towns in New Mexico. These frontier towns grew at such a slow pace that very few of their police forces reached important thresholds—such as the adoption of uniforms—until late in the territorial era. Santa Fe may have been the first village in either New Mexico or Arizona to take this important step. The *Weekly New Mexican* announced this new step toward professionalization in February 1881.[17]

In Arizona, the growth of towns proceeded even more slowly. Tucson made do with precinct status for many years. One observer noted with surprise that one officer, the nightwatchman, doubled as chief of police and detective. With a population of 8,000 by the early 1880s, the town finally boasted a chief of police, four regular and two special policemen, and one nightwatchman. This latter official also served as city jailer. One of the regulars served as desk sergeant. By 1910, the population of Tucson had only reached 13,000. However, the police force now included ten members. Phoenix possessed a population of 8,000 about this time and supported a three-man force of marshal, policeman, and jailer.[18]

The town marshal or chief of police performed duties akin to those the sheriff, but confined them to his (city) sphere. The marshal served the process of justice of the peace court, or mayor's court, collected license fees of businesses, and served as street commissioner, poundmaster, and health officer. He maintained the peace and kept the town jail, if his community could afford one separate from the county jail. Towns that could not afford a place of incarceration rented space from the county sheriff. Since the town marshal possessed the powers of a constable, he might hold both offices simultaneously. This post of town lawman was usually elective. The *Silver City Enterprise* made a good plea for its importance as elections approached in 1883:

The [city] marshalship is probably the most important office in a new and fast growing town [such as Silver City], for upon his efforts in keeping the peace and driving out disreputable characters the citizens must rely. We want an officer whose time is not engaged in his own private affairs, and a man who can be relied upon to do his duty. . . .[19]

The town marshal was often very controversial and was "the low man on the municipal totem pole," according to one historian. Men from the rougher element—the very segment of society that created disturbances—were often the only persons willing to accept the post. Some town policemen cultivated a reputation for dexterity with guns. The tragic quarrel of City Marshal Virgil Earp and his brothers with Sheriff John H. Behan in Tombstone was only the most spectacular instance of such rivalry. A vicious vendetta involving similar official parties erupted in Santa Fe a decade later. This vendetta resulted in the murder of former sheriff Frank Chavez and others. George Hochderffer, veteran city marshal of Flagstaff, Arizona, lamented the evil reputations that a few town peace officers, such as Virgil and Wyatt Earp, had given this important local law enforcement office. The selfish desire to earn fame as a gunman could only bring harm to the peace officer's community. Hochederffer had a much more modest goal for these city lawmen. "No officer had any special claim to glory," said Hochderffer, "as long as he did his best to maintain law and order. . . ." While he concluded that Flagstaff "was no worse than other western towns," he boasted that this community's lawmen "were never mixed up in crime" like the policemen of some other towns. Nor did this Flagstaff lawman quarrel with Sheriff Ralph Henry Cameron. Hochederffer averred that "the county and town officers worked together without rivalry.[20]

Sheriffs and city policemen often clashed over jurisdiction. In September 1886, Sheriff Santiago Baca and Deputy Elfego Baca (a former Socorro deputy) were accused of assaulting an Albuquerque policeman. Since the victim was an Anglo, this incident nearly provoked a race riot. Difficulty also occurred between city officers and the sheriff's office in Santa Fe in January 1884. The *New Mexican Review* noted that deputy sheriffs were patrolling the streets at night, while the city police were "conspicuous by their absence from the streets, as usual. . . ." When a Santa Fe policeman complained in February 1893 that Sheriff Charles Conklin's men were infringing upon his sphere, Deputy Sheriff Antonio Alarid denied this charge. Through a local newspaper, Alarid protested that, far from interloping, he had assisted his city counterparts "as far as I have been able. . . ."[21]

Of all frontier lawmen, the county sheriff and the United States marshal resembled each other most closely. Not to be confused with the city marshal, one United States marshal served each territory. Like the sheriff, this officer served process and had charge of prisoners, but only at the federal level. In the absence of adequate funding, he could employ few full-time deputies and therefore commissioned sheriffs and deputy sheriffs. He also rented county jail space for United States prisoners. Marshal Creighton M. Foraker frankly admitted this dependence upon the county lawmen. When the Department of Justice proposed to reduce the daily rate paid sheriffs for housing federal prisoners, Foraker strongly objected. In a letter of 17 June 1901 to the Attorney General, Deputy Marshal John H. Campbell explained his superior's case:

> We have to rely a great deal upon Sheriffs and other local officers for information and assistance. . . . The [marshal's] district is so big, and settlements so widely scattered that 'hold-ups' [bandits] would get too much start if we could not obtain information from local officers. It is very profitable [for sheriffs] to keep U.S. prisoners and the marshal feels that if he took steps to force the price [of contracting prisoners] down he would antagonize the Sheriffs, and lose their help. . . .

In the routine of cooperation between the various spheres of lawmen, practical trade-offs were necessary. A similar dependency prevailed in Arizona.[22]

The authority of the United States marshals was very restricted. They could not interfere with the county sheriff or any other lawman in the territories. In the American Republic, the founders divided the power to coerce among many separate spheres, each one being to some degree autonomous. The United States marshal and the sheriff were colleagues, but separate, and possessed equal stature within their respective bailiwicks. The founders also assumed that men and women were rational human beings and would generally conduct themselves as reasonable people. They would live in harmony most of the time. At the same time, the founders had a healthy respect for occasional outbursts of human passions and abuse of power. Hence, the Constitution clearly defined the purview of various offices, among them the sphere of the United States marshal. The awesome prestige and power of the United States government today is largely a product of this century. In the nineteenth century, the federal government lacked the financial resources and the support of the public to create such an overwhelming system.[23]

Popular writers of Western history and fiction have elevated the frontier United States marshal far above his actual authority. When the Hollywood screen creates a fictitious marshal and causes him to override the sheriff or city marshal, such wild assumptions are totally false. In a recent article in a Las Cruces newspaper, a writer erroneously maintains that the United States marshal directed all law enforcement in New Mexico Territory until the turn of this century. Only then, he says, were the sheriffs and other lawmen emancipated from federal control, presumably through some imaginary Congressional law. In fact, nineteenth-century frontiersmen respected the separate spheres of law enforcement and decried any infringements. Only when a person violated federal statutes did the United States marshal enter a case. Even then, the federal lawman did not necessarily assume leadership of the investigation but cooperated with the sheriff. The marshal possessed so few financial resources that he often graciously remained aloof.[24]

Arizonans witnessed several disputes between sheriffs and United States marshals. The most regrettable took place in June 1878 when Deputy Marshal Joseph W. Evans took possession of two suspected mail robbers from the jail of Yavapai County. Sheriff Edward F. Bowers was away, leaving a deputy on duty. The federal lawman convinced the deputy that he held a proper United States commissioner's warrant. The suspects, including pioneer Arizonan Jack Swilling, were already under territorial indictment. The *Arizona Miner* opined that Deputy Marshal Evans was guilty of "sharp practice" and had "perhaps unlawfully" taken custody of the prisoners. This editor scolded sheriff's personnel for failing to get legal advice before turning over the accused men. Swilling died in the Yuma County jail before trial in federal court. Three years later, Yuma experienced two additional county-federal confrontations. Deputy United States Marshal Robert H. Paul—later sheriff of Pima County—used a heavily armed posse to overawe a deputy sheriff and a probate judge in order to take possession of a bankrupt mercantile house. The Prescott *Arizona Miner* urged Marshal Crawley P. Dake to reprimand his high-handed deputy. Although Paul had the law on his side, his error lay in the roughshod and tactless manner in which he publicly humiliated the sheriff's office. The sanctity of this county officer, the primary law enforcer at the local level, was very dear to frontiersmen.[25]

The county sheriffs encountered a wide array of governmental and private agencies. The Departments of the Treasury and Interior dispatched investigators to Arizona and New Mexico. Congress sent specially empowered committees—the most notable being the Land Court—to conduct investigations. The Department of Treasury maintained customs officers along the international boundary. The United States Army often assisted law enforcement officers. On the territorial level, the militias served as sheriffs' posses. At the turn of the century, Arizona and New Mexico created territory-wide police forces, the Rangers and the Mounted Police, respectively. Although outside the United States, the Mexican *rurales* (rural police) cooperated with the sheriffs of border counties.[26]

In addition to publicly supported lawmen, many private companies maintained policemen. Arizona and New Mexico granted mining, cattle, railroad, and express companies this right. In some instances, the sheriffs deputized these company men for limited and specific purposes. Private detectives were also common on the late nineteenth-century frontier. William Pinkerton founded the Pinkerton National Detective Agency before the Civil War with the purpose of protecting the Illinois Central Railroad from thieves. Soon, the Pinkerton's "eye that never sleeps" became identified with the protection of big business. This explained the active presence of the agency in the New Mexico and Arizona territories where bandits often preyed upon stage, express, and railroad companies. When Pinkerton set up a branch office in Denver, Colorado, his operatives became a common sight in the two territories to the south. Operative Charlie Siringo conducted many investigations in New Mexico and eventually retired in Santa Fe, where he wrote books— very critical ones—about his former employer.[27]

The popularity of private detective agencies prompted the creation of local counterparts. The Rocky Mountain Detective Agency, with headquarters in Denver, maintained affiliates in New Mexico and elsewhere in the Rocky Mountain West. David J. Cook, a Colorado sheriff, founded this organization after the Civil War. Some form of cooperation between law enforcers was needed in the Rocky Mountain West, although the primitive communications of that day made mutual assistance difficult. Cook described the experiences of his organization in *Hands Up! Or, Twenty Years of Detective Life in the Mountains and on the Plains*. This agency should not be confused with the highly organized and profitable Pinkerton operation. Cook's concern was not a formally chartered and self-sustaining company, but consisted of sheriffs, city lawmen, and other authorities who served without salary. Cook did distribute reward money if available. The Rocky Mountain Detective Agency provided very real services, and a branch appeared in New Mexico. In May 1883, Tony Neis, a veteran deputy sheriff and deputy United States marshal, opened an office in Albuquerque, with branches in Santa Fe and Silver City.[28]

A market for local private detectives soon arose in New Mexico and Arizona. Elfego Baca opened an agency in Albuquerque about 1890. He also practiced law. Baca's official business card advertised his detective skills on one side and legal trade on the other. In March 1901, two residents of Phoenix, Arizona, opened a detective agency. In C. W. Johnstone and Hi McDonald, said the *Arizona Republican* proudly, the territory had sleuths better than the Pinkertons.[29]

Some frontiersmen expressed skepticism about the effectiveness and propriety of these public and private agencies. When Azariah F. Wild, Secret Service Agent of the Treasury Department, investigated counterfeiting in Lincoln County, he failed to keep his identity a secret. The public soon knew his every move. The *Daily New Mexican* poked fun at detectives in general and Wild in particular and declared that they should possess "a small amount of sense and discretion." This "namesake of Jonathan Wild," continued the *New Mexican*, "told every one of his business." Furthermore, Wild "was withal a rank coward." When Wild visited White Oaks, the roughhouse miners reportedly manhandled him "without gloves." A more controversial encounter took place in Arizona in the summer of 1877 when Post Office Detective John Mantle infiltrated a band of stagecoach robbers in Yavapai County. Mantle made the serious error of failing to alert Sheriff Edward F. Bowers. When Mantle actually participated in a robbery, the sheriff was a passenger on the victimized coach. Bowers lost $450 to the bandits! A grand jury concluded that the Post Office's conduct was "deplorable in the extreme"; "we cannot too severely condemn this light-handed experiment." The Mantle operation showed "an almost criminal lack of common sense." The jury opined that such irresponsibility should be "a public caution to the world at large" against such reckless escapades. The jurors deplored the excesses "within the reach of the detective's peculiar intellect." This panel expressed the belief that the government agents could depend upon the discretion and assistance of the sheriff. When the prosecutor placed Bowers on the witness stand, he asked the lawman, "could you not have captured or taken the other [outlaw] parties . . ." if Detective Mantle had taken the sheriff into his confidence? The sheriff replied affirmatively, "I could."[30]

Private sleuths also came into question. Many persons regarded railroad detectives as boorish, "fat and lazy," and incapable of holding respectable law enforcement jobs. In September 1887, the *Silver City Enterprise* reported that the Pinkertons had arrested train robbery suspects in Arizona and illegally spirited them to Los Angeles. However, the detectives lacked sufficient evidence to hold the accused men. When the California judge released the suspects, the Pinkertons refused to pay their victims' expenses home. The *Enterprise* concluded that such insensitive behavior made the agency a "laughing stock" and fostered hard feelings in the Southwest. When the Pinkerton Detective Agency assisted steel magnate Andrew Carnegie in the breakup of a strike in Pennsylvania, a Las Cruces newspaperman characterized such brutal activities as "un-American." This angry editor approved of efforts of detectives to unearth crime but objected to the employment of "an army of soldiers of fortune" against hardworking laboring men.[31]

Relations between New Mexico sheriffs and the Pinkertons were uneven. Personality conflicts did occur. Pinkerton Operative Charlie Siringo cultivated good relations with New Mexico sheriffs during his pursuit of the Butch Cassidy band in 1901. Siringo applauded Sheriffs Arthur Goodell and James K. Blair of Grant County. They were "model officers." Sheriff Pat Garrett obviously resented the interference of a Pinkerton agent in the search for the assassins of lawyer Albert J. Fountain and his son in Doña Ana County in 1896. Garrett refused to cooperate and called upon a friend, Chaves County Sheriff Charles C. Perry. Perry poked fun at the detective and refused to share information. In reflecting upon the general unwillingness of Southwestern sheriffs to cooperate with his agents, William Pinkerton concluded that these peace officers probably feared reprisal or assassination, although other motives— he did not specify—might contribute to this reluctance. In one instance, Pinkerton recalled that an unidentified Southwestern lawman agreed to secretly deputize an operative, but refused to openly assist him. In spite of a spotty success record, the Pinkertons continued to obtain employment in New Mexico and Arizona territories. Operatives worked for the Maxwell Land Grant against the anti-grant movement in Colfax County, and Governor L. Bradford Prince hired the Pinkertons to infiltrate the White Cap movement in neighboring San Miguel County in the early 1890s.[32]

The governors provided many services to law enforcers. The sheriffs were especially dependent upon them, although the executives possessed little or no statutory authority over the day-to-day conduct of county officers. (The sheriffs had belonged to the counties since Anglo-Saxon England.) The governors proclaimed rewards, processed extraditions, exchanged information about criminal movements, made the militia available to sheriffs, and appointed agents in special cases. The governors employed private detectives and exercised the pardoning power. They also set the tone and the example for lovers of law and order. The hardier territorial executives made on-the-spot visits to troubled areas. Lew Wallace took personal charge of the campaign against outlaws in Lincoln County in 1879. William T. Thornton did the same against violent secret societies in the 1890s. Governor George Curry played a part in the investigation of the murder of former Sheriff Pat Garrett in 1908, albeit unsuccessfully. In Arizona, the governors were also active. In the 1870s, Governor Anson Safford led a posse after murderers, while Acting Governor John J. Gosper personally investigated the Earp-Clanton feud in Tombstone in the following decade. Governor C. Meyer Zulick took a direct interest in the suppression of the Tewksbury-Graham feud in 1887.[33]

The governor was the prime mover in extradition proceedings. To place a properly worded requisition before the proper authority in another land was very difficult. Each requisition—the formally written request for a fugitive—had to be precisely copied, notarized, and signed. When the governor placed the official documents in the hands of a sheriff, the package included a certified copy of the indictment, affidavits as to the commission of the crime, the requisition, and verification of the official status of the agent (sheriff or deputy). Only then did the host state or country consent to extradition—the actual surrender—of the wanted person. The formal notice of this consent took the form of an official document, a mandate, in which the host government honored the requisition.[34]

The web of law enforcers grew more complex as the nineteenth century drew to a close. Indian policemen patrolled the reservations. Game wardens and livestock association detectives traveled remote lands. The wardens held the authority of deputy sheriffs but could only make arrests when game laws were violated. Customs officials guarded ports of entry from the Republic of Mexico. Sheriffs of counties on the border were very familiar with these customs officials, both Mexican and American. The list of persons engaged in law enforcement seemed endless. One person not yet mentioned is the bounty hunter, that "professional" manhunter who allegedly prowled Arizona and New Mexico territories in search of criminals with rewards on their heads. While some aficionados of the Wild West may be disappointed, the professional bounty hunter did not exist in the Southwest. That is not to say that lawmen and private citizens did not seek reward money. They did. However, an individual could hardly earn enough money to support a family while merely engaged in bounty hunting. Sheriffs and other lawmen did supplement their regular incomes from rewards.[35]

The sheriffs of Arizona and New Mexico territories were members of a complex fraternity of law enforcers, both public and private. At first glance, it would appear that the county sheriffs would be unable to perform their routine duties without infringing upon colleagues. However, certain rules of conduct applied to all, even on this remote frontier. The sheriffs and their comrades remained within prescribed spheres. Friction did exist between the sheriffs and their counterparts in the other spheres. Some embarrassing incidents took place. Since the counties constituted the most important foundation of local government in the Anglo-American tradition, the sheriffs held a central place in territorial law enforcement. The many private and public lawmen in Arizona and New Mexico could accomplish very little without the consent of the local sheriff. A give-and-take relationship was necessary among these many echelons. The sheriff bestowed favors upon many persons, such as deputy commissions, jail space, and information. In other instances, he made concessions to counterparts at the precinct or town level by permitting the constables or city policemen to make arrests and thus earn fees. The sheriffs and the many other peace officers were a quarrelsome lot and guarded their prerogatives jealously. Yet, the system worked—with some notable exceptions—in a rough and tumble way.

4

Getting in Office
Seeking Preferment to the Shrievalty

 Aspiring politicians of Arizona and New Mexico eagerly sought the shrievalty. Within the limited spoils system of poor territories, this position was a plum. Political infighting began at the first inkling that the assembly contemplated the creation of a new county. If the aspirants lacked money in the territories, they substituted energy and imagination. Candidates for the sheriff's office confronted many campaign obstacles: vast distances, scattered settlements, Indian hostilities, ethnic divisions, and even corruption and violence at the polls. Even when the governors made appointments, candidates found it necessary to campaign for the selection. If resources were lacking for waging a sophisticated Eastern-styled campaign, these frontier New Mexicans and Arizonans conducted crude, but sometimes imaginative, battles. Although difficult to imagine today, the stakes could be very high in the race for sheriff, and passions often soared. Campaigns could explode into lethal confrontations. This passionate undercurrent was present throughout the territorial era.

Electioneering and political maneuvering became a consuming passion in the southwestern territories. Since the residents of territories were unable to participate in most elections at the federal level—President, United States senators and representatives—frontiersmen seemed to channel their political fervor into local elections. Organized political parties were slow to materialize in New Mexico and Arizona territories; individuals sought offices based upon personal popularity, and factions thrived. In counties with minimal population, persons from various political persuasions formed temporary alliances of convenience to present "county tickets." Loyalty to candidate or ticket extended beyond the ballot to everyday conduct. The faithful follower traded only with the storekeeper in his faction. As one historian humorously observed about Holm Olaf Bursum's term as Socorro County sheriff, if a local GOP member had an appendectomy, the excised tissue better have "Republican" stamped on it. As George Curry put it, "Personal enmities were engendered that lasted for years, extending into business as well as political affairs, and leading . . . a number of times to violence and death."[1]

The behavior of candidates for local offices often appeared mindless and grasping. Idealism and exalted notions about the principles of republican government were sometimes hard to find. In the 1863 campaign, Albuquerque editor Hezekiah Johnson reminded candidates for the sheriffalty, coronership, and other Bernalillo County offices of "the importance of their trust regarding the wellbeing of Society." Government, said Johnson,

> is not a farce gotten up for public diversion, nor a game invented to displaying the chicanery and skill of politicians, but an institution necessary for man as a social being, and to protect and promote his pursuit of his true and substantial happiness. . . .

If all newly elected officials will enter into "the spirit of their oath[s] of office," continued Johnson, "the prosperity and good name of New Mexico will . . . progress. . . ." Such exalted notions on this remote frontier were refreshing, but whether the Bernalillo County candidates would take this preachment to heart remained to be seen.[2]

Each shrievalty candidate boasted some attribute or quality that fitted him for this important post. Sanford Rowe, who desired the Coconino County, Arizona, office in 1900, was a "straight-forward business man," while James A. Tomlinson, candidate in Lincoln County, New Mexico, in 1882, was "a genial gentleman of positive tendencies, and . . . will make things buzz . . ." in the shrievalty. Charles F. Hunt of Albuquerque was gifted at "getting around the voters and gaining their good will." In 1892, Scott White, a Cochise County hotel owner, was touted as "a young man 35 years of age, and a fearless, active man of good sense and Judgment." L. K. Drais, of Florence, Arizona, not only fought with General Ulysses Grant at Vicksburg and Atlanta, but stood in "the ranks of labor and is recognized as a skilled mechanic." Edward F. Bowers, candidate for sheriff in Yavapai County, Arizona, in 1878, had the reputation of peacemaker. A friend who had known him in the

California goldfields praised Bowers for his mediating ability. "When any trouble got among us [miners]," said this informant, "he never decided wrong in his life. . . ." Bowers "hasn't got one dishonest principle, no sir, not one . . . ." Bowers disagreed with his old friend and averred that he was "not a man of words but action." In the 1884 Santa Fe County race, the *Weekly New Mexican* supported a promising young man, Celestino Ortiz. "The shrievalty is as near a war office as any civil position can be," said this writer. "'Old men for counsel and young men for war,'" declared this journalist.[3]

In periods of lawlessness, law and order campaigns were common. Since frontiersmen generally had some familiarity with weapons, voters could be assured of a minimal ability with guns in most shrievalty candidates. Voters were more concerned that the candidate possess nerve and determination to use their guns. Whether the office seeker had "killed his man" did not seem to loom large with voters. Pat Garrett promised law and order in the 1880 Lincoln County campaign, and supporters advertised his "quick gun." But they were not referring to an ability to draw quickly. Garrett may not have had this aptitude. He was known to have killed only one man, an acquaintance, in regrettable circumstances. Garrett often employed a rifle rather than revolver. This long gun was a less dramatic but more effective weapon and a habit from his buffalo-hunting days. Garrett partisans really believed that his strongest suit was a willingness to shoot sooner—not draw faster—than opposition candidates. When Commodore Perry Owens ran a similar campaign in Apache County, Arizona, six years later, he could not point to a man-killing record. Yet, close associates regarded Owens as a nervy person. A frequently used slogan for such candidates was "a man who knows no fear." Even when frontier voters desired a "quick gun" in the sheriff's office, the public usually confined him to only one term. The people much preferred that a Garrett or an Owens be confined (if given a law enforcement position at all) to the deputyship.[4]

Candidates for the sheriff's office sought opportunities to demonstrate nerve. Service in posses was one means, although the results were sometimes tragic. John A. Gillespie, a Tombstone miner, desired the nomination in the 1882 campaign. In March he joined in a manhunt, only to be killed in a murderous confrontation with the bandits. In September 1911, Thomas Hall volunteered to serve in a Grant County posse which was pursuing the John Greer band, a hard set of badmen. Robert Bell, an acquaintance of this posseman, recalled years later that Hall "was gonna run for sheriff in the next election" and thus joined the posse in order to build up merits with the voters. A Graham County man recommended a novel scheme to test the manhunting qualities of shrievalty candidates during the 1900 elections. The proposal was that the major political parties choose candidates early. Sheriff Ben Clark would then deputize them and assign these aspiring politicians the task of capturing the notorious escaped murderer, Augustin Chacon. The successful candidate would then be elected sheriff. In a reference to the growing demand for a professional class of educated and trained public servants, the Lordsburg *Liberal* observed that the Graham County proposal "would be a first class civil service examination." This firsthand test would also be "a more practical one than was ever made by the government's [Civil Service] commission." While the Arizonans did not seriously consider such a plan, the discussion surrounding it registered the public skepticism that the electoral process was the most effective way to choose the chief county lawman.[5]

A surprising amount of resources and planning went into these campaigns. Each faction desired the support of a newspaper, which prominently displayed its ticket near the banner. Alphie A. (Pap) Anderson, candidate for Graham County sheriff in 1906, distributed a campaign book, which contained a biographical sketch of each person on his party's slate and formal positions on critical issues. Travel over lonely trails was an accepted part of campaigning. William Eugene Brooks, a young lawyer, recalled this particular election campaign. When Anderson learned that the young barrister planned a trip from the mining camp of Metcalf to the remote Double Circle Ranch, the candidate asked permission to accompany him. Brooks quickly consented. "I was glad to have company," said Brooks. The *Arizona Miner* noted the departure of Sheriff Edward Bowers and aspirants for other offices for outlying settlements in the 1878 campaign. Bowers sought reelection. He and his colleagues "were armed with all the modern electioneering appliances," according to this writer. Bowers lost the campaign to Joseph Rutherford Walker, nephew of the famous Joseph Reddeford Walker, who helped to found Prescott.[6]

There were many ways to communicate with potential voters. Ash Upson, a close friend of Pat Garrett, wrote letters on his behalf in the campaign for sheriff of newly created Chaves County in 1890. "I have a pile of letters before me . . . ," moaned Upson, and "have pretty much all the correspondence to attend to. . . ." Campaign jingles were common. Wayne Whitehill, son of the longtime sheriff of Grant County, New Mexico, Harvey Whitehill, sang a campaign song for his father in an election parade through Cook's Peak mining camp:

Vote for Harvey Whitehill
Vote for Harvey Whitehill
Vote for Harvey Whitehill early in the morning
Vote for Harvey Whitehill early in the morning
Cook's Peak gallant band.

Charles F. Blackington had a great advantage over opponents in So- corro County. Better known as "Doc," "He combined medicine and free services as a physician and surgeon," according to New Mexico pioneer and historian William A. Keleher, "with an occa- sional bit of practical politics." "On election day 'Doc' Blackington could not be defeated. . . ," concluded Keleher.[7]

Liquid refreshments flowed freely in frontier election campaigns, although the importance of the role of alcohol can be over- emphasized. When Louis Dupuy canvassed Pima County, Arizona, to determine his chances for the shrievalty in the late 1870s, this former constable distributed whiskey and cigars. In spite of such generosity, he lost to Charles Shibell, a well-known restauranteur and veteran office holder. In neighboring Yavapai County, lawyer John Wentworth recalled that he set out to politick for Buckey O'Neill "with a buckboard load of whiskey." Another pioneer of Prescott, John A. Edmunson, met one troop of frolicsome O'Neill supporters in this campaign. They distributed spirits to everyone, he recalled, "regardless of their voting qualifications." In New Mex- ico, Miguel A. Otero recalled canvassing San Miguel County with "five gallon kegs filled with the customary XXX whiskey, calculated to encourage fights and provide votes." Candidates were also ex- pected to hold their liquor, said Otero, and "You would lose votes if you refused to take the proffered drink. . . ." Whiskey did not al- ways work, as George Curry learned in Pat Garrett's campaign for the Lincoln County shrievalty in 1880. While Garrett won the elec- tion, he failed to hold Las Tablas Precinct. Curry dispensed free li- quor and cigars on behalf of Garrett, but the voters—primarily Hispanos—supported the incumbent, George Kimbrell. Although it was only a minor setback, George Curry became convinced that "whiskey and tobacco did no voting." Hard issues still counted for something.[8]

Alcoholic beverages worked more effectively when combined with other festivities. Citizens of St. Johns, Yavapai County, gave candidates a dance during the 1878 campaign. Among these aspirants was Sheriff Edward F. Bowers, who sought another term. After a clumsy attempt at speech making (and Bowers admitted his ineptitude), the various candidates were given the opportunity to exhibit aptitude on the dance floor. "The most amusing part of this dance," observed one writer, "was [the] skill—I won't say grace—with which Sheriff Bowers engineered his towering head (he is over six feet tall and built in proportion) among the glittering chanceliers [sic]. . . ." Bowers lost his bid for reelection in spite of his nimbleness of foot. Miguel A. Otero recalled how Don Juan Gallegos, Republican strongman in San Miguel County, generously provided facilities for a grand *baile* for candidates. "We soon finished a very successful meeting," wrote Otero. Santiago Baca, candidate for sheriff in Bernalillo County in 1886, attempted to gain control of the only brass band in Albuquerque in order to prevent the musicians from playing for the Republican opposition. When Baca learned that these music makers owed money on their instruments, he purchased their note from the creditor and seized their horns during a hotly contested campaign. Baca, who had already upset his followers by changing parties, lost this election.[9]

The incumbent sheriff possessed considerable advantage over contenders in the race for office. William C. Truman, an experienced Pinal County politico, had no qualms about using his deputies as campaigners. Truman also shrewdly utilized the Young Men's Democratic Club to attract the newly qualified voters. Billy Breakenridge, a Cochise County deputy, admitted using his position to influence voters on behalf of the Democratic ticket in the 1882 county elections. His assignment—to distribute blank ballots—provided some official cover. On the eve of election day, Breakenridge stopped at a newly established ranch staffed by Texans who were unfamiliar with the candidates. The deputy persuaded all seventeen men to vote the straight Democratic ticket. Given their ex-Confederate backgrounds, these herders probably would have voted this ticket anyway.[10]

Masterminds behind these shrievalty campaigns carefully courted all voting blocks. The candidate whose area included large ethnic communities, such as the heavily Mexican and European sections of the mining camps of Clifton and Morenci, Arizona, needed to win over these groups. The Parks family, which participated heavily in Graham County politics, often won the support of ethnic groups, especially the new arrivals from Europe. In one of Jim Parks's campaigns for sheriff, his brother, Deputy John Parks, sought out Jack Laustenneau, who was believed to be part Spanish and a spokesman for many foreigners. "Whenever the [law] officers saw one of the foreigners becoming a leader," recalled sister Jennie Parks Ringgold, "they cultivated his friendship . . . for political reasons." Laustenneau later led a major strike and was sent to prison. In counties of predominantly Spanish-speaking heritage, the wise Hispano candidate courted the Anglo minority. However, Don Hilario Romero, who ran for the San Miguel County sheriffalty in 1884, caused some concern among his Republican friends. Although an experienced campaigner, Romero incautiously promised to appoint a Hispano friend to the post of deputy sheriff in East Las Vegas, an Anglo stronghold. These new arrivals demanded one of their own in the deputyship. Although Romero won in spite of this faux pas, his followers worried about the alienation of this important block.[11]

Political indiscretion, such as that of Hilario Romero, played an important part in shrievalty campaigns of all groups. Anglo politicians commonly believed Hispanic voters could be easily manipulated, since they lacked formal education and training in democracy. However, the liberal distribution of whiskey among grassroots Anglos revealed that American office seekers held their own kind in equal (if more cleverly veiled) contempt. After the 1902 elections in Florence, Arizona, observers told a story to illustrate the condescending attitude toward persons of Spanish heritage. William C. Truman, longtime sheriff, had just lost a bid for reelection. A curious bystander asked a Hispano, "'Whom did you vote for for sheriff?' The reply was, 'Truman.' 'Whom did you vote for for district attorney?' Again the answer was, 'Truman.'" In nearby Pima County, veteran Deputy Sheriff Jeff Milton recalled that Matthew F. Shaw openly steered the Hispano vote in the 1890 campaign. On the night before the polls opened, candidates for various offices rented halls and sponsored parties. Liquor flowed freely all night. When the voting booths opened, said Milton (a supporter of Shaw), the politicians gave voters "a registration receipt and a ticket apiece and flanking them with squads of guards marched them to the polls."[12]

The entry of the railroads into New Mexico and Arizona territories provoked a significant change in political behavior. This change was not lost on candidates for the sheriffalty. In counties fortunate enough to be in the pathway of the iron horse, the office seeker could benefit if identified as "the railroad candidate." Company officials contributed in a variety of ways. They provided candidates with money and free rail passage and also encouraged employees to vote for their candidate. A negative recommendation by the railroad could just as easily block an aspirant to the shrievalty. In the 1880 campaign for this office in Pima County, Arizona, opponents of Robert H. Paul accused him of being "the railroad candidate." Paul had been a Wells Fargo Express Company detective. This company was a close associate of the railroad. Both companies used their influence on behalf of Paul. Paul won this and two successive elections, although not without much controversy. Frank E. Murphy relied upon the Southern Pacific in the 1900 campaign in this same county. When Murphy had to leave Tucson on a business trip, W. P. B. Field, a campaign worker, wrote excitedly that he should return quickly. The nominating convention would meet soon. Field assured Murphy that "The majority of the railroad boys are tied up [confirmed] for you . . ." but they "want to see you on the ground . . ." in Tucson. The opposition was "working hard" to unseat Murphy in the convention, said Field, and "The point has been reached when you must be personally present." Murphy apparently complied. He won the race.[13]

As railroad, mining, cattle, and other economic enterprises began to wield political influence in Arizona and New Mexico in the 1880s, some voters began to develop suspicions about them. When this skepticism began to influence the public mood, the shrievalty candidates detected such misgivings. Insurgent politics briefly added new vigor and liveliness to races for the sheriffalty in the 1880s and 1890s. Buckey O'Neill played successfully upon public hostility toward railroads and mining companies in the race for Yavapai County sheriff in 1888. His "anti-establishment" campaign singled out the Atlantic and Pacific Railroad as a target. This company owned thousands of acres of improved and unimproved land but paid only minimal taxes. O'Neill brazenly promised that as sheriff and collector he would strive to make the company pay a fair share. (Voters evidently forgot that the sheriff-collector only executed, and did not make, the law.) On election day, the A and P responded by shipping its employees into Prescott free of charge with instructions to cast their ballots against this troublemaker. O'Neill won in spite of the railroad's efforts, and his two years as sheriff were among the most memorable in the history of the Arizona shrievalty. In spite of his gift for flamboyance, O'Neill could not keep his campaign promise to force the railroad to pay its fair share of taxes. Ten years later, John Munds employed this same theme in a Yavapai County sheriff's race; except that the United

Verde Copper Company was the villain. In San Miguel County, New Mexico, Don Jose Lopez was accused of garnering grassroots support in his race for sheriff by catering to the people's hatred of land grant owners.[14]

The livestock industry also became a powerful force in the shrievalty campaigns. In the 1880s, newly formed stock associations lobbied very effectively for their self-interests. "What was important to them [cattlemen] was the race for sheriff," said Jeff Milton, a longtime deputy. In Grant County, Henry Brock, manager of the vast Diamond A ranch, admitted that his company profitted by having an efficient and friendly man in the shrievalty. Brock protested that he voted for "the proper man," not the party candidate. However, he probably found that one candidate filled both categories. When George Curry entered the sheriff's race in Lincoln County in 1892, the large cattle companies opposed him. "I was too friendly with the small cattlemen," admitted Curry. The big spreads assumed that all lesser ranchers were rustlers or in league with wielders of the "long rope." After winning this bid, Curry maintained that his firm stand against all rustlers so impressed the large spreads that they offered to help finance his next campaign. He refused the offer.[15]

The combination of these various powerful interests began to challenge the traditional political regimes in the 1880s. The accusations that small ranchers and farmers fostered cattle thieves and train robbers and general lawlessness provided the rationale for the efforts of big companies to win control of county sheriff's offices. The campaigns for these critical offices were often tense and explosive. In the 1886 election in Apache County, Arizona, the Atlantic and Pacific Railroad and various cattle companies challenged the clique of Indian traders and Hispano sheepmen who had settled the Little Colorado Valley after the Civil War. (The Mormons, also recent arrivals, remained neutral or were shunned by both parties.) John Lorenzo Hubbell, representative of an influential New Mexico–based mercantile family, won the shrievalty in 1884, although not without the opposition of the railroad and cattle companies. If Hubbell's memoirs are to be believed, he expressed open contempt for these interlopers and detested the roughshod way the cowboys harassed the Hispanos. He also believed sheepmen used the land more wisely than stockmen.[16]

When the 1886 campaign for sheriff came around, the railroad and cattle companies were more firmly entrenched. Even some sheepmen, including the great California-based company of A. A.

and P. P. Daggs, desired the defeat of Hubbell. Although the Mormons may not have voted, they looked back upon this election as an important one in the effort to impose law and order. Samuel Brown, sheepman and Holbrook livery stable owner, was the local representative of the Daggses as well as chairman of the Apache County Democratic Party. Frank Wattron, druggist and constable, assisted Brown in the search for a candidate. These law and order men selected Commodore Perry Owens. Owens was born in Tennessee in 1852; his mother reportedly named him for the great naval hero. It's unknown when Owens moved west, but it is known that he became manager of a stagecoach station in Arizona in 1881. He won local approval for killing a Navajo Indian, although the Indian agent unsuccessfully prosecuted him. As range foreman for a cattle company at Navajo Springs, he quietly but efficiently combatted rustlers. Although he sported long hair—Buffalo Bill style—Owens's prowess with weapons discouraged any criticism. The *St. Johns Herald* enthusiastically supported the Apache County Democratic Central Committee's selection:

> There is a good time coming when Commodore Owens is installed in the Sheriff's Office. The cattle and sheep will be able to browse unmolested upon the plains, lawbreakers must seek another climate, cattle and horse thieves must adopt a safer business. . . . The Commodore possesses all the traits of a good and efficient officer; temperate and discreet, yet at the same time fearless and conscientious. . . .[17]

Commodore Owens was a part of a "team" that the Democrats envisioned as necessary to rid the county of rustlers. These politicos selected Harris Baldwin for the district attorneyship. A fearless prosecutor was as essential as a brave arresting officer. The *Herald* admitted that "Reform is staking all and everything on this team. . . ," but this writer added, "We make the assertion that these two men will make the fur fly all over Apache county. . . ." The Owens-Baldwin ticket won this critical county election, although the margin of victory was probably closer than desirable. Commodore Perry Owens won 499 votes, to 419 for Don Lorenzo Hubbell. Unfortunately, Hubbell's memoirs do not reveal his efforts in this campaign. Harris Baldwin won the attorneyship unopposed.[18]

Elsewhere, in both territories, law and order campaigns were successful. The emerging cattle interests played a decisive part in installing a law and order administration in Lincoln County, New Mexico in 1880. Cattleman Joseph C. Lea and fellow range barons not only desired to suppress cattle rustling but to prevent the possibility of the resurrection of the bloody vendetta that had ravaged the region two years earlier. A similar sentiment prevailed among stockmen in Cochise County, Arizona. They spearheaded the movement to elect one of their own, John H. Slaughter, to the sheriff's office in 1886. Billy King, a Slaughter deputy, recalled later that this new lawman's purpose was to run off "the Wild Bunch" of rustlers. James Wolf, another subordinate of this famous manhunter, believed that other property owners equally desired Slaughter. "Such a sad state of [lawless] affairs was reached," said Wolf, that "the business men met and induced John Slaughter to run for sheriff." Mining companies and other property owners united in Pinal County to rout the troublesome element in 1881. These middle-class men persuaded Andrew J. Doran, manager of the Silver King Mine, to seek the office of chief county lawman. Doran recalled that "whiskey men, gamblers and [the] rough element were running the county." The "decent element of the county organized to bring about a change," added Doran, who won his bid for office.[19]

If the incumbent sheriff desired to remain in office, his past often played a critical part in his bid for reelection. When Sheriff William Sanders Oury announced this desire in fall 1874, a rival faction in Tucson went into action. James E. McCaffry, United States district attorney, distributed a handbill which enumerated many alleged shortcomings of the sheriff. Among other offenses, Oury failed to assess taxable property fairly; assigned prisoners to work on private property rather than public projects; failed to maintain the courthouse properly; refused to serve a warrant, alleging that the fee income was too meager; and failed to arrest disturbers of the peace. Oury's standing as an original settler and brave pioneer helped him overcome these charges and win again. In subsequent campaigns in this county, Bob Paul fought a hard but ultimately successful fight to overcome public disgust over two big jailbreaks. Later, Frank Murphy lost a reelection try in Tucson because he had refused to hang a condemned man in his prior term. The intended victim was insane. Voters evidently concluded that Murphy lacked an essential quality for a sheriff—nerve.[20]

Elsewhere in Arizona, Navajo County voters refused to return Sheriff Chester Houck to office in 1906 because he would not arrest a friend and former deputy who had killed a man under questionable circumstances. In 1888, the citizens of neighboring Apache County refused to reelect Tomas Perez because two of his deputies from an earlier term were serving prison sentences.

Edward Beeler, a candidate in this same county some years later, lost a reelection bid because he failed to run down outlaws who senselessly murdered two of his possemen. Sheriff Jerome L. Ward, who had the distinction of winning the first sheriff's election in Cochise County in 1882, failed to arouse voter confidence for a second term. Fred Dodge, a resident of Tombstone, concluded that the people suspected Ward of deliberately exposing a prisoner to the clutches of a lynch mob. Ward's alleged purpose was to garner the favor—and hence, votes—of the Bisbee miners at the next election. Robert Hatch, who defeated Ward in this 1882 campaign, had no chance two years later because of sexual indiscretions. He had an affair with a neighbor's wife and earned the reputation of "home wrecker."[21]

In such passionate shrievalty campaigns, violence could easily erupt. An unfortunate death took place in Pinal County when former Sheriff John Peter Gabriel and Joseph Phy vied for this coveted office in 1888. As Phy's superior two years earlier, Gabriel had revoked his commission. Phy resented this slight and began to amass other grievances, real and imagined. Gabriel suspected that Phy was paying undue attention to his (Gabriel's) wife. Finally, a Florence journalist unwisely printed a story to the effect that Gabriel was the more popular of the two candidates and would easily win. Friends of Phy noted that he became very agitated and possibly "mentally unbalanced." In May 1888, Phy stormed into a Florence saloon and opened fire upon his former boss. In a murderous fight that became legendary, the two men inflicted terrible wounds upon each other. Phy died. Gabriel miraculously survived, but the death of his former deputy preyed upon his mind. Gabriel experienced nightmares for the remainder of his life. Although it is not clear that this grisly event turned voters away from Pete Gabriel, he lost the election to incumbent Jere Fryer. As voters looked forward to their first general elections in newly created Maricopa County in 1871, a tragic quarrel erupted between two candidates for the sheriffalty, John A. (Gus) Chenowith and James Favorite. The former shot and killed the latter.[22]

A hotly contested campaign in Doña Ana County, New Mexico erupted into one of the most regrettable election episodes in 1871. The Republicans and Democrats presented a slate of candidates for county offices and the territorial delegateship. Don Mariano Barela, sheriff from 1865 to 1869, was the Democratic candidate again. The rival parties made the error of staging rallies simultaneously in the Mesilla plaza on Sunday, 27 August 1871. As the opposing crowds jeered and taunted each other, tensions mounted. Someone fired a shot, which set off a bloody exchange of clubbings and gun-fire. A bullet evidently meant for Barela struck a young mental de-fective and killed him. Partisans took up positions on rooftops, and the plaza fell into a state of siege. Seven persons died from wounds acquired on that day. Twenty were injured. Sheriff Fabian Gon-zales, who had won a taut election two years earlier, made a desper-ate ride to a nearby United States Army post and obtained assis-tance. The precise cause or causes of this violent outburst are unclear, although lingering Civil War hatreds may have contrib-uted. When it became clear that this election hatred would not sub-side, some citizens, including Sheriff Gonzales, pulled up stakes and immigrated to Chihuahua. Barela won the election by a 300-vote majority and dominated the shrievalty for many years.[23]

Even on the frontier, the expense of electioneering caused finan-cial difficulties. Harvey Whitehill, a perennial shrievalty candidate in Grant County, New Mexico, complained about campaign costs in a letter to a creditor in December 1881. In reply to a dun letter, Whitehill assured Joseph Collier of White Oaks that "everything I owe you . . . will be paid":

> You speake [in your letter] of me being so well off [financially]. It is quite a mistake but I think next year will give me a good stake as the county is growing and my fees [as sheriff] will be as large again as it has ever been and I do not have to run for the office again[.] It has took [sic] all I made the last year [to] pay up for my run last year. . . .

A Prescott, Arizona, district attorney, E. M. Sanford, informed the Denver *Rocky Mountain News*, in September 1890, that a "red-hot campaign" was underway in his hometown. Since elections were fervently contested in his district and Yavapai County was so large—300 by 200 miles—it "will cost a great deal of money if the present pace is kept up." In addition to "the wickedest ballot box manipulation," Sanford estimated that "It costs a candidate about $5,000 to make a tour of the county and fix up the small-fry politicians. . . ."[24]

Some candidates for sheriff were not above dishonesty and fraud. The procedure for voting was very open, and management of the polls was clumsy and inefficient. On one occasion, a rancher rode into Alma, New Mexico, to exercise his franchise. The admin-istrator of the poll, who apparently could neither read nor write, insisted that the cowman serve as poll judge. He was the only literate man available for the task! Since the number of eligible voters in these thinly populated frontier counties were few, a contest for the sheriff's office might hinge upon one or two votes. Such narrow margins accentuated the possibility of fraud. Dee R. Harkey, a veteran deputy sheriff in Eddy County, New Mexico, later admitted to the theft of a ballot box. As a deputy sheriff, he also investigated the disappearance of other ballots in heated elections in the 1890s. Partisan sheriffs sometimes deputized large numbers of loyal party men, allegedly to guard the polls. Voters were keenly aware that their purpose was intimidation of the opposition.[25]

Accusations of voter fraud became commonplace in a series of shrievalty elections in Pima County, Arizona, in the 1880s. Robert H. Paul, a former Wells Fargo detective, played a central role in these elections in 1880, 1882, and 1884. This stalwart Republican was closely tied to the Southern Pacific Railroad. At that time, the boom in mining and cattle promoted prosperity. The income of the sheriff increased proportionately and made the office much more attractive. Not only did the lawman earn more from the collection of taxes, but his fee income rose from the natural increase of court business. The growth of powerful economic institutions stimulated the growth of the Republican Party. The Democrats—traditionally dominant in southern Arizona—naturally felt beleaguered. They went to great (even illegal) lengths to bring in rural voters at election time. John P. Gray served as a tally clerk in Tombstone in 1880. (This area was still a part of Pima County at that time.) Gray remembered that "each candidate had runners out to bring in all available voters. . . ." "They came into town by wagon loads," he said. Rumors circulated that zealous campaigners used illegal aliens and even brought Mexican citizens from Sonora.[26]

While the early voting was brisk in the 1880 election, Robert Paul appeared to be well out front of Charles Shibell, the incumbent Democratic sheriff. However, Pima County was very large. Some precincts were 100 miles distant from Tucson. San Simon, one faraway polling station failed to deliver its ballots until daybreak of the second day of voting. (San Simon apparently registered its votes in Tombstone which, in turn, relayed the count to Tucson.) Tombstone Democrats relied heavily upon these San Simon adherents. John Gray recalled that "there seemed to be an unaccountable confidence among the Democrats that they would win. . . ." These partisans "kept repeating, 'Wait 'till the returns from the San Simon [poll] get here,'" said Gray. "With all formality we opened the [San Simon] package and tallied the votes—one hundred straight

Democratic votes for Shibell. . . ," he added. The Republican, Paul, won only one vote in San Simon! When the entire body of votes for Pima County were counted, the San Simon box gave Shibell a clear victory.[27]

The Republicans suspected foul play in this miraculous turnout in the tiny hamlet of San Simon. By common agreement, only ten or twelve voters resided there. Robert Paul visited this remote precinct and found clear evidence of fraud. The culprit appeared to be William "Curly Bill" Brocius and his rustler friends. Brocius, Newman H. Clanton, and others feared Paul, the Republican "law and order" candidate. J. C. Hancock, who lived through these exciting times, wrote that Curly Bill and his band occupied San Simon on voting day. They voted several times, and then gathered "all the white people of the little place—men, women and children, probably eight or ten in all—and voted them in the same manner." The outlaws voted the Mexicans and Chinese aliens and then descended to horses, cats, and dogs. "To make sure that no one had been neglected . . . ," added Hancock, "they voted everyone over again. . . ." To explain the single ballot for Robert Paul, a participant in the San Simon voting later declared that near the end of the day, one of the voting judges remarked, "This election is too d—d one-sided to suit me. I believe I'll put one in for Paul." Hence, the Republican's lone San Simon vote.[28]

Paul formally contested this election, and the court ruled against the San Simon ballots. This ruling was not difficult to arrive at since Curly Bill, Ike Clanton, and other rustlers, refused to answer subpoenas to testify in Tucson. Charles Shibell, who had remained in the shrievalty through the court proceedings (and enjoyed the financial fruits thereof) appealed to the territorial supreme court. In April, this exalted bench upheld the lower court ruling in favor of Robert Paul. On 18 April 1881, the new sheriff took possession of the much fought for office. The Tucson *Arizona Weekly Star,* a Shibell advocate, commented upon the "stubborn and vigorous fight," but concluded that the supreme court's decision rendered Shibell's claim "hopeless." This writer recommended "a graceful yielding." The sheriff's office was too important to permit its prestige to be compromised. If the people harbor "A feeling of doubt and distrust as to the legality of the acts of the chief executive officer of the county . . . ," wrote this journalist, "such feeling can . . . but deleteriously affect the public welfare."[29]

This controversial Pima County election may have had the unexpected effect of accentuating the growth of party consciousness across the territory. Political party lines had been faint at best in early Arizona. C. D. Reppy, a pioneer Arizona journalist, observed that "Never before this [1880] election [in Pima County] had party lines been drawn in the territory. . . ." According to Reppy, candidates were usually independents and merely presented themselves to the voters. Electioneering "was a go-as-you please affair." This hotly contested Pima County election—a shrievalty campaign only—had significant and long-lasting results. Robert H. Paul remained a controversial figure. He won reelection in 1882, but encountered strong opposition in Eugene O. Shaw two years later. Shaw charged that on election day, 1884, the Southern Pacific Railroad—Paul's corporate patron—shipped in illegal voters from as far away as Yuma, Arizona, and El Paso, Texas. The Democrats also charged that Paul and a crony burgled the safe of an election official, broke the official seal on a package of ballots, and changed the number necessary to win. Significantly, the ballots were stored in the Wells Fargo Express Company safe, which also aroused some suspicion. This company had employed Paul earlier. Nonetheless, on the strength of a recount, Paul won the 1884 election and took possession of the shrievalty.[30]

The vanquished Pima County Democrats did not give up so easily. The Democratic presidential candidate, Grover Cleveland, won the longtime Republican-controlled office in Washington. Cleveland's appointees to territorial posts in Arizona were, naturally, from his party. These partisans ordered a grand jury investigation into allegations of Republican voting fraud in the most recent Pima County elections. This case became especially unsavory. Paul published affidavits in which he alleged that opponent Eugene O. Shaw employed underhanded tactics. The case dragged on until April 1886, a year and a half after the election. The district court granted the shrievalty to contestor Shaw! Shaw pointed out that he had lost the income from the shrievalty for eighteen months and deserved recompense. However, Paul was unwilling to concede this claim. Shaw served out the last months of Paul's term, but Paul kept the profits of office to the time Shaw took over.[31]

Unsuccessful candidates for the sheriff's office sometimes carried grudges and awaited an opportunity for revenge upon the victor. Mike Rice, a longtime Arizona peace officer, recalled how former Cochise County Sheriff Robert Hatch refused to forget an election slight by Jerry Barton, a Tombstone saloonkeeper. When Hatch became captain of the guard at Yuma Prison, he gleefully noted the presence of Barton, recently convicted of murder. Hatch assigned him to "the hardest tasks in the yards," including "Wheel barrow and pick and shovel work," said Rice. The first two shrievalty elections in Eddy County, New Mexico, provoked intense hatred between David Kemp, the first sheriff, and contender James L. Dow. When the latter won the November 1896 campaign, Kemp shot Dow to death only a few days after the victor took the oath of office. Dow was one of the few sheriffs of either Arizona or New Mexico to die violently in office. The frequent use of violence to eliminate political rivals from New Mexico politics—at the county and territorial levels—has prompted historian Richard Maxwell Brown to conclude that "virtually all political factions . . . accepted and used assassination as a way of eliminating troublesome opponents."[32]

Some disgruntled aspirants to the shrievalty sought other means to acquire this coveted position. If they could not have the office in their hometown, why not create a county and obtain the new sheriffalty? County building was a favorite sport of budding politicians in both territories. The failure of Harvey H. Whitehill's bid for reelection to the Grant County shrievalty in November 1886 encouraged some dissatisfied persons to demand that a new (Logan) county be set aside from the present bailiwick. One observer concluded that "'Whitehill wanted to be sheriff very badly'" and that his supporters, who apparently anticipated some spoils, were even more disappointed at this setback. When they failed to obtain a court-ordered recount, some Whitehill partisans in Deming proposed "the scheme to cut loose from Grant County." In the process of creating the new county, the governor normally appointed a temporary sheriff. Whitehill could (presumably) receive this appointment. This plot failed, although a new county—Luna—did eventually emerge in that region. By that time, Harvey Whitehill's political fortunes had waned. After winning one more term, in 1889–90, he left office for good. Whitehill had occupied this important local position for a decade.[33]

Harvey Whitehill's scheme to create Logan County and seek the governor's patronage in a new sheriffalty was not so farfetched. Upon the initiation of a new county, the territorial executive selected not only the first sheriff but the entire cadre of officials. The politicking for the shrievalty of the new county of Cochise provides an example of this process. The contenders began their maneuvers sometime before the inauguration of this new governmental unit in February 1881. Two deputy sheriffs in Tombstone, John H. Behan and Wyatt Berry Stapp Earp, were the candidates. Behan, a Democrat, had served one term as sheriff of Mohave County and had the much-coveted stamp of native son. The credentials of Earp, a Republican, were somewhat suspect. Although a lawman in Kansas, he devoted much time to gambling. In Tombstone, he and his brothers invested in mining property but continued their association with the saloon and gambling crowd. In the meantime, the brothers—all Republicans—sought law enforcement positions in Tombstone: Virgil, deputy United States marshal and city marshal; Wyatt, Pima County deputy sheriff; and Morgan, on occasion, special city officer and posseman. An undocumented story circulated that Wyatt Earp won his badge as Pima County deputy sheriff in a poker game. However, Sheriff Charles Shibell, a Democrat, accepted Earp's resignation as the movement to create Cochise County gained momentum in late 1880. Behan, also a Democrat, obtained Earp's place.[34]

Considerable infighting took place in Prescott in the first weeks of January 1881, as the nominees for new posts in Cochise County put in their bids. The candidates waged a "law and order" campaign in the assembly and sought the nod of John C. Fremont, the Republican governor. The mining and mercantile interests, largely Republicans and outsiders, desired a "two-gun man," recalled Billy Breakenridge, later a deputy sheriff in the new county. Their choice was Wyatt Earp, presumably a man who could curb the growing problems of stagecoach robbery and rustling along the border with Mexico. However, John Behan felt confident of the appointment. Josephine Sarah Marcus, Behan's lover at the time, recalled that he pulled unnamed "political strings" and "counted on getting the job." Behan later admitted, "I knew I would get the appointment." The rustling and smuggling element, led by Newman H. Clanton (also a Democrat), enthusiastically supported Behan. Behan "made sure," recalled Marcus, "that they [the outlaws] knew he was *their kind of man*." While Behan was not an outlaw, he would presumably fail to enforce, or ignore, some laws against these Democratic freebooters on isolated farmsteads and ranches. Marcus's recollections are not fully reliable, since she deserted Behan for Wyatt Earp during his political wheeling and dealing! Perhaps Behan's slaveholding and Democratic background had much to do with his ability to win support in southern Arizona, since this region was a haven for ex-Confederates. The Clantons and some of their followers were of the Democratic persuasion and voted faithfully—many times over—at every opportunity.[35]

Behan was so assured of the appointment that he convinced

Wyatt Earp to withdraw at the last minute and accept the post of undersheriff. Earp later declared that Behan promised to "hire a clerk and divide the profits" of office. Behan later admitted informing Earp that he "would like to have him [Earp] in the office with me." Whatever the details of this agreement, Earp accepted but informed Behan that he would enter the first general elections, in November 1882. Governor John C. Fremont announced the appointment of Behan as sheriff of Cochise County in mid-February 1881. This selection remains a puzzle, although political inconsistencies were common in frontier Arizona. The Republican regime in Prescott made many accommodations to the Democratic south. Perhaps Fremont desired to continue the "healing" policy of his predecessors in Prescott, who consciously conceded Democratic control of the southern counties. Mining and land development schemes also preoccupied Fremont, whose political and financial fortunes had disappeared since the Civil War. Arizonans in general were miffed at their "absentee" governor. Territorial Secretary John J. Gosper often tended official matters, although Fremont was present during the appointment of Cochise County's first officers. That the new sheriff reneged on the offer to Wyatt Earp goes without saying. The enmity thus generated helped fuel the hatred that led to subsequent bloodshed in Tombstone.[36]

Some indications of the political dealing that took place in the appointment of John Behan can be gathered from the simultaneous process of creating Gila County. John C. Fremont selected the first battery of officials for both counties. Gila County residents complained almost at once. The *Silver Belt* of Globe indicated that citizens "were not satisfied with some of the officers appointed by Fremont." The governor "ignored the rights of our Representative [Donald Robb]," added this editor, "who alone was our [only] means of communication with him." The *Silver Belt* charged that the executive "sold out offices in this county in order to secure another vote." Among Fremont's pet projects were the removal of the capital from Prescott to Tucson and the repeal of a bullion tax for the benefit of his fellow mining speculators. "If he held a deed to Heaven [Fremont] would give the best lots in it to any member of the Eleventh Legislature that would vote for his pet schemes . . . ," concluded this journalist in disgust. Perhaps Fremont conceded the appointment of Behan as sheriff of Cochise County in order to obtain much needed support in another matter.[37]

Residents of Arizona and New Mexico territories should have been accustomed to political trade-offs in the appointments of sheriffs. In 1864, Van Ness Smith reportedly gave up his squatter's rights to the ground that became Prescott, with his reward being the sheriff's office. When Colfax County Sheriff Mason Bowman died suddenly in June 1883, three interest groups presented names to the county board of commissioners: the Reverend Oscar P. McMains and his anti-Maxwell Grant followers; the county seat residents known as "the Springer people"; and Raton and vicinity. This latter region won when the governor appointed Matthias B. Stockton. When John Poe resigned the Lincoln County office on 31 December 1885, he submitted a letter to Governor Edmund G. Ross on behalf of his deputy, Jim Brent. Lawyer Harvey B. Fergusson and "the Albuquerque Ring" desired that Poe's replacement come from the White Oaks area rather than the county seat, Lincoln. However, a Lincoln lawyer, William T. Thornton, law partner of the Santa Fe power broker, Thomas B. Catron, had prearranged the Brent nomination. "We succeeded in getting Jim Brent appointed Sheriff some days ago," Thornton boasted to a client on 16 January 1886. While the *Weekly New Mexican* was aware of other nominations (not named), the editor believed that Brent was "almost as good . . . as could have been made." Sophie Poe, wife of the former sheriff, declared that "There was no doubt that Brent was the man for the place. . . ." "Everyone was delighted" upon the announcement, she said.[38]

Possession of the sheriff's office constituted a great prize on the southwestern frontier. The politicking that surrounded campaigns for this office in New Mexico and Arizona territories included every imaginable ingredient, from idealistic platforms to the crassest possible motives. Nonetheless, candidates exhibited much creativity and even more energy. While the issues were generally local, changes at the national level were sometimes felt. This was especially true during protests such as that of the Populists. More often, the greatest upheavals took place at the local level when new economic interest groups, such as the railroad and mining companies, began to demand control of the shrievalty. Elections took on a new seriousness, and candidates went to great excess in order to command the necessary ballots. The voters also demanded that candidates possess stronger qualifications, including the nerve to stand up to bands of lawless men. Some important law and order campaigns were waged on this score. Whatever their outcome, the fervency with which the participants waged these campaigns for the shrievalty revealed strength in the republican system on the Southwestern frontier and, even more, a significant degree of ability on the part of the candidates.

Top: Samuel G. Bean, one of the pioneer sheriffs of the Southwest, occupied the Doña Ana County office when its jurisdiction extended to the California border in the 1850s. (Courtesy Doña Ana County Sheriffs Photograph Collection, University of Texas at El Paso Library, Special Collections.) *Bottom left:* Mariano Barela served as Doña Ana County sheriff through some of the most lawless times. He entered the office in 1865 as a young man and held the post intermittently until his death in 1892, for a total of fifteen years. (Courtesy Doña Ana County Sheriffs Photograph Collection, University of Texas at El Paso Library, Special Collections.) *Bottom right:* William Brady (Lincoln County, New Mexico, 1877–78) was one of the few sheriffs in Arizona or New Mexico to be killed in the line of duty. (Courtesy Maurice G. Fulton Collection, University of Arizona Library.)

Top: George Kimbrell (Lincoln County, 1879–80) used his good offices to begin the reconciliation of feuding factions. (Courtesy Museum of New Mexico, neg. no. 104913.) *Bottom left:* Charles T. Russell (Socorro County, New Mexico, 1885–88) represented the newly emerging cattle interests in a region of Hispanic domination. (Courtesy N.S. Haley Memorial Library, Jeff Milton Collection.) *Bottom right:* Believed to be Francisco (Frank) Chavez, controversial Sheriff of Santa Fe County, 1885–91. He was murdered shortly after resigning from office. (Courtesy Museum of New Mexico, neg. no. 9836.)

Three men who served as Lincoln County sheriffs are captured in one sitting: *(left to right)* Patrick Floyd Garrett (1881–82), James Brent (1886–88) and John Poe (1883–86). (Courtesy Mullin Collection, Haley History Center.)

Charles C. Perry (Chaves County, New Mexico, 1895–96) cast aside the reputation of manhunter when he absconded to South Africa with tax revenues. (Courtesy Chaves County Historical Museum, Pecos Valley Collection.)

Top: Solomon Luna (Valencia County, New Mexico, 1892–94) was just one of at least six Lunas to serve as sheriffs in "The Kingdom of Valencia." (Courtesy Museum of New Mexico neg. no. 50606.) *Bottom left:* William Price Cunningham (1893–96) was brought in to help clean up the criminal element in Santa Fe County, New Mexico. He made many enemies and departed office under a cloud. (Courtesy Center for Southwest Research, UNM General Library, 000-21-0063.) *Bottom right:* Thomas A. Hubbell (Bernalillo County, New Mexico, 1895–1905) was part of a family dynasty and political machine until removed from office. (Courtesy Museum of New Mexico, neg. no. 51712.)

Patrick F. Garrett, perhaps the most notable of all frontier sheriffs, is shown here at the peak of his professional career as sheriff of Doña Ana County about 1900. (Courtesy Doña Ana County Sheriffs Photograph Collection, University of Texas at El Paso Library, Special Collections.)

Families often dominated county shrievalties. The Romeros were very influential in San Miguel County, New Mexico. *Seated left to right:* Hilario (sheriff), Trinidad (United States marshal), Eugenio (sheriff). *Standing left to right:* Benigno and Margarito. (Courtesy Denver Public Library, Western History Department.)

Top: John Thomas Hixenbaugh (Colfax County, New Mexico 1885) served only a few months after receiving a debilitating wound. The legislature provided benefits for sheriffs injured in the line of duty after the Hixenbaugh case. (Courtesy Museum of New Mexico neg. no. 105057.) *Bottom left:* Men with Hispanic background often dominated the sheriff's office in New Mexican counties. Shown here is Benigno C. Hernandez (Rio Arriba County, 1905–06) who held office in a peaceful period. (Courtesy Museum of New Mexico, neg. no. 105452.) *Bottom right:* George Curry, sheriff of Lincoln (1893–94) and Otero (1899) counties, eventually rose to the governorship of New Mexico Territory. (Courtesy Center for Southwest Research, UNM General Library, 000–21–0065.)

Robert H. Paul (Pima County, Arizona, 1881–86) was a noted manhunter but controversial politician. (Courtesy Arizona Historical Society/Tucson.)

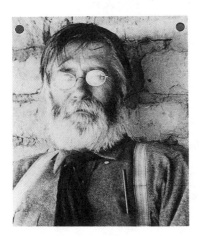 

Top: Adolph G. Buttner, veteran Tucson Chief of Police, also served many years as concurrent Pima County deputy sheriff. (Courtesy Arizona Historical Society, Tucson.) *Bottom left:* John Lorenzo Hubbell (Apache County, Arizona, 1885–86), a member of a famous family of law enforcers, represented that group of transitional politicians of mixed Anglo-Hispanic background. (Courtesy Museum of New Mexico, neg. no. 7315.) *Bottom right:* William J. Mulvenon (Yavapai County, 1885–88) played an important part in breaking up the Pleasant Valley War. (Courtesy Arizona Historical Society, Tucson.)

William O. "Buckey" O'Neill (Yavapai County, Arizona, 1889–90; second from right) poses with his famous posse that captured the Canyon Diablo train robbers. (Courtesy Arizona Historical Society, Pioneer Museum.)

James R. Lowry, Sheriff of Yavapai County for eight years in the territorial era, was later killed in the line of duty. He is shown here with his family in Prescott. (Courtesy Sharlot Hall Historical Society.)

An interior view of the Yavapai County, Arizona, sheriff's office about 1900. *Seated:* Fred Munds, brother of Sheriff John L. Munds (1899–1902). *Right:* Deputy Tony Johns. *Left:* An unidentified prisoner stands in handcuffs. (Courtesy Sharlot Hall Historical Society.)

Left: Henry Lovin (Mohave County, Arizona, 1901–4) won recognition for his relentless pursuit of killer Jim McKinney across the Mohave Desert of California. (Courtesy Research Division, Department of Library, Archives & Public Records, State of Arizona, Phoenix.) *Right:* Gus Livingston (Yuma County, Arizona, 1901–12) was one of the longterm county lawmen of the Southwest. (Courtesy Arizona Historical Society/Tucson.)

5

Servant of the Court

Sheriffs were routinely called upon to cooperate with many public officials. One of the closest associations was with the personnel of the court system. Like most tasks of the sheriffs, service to the bar of justice presented many difficulties. Since the lawmen performed many duties in the field while the court personnel remained in town, the latter often failed to comprehend the problems that arose in the service of warrants and subpoenas in the hinterland. The sheriffs' duties also preceded court sessions by several weeks and then continued through the sittings. In addition to the presiding judges, there were clerks, public prosecutors, and lawyers as well as crowds of spectators at each sitting. During especially tense trials, the sheriffs were constrained to keep the peace inside the courtroom.

The county sheriff maintained an ancient and noble association with the courts. In the justice system, one could hardly exist without the other. The Kearny Code of 1846 laid upon the sheriff the duty of serving the process of court and also directed the lawman to "attend upon such courts during their sittings." The *Revised Statutes of Arizona* were more specific, adding that the sheriff should "call the parties and witnesses, and all other persons bound to appear at the court, and make proclamation at the opening and adjournment. . . ." These few words hardly captured the many and sometimes dangerous duties that the sheriffs performed during court sessions.[1]

While the sheriff served the courts the year round, these duties peaked during the spring and fall sessions. Preparations began well in advance of opening day. In early Arizona and New Mexico, sheriffs participated in the selection of jury panels for the territorial side of district court and then served the venires (writs issued by the judge ordering a lawman to summon a panel). The United States marshal, the federal counterpart to the county lawman, performed the same duty on the United States side of district court. Many persons complained about involvement of the sheriff in jury summoning, which could open the way for corruption of the jury system. In the 1880s, both territories excluded the sheriff from this process and established jury commissions that included the district judge and prominent citizens. The sheriffs continued to play a part in jury selection in a roundabout way. If they failed to deliver summonses to all the prospective jurors, the size of the panel was inadequate. The presiding judge then had to draw upon hangers-on around the courthouse. The sheriffs sometimes had the duty of drawing the names of the prospective jurors after the jury commission prepared the list. These lawmen were so conspicuous during the work of the jury commission that the public continued to imagine (erroneously) that the sheriffs still selected the jurors. Leonard Alverson, whom a jury in Las Cruces convicted of mail robbery in 1898, accused Sheriff Pat Garrett of manipulating the panel and packing it with "professional jurymen" who loitered around the courthouse.[2]

The clerk of the district court also played an important part in the preparations for each court session. He served as a point of contact for the sheriff. When the jury list and the subpoenas for witnesses were readied, the clerk handed them to the sheriff for delivery. Upon successful completion of this job, the sheriff wrote a "return" (description of his official action) on each document. The lawman returned it to the clerk, who recorded the sheriff's action, filed the paper, and noted the fee expenses for such service. The sheriff also stored physical evidence, such as weapons, in the clerk's vault.[3]

The failure of the clerk to perform his duties promptly could adversely affect the sheriff. When Judge Perry Brocchus called for a special session of district court in Taos, New Mexico, in May 1855, the order caught Clerk Elias Clark by surprise. Clark delayed the issue of a writ of *venire facias* (special call for jurors) to Sheriff Ezra N. DePew until the day court was to open. The clerk presented the lawman with a hastily compiled list of jurors and suggested that they antedate the venire so that it would conform to law. Such a proposal contradicted all formal practice and was probably illegal. Judge Brocchus accused Clark of "gross and inexcusable neglect" and of attempting to lure the sheriff into a criminal act. This issue became a momentary *cause celebre*. The participants wrote explanations to the *Santa Fe Weekly Gazette*. Sheriff DePew did not consider Clark's actions a serious offense and attempted to smooth the matter over. The clerk was not guilty of "inducing me, as an officer, to do any act inconsistent with my duty," declared the sheriff. Apparently, Clark merely intended to expedite the jury selection process in order to correct the results of his carelessness. A similar muddle took place in Mohave County, Arizona, when the district court clerk failed to formally open a court session for Judge Charles Silent, who could not arrive in time to perform this essential ritual. The clerk neglected to carry out these instructions, and Silent had to cancel the sitting.[4]

Many judges in these frontier districts were equally controversial. Presidential appointees, they represented all aspects of human character. Commonly referred to as "Hizzoner" (a play on His Honor), some were men of learning and integrity, while others were of inferior stuff. Judge Kirby Benedict embodied both strong and weak characteristics. In his many years on the New Mexico bench, he performed yeoman service in the gargantuan southern, or Third, judicial district. Yet, he thrived on the "good life." Franz Huning, a New Mexico merchant, recalled, in playful understatement, that Benedict "did not belong to any temperance society and . . . was fond of a game of cards." Huning added, in humorous malevolence, that the good judge was a noted cheat at the poker table. Acting Governor W.F.M. Arny complained to President Abraham Lincoln in December 1863 that the veteran judge "has lapsed into his old habits." Benedict "visits the gambling halls and drinking saloons and . . . defiles his judicial robes. . . ." President Theodore Roosevelt felt compelled to remove Judge Daniel H. McMillan from the New Mexico Supreme Court in June 1903. McMillan's constituents accused him of "general immorality." While he left his wife in El Paso, Texas, this errant occupant of the bench took his mistress on his circuit rides through New Mexico. "The removal was long a foregone conclusion," boasted the *Capitan Progress*. The citizens of Prescott, Arizona, became miffed at Judge Richard Sloan in December 1899. When the jury retired to reach a decision in a murder case, Sloan expected lengthy deliberations. He departed the courthouse. However, the panel returned to the courtroom very quickly and ordered him searched out. The bailiff found him on the "golf grounds" practicing for an upcoming tournament![5]

The process by which the President selected judges for the territories mystified many Southwesterners. To obtain a competent judge required a lot of luck. But good appointments did happen. In September 1872, the *Daily New Mexican* noted that Judge Joseph

Palen "has done more than all of his predecessors together to elevate the judiciary generally throughout the Territory." In an evident reference to the scandalous behavior of Judge Kirby Benedict, this writer remarked that "the time has passed when the bench . . . can be disgraced or defiled by a drunken judge, fresh from a night's debauch. . . ." Judge Henry L. Waldo was noted for his fervent devotion to the law. He introduced an era of openness through "free, outspoken & comprehensive charges" to grand juries. When two influential Rio Arriba County dons complained about lawlessness in their district, but were too frightened to sign complaints against the criminals, this forthright judge replied that "they would have to suffer." Judge LeBaron Bradford Prince won a reputation for hard work and the largest caseloads in New Mexico. Frank W. Clancy, who practiced law in Prince's court, could find only one shortcoming in this official's performance and that "was in the excessive amount of work which he performed and imposed upon the members of the bar and court officers. . . ." Thomas Smith, who eventually became chief justice, won the praise of the *Daily New Mexican* in January 1895 for "lifting from the fair name of New Mexico the accusation of lawlessness." Smith had just won sixteen criminal convictions in Las Vegas, an area that had been riddled with lawlessness for five years. This journalist urged colleagues of Smith to follow his example and not permit "criminals . . . to stalk abroad in our midst."[6]

When the clerks drew up and certified a jury venire, the sheriffs set in motion the process that led to the convening of grand and petit juries in the district court. The grand jury originated in medieval England and possessed much power. It listened to complaints and could initiate investigations into any alleged wrongdoing. The petit jury was the trial jury. The duty of summoning jurors and witnesses imposed a sizeable burden upon sheriffs, since most counties in Arizona and New Mexico were so extensive. Prospective jurors also deliberately avoided process servers from the sheriff's office. Jack Potter, a rancher in "No-Man's Land" (now the Oklahoma Panhandle), recalled how his neighbors dreaded the tiresome journey to court in Springer. The Colfax County sheriff was aware of this truancy and attempted to surprise the cattlemen. However, the stockmen posted signs to warn their neighbors of the approaching sheriff. "A bleached cow head was . . . hung on the fence as a notice to all who wanted to avoid jury duty," said Potter. An Arizona rancher recalled that his neighbors resented the call to court. Spring sessions were especially bothersome since ranchers and farmers were distracted from roundups and planting. On the other hand,

cowboys and other laborers welcomed the visit of the county lawman. Jury service meant that they could earn the juror's and mileage
fees as well as their regular $35 monthly wage while avoiding their
work.[7]

The sheriff's office labored mightily to deliver all court process in
order to make the session successful. Other important tasks had to
be set aside. On 4 January 1884, the *Silver City Enterprise* noted that
Sheriff James Woods had suspended the investigation of a train robbery. He and his staff were "occupied attending court." Wells Fargo
detectives, who were anxious to continue the search for clues, were
very upset with the sheriff. To deliver court process involved long
horseback and buggy rides. Peter Brady, Jr., son of a Pima County
sheriff, recalled that "the official duties of his father meant covering
many miles of wild country. . . ." In December 1883, a Tucson
newspaperman observed Deputy Sheriff Vosburg returning from a
jury summoning mission. Vosburg said he had ridden more than
500 miles and was so saddle sore that "he now takes his meals
standing." The Holbrook *Argus* noted Sheriff Frank Wattron and
Undersheriff Bargman "scouring the country serving papers, and
summoning grand and trial jurors" in December 1898. When trial
lawyers could not form a jury from the original venire in a
Tombstone session in June 1885, Sheriff Robert Hatch was required to summon a new one. Since the sheriff and deputies often
held commissions as deputy United States marshals, they served
writs for the federal side of district court on the same journey.[8]

In the long history of relations between sheriff and judge, the
lawman had extended the courtesy of an official greeting at the
county line. While English sheriffs had continued this gesture,
American peace officers had apparently permitted this protocol to
fall into disuse. In an apparent effort to resurrect this ancient usage,
the sheriff and citizens of St. Johns, Apache County, rode out to
greet Judge C.G.W. French in 1879. Richard E. Sloan, judge and
later governor, recalled with a chuckle French's surprise and
discomfiture:

> It was with extreme difficulty that he [French] was finally persuaded
> that these heavily armed and ferocious-looking men, led by the tough
> *hombre* at their head, were only a committee of good citizens, headed
> by the sheriff who had come out to meet His Honor and properly
> escort him. . . .[9]

The sheriff played a conspicuous role in the opening of a court
session. According to the *Revised Statutes of Arizona,* he was to

make "proclamation at the opening and adjournment." The traditional exhortation to open the court followed a prescribed formula: "Oyez! Oyez! Oyez! This Honourable Court is now in session!" Evidently, variations existed in this formula. In June 1898, the Prescott *Weekly Journal Miner* noted a Yavapai County officer in this role. "A deputy sheriff appeared on the court house porch this morning and yelled out in stentorian tones 'John Smith, John Smith, John Smith, come into court," said this writer. "Immediately from the four sides of the plaza," he continued, "small processions were seen to head towards the temple of justice. . . ." One bystander failed to hear the bailiff's call and concluded that the commander of volunteers—the Spanish-American War was on— had issued a muster call. "When told it was only John Smith obeying a summons," said the *Miner,* this anonymous person "ejaculated 'Oh!' and disappeared into the Comet [saloon]." This hallowed call to the bar of justice was not sacred to all. When Judge W. F. Fitzgerald suddenly fell ill at his home in Tucson in June 1884, he had to delay a scheduled session of court in Florence. Fitzgerald telegraphed Sheriff Andrew J. Doran to formally open court and then adjourn it until the judge could preside.[10]

The first session in a newly created county often was not only the most memorable but the most difficult. When Grant County held its opening session in Silver City in July 1868, the judge presided under a juniper tree. Apparently, the first sheriff, Richard Hudson, was unable to rent adequate quarters for this important event. Residents of Lincoln gathered in John B. Wilson's saloon for their premier session, probably in 1869. One of the earliest meetings of court in Prescott, Yavapai County, Arizona, in September 1865, was interrupted by an Indian raid. Participants and spectators alike sprang out of the building, guns in hand. Judge William T. Howell, who presided over the first session of First Judicial District Court in Tucson in May 1864, sensed the historical nature of the occasion in his charge to the grand jury:

> Gentlemen of the Grand Jury:—You are the first grand inquest ever duly empaneled and sworn by authority of law, in this territory. With your action to day, commences the judicial history of a country which area is sufficiently extensive to form the seat of a powerful empire.[11]

A backlog of judicial business awaited the first session of district court in Graham County, Arizona. Although created in 1881, the new county was slow to organize. The first session of court did not convene until 5 November 1883. When Judge A. W. Sheldon arrived in Safford, the first county seat, he faced a crowded docket. The grand jury returned thirty-five indictments, including ten for murder. Even the sheriff, George "Little Steve" Stevens, was subject to the charge of allowing two prisoners to escape. In spite of threats and intimidation, the jury made a courageous stand. The panel sentenced nine convicted persons to prison. An additional three were sentenced to hang. In an ironic twist, these same three escaped the Graham County jail and fled to neighboring Cochise County. They committed one of the most brutal and heinous crimes in Southwestern history—the Bisbee Massacre—and were hanged in Tombstone in the following year.[12]

These sheriffs performed their duties in very spartan court facilities in the early decades of the territories. An anonymous spectator at the trial of rustler kingpin John Kinney in Mesilla, New Mexico, in 1883, was unimpressed with the condition of the courtroom:

> The courtroom . . . is a room about fourteen feet wide and twice as long, with whitewashed walls and a wooden floor. At the back end of the room is a small platform on which are a table and chair for the judge. On either side of the platform is a small table with two chairs. In one corner of the back wall is a large bookcase with the glass missing from one door. At the other corner is a stove in front of the fireplace. There is no other furniture in the room except sixteen or eighteen wooden benches without backs.

This facility normally served as a school building. A young schoolgirl wrote in her composition book, "There will be no school next week because the schoolroom is needed to hold court trials." Rancher William French attended court in Socorro about this time. While lawyers "sat about promiscuously wherever they pleased. . . ," wrote French, witnesses reposed in "One rather rickety chair on the right of the Bench. . . ." "There seemed to be no objection whatever to the use of tobacco. . . ," said this Englishman in surprise.[13]

The use of the Spanish and English languages simultaneously in these Socorro proceedings also surprised William French. "Neither the Bench nor the Bar understood the former [Spanish]," he observed, "while the jury was entirely ignorant of the latter. . . ." This mixture of tongues was an accepted fact in New Mexican courts and, to a lesser degree, in Arizona. In 1902, United States Senator Albert Beveridge led a committee to New Mexico to investigate a bid for statehood. The committee members were amazed that "Interpreters are required in the courts to interpret Mexican testimony to the American half of the jury and American testimony to the Mexican half. . . ." The Beveridge Committee also noted that mixed juries employed translators. New Mexico "is very much Mexicanized," concluded the senator. Had they searched further, the lawmakers would have discovered even more startling language gymnastics in the courtrooms of both territories. When Indians were involved, three-way translations took place. In such instances, some sheriffs—especially Hispanics who possessed Indian language skills—served as interpreters.[14]

A large delegation accompanied official court personnel on their biannual trips around the judicial circuit. William French characterized the members of the bar at the Socorro session as "a scratch lot." Other observers made similar assessments. This was not uncommon on the frontier, since admission to the bar normally required only some reading in a law office. A humorous anecdote told on the Attorney General of New Mexico, apparently William Breeden, reveals the rather coarse behavior of some frontier attorneys. This anonymously penned story is entitled "A Drunken Atty. Gen. With An Important *case pending* As Related By Those Who Were There." Breeden accompanied the official party of Judge Joseph Palen to a session in Mora in 1875. After a day's work, the judicial delegation retired to a saloon, whereupon the attorney general went on "a big drunk." The embarrassed judge ordered bystanders to put the lawyer to bed, but he escaped his hotel room dressed only in "shirt & drawers." Breeden soon gathered up "an old one-eyed hag and her daughter" in a neighboring bagnio and returned to Judge Palen's hangout. The disgusted bench ordered the attorney general taken to his room "by main force." But the tipsy attorney general was unsinkable. He demanded a new bottle and the presence of female companionship, to which his friends acquiesced on the condition that he remain in his room.[15]

The sheriff was responsible for collecting all weapons of spectators in the courtroom. In one trial in Las Vegas, New Mexico, Judge Samuel Axtell, who had received a death threat, ordered the county lawman to examine every visitor. The surprised bailiff reportedly collected forty-two revolvers, some of which belonged to the attorneys! Axtell found every pistolero guilty of contempt and fined each ten dollars. Even court officers abused the weapons policies of district judges. In April 1870, Sheriff Peter Brady policed the trial of former United States Marshal Milton Duffield in Tucson,

Arizona. Duffield was accused of assaulting a newspaperman. The former federal lawman, who had a reputation for violent and often irrational behavior, entered the courtroom heavily armed. When the judge ordered him disarmed, Duffield pulled a gun (he reportedly carried a dozen arms at one time!) and threatened Sheriff Brady. Observing this threatening movement, District Attorney James E. McCaffry placed a pistol against Duffield's back and pulled the trigger. Although McCaffry's weapon misfired, his action distracted the defendant and probably saved Sheriff Brady's life. The court later convicted Duffield for this assault upon the county gendarme and sentenced him to one year in prison and a fine of $1,000 and costs. A higher court overturned this sentence. New Mexico Deputy Sheriff Dee Harkey may have been referring to similar tense courtroom experiences when he observed that "Any trial in those days involved more law enforcement than that on the court's books."[16]

An especially taut atmosphere existed during the murder trial of Barney Riggs in Cochise County in the mid-1880s. Deputy Sheriff Fred J. Dodge performed guard duty inside the Tombstone courtroom. The Riggs family was noted for independent and often violent behavior. Dodge sat at one end of the judge's platform with a shotgun nearby. When Prosecutor Marcus Aurelius Smith let his courtroom oratory go to excess and accused the defendant of an "Indian-like" (cowardly) murder, Barney Riggs jumped to his feet, grabbed a heavy inkstand, and shouted, "'Yes, you Son of a Bitch and I will murder you!'" Dodge recalled that he reacted spontaneously:

> All in a few seconds, I left my chair and jumped. I just touched on the table and then onto Barney Riggs' shoulders, crushing him to the floor and taking and throwing aside the Ink stand, [and] jerking Barney up and throwing him into his chair. . . .

Lawyer Smith—destined to become a United States senator—soon regained his composure. He quietly turned to the deputy sheriff and said, "'Thank you. Fred,' and continued his address to the jury."[17]

Danger could enter the courtroom in the most innocent form. Sheriff John Britt Montgomery patrolled a potentially explosive event in Phoenix in 1891. The occasion was the trial of John Rhodes for the murder of Thomas Graham, a holdover from the bloody Tewksbury-Graham Feud, or Pleasant Valley War. The bereaved widow of Graham attended faithfully, all the while becoming noticeably more emotional. Suddenly, in a fit of hysteria, she bolted from her chair, dashed toward defendant Rhodes, placed a revolver against his chest, and pulled the trigger. Nothing happened. The gun failed to fire! The hammer of the weapon had caught in Mrs. Graham's scarf and could not fall upon a cartridge. Sheriff Montgomery and his deputies raced to her in time to prevent a second opportunity. She cried out in despair: "'But he killed my husband! Oh, God! Let me kill him!'" The grieving widow was so strong that several deputies were required to disarm her.[18]

The unexpected could always take place in the courtroom. Sheriff John Henry Thompson had the pleasure of arresting a wanted man in a Globe courtroom. During the trial of an accused bandit, District Attorney John W. Wentworth observed a suspicious-looking person among the spectators. Although the man was in a disguise, Wentworth recognized him as Nick Booth, a partner of the man on trial. The district attorney passed a note to Sheriff Thompson, who promptly arrested Booth. The outlaw's curiosity had gotten the best of him. In a reversal of this incident, Sheriff Arthur Goodell experienced the embarassment of losing his prisoner, Perfecto Rodrigues, during a trial in Silver City. Rodrigues escaped from the courtroom just before sentencing. The sheriff eventually recaptured the fugitive and lodged him in the penitentiary in Santa Fe.[19]

In the controversial trial of Oliver Lee in Hillsboro, New Mexico, Sheriff Max Kahler faced an extremely dangerous situation. Lee was accused of the murder of Albert Jennings Fountain and his eight-year-old son in neighboring Doña Ana County. This case aroused great indignation and became politically explosive, since Lee led some powerful cattle interests in his region. His colleagues would certainly attend the proceedings. Many of them also believed that the Doña Ana County sheriff, Pat Garrett, had embarked upon a vendetta against Lee. For these and other reasons, the Lee trial landed in Max Kahler's Sierra County bailiwick. Fortunately, Garrett and Sheriff George Curry of Otero County also attended. The presiding judge wisely directed the sheriffs not only to disarm all spectators but to register every lawman's weapon. George Curry recalled that he was "technically in charge of the prisoners" but "I placed myself at the disposal of Sheriff Kahler. . . ." Even Garrett, whom defendant Lee profoundly distrusted, "was active in maintaining order and in quieting wild rumors," he added. Curry had nothing but compliments for Sheriff Kahler and the battery of special deputies he had deputized for this occasion. They were "entirely impartial," said Curry, as they maintained good order among the many partisan spectators. The trial passed without serious incident. Oliver Lee was acquitted.[20]

The tense atmosphere that arose in the court room could spill over into the streets, as Sheriff William Mulvenon learned in Prescott, in the fall of 1887. The occasion was the trial of several feudists in the Pleasant Valley War—the same conflict that prompted the near fatal scene in the Phoenix courtroom four years later. The streets of Prescott were crowded with partisans of both factions. Sheriff William Mulvenon fretted considerably about the need to protect the grand jury, which investigated this tragic bloodbath. The jury rendered indictments. When the panel summoned participants from both sides to testify, Mulvenon had to employ additional deputies to patrol the streets of Prescott. Fortunately, the followers of both factions carefully avoided each other. Some even used this rare visit to the county seat as an opportunity for some recreation. Apache County Deputy Sheriff Joe T. McKinney, who assisted Mulvenon, was surprised when members of one of the warring parties requested that he consent to a photograph with them.[21]

The moment of truth in any trial arrived when the judge pronounced sentence and said, "Mr. Sheriff, remove the prisoner from the courtroom." The anxiety that had accumulated in the defendant throughout the trial could explode into violence. When Frederick Falkner, accused of murder, realized that a San Miguel County jury was about to find him guilty in April 1892, the prisoner burst into abusive words and "used blasphemous language toward the jurors." Had not two deputy sheriffs restrained Falkner, wrote a local journalist, the defendant "would have assaulted the prosecuting attorney." A similar event took place in the McKinley County courthouse in Gallup, in 1911. The bench sentenced a defendant to ninety-nine years in prison for murder, whereupon the condemned man let out a threatening oath. Deputy Sheriff Patrick Dugan, who attended the prisoner, became visibly upset and took this outburst as a personal affront. As A. T. Hannett recalled, the sheriff angrily "planted his foot between the prisoner's shoulders and gave him a shove that sent him head first" down the courthouse steps. "'You can insult the Judge," exclaimed Dugan, "but you can't insult me.'"[22]

Among the courtroom duties of the sheriff was care of the jury. The lawman provided meals and lodging and also ensured privacy and protection. These duties were difficult since the crude frontier courtrooms seldom contained secure, private jury rooms. The sheriffs had to take extra precautions to isolate the jurors from litigants who sought to compromise them. The judge would declare a mistrial in such events. When lawyer Alexander L. Morrison, Jr., learned that jurors had taken alcoholic beverages into the jury room in Albuquerque, he asked for a new trial for his client. The seemingly routine task of feeding the jurors could become complicated, as Deputy Sheriff Fred Dodge learned during the trial of Barney Riggs in Tombstone, Arizona. Bannock Riggs, the patriarch of the family, vowed to assist his son in some way. The senior Riggs chose to do this by trying to discredit the jury. Dodge and fellow Deputy Charles Smith carefully shepherded the twelve-person panel to the Can Can Restaurant for meals. The delegation sat at an isolated table in the rear. As the lawmen led the file of jurors back to the court after one meal, Bannock Riggs and a friend suddenly fired their weapons into the air. The jurors were panic stricken, as the elder Riggs had hoped. However, they did not scatter, which was also a part of Riggs's plot. Instead, the twelve huddled about their guards. Had the panel taken refuge out of sight of the deputies, Barney Riggs's defense attorney could have claimed that some of them talked with bystanders and won a mistrial. Barney Riggs was convicted and sentenced to a prison term.[23]

The fact that the sheriff maintained such a close relationship with the jury could expose the lawman to accusations of wrongdoing. In 1885, Cochise County Sheriff Robert S. Hatch was accused of irregular conduct in providing for the needs of a jury in Tombstone. During a trial of the Cooper Queen Mining company vs. The Arizona Prince Copper Company, Hatch had allegedly "feasted and wined" the trial jury. Although he replied that both parties to this case had requested that he fete them, the charge could not be ignored. Upon review of the case, the Territorial Supreme Court scolded the sheriff for his indiscretion, but concluded that there was "no evidence that any juror was so drunk that he could not perform his duty. . . ." This tribunal let the original decision in the mining case stand. As a Bernalillo County deputy sheriff, Thomas S. Hubbell had a near calamity with an Albuquerque jury in 1893. During the deliberations of a jury in a controversial rape case, a juror emerged from seclusion and asked for instructions about the proper form of a written decision. Hubbell innocently responded with the desired information. When defense counsel learned of this improper contact between jury and lawman, the attorney appealed to the New Mexico Supreme Court. The high court took the case under study but concluded that the deputy sheriff had had no criminal intent. After reading Hubbell's written affidavit, the supreme court concluded that his explanation "made apparent the harmlessness of the communication." The original decision of the district court in the rape case was upheld.[24]

The relationship between sheriff and district court followed prescribed rules. Twice annually, in spring and fall, the presiding judge and his entourage of representatives of the bar made the pilgrimage to each county seat in the appropriate district. The sheriff awaited the arrival of this delegation and answered to its demands. However, this tradition was overturned momentarily in Colfax County, New Mexico, in the mid-1870s. Squatters had become embroiled in a violent "war" with the absentee-owned Maxwell Land Grant Company. In January 1876, the New Mexico Legislature peremptorily withdrew sessions of district court from Colfax County and assigned all of its cases to the sittings in Taos. Although Taos was in the same circuit of the judicial district, the residents of Colfax County were outraged at such arbitrary behavior. To be tried in the community where the crime was committed was an ancient right in Anglo-American jurisprudence. These irate frontiersmen blamed this legislative action on the Santa Fe Ring, that is Thomas B. Catron and his land-grabbing followers. The *Daily New Mexican,* the official organ of the governing regime in Santa Fe, replied that Colfax County was "full of crime."[25]

For Sheriff Isaiah Rinehart, the disabling act had immediate and discomfiting results. He and his deputies now had to escort prisoners on a long, dangerous journey across a mountain range to Taos. On one such trip, Rinehart had in charge the legendary and intimidating badman Robert Clay Allison, one of the squatter leaders. The citizens of Colfax County cried out against this deprivation of judicial rights. Mrs. Ada McPherson Morley, whose husband was a defendant in a case sent to Taos, declared that her county had been "robbed." Residents of Cimarron petitioned Governor Samuel Axtell, who replied vaguely that "certain objects" of the crippling law had not yet been accomplished. Apparently Frank Springer, a rising political star and opponent of Axtell, reached influential ears in Washington, D.C. Upon instructions from the secretary of interior, the New Mexico Legislature restored the district court session of Colfax County in 1878. The new sheriff, Peter Burleson, had the pleasure of serving a local session some time later. The frontiersmen knew their rights to convenient, fair, and speedy trials.[26]

Since the sheriffs conducted investigations and collected evidence in criminal cases, they often testified in court. Sheriff Harvey H. Whitehill's testimony saved a Jewish peddler from a murder conviction in Grant County, New Mexico. In the mid-1870s, this itinerant merchant stopped at the Whitehill residence. The sheriff's children observed the striking similarity of the noses of the two men and charcoaled their profiles on a wall. A short time later, Whitehill received a summons to testify in a trial in El Paso, Texas. This very same peddler stood accused of murdering his business partner. The Grant County lawman's testimony was crucial to the defense, since the murder had taken place on or about the day of the merchant's visit to the Whitehills. The Silver City peace officer could point to the physical evidence of this visit—the drawings of the "Roman noses" on the wall of his living room. Sheriff Pat Garrett was the primary witness in the controversial case against Oliver Lee, charged with the murder of lawyer Albert Fountain and his son, in 1896. Although the famous manhunter had worked diligently to assemble the necessary evidence, Garrett's testimony failed to win a conviction. Lee went free.[27]

Although the sheriff officially belonged to his county, the district judge possessed authority over the lawman in matters pertaining to the bench. Andrew J. Doran, sheriff of Pinal County, Arizona, was surprised to receive a citation from Chief Justice Daniel Pinney to show cause why the lawman should not be punished for contempt of court. This case arose in the wake of a tragic stagecoach robbery and murder at Riverside, a small stopover near Florence, in 1883. The sheriff arrested one man, Len Redfield. However, the United States marshal desired custody of the outlaw, since he and his band had robbed the mails. Doran refused to relinquish Redfield, thus prompting Judge Pinney's summons to Phoenix. Sheriff Doran recalled that in an interview with Pinney,

> I showed him . . . the evidence which I had obtained in reference to the robbery; showing conclusively that Redfield had planned the robbery; had received the [stolen] money, and that [Joseph] Tuttle had done the shooting. The judge studied a few moments and said: 'Mr. Sheriff, go home and attend to your duties; when I want you for contempt of court I will send for you.' . . .

Sheriff Felipe Lucero ran afoul of a district judge in Las Cruces in 1908. The occasion was Wayne Brazel's brutal murder of former Sheriff Pat Garrett. When Brazel rode into the county seat and surrendered, he asked Lucero if he intended to jail him. The lawman reportedly replied, "'No, you came in and gave yourself up when you . . . could have been hiding out by this time.'" When Garrett's friends observed this nonchalant behavior of the county lawman, they complained to the district judge. He promptly reprimanded Sheriff Lucero, had a warrant issued for Wayne Brazel, and set a stiff bond for the killer.[28]

As servant of the court, the sheriff had duties extending beyond service of process and care of the jury to the upkeep of public buildings. He not only rented court space but handled such mundane services as providing a desk for the judge and firewood and lighting during court sessions. The *Mesilla Valley Independent* noted Sheriff Henry J. Cuniffe going about such activities in May 1879. Not only did the lawman repair the doors to the courtroom and add a sidewalk in front, but he whitewashed the building. "The old sign over the door which so long served as a bat roost has been removed," added this writer. But "it is not considered worth while or economical to put glass in the windows," he lamented. A Florence journalist complimented Sheriff Andrew J. Doran for applying similar remedies to the hall of justice in Pinal County, Arizona. Doran put prisoners to work with calcimine on the interior of the court and added tapestry to the judge's stand. These improvements gave the inside of the court "a more respectable appearance," noted one newspaperman. When Chaves County opened a new courthouse in Roswell in 1891, the board of commissioners gave Sheriff Campbell C. Fountain strict orders to limit the use of the building. Only sessions of court, public school meetings, and preaching and Sunday school were permitted. The county fathers also enjoined him to sod the courthouse square—bluegrass was specified.[29]

In the 1880s, sheriffs acquired additional duties when New Mexico and Arizona established county courts. These lawmen had served local probate and justice of the peace courts all along. But the new county courts constituted an additional burden and evidently represented an effort to acquire more "home rule," according to one newspaper. Said this writer, Arizonans believed that by taking away some jurisdiction from the district courts, smaller communities would have an opportunity to make some decisions in the justice system. Arizona began this experiment in 1885, and New Mexico followed eight years later. In both sets of courts, the sheriffs summoned jurors and attended sessions just as at the district level. However, these new tribunals proved to be too expensive for the relatively poor counties. The burden upon the sheriffs was also oppressive. Arizona abolished this new creation after only two years of service. Just when New Mexico followed is not clear.[30]

Whatever the echelon of court, every session led to welcome by-products for the county seat. Rural families were prompted to make a rare trip to the county seat. Businessmen oiled their cash drawers. Perhaps the head of a family had been summoned to jury duty or as a witness. Fees for this service provided some spending money. Others came simply for the drama and excitement of court proceedings. In February 1873, the *Daily New Mexican* observed that a session of court attracted "quite a crowd of strangers . . . and for a short time . . . has broken up the monotonous stagnation" of Santa Fe. The crowd about the courthouse, said this writer, "looks enlivening and refreshing." A similar air surrounded a sitting in Silver City in April 1893. The village is a "thriving and busy metropolis," said one observer.[31]

Social life received a stimulating injection of new humanity. Sophie Poe, wife of the Lincoln County lawman, recalled how the arrival of the wives of the judicial delegation contributed to the social life in this remote county seat. "During the day interest centered in the court proceedings," she wrote, "but at night the absorbing matters were dances and other festivities." "Everybody was expected to have a good time," added Sophie Poe. The wife of Saturnino Baca, another former sheriff, kept an open house during each session. During a notable trial in Tombstone, Arizona, the gambling fraternity became very conspicuous. The occasion was the trial of William Greene, the future mining baron, in 1897. Greene had killed the bullyish and temperamental Jim Burnett, a former justice of the peace. The sporting crowd took bets that Greene would win his liberty. They were right.[32]

When the sheriff instructed all present to rise for conclusion of a district court session, he and his staff must have breathed a sigh of relief. They could now reflect upon the results of this latest burst of frenzied energy. A session of court brought together a host of conflicting personalities, among both officials and spectators. Just as the sheriff negotiated his way through a labyrinthine series of lawmen each year, he did the same among court officials twice a year. The sheriff was a conspicuous feature as executive officer of the court from the beginning of the process—summoning witnesses and jurors—to the end, when he sealed the jury in its quarters to deliberate. As policeman or bailiff, the sheriff sought to protect participants and spectators alike. While most trials were peaceful, the courts were places for the adjudication of grievances. Human passions naturally came out in every trial. It was the sheriff's job to police such outbursts and guard this sacred precinct against potential violence. In particular, it was his task to protect the inner sanctum, the jury room, from alien or corrupting influences. Ironically, such close association with the panel exposed sheriff and deputies to charges of interference or tampering. In spite of such nettlesome problems, the sheriffs of Arizona and New Mexico territories managed to provide the presiding judges and their assistants with the necessary services for some measure of justice.

Top: Cleofes Romero (San Miguel County, 1899–1910) was a member of the in-fluential family that provided his county with several sheriffs. The cartoon appar-ently refers to a train robbery in eastern New Mexico in 1904. (Courtesy Special Collections, University of New Mexico Library.) *Bottom left:* Jose R. Lucero (Doña Ana County, 1901–1908) occupied the shrievalty at the time of Pat Gar-rett's death near Las Cruces. (Courtesy Special Collections, University of New Mexico Library.) *Bottom right:* Patricio Sanchez (Mora County, 1912) was elected sheriff in the special November 1911 elections for officials who assumed the helm of government at statehood in the following year. (Courtesy Special Collections, University of New Mexico Library.)

Saturnino Baca (Lincoln County, 1875–76) was a Union veteran and founder of Lincoln County. He is shown here with a daughter Saturnina. Baca lost an arm in a shooting between cattle and sheep men. (Courtesy Museum of New Mexico, negative no. 105385.)

6

Keeper of the Keys
The Sheriff as Jailer

 The care of the county jails and their inmates proved to be one of the most vexatious of the sheriff's tasks. Not only were the impoverished counties of New Mexico and Arizona unable to afford secure jails, but the Hispanic and Indian populations were generally unaccustomed to imprisonment as punishment for crime. Nonetheless, the Americans insisted upon a penal system at the county level. To secure prisoners in preparation for trial was fundamental to the Anglo-American judicial system. A host of obstacles obstructed the sheriffs. Incredibly primitive facilities, vigilante action against flimsy jails, and frequent breakouts were just a few problems. Attentive jail guards seemed to be impossible to find. Most jails were overcrowded, since other lawmen lodged their prisoners in the sheriff's lockup. And the frontier citizenry did not respond to the occasional cries for prison reform. Sheriffs generally lacked the public support necessary to maintain large jail staffs. Still, some progress in improved jail construction was made as the territorial era drew to a close.

The American conquerors arrived in the Mexican southwest with a firm resolve to impose the Anglo-American judicial and law enforcement system upon the native population. While General Kearny and his successors did not force the complete apparatus upon them all at once, the necessity for a network of county jails and a territorial prison was an uppermost concern in the governor's office in Santa Fe. The Kearny Code, which went into effect in September 1846, vested each sheriff in New Mexico with "charge of the jail within his county." An alarmed Governor Charles Bent informed Senator Thomas Hart Benton of Missouri, who acted as a spokesman for many territorial interests in the national capital, that "there is not . . . a single jail or prison in the whole territory." Shortly after the creation of Arizona Territory, Governor Richard C. McCormick reminded the legislature of the conspicuous absence of county jails. "The officers of justice find it difficult to retain their prisoners," said the alarmed executive. Army guardhouses offered sheriffs the only hope of securing prisoners, although the civilian lawmen resented dependence upon the military.[1]

Elsewhere sheriffs and other local lawmen had recourse to unique penal expediencies. In many communities, lawmen tied prisoners to trees or buried logs dubbed "snubbing posts." One deputy sheriff, Hurricane Bill Smith, lodged troublemakers in an empty railroad car at Otero, New Mexico. Samuel Bean, sheriff of Doña Ana County in its earliest days, erected an open air stockade in Mesilla. The first jail of Pinal County, Arizona, recalled Jailer Oliver Stratton, was primitive. Since this structure had no door, Stratton chained prisoners to a large rock in the floor and slept in the open doorway. A local journalist compared this calaboose to the torture rooms of the Inquisition. In Arizona mining districts, such as Clifton, abandoned shafts served as jails. Jennie Parks Ringgold remembered the infamous "Rock Jail" at Clifton:

> The interior consisted of two compartments. One was a large cell about twenty feet square which housed the common drunks, misdemeanor prisoners, and . . . less dangerous types. It had two ventilator windows. . . . The other cell was much smaller and had no windows or ventilators. Here the dangerous criminals were confined. Both cells had regulation steel-barred doors. . . .

As local badman Red Johnson remarked upon completion of his stay in this bizarre carcel, "'This is the damndest hole to put a white man in I ever saw!'" In 1904, an article in *Wide World Magazine* gave the Rock Jail nationwide notoriety.[2]

Some county governments were slow to provide adequate penal facilities. The citizens of Lincoln County, New Mexico, failed to erect a county jail for eight years. When Sheriff William Brady finally constructed a carcel in 1877, he could hardly boast. It was an underground cavern, twenty by thirty feet and ten feet deep. This dungeon was lined with logs and consisted of two cells with ingress through a trapdoor in the roof. The jailer, whose office was above ground, lowered a ladder to serve the prisoners. The *Las Vegas Gazette* described the lockup as "literally a hole in the ground, where candles were constantly burning to enable the prisoners to recognize each other." This "cellar" jail was very insecure, and escapes were common. By the time Pat Garrett entered the shrievalty in 1881, it was closed. He recalled it as "a horribly dismal hole, unfit for a dog-kennel." One of the first inmates was reportedly William Bonney, alias Billy the Kid. After scratching his dates of confinement on a log, he added, "and hope I never will be [in here] again." The absence of a secure jail in this remote county had serious repercussions for the reputation of Sheriff Brady. When the notorious Jessie Evans and his rustler band escaped the flimsy *calabozo* in November 1878, the public lost confidence in the lawman. This loss of faith in Brady contributed to the growth of tensions that led to the Lincoln County War.[3]

After the interruptions of the Civil War had passed, some progress was made toward the construction of new jails. Pima and Yavapai counties were among these innovators. In New Mexico, at least four counties—Grant, Socorro, Rio Arriba, and Colfax—built new jails within a twelve-month period. Some were constructed with new courthouses. Citizens waxed enthusiastic about these public buildings and hailed them as signs of progress. As one man gazed upon a new courthouse in Plaza Alcalde, New Mexico, he was moved to boast that "Our little town is improving fast. . . ." As Grant County's calaboose went up in Silver City, another person mused to the *Daily New Mexican* that his county "will soon lead the territory." Unlike the counties of the 1850s, which began without jails, many new units of local government after the Civil War constructed jail buildings at the outset. When Tom Murphy assumed his duties as sheriff of the new Sierra County, New Mexico, in 1884, he began with a jail at hand.[4]

These new jails represented a significant step forward, although modest in size and flimsy in construction. The new Colfax County Jail in Cimarron consisted of three cells on one side of a central passageway and a "minimum security" general lockup and jailer's rooms on the opposite side. After lynchers broke in, Sheriff John J. Turner added a jailyard enclosed by a stone wall. In Tucson, the Pima County jail sported iron-barred cells and a walled exercise yard. However, unseasonable rains soon began the premature deterioration of this new adobe structure.[5]

The selection of a reliable person as jailer posed a problem for the sheriff. Few men on the frontier had prior experience. In the absence of professional penal training, jailers learned on the job. The sheriff preferred someone of mature years, settled, cautious, and with some management experience. The jailer also held a commission as a deputy and performed other tasks. He usually received a fixed income, since jailers did not have as much opportunity as other deputies to earn fees. He and his family often lived in quarters in the jail building. While some early county jails were unattended at night, county officials eventually insisted upon a nightwatchman. This slot was a luxury in some early jails. Like the deputy sheriffs, the jailer was an employee of the sheriff, rather than an official employee of the county. This nebulous situation could cause some questions when a jailbreak or other emergency occurred in the jail.[6]

The backgrounds of the two Pima County jailers provide some examples of their qualifications. During the six years that Robert Paul occupied the shrievalty, the security of the jail was a constant source of concern. Paul hired George Cooler as jailer in 1881. Cooler had immigrated from Holland. He joined the United States Army and served against the Indians in New Mexico and later against the Confederacy. After the Civil War, Cooler continued to work for the military in civilian capacities. While operating a saloon in Tucson, he made the acquaintance of Sheriff Paul. Shortly after assuming the post of jailer, Cooler had the misfortune to be the victim of a jailbreak. The public outcry was so great that the sheriff had to arrest and imprison his own jailer! The outcome of Cooler's court case is not known. Paul selected Andrew W. Holbrook as the new Pima County jailer. Holbrook was born in Upton, Massachusetts, on 13 May 1830. He migrated to California and served on the San Francisco police force, where he earned a reputation for efficiency. Robert Paul met Holbrook when Paul was a detective for the Wells Fargo Company in that state. Paul evidently approved of Holbrook and called him to Tucson as jailer. Holbrook was unmarried and regarded as quiet and unassuming. He too was the victim of a breakout. Joseph Casey, one of Arizona's most vicious criminals, callously shot Holbrook to death in May 1883.[7]

In spite of the responsibilities, the income of the jailer was paltry. It is difficult to determine in all instances the precise salary of this official. The method of paying him, as well as the support of the jail, changed during the territorial era. While the sheriff continued to employ the jailer of his choice, Arizona eventually placed a ceiling upon the salary of jailers and guards. In New Mexico, the pay of jailers became uniform from county to county. In 1891, Chaves and Doña Ana counties paid them $600 annually. Since the Assembly in Santa Fe specified this figure in an 1897 law, presumably all turnkeys received this same sum. This law also limited each jail to one additional guard at $480 annually. If additional guards were needed, the district judge certified to this need.[8]

Arizona and New Mexico authorized the chief county lawman a daily rate, per prisoner, for all jail expenses. This was, presumably, the source not only for money to pay the routine costs of upkeep of the jail and prisoners but for the jailer's pay. In 1866, New Mexico fixed this daily rate at fifty cents per prisoner per day with the understanding that the jailer provide from this income "all necessary things" for the jail: firewood, candles, kitchen furniture, food, leg irons and handcuffs. The lawmakers raised this figure to seventy-five cents in the 1880s. However, much controversy surrounded the management and means of support of county jails in both territories. New Mexico took the management of county jails from the sheriffs and implemented a contractual system in 1890, returned to the fixed rate of seventy-five cents in the following year, reduced it to forty cents in 1898, and returned to seventy-five cents in 1899 (but only for the first ten prisoners, and fifty cents for any excess).[9]

New Mexico lawmakers gave county jail policy a good airing in their 1891 session. The decision of the previous session to raise the daily allowance to seventy-five cents provoked some outcry. Many people believed the sheriffs were earning too much money already from fees of office. Since the population was growing, the business of courts, and hence that of the sheriffs, increased accordingly. When the legislators changed to a contractual system for the jails, many sheriffs were upset. This new procedure permitted any private citizen to bid for a contract to administer the jail. The lowest bidder received the contract. Through the New Mexico Sheriffs Association, the lawmen lobbied against the law at the 1891 session. When the *Daily New Mexican*, a leading journal in New Mexico, supported the contract system, Socorro County Sheriff Clarence A. Robinson sprang to the defense of the seventy-five cent allotment system. Robinson asserted that the contractual plan weakened jail security because it permitted outsiders—perhaps, a contract jailer over whom the sheriff had no control—to roam freely in and out of the facility. To permit "a lot of irresponsible parties to be going in and out of your jail at will . . ." continued the angry sheriff, would cause many problems. He predicted major jailbreaks, because "Some one will soon bribe some person . . ." on the contractual jail staff. To some degree, the sheriff would continue to be responsible for jail security. Yet, this new law divided the day-to-day task of supporting the jail between the contractor and the lawman.[10]

Sheriff Robinson also did not agree that the seventy-five cent fee provided him with an exorbitant income. He informed the public that he did not retain any surplus that might remain after the expenses of the prisoners were paid, but permitted his jailer to keep as his income everything the jail earned (presumably, after expenses). The Socorro County lawman believed the sheriff should be "the sole custodian" of the jail, but admitted that the assembly should "hold him responsible for the management of the same." The contractual system tied the sheriff "hand and foot," threw him in the lake and told him "to swim or drown," said Robinson. Apparently, the lawmakers agreed with him. On 24 February 1891, the governor signed a bill to reinstate the seventy-five cent proviso. Some newspapermen continued to maintain that this system permitted the sheriffs to earn too much money.[11]

Regardless of the method of support of county jails, the sheriffs provided the barest amenities for prisoners. Some peace officers begrudged every cent of jail upkeep. Such an attitude resulted from many sources. The povertied status of new frontier counties, lingering prejudices of many natives against costly penal systems, and the traditional disdain for criminals were possibly contributory. As late as the Civil War, New Mexico law required prisoners (or their families) to pay for their own support while in jail. This procedure was common practice in the Republic of Mexico and may have been one of the many native traditions that the Americans permitted to continue after the conquest. Arizona Territory required the sheriff to provide minimal, necessary clothing and bedding for each inmate. This expense could be worked off through public labor. Arizona and New Mexico codes charged the sheriff to provide "wholesome" food, although such quality lay in the eye of the beholder. In 1866, the latter territory declared that the food should be "healthy" and served "at proper hours, . . . three times a day." "Bread and water" was authorized for recalcitrants.[12]

The sheriffs provided food for prisoners in various ways. Where the lawman's family lived in or near the jail building, his wife often cooked for inmates. Sheriff Marion Littrell's spouse provided this service to Colfax County prisoners. Local restauranteurs eagerly sought the contract to provide food for the county jail, and bidding could be keen. When the Pima County (Arizona) Board of Supervisors opened bids for the year 1871, three Tucson restaurant owners competed. J. Neugass bid one dollar per prisoner per day; D. A. Bennet[t] offered "cooked provisions . . . at the rate of 95 cents per . . . head," while Frank S. Alling would provide two meals per day for 99.9 cents per prisoner with "two extra dishes on the sabbath." Just who received the contract is unclear, but the Bennett proposal was probably the most attractive.[13]

Inmates in these county jails complained routinely about the poor quality of the food. One unnamed New Mexico grand jury—evidently in Albuquerque—reported complaints of prisoners in 1891 and 1892:

> The prisoners complain of receiving very bad food. The coffee is made from grounds that have been used before. The bread is badly made. The meat is bad and the soup very thick and the prisoners get bad language from [Jailer] Jose Barera [Barela?] if they complain. . . .

In February 1893, federal prisoners housed in Sheriff Joseph B. Scott's jail in Tucson became dissatisfied. They petitioned Robert H. Paul, now United States Marshal, and urged him to investigate "the kind of board furnished U.S. Prisoners." "The food is to[o] horrible for even Mexicans," they alleged. Since the United States Government paid Sheriff Scott one dollar per day for support of each federal inmate, these prisoners believed that the marshal should "act with a little magnaminity in their behalf." Whether they obtained assistance is not known.[14]

To provide adequate water and sanitation services was a considerable task. Each jail normally kept a well or pump, and a trustee fetched water. All inmates drank from the same dipper. In September 1886, the twenty-one inmates in the Pima County jail complained to the grand jury that Sheriff Eugene O. Shaw neglected to provide enough water. Shaw replied that the water tank atop the courthouse—the source of jail water—had gone dry during the previous summer's drought. Water had to be carried from the courtyard. This proved to be difficult since the large number of inmates required about 100 buckets daily. The jury recommended the installation of a hydrant in the jailyard.[15]

Sanitation measures were crude to nonexistent in these early penal facilities. A bucket—"slop jar"—served as a waste station in many jails. As late as 1877, the Santa Fe County jailer used open barrels for privies. The indoor toilet facilities in an early Colfax County jail—a one holer—represented a great improvement. Where the jail possessed a yard or walkabout, the prisoners had the luxury of an outdoor station. Deputy Sheriff Jeff Milton recalled that one of his duties at the Sierra County jail, in Hillsboro, was to escort prisoners "to the brush." This facility lacked indoor accommodations. The accumulation of trash in the cells also posed a problem. Billy Breakenridge, a Maricopa County deputy, in 1879 recalled that the jailer merely swept trash under a loose floor plank rather than dump it outside. The occupants of Sheriff Edward Bowers's Prescott *calabozo* could count themselves fortunate. The *Arizona Miner* complimented him for a "well regulated jail" which he swept each day.[16]

Diseases were common among prisoners in such filthy conditions. Sheriffs were often hardpressed to provide adequate medical service, although territorial law required it. In July 1901, Sheriff William C. Truman informed United States Marshal William Griffith that a federal prisoner in the Florence jail "has a number of carbuncles and odd things on his penis." "It looks . . . like a case of syphillis," concluded the sheriff. A federal prisoner in the Pima County jail complained to Marshal Benjamin Daniels some years later that "I am suffering from too [two] fistulas, one beside the rectum and [another on] the penis. . . ." These sores "are very painful," he complained, "as when I pass water it comes through the holes. . . ." "Please do what you can for me," this unfortunate man begged. The territorial authorities were not insensitive to the medical needs of prisoners. The Arizona Assembly ordered the county sheriffs to prevent "pestilence or contagious disease" in their jails. To do so, they contracted with a physician to care for ailing inmates. In August 1871, J. C. Handy, a Tucson doctor, bid for the contract as Pima County physician: "I propose to attend upon the county prisoners and upon such sick . . . for ($50) fifty dollars per month and furnish medicines free." Handy averred that he would also "take full charge of helpless [indigent] persons and furnish hospital accommodations . . ." for eighty dollars each month.[17]

The sheriffs normally made some effort to obtain medical attention for ailing prisoners. Even the most backward officer realized that a healthy prisoner reduced jail expenses and warded off public criticism. Daily exercise was encouraged in jailyards. Mrs. O. P. Church, who resided in Lincoln, New Mexico, in the 1870s, recalled seeing the jailer bring prisoners up from the cellar jail for exercise. Sheriff Jose D. Sena was observed arranging for an ill prisoner to enter Sister's Hospital in Santa Fe in May 1880. Morphine addiction was a common problem. Sheriff George Ruffner encountered many such cases in the Yavapai County jail in the late 1890s. Among them were Genz Leander, a professional tightrope walker, and a man who attempted suicide when he could not obtain drugs in his cell. The Maricopa County physician in Phoenix attempted to cure prisoner Harry Smith of his drug habit. "Smith does not take well to the doctor's kindly intention," remarked a local journalist.[18]

Sheriffs attempted to separate the various categories of inmates, although this was difficult to impossible. Where possible, youthful offenders were kept away from hardened criminals. One cell, without lights or amenities, served as a place of solitary confinement. If the town did not have a separate city jail, the chief of police sometimes rented one cell as a "tank" for his troublesome citizens. In the absence of adequate space for such an elaborate distinction between inmates, the sheriffs simply made do. As late as the 1880s, the Santa Fe County jail still consisted of one long room. To segregate the more dangerous prisoners from first-time offenders, the sheriff chained the former to a post in one end of the cell. Some troublemakers were subjected to the "Oregon boot," a heavy metal anklet, while others were attached to an iron ball. Solitary confinement could mean being shut in a small, windowless cell or merely being chained alone in the darkened corner of a larger room. Insane confinees were also bound in order to prevent them from harming themselves or others.[19]

There is little doubt that brutalization was an everpresent prospect for these county prisoners, whether inflicted upon one another or by the jailers. Some abuses took the form of harassment, including ugly or threatening language or the withholding of routine services. When Pat Garrett lodged the Billy the Kid band temporarily in the San Miguel County jail, in Las Vegas, the lawman expected standard treatment for his wards. However, Sheriff Desiderio Romero's jailers, who were Hispanos, harbored much ill will not only against Garrett but his prisoners. The jailers ate the food designated for the outlaws. Needless to say, the Lincoln County officer was irate, and he complained to the local newspaper. Although located in the territorial capital, the Santa Fe County jail apparently had a reputation for harshness. When an accused embezzler was transferred from Rio Arriba County to Santa Fe in May 1886, he reminded the jailer at the outset that, "'I ain't a bad man and I want you to treat me right.'" Sheriff Frank Chavez won notoriety for roughing up his wards in this facility. One prisoner, Lee White, obtained a grand jury indictment against the sheriff for assault. Chavez allegedly beat up Francisco Borrego, another inmate, while the helpless man was chained to a post in his cell. This senseless act helped to set off a regrettable series of violent incidents in Santa Fe and led to the assassination of Chavez a short time after he left office.[20]

Although remote from the larger centers of civilization, the frontier county jails often housed a very cosmopolitan clientele. These often included offenders against United States laws, both white and Indian. Violators of city ordinances in the county seat also resided in the county jail. Foreign lawbreakers included citizens from Mexico and as far away as China. In addition, the sheriffs were also responsible for safekeeping insane persons until they could be transferred to an asylum. United States prisoners probably constituted the larger group of nonterritorial inmates. The United States marshal, who was custodian of all federal violators, contracted with sheriffs to guard Uncle Sam's lawbreakers serving short-terms. Congress preferred this expediency rather than go to the expense of transporting them to Eastern penitentiaries. These offenders usually remained in county jails if their terms were for twelve months or less. The United States marshal could only place federal lawbreakers in the county jail if the sheriff agreed to wear the badge of a deputy marshal. In effect, the county officer became a "U.S. jailer." The sheriff charged the federal lawman a contracted amount per prisoner for each day in the county jail. This amount, sometimes one dollar per day, provided the sheriff with welcome additional income. The county lawman also housed prisoners arrested by the town marshal of the county seat. Sheriff Holm O. Bursum gave Socorro officers a break. He charged them ten cents less than the United States marshal for each prisoner. Bursum's cooperative attitude had some calculation behind it. He relied heavily upon these town and federal counterparts. This feeling was mutual.[21]

While women were only a small part of the body of prisoners, they posed many problems. To keep them separated from male inmates and provide them with any additional necessities was difficult. Some statistics might provide an insight into this problem. The Pima County jail contained twenty-two prisoners in July 1891, five of whom were females. The Bernalillo County lockup held twenty inmates in March 1908, three of them women. These unfortunates represented all of the races and ethnic groups in the Southwest. Sheriff Robert Hatch arrested a Mescalero Apache woman, Na-di-sah, for horse theft in 1886. Camillus S. Fly, Tombstone photographer and future sheriff, took her picture for a tourist postcard. She "looks quite fashionable in her neatly fitting calico dress," said the *Daily Epitaph*. The court dismissed her case. Women of Anglo and Hispanic backgrounds were most commonly incarcerated. A Las Cruces newspaperman overheard "lady boarders" singing "Wait Till the Clouds Roll By" in August 1893. Paula Angel, the only female to be hanged in either New Mexico or Arizona territories, sat on "death row" in jail in Las Vegas until her execution in 1863. Many years later, a Department of Justice investigator accused the jailer of this county of abusing female prisoners. A Pima County physician charged Sheriff Robert Paul's jailer with impregnating a female prisoner. Alice Parker captured the attention of the New Mexico press when she was arrested as a member of a band of horse thieves and lodged in the Doña Ana County jail in December 1892. The *Daily New Mexican* lamented the consequences of her errant ways and painted a sad picture of her children standing helpless in front of her cell and crying out for her. The waifs would now become charity cases. This county facility soon added a "woman's room" to its cell block. Yavapai County, Arizona, followed suit.[22]

An occasional female inmate rivaled the more infamous male wrongdoers in public attention. "Bronco Sue" Yonkers, accused of murdering a man, graced the Socorro County jail in 1886. Pearl Hart, a would-be stagecoach robber, presented the sheriff of Pinal County, Arizona, with many problems in 1899. Since the jail in Florence had no cell for women, William Truman transferred Hart to the more secure jail in Tucson. Sheriff Lyman Wakefield soon regretted this decision. The young outlaw used her cell as a forum to speak out for women's rights! She impressed the Tucson *Star* with her fervency when she declared that she "would never consent to be tried under a law she or her sex had no voice in making." Hart caught the attention of *Cosmopolitan Magazine,* which featured this outlaw-crusader. Meanwhile, she employed her feminine wiles on a gullible trustee—he "fell in love with me," she boasted—and escaped Wakefield's supposedly secure jail. Authorities in Lordsburg, New Mexico, soon recaptured her. After serving a short term in Yuma Prison, Pearl Hart disappeared.[23]

The lawmakers of Arizona and New Mexico territories insisted that prisoners perform useful work. Idleness not only violated the Puritan ethic of the pioneers but permitted jailbirds the leisure to plot escapes. New Mexico's 1866 penal code contained the provision that prisoners, rather than the taxpayers, pay for their own upkeep. If an inmate or his family could not pay for this subsistence, the sheriff put him to work. The code provided that the prisoner perform street cleaning chores or "any other public work." Persons accused of murder were excepted and kept in confinement. Sheriff Andrew J. Doran of Pinal County, Arizona, assigned his wards the task of painting the courthouse in 1883. A Lincoln County inmate who possessed some artistic skills drew frescoes on the cell walls. A Phoenix sheriff put his prisoners to work cleaning the cemetery. In

June 1875, the Pima County supervisors ordered county inmates "to dig [a] grave and bury a man that was found dead last night." Sheriff William "Buckey" O'Neill directed his prisoners to plant trees in downtown Prescott.[24]

Prisoners responded in various ways to work details. After all, they may have gotten into their predicament from the desire to avoid labor. In 1879, a Phoenix jailbird feigned insanity to avoid a work detail. The sheriffs rationed the food allowance of uncooperative wards. A Florence newsman observed that Sheriff Andrew Doran "had to place [inmates] on a diet of bread and water to conquer their disinclination to toil." "After a few days . . ." continued this writer, "the boys felt industrious" and began "digging like dredging machines." Other prisoners passed their sentences profitably. In 1893, two Mohave County inmates became "Jack-knife carpenters." One Hispano fashioned a guitar; the other a miniature brigantine. An unusually industrious time-server in the Cochise County jail found a way to make money. Mack Axford, the jailer, permitted Chicago Whitey, a tramp charged with robbery, to purchase a small cookstove. Among other foods, Whitey's "Mexican pies" sold very well. By the time of his release, Whitey had accumulated $100.[25]

Time still weighed heavily upon these inmates. Axford, who became jailer in Cochise County shortly after the turn of the century, attempted to fill this enforced leisure with recreational activity. He provided his inmates "a set of boxing gloves, checker boards and a couple of harmonicas." Mexican prisoners obtained guitars from their Tombstone friends. Axford also permitted a prisoner with barber skills to set up shop in the jailyard. The occupants of the Chaves County *calabozo* organized a mock court in May 1903 to try a German, Carl von Stoffen, for cursing Uncle Sam. The sentence—a lashing. When citizens of Santa Fe provided prisoners with flowers and reading material in November 1884, they responded with a letter of thanks "for the kindness shown." Inmates of the Pima County jail responded in like manner when a Tucson merchant gave Sheriff E. O. Shaw's boarders a box of cigars at Christmas. The recipients, giving their address as "Hotel Shaw," thanked this thoughtful giftgiver and concluded the letter, "May his shadow never grow less." Mrs. O. P. Church recalled how sorry she and her mother felt for young William Bonney and other prisoners in the Lincoln County jail. The elder Church made tea and cookies for them and the daughter delivered the food.[26]

The presence of unoccupied time in flimsily constructed jails made breakouts an ever-present prospect. Ingenious inmates used every conceivable means to escape. Many jails were made from adobe, a rather soft substance that prisoners often dug through with hastily fashioned tools. Que-cha-co, the Yuma-Mohave Indian who murdered Yuma County Sheriff James Dana in 1873, made his escape this way. He was never recaptured. Jailbirds used clever ruses upon unsuspecting jailers. Bill Smith, a vicious Arizona outlaw, feigned deep sleep several mornings in a row. Eventually the frustrated jailer violated procedure and carelessly walked into Smith's cell with his weapon on. The outlaw jumped the jailer and made his escape. Youthful William Bonney (later Billy the Kid) scrambled out of the Grant County jail by way of a chimney. Some escapees had outside help. The friends of two Cimarron toughs, Gus Hefferon and Bill Lowe, threw a rope over the jailyard wall one night in October 1876, enabling the two to run free. Sheriff Carlos Conklin was accused of being too compassionate toward prisoners in his Santa Fe lockup. When he permitted one young first offender the privilege of sleeping in the jailer's room rather than a cell, the budding thief skipped out. Clever inmates of the Colfax County jail took advantage of an inexperienced fill-in jailer in January 1892. They fashioned the form of a body in their cell, informed the turnkey that he was ill, and overpowered the unsuspecting jailer. One Lincoln County badman was able to escape the jail in White Oaks because he had helped construct it. He had the foresight to leave a log loose and thus escaped.[27]

A secure and commodious system of county jails lay at the foundation of the law enforcement and judicial system, as the governors of New Mexico and Arizona often reminded the citizenry. This problem had bothered territorial executives since Charles Bent assumed the New Mexico office in 1846. At the height of a cycle of lawlessness in 1884, New Mexico Governor Lionel Sheldon reflected at length upon the impact of inadequate county jails. While he admitted some improvements had been made in recent years, Sheldon went on to observe that in many counties the jails were "small, filthy, frail and insecure." Not only did the confined person run a risk of acquiring diseases but, continued the governor, "escapes are almost as easily made as from a paper [rubber] bandbox." This executive expressed disgust that while special jail guards were needed in these circumstances, some county boards refused to authorize this emergency expenditure. "There can be no certainty that criminals will be tried and punished," added Sheldon, "when there is so much insecurity. . . ." This law-and-order executive had gone to the heart of the jail controversy. Jails were the foundation of the judicial system. If the sheriffs failed to hold accused persons securely and present them at the bar of justice for trial, the courts could not mete out just sentences. Governor Sheldon urged the assembly to give district courts the power to persuade reluctant counties to either pay for extra jail guards or improve their physical facilities. At another time, Governor Sheldon made the additional observation that vigilantes were more inclined to take the law into their own hands when jails were insecure.[28]

The death of a jailer or innocent bystander during an escape was cause for great embarrassment to the sheriff. Toward the end of the territorial era, a New Mexico law provided for the death penalty for the murder of a jailer or sheriff. Residents of Las Vegas, New Mexico, were prepared to lynch bandit David Rudabaugh who murdered Jailer Antonio Lino during an escape in 1881. When Jim Casey led a break in Tucson two years later, he shot and killed Andrew Holbrook, the jailkeeper. Sheriff Bob Paul, a longtime friend of the dead man, upheld the law and fended off a lynch mob but later had the satisfaction of presiding at Casey's hanging. Yavapai County Sheriff George Ruffner had a similar experience in Prescott in 1897. Train robber Jim Parker murdered an innocent bystander during a jailbreak, but Ruffner soon recaptured him. Ruffner hanged Parker in the following year.[29]

After a jailbreak, the public often registered its displeasure by demanding an investigation. Residents of Tucson expressed much displeasure at the breakout of four men, two of whom were murderers, on New Year's night, 1875. One man concluded that the capture and conviction of the four badmen had cost the taxpayers $12,000. Sheriff William Sanders Oury reportedly took the incident nonchalantly. When informed of the breakout, Oury allegedly replied flippantly, "'Well, damn it, let them go. It will save the county a lot of trouble.'" The county supervisors held a hearing which revealed very lax security arrangements. Jailer Ad Linn was often absent from duty and spent much time drinking and gambling at a local saloon. Nightwatchman J. B. Sawyer admitted disobeying jail rules and opening cells when alone at night. Apparently, this inquiry was directed at the jailer and watchman and not Sheriff Oury. Oury asked Sawyer: "'Did I ever show any friendly feeling to any of the prisoners?'" "'No, you did not,'" he replied. The action of the board is not clear. The prisoners were never recaptured. William Sanders Oury was elected mayor of Tucson at the next election. Charles Shibell became the new sheriff.[30]

The escape of Augustine Chacon from the Graham County jail in Solomonville in June 1897 caused considerable public outrage. This infamous border bandit was scheduled to hang on 18 June. The supervisors found that Chacon cut his way through the wall, although Sheriff Billy Birchfield placed two special guards in the structure each night. Both men had been sleeping. The *Arizona Republican* reported that the bandit cut through a ten-inch adobe wall lined with "a double layer of two-inch pine boards . . . spiked together with five inch spikes." Chacon performed this miraculous, but noisy, feat while shackled. This journalist speculated facetiously that "The guards imagined that they were hired to sleep . . ," since the supervisors failed to specify that they could not sleep in a written contract. The writer added caustically that perhaps the guards obliged the busy outlaw by supplying "novelties in the way of snoring," that "enveloped the sound of the patriot, Chacon's saw. . . ." Another observer called attention to the fact that Sheriff Birchfield's duty was to examine the jail regularly and see that the guards remained on "active duty" rather than asleep. Chacon remained at liberty for five years; he was hanged in Solomonville in 1902.[31]

When a series of embarrassing breakouts beset the Cochise County jail between 1901 and 1904, Sheriff Del Lewis felt compelled to find a new jailer. Lewis's head turnkey was aged and overweight and could no longer maintain the necessary vigil. The sheriff sought a replacement in Mack Axford. "I was surprised one day while crossing the street [in Tombstone]," recalled Axford, "to have [Lewis] stop me and ask what I was doing." When Axford replied that he was unemployed at the moment, the lawman asked "if I could handle the jail job and guarantee that no prisoners would escape." After an examination of the jail facility, Axford informed Lewis that he could guarantee that no breaks would occur. However, Axford added the proviso "that I would be the boss and not subject to interference from anybody. . . ." "If I found a guard was not dependable," he continued, "I wanted the right to remove him without political interference. . . ." (The jail sometimes became the dumping ground for supporters of county politicians.) Axford concluded rightly that the sheriff—"Big Del"—was so embarrassed by the wave of jailbreaks that he "was willing to agree to almost anything." Axford kept his word, and no escapes took place while the ex-cowboy was jailer. Although inclined to boast in his later years, Axford asserted that prisoners often betrayed their intentions to make a break for liberty. Such plots usually arose as the spring or fall sessions of court approached. Inmates became "nervous" and their level of desperation increased.[32]

When a prisoner died inside the jail, the public naturally desired to know the circumstances. There were many causes. Sheriff Carl Hayden had an unsettling experience in 1911 when Francisco Rubio, a Mexican citizen, died in his jail in Phoenix. The Mexican consul requested an investigation. County Physician R. M. Tafel, the contract medical man, found that Rubio suffered from peritonitis upon incarceration and had admitted "being on a drunk for two weeks." Tafel "did not find any marks on the body that would cause me to think he had been injured . . ." during the arresting process. Constable J. T. Murphy, who arrested Rubio for disturbing the peace, declared that "no violence whatever was used." These explanations evidently satisfied the complainants. Suicides were also common. A soldier in Sheriff Edward Bowers's Prescott lockup slipped a gun from the lawman's holster and shot himself. Lincoln County Sheriff Alfredo Gonzales was shocked when two brothers attempted suicide in his lockup in 1902; one died and the other was injured. Two Apache Indians took their own lives in the Gila County jail, in Globe, in 1889.[33]

The occupants of these crude frontier lockups lived under much emotional stress. The possibility of fire and other calamities loomed very large. Would the sheriff and citizens remember them in event of fire? A near disaster occurred in Prescott, in 1884, when fire ravaged part of the town and put the jail in jeopardy. The prisoners "barely escaped with their lives," said one journal, "and had nothing on but night clothes. . . ." Flames engulfed Flagstaff in April 1896 and threatened the jail, commonly called the "rookery." City Marshal George Hochderffer recalled that the fire lapped at the jail door and prevented firefighters from approaching the building. For a moment the inmates appeared doomed. However, resourceful citizens came to the rescue. They "poured a stream of water upon the back of the jail," wrote Hockderffer, while "one man at a time plied the axe . . ." to an unexposed wall. The city marshal took a turn with the ax because "I felt a greater responsibility and anxiety to get them out." Some horrible tragedies did occur elsewhere. In January 1907, two of Sheriff Pedro Schuberts's prisoners burned to death in Estancia, New Mexico. When a drunken prisoner set afire the Yavapai County branch jail, he was also consumed in the flames. A female Mexican prisoner did the same to the Nogales jail in April 1900. She also died. Five occupants of the infamous "Rock Jail" of

Graham County, Arizona, would have drowned during a flood had not Deputy Sheriff John Parks risked the high waters and taken them to safety on horseback. Traumatic experiences in these oppressive county jails even included the occult. Some inmates experienced a shock after vigilantes took bandits Joe Tuttle and Len Redfield from the Florence jail, in 1883, and hanged them. The shaken prisoners claimed to have seen the ghosts of the lynching victims. "Old Joe Tuttle's spectre . . ," said one reporter, "renders itself especially annoying and odious by prowling about and knocking around the jail corridor every night. . . ."[34]

The degree of occupancy of these frontier jails varied. In spite of the popular notion of the lawless frontier, empty county jails existed in Arizona and New Mexico territories. In November 1884, the Mineral Park *Miner* reported that the Mohave County branch jail was unoccupied and concluded that "This tells a good story of the morality and love of order in our community." The writer admitted that the absence of inmates "must be hard on Bill Jackson, the deputy sheriff." "An empty jail does not pay," added this writer, "and unless something is done Bill's cloak of office will get pretty thin." In larger communities, the jails were regularly filled. Sheriff Edward Bowers's Yavapai County jail bulged to capacity in May 1878. A local newspaperman remarked humorously that "In the daytime he herds them in the backyard," and "he will have to hang them up on nails at night." The lockup in Grant County, New Mexico, brimmed with so many inmates in January 1890 that it reportedly contained more than all other county jails in the territory combined! An Arizonan took some pleasure in this adverse reflection upon the neighboring territory and blamed the condition on lenient juries. After years of coddling criminals, the courts had suddenly decided to punish them with stiff penalties, hence the glutted cells.[35]

The typical group of county prisoners had committed a wide variety of crimes. Sheriff William Sanders Oury's quarterly jail report on 6 October 1873 contained the following:

Committed	Offense
July	9 prisoners (4 disturbing the peace, 4 assault, 1 grand larceny)
August	9 prisoners (1 sentenced to six months for improper use of deadly weapons and who escaped 17 Sep.; 3 arrested for murder and hanged by a mob on 8 Aug.; 2 arrested by sheriff and city marshal)
September	14 prisoners (jailed by justice of peace)[36]

According to the annual report of Matthew Shaw, sheriff of this same county, the Pima County jail contained a total of 252 persons in 1887:

Number	Charge
135	petty offenses
88	higher crimes
29	United States prisoners

In 1888, the jail received 279 inmates:

Number	Charge
148	misdemeanors
38	higher crimes
80	United States prisoners
9	insane
4	arrested and turned over to other counties

The ethnic or national background of these prisoners was not addressed in these reports. There is little doubt that a large number were Hispanos or Mexican nationals. In July 1906, the United States Immigration Bureau found that fifty percent of the occupants of insane asylums and prisons in (presumably) Arizona and New Mexico were Mexicans. (The term "Mexican" may have included both citizens and aliens.)[37]

As New Mexico and Arizona acquired additional population and modest resources after 1880, substantial jails began to appear. This "second wave" of carcels usually accompanied a courthouse. To construct such a costly edifice became a matter of civic pride. Civic-minded boosters regarded these "justice complexes" as weathervanes that pointed to a brighter, more secure future. The bell tower of the new courthouse constituted the skyline of these frontier county seats. In 1883, Grant County, New Mexico, built a new courthouse and jail. It was a three-storied brick building with the cell block in the basement (first floor). This block contained ten cells with an encircling hallway and thus separated prisoners from the outside wall. The offices of the sheriff and other public servants were on the second floor, with courtroom and jury rooms on the third. As other counties undertook new jails, they hired professional prison architects. The county administrators of Bernalillo employed an official of the Kansas Penitentiary to help design a new jail in Albuquerque. Some counties contracted with the Pauly Jail

Building and Manufacturing Company of St. Louis, Missouri. This company boasted about its "Celebrated steel-clad jail cells, saw and file proof." There was always danger of overextending the meager tax base of thinly populated counties. The board of supervisors of Mohave County, Arizona, committed near financial disaster in 1883 when they underestimated the cost of a new jail. What began as a $4,800 endeavor concluded at $6,995. To exacerbate matters, the county seat soon moved to Kingman, located on the railroad. Naturally, a new jail had to be erected there.[38]

As might be expected, this "second generation" of county jails soon failed to accommodate the growing criminal population of the Southwest. New and stronger penal facilities were needed. In 1897, a Santa Fe County grand jury reminded citizens that the capital "needs a new jail building." However, nearly a decade passed before the taxpayers concurred. Not until 1906 could a grand jury congratulate the county on possessing "the best appointed jail in the Territory":

> It is composed of concrete, and in the walls steel bars run across every twelve inches, and horizontally every twenty-four inches, thus making the escape of a prisoner practically an impossibility. The residence portion of the jail is composed of brick, with stone trimmings, and with a deep and strong stone foundation throughout the whole building, the basement of the cell portion being composed of solid concrete. . . .

Through an oversight, the expense of plumbing and furnishings were not included in the original estimate of $7,390. Nonetheless, the grand jury predicted that the new jail would "be an ornament to the City and a living monument to the integrity and progressiveness of the Board of County Commissioners. . . ." In the "chamber of commerce" atmosphere of rivalry that prevailed in that day, all new public buildings added luster to growing frontier communities. Albuquerque boasted a new jail in the following year.[39]

The long delay in the construction of territorial prisons strengthened the arguments for new county jails. Some long-term Arizona prisoners, who ordinarily would have resided in a penitentiary, served their sentences in the county jails. New Mexico lodged convicted felons in the Kansas Penitentiary, at considerable expense. In both territories, short-term prisoners remained in county facilities, usually the most secure ones. The establishment of penitentiaries represented a giant step in law enforcement in both territories. Arizona opened the Yuma Penitentiary in 1878, and New Mexico followed in 1885. Short-term territorial prisoners (less than one year) still served out their time in county jails.[40]

That a reliable county jail system lay at the heart of a successful judiciary was common knowledge among residents of New Mexico and Arizona territories. Yet, the failure to provide such facilities remained a glaring inconsistency. While the territories imposed the responsibility for jails and prisoners upon the sheriffs, the lawmakers of both territories expected the counties to find the resources necessary to fulfill this task. Throughout the entire territorial era, these hardworking local lawmen labored uphill to maintain secure quarters for prisoners. Such facilities grew from primitive and often bizarre substitutes to modern jails by the standards of that era. Even so, inmates endured much abuse and discomfort in filth- and disease-ridden cells. Escapes were common, even from the newer jails. In spite of the miseries of confinement, the occupants of these dreaded lockups managed a crude sort of society. Some actually improved themselves, although the sheriffs betrayed little or no desire to introduce modern penal reforms. The problem of maintaining adequate and secure jails was never-ending. As New Mexico and Arizona approached statehood, the older generation of jails had begun to decline. The cycle of deterioration and new construction began again.

7

The Sheriff and Extralegal Justice

 The county jails of New Mexico and Arizona were the focus of much public attention in the territorial era. The pioneers often expressed concern about the fragility of this important public facility, and they betrayed this feeling by spending ever-increasing amounts of hard-to-find public revenues upon these structures. The people also focused upon these often vulnerable jails in another fashion—in the form of vigilante actions. Lawless groups of citizens embarrassed the sheriffs on numerous occasions by storming the county carcel and administering summary justice upon defenseless prisoners. While the law clearly imposed upon this lawman the responsibility for defending the jail and its residents, this was a very difficult task. These early jails were very flimsily constructed and the sheriff often stood alone against overpowering mobs. To summon a *posse comitatus* was often impossible. The fact that members of the vigilance committee were sometimes friends or neighbors made defense of the jail doubly difficult. Some sheriffs made strong efforts to uphold the law. Others may have secretly welcomed the formation of vigilante organizations in troubled times. More often, the sheriff probably held equivocal feelings about such mobs. Occasionally, the lawman and courts attempted to prosecute members of vigilance committees. The incidence of Judge Lynch eventually began to subside as statehood approached.

Many misconceptions exist about lynch law. This term originally referred to nonlethal, as well as lethal, forms of extralegal punishment. Among the former were whipping, tarring and feathering, and banishment. When the mob inflicted death, the means employed might be hanging, shooting, or other forms of force. Nonetheless, Southwesterners clearly regarded suspension by rope as the primary function of Judge Lynch. Nor were groups necessary to perform this grisly business. One man could commit such a deed. These violent acts could occur spontaneously or through premeditation. Some lynchings took place in daylight hours with the participants unmasked; other vigilantes wore disguises and prowled the nighttime. Occasionally, Judge Lynch boasted a formal organization and followed "procedures," while other groups formed spontaneously and made no such pretense.[1]

Vigilantism became a common means to keep order in Arizona and New Mexico during the early decades of the territorial era. It appears that the Americans introduced this practice, although the native population may have occasionally exhibited this lawless tendency. As early as January 1851, an American survey party joined local residents to lynch Anglo outlaws at Socorro, south of present-day El Paso, Texas. This grim incident was widely publicized in the Eastern press. Thus Judge Lynch became conspicuously associated with the entry of the American justice system into this newly acquired region. District Judge John S. Watt was constrained to charge a grand jury in Mora County, New Mexico, to investigate a double lynching in November 1852. In the following month, residents of the village of Doña Ana (only a few miles north of El Paso) imposed peremptory "justice" upon an Anglo suspected of murder. In a reference to the Mora County incident, the *Santa Fe Weekly Gazette* described this latest lynching as "hung a la Mora!" Although chagrined, this newsman admitted that "This is the fifth execution . . . [in less than a year], under sentence of the high court of Judge *Lynch*. . . ," while only one man was currently under legal death sentence in a New Mexico district court. While the *Weekly Gazette* did not condone such lawlessness in principle, the journal noted a few months later that citizens complained loudly of "imperfect" criminal laws and the uncertainty of punishment in the new territory. "Whenever this is . . . the case," the editor continued, "communities are sometimes destined to take the administration of justice into their own hands. . . ."[2]

This journalist could hardly have known how prophetic his statement would be. The inhabitants of New Mexico and Arizona territories set off on a remorseless binge of lynchings that endured for many years. When nine-year-old Abe Spiegelberg arrived in Santa Fe in 1857, the first sight to greet him was three or four corpses hanging from a tree. In March of this same year, soldiers from nearby Fort Marcy raided Sheriff Jesus Maria Sena y Baca's jail in an effort to lynch prisoner George L. Gruber. These bluecoats were evidently so blinded by alcohol or rage (or both) that they mistakenly shot and killed another confinee and only wounded their primary target. In the far southwestern district of New Mexico Territory, "Arizonans" resorted to mob action just as quickly. In the absence of effectively organized legal courts, perhaps they had no alternative. In June 1859, citizens of Tubac met formally and resolved that they would "organize temporary courts, and administer justice to murderers, horsethieves, and other criminals . . ." until New Mexico Territory provided legal bars of justice. This hastily contrived Tubac tribunal immediately ordered its "constable" to administer fifteen lashes to the back of a horsethief. "Thus, our citizens have at last taken proper steps to guard their property and lives . . . ," one resident noted cheerfully.[3]

New inspiration for vigilante action arose after the Civil War. Many former Union and Confederate veterans turned to outlawry. Other troublemakers arrived with the influx of miners and cattlemen in the 1870s. Even more lawless men and women accompanied the railroad construction gangs in the late 1870s and early 1880s. Although the vast majority of these new immigrants were industrious and responsible citizens, they were contemptuous of the native inhabitants. Rather than settle within the Hispanic communities, they constructed "new towns" near the rails. Such exclusiveness could only lead to trouble. The Hispanos and Indians reciprocated with similar signs of disdain. Vigilante movements soon appeared among the "new towns" of Raton, Las Vegas, Bernalillo, Albuquerque, Socorro, and other villages. Confrontations took place regularly, and the first manifestations of Judge Lynch quickly followed. In December 1880, the Anglo residents of Socorro formed a Committee of Safety when two Hispanos murdered newspaper editor A. M. Conklin.[4]

The membership of these vigilante organizations represented a cross-section of the population. Prominent merchants and other property holders often took the lead. Ethan Eaton, a wealthy storekeeper, led in the formation of the Socorro mob. In 1873, storeowner William Zeckendorf convened an extralegal body in Tucson. John Spring, a schoolteacher, admitted that "I joined that committee and stood by its decisions and helped to execute them [regulations] to the end. . . ." George W. P. Hunt, a future governor of Arizona, marched with Globe vigilantes in 1882. When Bisbee miners lynched John Heith in Tombstone, Mike Shaughnessy, a shift foreman at the Grand Central Mine, was the alleged leader.

Henry Hoyt, a physician and assistant postmaster, joined a similar organization in Las Vegas, New Mexico. Hoyt's superior in the post office held a prominent place as well. Another member, James A. Lockhart, later became a Grant County sheriff. David K. Udall, a prominent Mormon bishop, admitted joining lynchers in Springerville, Arizona. Hispanos sometimes joined Anglo mobs but formed separate mobs as well. These ruthless bands of errant citizens did not spare the opposite sex. In September 1884, several misguided men who suspected an eccentric woman of being a witch and "in league with the devil," seized the unfortunate female and dispatched her near Chimayo, in Rio Arriba County.[5]

Vigilante groups usually carried out the death sentence with unenviable thoroughness. However, a bizarre exception occurred in Springer, New Mexico, on the night of 30 December 1885. An outraged citizens' group extracted accused murderer Theodore Baker from Sheriff William J. Parker's jail and suspended him from a telegraph pole. (Baker and Mrs. Frank Unruh had allegedly conspired to murder her husband.) As the lynchers proceeded with their grim work, a counter-mob appeared. These good citizens cut down the victim—apparently in his death throes—and whisked him off to Santa Fe. Baker was miraculously revived after several hours of unconsciousness. He soon set out on the lecture circuit and won much publicity in a widely reprinted article, "How It Feels to Be Hanged."[6]

Practitioners of this deadly hanging art defended their summary measures in several ways. The judicial system was slow and inefficient, they said, and crafty lawyers manipulated it to the disadvantage of society. Popular justice was more economical and saved the taxpayers exorbitant court expenses. Vigilantes seldom interfered in minor cases, but boasted a keen interest in "black" crimes, to include rape and murder. The fate of Henry Thomas was sealed when Las Vegans accused him of raping an eleven-year-old girl in January 1885. In addition, the *Weekly New Mexican* reported that Thomas had "communicated to her a nameless [social] disease, from which she is now suffering the torments of a thousand deaths. . . ." Some more nimbly minded journalists defended lynching by resorting to "constitutional" arguments. The *Gringo and Greaser* of Manzano, New Mexico, declared that since the people were the source of governmental power in American democracy, they could take away what they had given to the state.[7]

Advocates of summary justice also accused the county sheriffs of contributing to the maladies in the judicial system. These county lawmen were allegedly weak-willed and inefficient. Their jails were insecure and incapable of holding desperate criminals through the trial period. Some of these charges were well founded, especially in the early decades of New Mexico and Arizona territories. During one cycle of lawlessness in New Mexico in 1893, the press castigated the sheriffs rather severely. When three women were brutally murdered in Valencia County, the citizenry lynched three suspected killers in Los Lunas on 5 May. The *Daily New Mexican* observed pointedly:

> Some of the county officers in New Mexico have been very forcibly reminded of late of Abe Lincoln's saying that you 'Can't fool all the people all the time.' The situation is simply this—if the law officers won't do their duty the people will take the matter in to their own hands and see that crime is suppressed.

The *Deming Headlight* concluded that the use of the hempen solution was a "natural result" of the incapacity of Valencia County Sheriff Solomon Luna. The *San Marcial Bee* recalled the calloused murder of a young girl in the county seat of Los Lunas and how the courts let the killer off. Referring to the triple lynching as "The Los Lunas Lesson," this latter writer hoped that this harsh method of "education" would not have to be repeated. The remarks of the *Bee* were obviously intended for county sheriffs across the territory.[8]

The presence of flimsy county jails invited the intervention of vigilantes. Where county revenues were minimal, hastily constructed structures were the rule. Very little force was necessary to breach these places of incarceration. When a jailbreak took place in Las Vegas in November 1880, the *Daily New Mexican* was moved to editorialize on the connection between insecure jails and incidences of lynching:

> It needed no further proof or evidence than has already been furnished to prove that the jails of New Mexico are little more than so many farces, but the Las Vegas jail authorities have just come forward with another one of these proofs. . . . From just about every jail in New Mexico, men have been taken out and lynched or have escaped. . . .

The sheriffs were just as aware of another connection between jail and mob. After seizing the intended victim, Judge Lynch sometimes carelessly left the jail door open and permitted all the other inmates to flee.[9]

The responses of the sheriffs to the threat of vigilantes varied according to the circumstances of the moment. When desperadoes murdered Joe Carson, city marshal of Las Vegas, New Mexico, townsmen soon took them into custody and placed three of the killers in Sheriff Desiderio Romero's jail. Early on the morning of 8 February 1880, the Committee of Safety appeared at the sheriff's home and ordered him to open his carcel. Henry Hoyt, a participant, recalled that Romero "showed no resentment" at this infringement upon his office and "marched in front [of the mob] on our way to the hoosegow." Romero ordered his jailer to open the door "'and be damned quick about it.'" The lynchers proceeded with their business. A few days later, Territorial Chief Justice L. B. Prince accused Romero of cowering in his home "in abject fear" as the Committee usurped his office. Whether Prince was commenting upon the sheriff's delinquency at this or a later lynching is not clear.[10]

Sheriff Hilario Romero reportedly cooperated with citizens of Las Vegas in January 1885. Henry Thomas, a black man suspected of rape, was the target. The Reverend Gambino Rendon, who witnessed this bloody event, recalled the circumstances. Rendon reported that the crowd gathered at the jail "to watch the sheriff and under-sheriff lead the condemned man out. . . ." From Rendon's description, it appears that Hilario Romero, whom Judge Lynch had victimized before, was resigned to the supremacy of the mob. He and his staff attempted to render the proceedings formal or "official," in the reverend's words. When the "milling mass of wild, yelling, sweating people" gathered around the makeshift gallows, "The sheriffs managed to clear a space around the platform so that even I [Rendon], small as I was . . . could see. . . ." Even the services of a Catholic priest were provided the doomed man in what one racist observer callously described as "a chocolate drop matinee."[11]

Some sheriffs simply left the jail unlocked and absented themselves in order to avoid any association with such lawlessness. They made up excuses—clearly transparent—for failing to defend their carcels. When vigilantes hanged two county prisoners in St. Johns, Arizona, in 1881, Sheriff Ephram S. Stover was conspicuously absent. Although the newspapers speculated about Stover's disappearance, he evidently thought no excuse was necessary. Sheriff William Sanders Oury carefully avoided his jail on 8 August 1873. The Tucson vigilantes had designated that day for the termination of three victims. Oury claimed that he was "ill," having eaten too much watermelon. Territorial Chief Justice John Titus—also a resident of the county seat—chose the same day to visit a nearby historic site, San Xavier Cathedral. Titus averred that he had long desired to make this excursion.[12]

Some sheriffs offered token or symbolic resistance in a futile effort to save the honor of their hallowed office. In the summer of 1879, Sheriff Reuben Thomas encountered "their majesties" in Phoenix, Arizona. Being forewarned of this advance upon his jail, Thomas ordered Deputy Billy Breakenridge to take a harmless elderly prisoner to the safety of the sheriff's ranch: vigilante groups were notoriously fickle and indiscriminate about the choice of victims. However, Thomas left in jail the targets of the lynchers, William McCloskey and John Keller. The sheriff then assigned Undersheriff Hi McDonald the uncomfortable task of remaining in the jail and making a meek act of defiance. Presumably Thomas believed that as the presiding officer of the shrievalty he should stay away and thus avoid becoming a public spectacle; somehow, he did not regard the overpowering of his subordinate to be a humiliation. When the vigilantes arrived, McDonald fired a few shots into the ceiling of the jail and surrendered his charges. On at least one occasion, Sheriff Hilario Romero ordered his jail guards to make the same hollow gesture against a mob in Las Vegas, New Mexico.[13]

Some lawmen sought to save a modicum of respect by defying the vigilantes after their business had been completed. In an effort to show his contempt for the mob, Sheriff Tip Lowther refused to cut down the objects of a "necktie party" in Globe, Arizona, in August 1882. He declared that he would have nothing to do with their vicious deed. Deputy Sheriff Fred Dodge gave several Bisbee miners a tongue lashing after they hanged John Heith. "'I think that you are all a lot of murdering, Law Breaking Bunch of Damn Scoundrels,'" the deputy sheriff blurted out and walked away. Dodge and fellow Deputy Charles Smith expressed contempt for Sheriff Jerome Ward for failing to resist this mob. These angry subordinates tore up their commissions in his face and resigned. The Pima County supervisors took an indirect slap at lynch law in 1877. They refused to pay the expenses of a justice of the peace after he examined a man found hanged. "Pima County don't pay for mob law," said a pencilled notation on the claim. Joe Chisholm, whose father served as a justice of the peace in Bisbee, recalled hearing him refuse to preside at such an inquest. The elder Chisholm told the townspeople that the county board would tell him to "go to hell" if he presented a claim for services for the subject of a lynching. John A. Rockfellow, a Tombstone physician, was referring to such incidents when he recalled that "No coroner's inquest was considered necessary" for a person fitted with the "California collar," that is, the vigilantes' noose.[14]

The sheriff could unwittingly play into the hands of vigilance committees and facilitate their criminal acts. Sheriff Tip Lowther learned this harsh lesson in Globe, Arizona. The residents of the isolated mining camp expressed much anger at the robbery and murder of a Wells Fargo messenger in August 1882. When Deputy United States Marshal Pete Gabriel arrested three suspects, Sheriff Lowther demanded custody. He argued rightly that the territorial charge of murder took precedence over the federal crime of mail robbery. While Lowther was alert to the anger of his constituents at this heinous crime, he assumed that the arrests would allay the public's desire for blood. He may also have believed that as sheriff he could persuade the people to let the court decide the fate of the bandits. But angry townspeople greeted him, and Lowther just managed to arrange a justice of the peace hearing. Although the bandits confessed, the presence of the widow of the Wells Fargo messenger aggravated public emotions. Someone further incited the crowd by unwisely raising the question of the stolen money, which the sheriff had not yet found. The fate of the highwaymen was sealed. At about 2:00 on the morning of 24 August, a solemn and unmasked procession marched the three outlaws to a sycamore—the fabled "hanging tree"—on the main street of Globe. Methodist Minister David Calfee offered spiritual consolation. The mob quickly completed its awful business.[15]

Even when a sheriff resisted a mob, such efforts might merely delay the inevitable. Sheriff Desiderio Romero made a flashy show of resistance to the Las Vegas Committee of Safety in 1880. When a crowd besieged the jail, Henry Hoyt observed that Romero:

> came dashing in at full speed, mounted on a superb stallion which he guided with his knees, a forty-five [revolver] in each hand. He plunged through the crowd until he reached the center of the street in front of the jail doors. Here he stopped and using his guns as clubs backed his steed through the mob until he was against the jail doors . . . swearing he would shoot the first man that touched him. . . .

The angry crowd melted away, only to return a few nights later. Sheriff Romero was conspicuously absent during this second try. Hoyt opined that the peace officer deliberately stayed away, "knowing the Committee was composed of many of the leading citizens. . . ."[16]

In spite of Judge Lynch's awesome reputation, many sheriffs and their deputies successfully protected prisoners. Sheriff Pete Gabriel eluded vigilantes in Florence, Arizona, and spirited an endangered ward to Tucson. Deputy Sheriff Bill Voris hid a prisoner in an outhouse in Globe until the man could be sent to Solomonville. John Rockfellow recalled how Sheriff Robert Paul outwitted a would-be lynch mob in Pima County. The friends of a prospector, whom a Mexican had killed at the Salero mining camp, planned to take the suspect from Paul as he escorted the murderer through Tubac. As Paul drove his prisoner through this village, a man whom Rockfellow called John C. (a good friend of the sheriff) planned to "grasp his [the sheriff's] hand in a friendly way and then throw his left arm around him and so hold him while the prospectors took the prisoner and strung him up. . . ." The plotters stationed a boy on a rooftop with instructions to signal at the approach of the sheriff's carriage. But one member of the mob could not contain his curiosity and prematurely looked out of the saloon door. Paul spotted this eager fellow and

> slapping the reins gently on the back of the horses and shifting his shotgun [toward the mob which had emerged] he smiled at the crowd. . . . John C. . . . ran out with 'Hello, Bob!' and his hand ready to shake. Bob's smile widened to a grin. In a jiffy he was past [the saloon], and then, looking back over his shoulder, he returned John's salutation with a wave of his hand and a still broader grin.

Paul was involved in another threatening case in Tucson. When Jim Casey murdered the jailer, angry citizens gathered at the jail. Paul pushed through them, joined his deputies, and forcibly cleared the hallway with a water hose. Soon "quiet reigned," said the *Arizona Weekly Citizen*. This may be the first instance of the use of water against a mob in the Southwest.[17]

New Mexico sheriffs occasionally scored successes against vigilante groups. The county lawmen of Colfax waged an ongoing struggle with vigilantes, winning some battles and losing others. A deputy sheriff in Elizabethtown successfully shielded Wall Henderson, a notorious bully, in 1868. Six years later, Colfax County Sheriff John Turner lost one prisoner to vigilantes but managed to save another a short time later. Sheriff Isaiah Rinehart's record was also uneven. While he lost some inmates, he saved Clay Allison after the psychotic gunman killed Pancho Griego, also a noted tough. Rinehart spirited Allison to the sheriff's ranch. In August 1884,

Sierra County Sheriff Tom Murphy stopped briefly in Lake Valley while en route to Sante Fe. A lynch mob was forming at this very time. Murphy "promptly arrested Boyd [the murderer] and concealed him . . . in a distant portion of town," reported the *Weekly New Mexican*. The alert sheriff then "spent some time among the excited miners and finally induced them not to interfere . . ." with the judicial process. In May 1882, Sheriff Perfecto Armijo learned that some 100 Albuquerqueans had gathered to lynch convicted murderer Milton Yarberry. When "Sheriff Armijo got wind of the meeting," said one writer, he "fearlessly barged in, and forced the crowd to back down." Later, Armijo deputized some of these same persons to assist him in keeping the peace among newly arrived railroad toughs.[18]

A determined show of force could discourage practitioners of this lawless art. Mike Rice, a Gila County undersheriff, accused his unnamed counterpart in neighboring Florence of being "spineless" and lacking in "nerve" for failing to prevent a double lynching in 1882. When a mob threatened his prisoners, Rice took the unexpected step of arming his wards! A "stunned look" appeared upon the faces of the mob, recalled the amused undersheriff, as they stared into the rifle barrels held by their intended victims. The townspeople quickly retired. In an unusual postscript, Rice's superior, Jere Fryer, attempted to "suppress" news of this standoff. While the sheriff could hardly argue with this successful defiance of "their majesties," the chief county lawman also knew that the vigilantes were voters. They might recall this humiliation at the next election and refuse to vote for Fryer. Fryer concluded, said Rice, that the humiliation had been "bad medicine for the stomachs of the 'strangling' fraternity."[19]

In a singular incident in the vigilante-prone community of Las Vegas, New Mexico, Sheriff Hilario Romero went to the extreme of firing upon his own townsmen in July 1882. The senseless murder of a well-liked butcher sparked a march on the San Miguel County jail. Apparently the Committee of Safety assumed that Romero would remain passive, since they had overawed him successfully in the past. But the sheriff had stationed guards at the jail and on nearby rooftops. When the crowd appeared about midnight, 12 July, he ordered his men to fire on a prearranged signal. In order to avoid killing anyone, the deputies aimed low. After three would-be lynchers received wounds in the legs, the crowd dispersed. One of them died from complications. While journalists deplored the need for such violence against citizens, the *Daily New*

Mexican supported Sheriff Romero's unusually firm action. It is inconceivable that Romero would take such resolute measures unless he knew the membership of the group. Perhaps these midnight marchers came from a nearby saloon and did not include the more substantial citizens who had participated in earlier vigilante acts.[20]

These beleaguered sheriffs left few personal records of their thoughts about lynch law. Perhaps they preferred to leave such embarrassing moments behind. Since the lawmen were oath-bound to protect their prisoners and uphold due process, some inner struggle must have taken place as they faced the prospect of confronting friends, relatives, and other voters among the vigilantes. Sheriff Charles Shibell revealed some of his thoughts to a Tucson journalist as rumors of mob action spread in 1879. The sheriff admitted that he was "nervous" about the renewed stirrings of vigilantism, which had been dormant for several years. The Pima County jail held nineteen prisoners at the time. Vigilante action could lead to a general breakout. This journalist reassured the readership that Shibell was certain as to his duty to protect the jail. He expressed the resolve to use force, if necessary. But he was more concerned about "how to avoid a scene of bloodshed in case the vigilantes came for his prisoner." In spite of Shibell's professions of determination, he still harbored doubts about the use of arms against his constituents. The biggest question in the mind of the sheriff was, in the words of this editor, "Was the game worth the candles? Was the question of how long . . . [the murderers] should live worth a score of brave men's lives?" One possible course of action open to Shibell was to "Call for a posse comitatus." The sheriff could muster a force "composed of the best men in town . . . [and] include every man of the vigilantes in the posse. . . ." In this way he could coopt the strength of the mob, deflect the anger of the townspeople, and "stave off the tragedy." Fortunately, the sheriff did not have to choose such a course of action. He rushed his prisoner to the guardhouse at nearby Fort Lowell.[21]

Efforts to take court action against suspected vigilantes were usually futile. Not only was the sheriff reluctant to investigate his fellow citizens, but these lawless bands were often oath-bound and maintained a conspiracy of silence. The Bisbeeites who dispatched John Heith in 1884 ritually placed their hands on the noose around the victim's neck. Gila County Sheriff Tip Lowther encountered a silent populace as he investigated the lynching of one of his deputies, Thomas Kerr. Kerr murdered a man while on a drunken spree in the mining camp of Pioneer on Christmas Eve 1882. The mob added insult by hanging the officer on Christmas Day. The only comment that Lowther could elicit was that "A big crowd did it." The justice of the peace rendered the verdict, "cause of death, hanged by neck, [by] parties unknown." To add to the sheriff's frustrations, a letter arrived shortly from Deputy Kerr's mother. She lashed out at the Pioneer mob and protested that her son "had always been kind and good." What the lynchers did in oath-bound silence left the sheriff helplessly exposed to the glaring light of public censure.[22]

When cases against alleged vigilantes reached the grand jury, the results were generally unsatisfactory. Don Rosario Colomo, a prominent resident of St. Johns, was indicted for participating in the hanging of an outlaw band near Springerville in 1877. A Santa Fe journal reported that Colomo, a former resident of Cubero, New Mexico, had been forced to fortify his home against the desperadoes and to employ gunmen to defend his property. Colomo surrendered to Yavapai County Sheriff Edward Bowers but evidently went free. In another court action against lynchers, jail guards "testified to being overcome by superior force" but would divulge no more information. When a Phoenix coroner's jury looked into a lynching in August 1879, the panel concluded that this act of popular justice "was aided and abetted by so large a number of our best citizens, that we have to admit with shame that this Grand Jury and Court cannot execute [the] laws. . . ." Judge DeForest Porter took up this case in a subsequent session. He castigated the citizenry for the "cowardly murder" but went on to abjure the coroner's jury of responsibility for further action. "If they deemed it best for the good of the community to let the matter rest," said the bench, "they were at liberty to do so. . . ." The Phoenix *Territorial Expositor* disagreed with such coddling of vigilantism and rightly characterized Porter's instructions as "queer jurisprudence." The mob had broken the law. Oscar P. McMains, the popular leader of the anti-Maxwell Land Grant faction in Colfax County, was convicted of murder in the fifth degree for leading a lynch mob. This conviction was overturned on appeal.[23]

The hanging of Socorro badman Joel Fowler may have served as a watershed in the grim record of lynch law in New Mexico and Arizona territories. In November 1883, Fowler senselessly murdered James Cale. William French, an Alma rancher, recalled that the Socorrans quickly "determined to take the matter into their own hands." However, partisans of the murderer threatened to liberate him if vigilantism loomed. Sheriff Pedro Simpson was in an unenviable position. His jail was very insecure, but the county commissioners refused to fund extra jail guards. Governor Lionel Sheldon, an ardent law-and-order man, authorized Simpson to employ the local militia company. Unfortunately, the governor's budget could only support them until 21 January 1884. Sheldon so informed Simpson by letter. To add complications, the sheriff departed in the midst of this crisis to pursue train robbers and left Jailer F. W. Gaddis in charge. Friends of Fowler continued to threaten to liberate him from jail, and Gaddis found a pistol under the murderer's bunk. When the Fowler partisans offered to guard the jail against possible vigilante action, the jailer felt compelled to accept. A newspaper noted with alarm that one volunteer was the father of a train robber whom the sheriff was pursuing! To suspicious Socorrans, the presence of such unsavory persons at the county jail indicated a breakout in the making. In the meantime, the militia were withdrawn at noon on 21 January.[24]

Between midnight and 4:00 A.M. on the morning of 23 January 1884, some 200 citizens took Joel Fowler from the Socorro County jail and hanged him to a nearby tree. While at least two eyewitness accounts exist, the details of this tragic event are still disputed. William French characterized the victim as "the most miserable and contemptible object I ever saw." "He was howling and begging for his life," wrote the rancher, and had even "lost control of his [bodily] functions. . . ." The vigilantes moved very expertly, according to French:

> He [Fowler] was hustled into a wagon. The whole procession moved quietly to the edge of town, where a convenient tree overhung the road. There they strung him up and drove the wagon out from under him. Somebody fired a few merciful shots into him, but I think they were unnecessary. I saw his face as they did the work, and I believe he was already dead before they swung him loose. It was a horrible sight; the face of a coward.

The mob disappeared "as quietly and mysteriously as it had assembled." W. H. Hardy, a local bank teller, joined the vigilantes after pledging to remain silent. Hardy declared that Fowler became violent and uncontrollable when the vigilantes refused to permit him to jump off the limb and to die quickly. A member of the mob hit him over the head. "Fowler was placed on the bed of a wagon," added this eyewitness, and "the wagon was driven out from under him. . . ." Hardy did not recall any shots being fired into the victim, and believed that Fowler deliberately incited the crowd, hoping that a jumpy member would shoot him and end his life with merciful swiftness.[25]

This tragic defeat of the justice system placed Sheriff Simpson and Governor Sheldon in an adverse light. Simpson declared that Sheldon had failed to notify him of the withdrawal of the militia. The governor averred that he had mailed the letter on Saturday, 19 January, and that he was sure this all-important missive arrived in Socorro on the following morning. Simpson "feels very badly over this affair," said the *Socorro Advertiser*. Governor Sheldon had exhausted every avenue open to him. At the outset of the case, Sheldon had attempted to move Fowler to the stronger Santa Fe County lockup. However, Sheriff Romulo Martinez refused to accept the Socorro County prisoner. Under the law, the sheriff possessed great autonomy in the administration of his affairs. The governor sat by helplessly as Martinez argued that he could not accept the assurances of Sheriff Simpson that the Socorro County commissioners would pay the costs of lodging Fowler. After all, these same Socorro County officials had refused to pay for extra guards at their own jail. While both sheriffs and the executive were probably on plausible legal grounds, this failure to defend the county jail after so much highly publicized effort reflected poorly upon the authorities. The absence of a spirit of cooperation between sheriffs and other county officials was deplorable. In all fairness to Sheriff Martinez, he realized the law held him financially accountable if Socorro County should default on the debt for lodging Joel Fowler. Every avenue to assure the protection of Joel Fowler appeared closed.[26]

To add more mystery to the events surrounding the Fowler lynching, Sheriff Pedro Simpson was, in fact, present in Socorro on the night of the hanging. However, he failed to take any action. He arrived by train at 1:35 A.M., 23 January, the morning of the lynching. Alfred Hardcastle, an English visitor, was present in the Grand Central Hotel that night. The sheriff had just stepped off the train and stopped at the hotel when a man rushed in and shouted that "'They've taken *Joe*[l] out!'" The sheriff was warming his feet against the hotel stove. Hardcastle, who could see the sheriff's expression, concluded that the news "caused Pete Simpson to be slightly less agitated than would have seemed proper. . . ." Simpson asked Hardcastle and others gathered around the fire what he should do. From this conversation, the nonplussed officer "decided the correct procedure would be for him . . . to go at the first streak of day to the fatal spot and cut Joe[l] down. . . ." Hardcastle, gambler Billy Minters, and a justice of the peace accompanied the lawman on this uncomfortable errand. The coroner's jury rendered the oft-repeated decision that Joel Fowler had come to his death by "strangulation at the hands of persons unknown." The passive behavior of Sheriff Simpson led Hardcastle to conclude that the peace officer "was not entirely taken by surprise by the action of the mob."[27]

The lynching of Joel Fowler caused some revulsion against the reign of vigilantism in New Mexico and adjoining regions. This particular incident had received widespread publicity, and the failure of the sheriff and other officials had been glaring. Neill B. Field, Fowler's attorney, moved away from Socorro as a protest against the lynching of his client. The *Santa Fe New Mexican Review* was prompted to declare that the days of lynch law had passed. An anonymous correspondent of the *Review*, "Pro Bono Publico," took Judge Lynch to task. He observed that the territory now had a population of 190,000. The judges dispensed justice diligently. Therefore, there was no reason for vigilantism. "Pro Bono Publico" also pointed out that the mob that lynched Fowler had selected an awkward moment to interfere with the course of justice. Fowler was in the process of appealing his death sentence to the territorial supreme court. The writer declared that the regulators' timing made a difference. Had they hanged Fowler immediately after he committed murder, his case would have been "far different." If a problem existed in the judicial system—a common justification for lynching—it was the delay in getting this hearing scheduled. A thirty-day wait was too long, asserted "Publico," since it gave the vigilantes time to form.[28]

Some observers concluded that a relationship existed between a decline in lynchings and an increase in the number of legal hangings. When juries assumed a firm position and imposed the death penalty, the public relaxed and resorted less to mob action. The *Daily New Mexican* made this connection in editorials:

> We are fast returning to the good old orthodox times and sentiments when a spade was called a spade, when murder was not called 're-moval,' and when men committed murder they are hanged. . . . Whenever the criminal class arrives at the conclusion that the weight of public sentiment is against that sort of thing . . , that a majority of any jury is likely to be in favor of hanging, there will be far fewer murderers to punish. . . .

In another connection, this same newspaper applauded the imposition of capital punishment and characterized the return to legal executions as the herald of a new era. The use of the scaffold "will show the capitol [Washington, D.C.] that New Mexico is becoming less of a 'hard' and more of a peaceful and law abiding country." The heyday of vigilantism constituted a "hard" era, while the return to legal executions indicated a march toward civilization.[29]

Although the tempo of lynchings began to decline in the 1880s, the problem had by no means disappeared. A notable atrocity occurred in Flagstaff, Arizona, on 19 January 1887. Vigilantes stormed the jail and shot to death two brothers named Hawks. Judge Lynch took two suspected rustlers from a Yavapai County deputy sheriff and hanged them in the Tonto Basin in the following year. Another incident, this time in Clifton, in November 1897, prompted the *Phoenix Herald* to speculate that "lynching will never be discontinued till the time comes when no guilty man can escape regular conviction by law and the penalty thereof. . . ." Mob law results from "the inefficiency of law in the protection of the people." Occasional instances of vigilante action occurred in Arizona throughout the territorial era. New Mexicans also resorted to lynching in at least five more cases between the death of Joel Fowler and statehood.[30]

It is difficult, perhaps impossible, to determine the total number of men to whom popular tribunals applied the "California collar" in New Mexico and Arizona. Historian Richard Maxwell Brown attempted to enumerate the larger, more conspicuous vigilante outbreaks in the Rocky Mountain West. In Arizona, he found six major outbursts between 1873 and 1884: at Holbrook, Phoenix, Globe, St. Johns, Tombstone, and Tucson. These eruptions took the lives of ten men. Robert L. Spude examined some of this same ground in Arizona mining camps. He counted sixteen such acts in the years from 1882 through 1884. However, there were at least fifty-three lynchings in the region that became Arizona Territory from 1859 to 1911. No doubt more incidents will be unearthed as research progresses.[31]

Richard Maxwell Brown found that eleven New Mexico towns experienced popular justice between 1871 and 1884. Sixteen persons died at the hands of these specific mobs. Brown lists only those movements—in the literal sense—which usurped the sheriffs and captured some wider attention. He does not list isolated hangings outside of his chosen period. Of the total number of lynching victims in Brown's study—343—in the eleven Rocky Mountains states and territories, Arizona and New Mexico claimed twenty-six. However, as Appendix C in this volume reveals, the total number of victims of Judge Lynch in New Mexico, from 1846 to statehood in 1912, is much higher. At least ninety-eight persons were subjects of extralegal actions in New Mexico. When added to the fifty-three who died at the hands of regulators in Arizona, some 151 people were victims of mobs. This figure stands out starkly when compared with the approximately ninety-six persons who were legally hanged in the two territories.[32]

As the territorial era waned at the turn of the century, Southwestern journalists continued to note the decline of vigilante justice in the two territories. They concluded that this moderation of the public temper was a sign of social maturity and a good argument that Arizona and New Mexico were now eligible for statehood. When the residents of Las Vegas, New Mexico, momentarily reverted to their extralegal ways in 1893, the *Daily Optic* expressed great surprise but rationalized that this interruption of Sheriff Lorenzo Lopez's routine "had to happen." The victim had brutally murdered his cousin. When the *Chicago Tribune* published lynching statistics for 1901, the *Phoenix Arizona Republican* was elated at the results. While lynch law had claimed 101 persons across the nation, Arizonans had refused to participate at all. Had he looked closely, the writer would also have noted that New Mexico did not claim one victim in that year. The territorial governors were especially anxious to maintain this clean record. Congress would bestow statehood only on law-abiding populations. When City Marshal J. J. Brophy of Clayton prevented a lynching in July 1906, Captain Fred Fornoff of the Mounted Police congratulated him on behalf of Governor George Curry. "The Governor is very anxious that no lynchings take place in New Mexico . . ." said the policeman, "and was pleased when I told him. . . ." Arizonans also continued to exercise similar restraint in tense moments that would have resulted in extralegal action in the past. When an alleged assault occurred upon a four-year-old girl in December 1906, the *Arizona Republican* surmised that conditions were ideal for summary justice. When the mob failed to materialize, the editor concluded that this was "evidence of good citizenship" in Arizona. At least one vigilante action took place in Arizona after the turn of the century. An unknown assassin shot and killed an accused murderer in the Globe jail.[33]

Among the many impediments to the sheriffs' performance of duty in the two territories, vigilantism ranked high. "Their majesties the mob" had accompanied the westward movement since the eighteenth century. Extralegal justice took many forms, although all interrupted the "due process" of the law. There were many wellsprings of hatred and insecurity to motivate would-be lynch mobs: racism, religious intolerance, drunkenness, fear, and disillusionment. The sheriffs, who bore the brunt of these popular tribunals, could seldom resist when the mobs were at their peak of strength. Only in isolated instances did the sheriffs forcibly resist. Governor Lionel Sheldon, who possessed a keen insight into the reasons for inadequate law enforcement at the county level, concluded that the public had failed to support the sheriffs in many ways. One of the primary failures was in financial rewards. "Encourage and support our officers of the law and confidence in them will exist," remarked the governor, and "their work will be well done. . . ." If such support was forthcoming, he continued, "people will cease to look to lawless courts [lynchings] for vengeance upon criminals."[34]

In no case did vigilantes of Arizona and New Mexico wield overwhelming power comparable to that of the San Francisco stranglers in the 1850s. In this latter instance, the vigilantes usurped the legitimate law enforcement agencies. Historian Philip J. Ethington has concluded that this overthrow of the sheriff's office and other police forces had an ironic and beneficial consequence—it provided "a grace period of stability during which the service ideal" of police professionalism could emerge in San Francisco. Vigilantism brought about no such transformation in law enforcement in the communities of Arizona and New Mexico Territories. While the larger movements—in Tucson, Socorro, and Las Vegas—possessed some organization and longevity, Judge Lynch usually made only fitful appearances. It does not appear that vigilantes ever prevented a session of district court from taking place in either territory, although some terms were not held for other reasons. These brief outbursts of mob action seldom usurped all of the sheriff's duties, but intervened only in instances of heinous or "black" crimes in frontier parlance. In areas remote from the county seat, ranchers, miners, and other isolated pioneers sometimes inflicted "justice" for lesser crimes. Most sheriffs adopted a pragmatic attitude toward the appearance of Judge Lynch. While the mob interfered in an area of the lawman's responsibilities, the sheriffs continued to perform other routine duties and permitted such irrational public outbreaks to run their course.[35]

Frontier society harbored the seeds of vigilantism. This wandering motley were searching for riches "out there," largely beyond its grasp. This "other worldly" frame of mind preoccupied the frontiersmen and prevented them from supporting the sheriffs. Even the sheriffs were sometimes infected with this "get-rich-quick" attitude. Many caught up in this higgledy-piggledy existence did not intend to remain in the Southwest. They felt no allegiance to a wilderness community, whose sheriff appeared weak and jail looked sickly. In their impatience, these seekers of wealth paid lip service to law and order and merely tolerated men of the badge. The small, propertied class, which brought its wealth from the East, sometimes felt very insecure among such lawless forces. Vigilantism thrived in this atmosphere of uneasiness and presented the sheriffs with one of their most severe tests. However, recourse to popular tribunals was usually temporary, and it passed as communities grew and the citizenry felt more secure. Individual citizens had to develop confidence in each other and produce public-spiritedness before these youthful communities could acquire faith in their sheriffs. The ardor of vigilantism began to dissipate well before these two territories acquired statehood in 1912.

8

Deathwatch

Of his many duties, the sheriff disliked most the task of hanging condemned men. This grim chore included more than the brief stay on the scaffold. It entailed the tense days of the deathwatch in the jail. The physical and mental stress imposed upon the sheriff and his staff sometimes became visible. Moral and ethical questions about taking human life might beset the sheriff. The men on the county death row were always potentially violent. As they squirmed under the stress of approaching doom, these condemned persons sought ways to cheat the gallows. Given the relatively meager resources of the frontier counties, the sheriffs often lacked the necessary resources to adequately guard the prisoner on death row—from angry mobs and from himself. Yet, the desire to extend a degree of humanity to the condemned man was ever-present, in the sheriff and in the public. The territorial governor was also an unknown factor, and both prisoner and public often became excitable as they awaited last minute executive clemency. As the day of execution approached, tensions mounted. The sheriff was as much under public scrutiny as the victim. A botched execution could blemish his standing and have political repercussions. Macabre scenes were possible on the gallows, and these legal executions could take on the atmosphere of a circus sideshow. Even the frontiersmen of the Southwest, who were enured to hardships, began to doubt the necessity for such public spectacles after the turn of the century. As statehood approached, the sheriffs could look forward to a day when the awful duty of hangings would be lifted from their shoulders.

Each territorial code provided for the infliction of capital punishment. In 1871, *The Compiled Laws of the Territory of Arizona* declared:

> When the judgment of death is rendered, a warrant, signed by the judge and attested by the clerk [of district court] under the seal of the court, shall be drawn and delivered to the sheriff; it shall state the conviction and judgment, and appoint a day on which the judgment shall be executed. . . .

The sheriff should carry out this sentence in not "less than thirty nor more than sixty days from the time of judgment." Section 449 specified that "The punishment of death shall be inflicted by hanging the defendant by the neck until he be dead." In 1846, the sheriff received a fee of fifteen dollars for conducting a hanging. By 1890, he earned $100. He also received funds for the erection of the scaffold.[1]

Within a few days after the judge pronounced sentence, the court clerk issued the death warrant. After receiving the governor's approval, the document passed to the sheriff, who then instituted the deathwatch. He placed the condemned man in a separate cell under special guard. The exact time that the watch began could vary, as the prisoner's attorney often appealed the sentence. In the case of Francisco Garcia, the court sentenced him to death in Prescott, Arizona, on 8 December 1899. Sheriff John L. Munds began the deathwatch on the 20th, preparatory to hanging on 2 February 1900. The district attorney ordered Munds to suspend this costly procedure on 31 January since the Mexican consul (Garcia was a citizen of Mexico) had set the appeal process in motion. Evidently, Garcia's sentence was commuted. Sheriff Bob Paul initiated the watch over Joseph Casey on the night of 9 April 1884, with execution to take place in Tucson on the 15th. Pinal County Sheriff L. K. Drais, who housed a condemned federal prisoner, sounded rather mercenary in a letter to the United States district attorney in July 1893. The United States marshal had asked Drais to begin the deathwatch, but the sheriff feared that through bureaucratic oversight the federal bureaucracy might neglect to pay him. The county lawman desired reassurance that the extra expense of the deathwatch would be covered.[2]

In the meantime, the sheriff engaged carpenters to erect the gallows. The scaffold prepared for the vicious desperadoes who committed the Bisbee Massacre was truly formidable. This frame, erected in Tombstone, had to accommodate Big Dan Dowd and his three comrades at one time. The structure consisted of six-by-eight-inch timbers. The platform was eight by sixteen feet and stood eight feet above the ground in order to accommodate the condemned men's fall. The deck could hold twenty-five spectators. The cross beam to which the ropes were tied rested eight feet above the platform. The trapdoors under the feet of Dowd and his partners in crime were supported by triggers, or bolts. When Sheriff Jerome Ward dropped a heavy weight, to which the triggers were tied by rope, all the bolts were simultaneously pulled. The carpenter who constructed this death-dealing device took pride in his work. Said the *Tombstone Republican*, he "proposes to have everything work perfectly." Since most executions took the life of only one person, the typical scaffold was a scaled down version of the one in Tombstone.[3]

Since the law neglected to specify the precise design of a scaffold, sheriffs were free to devise their own hanging apparatus. Sheriff Perfecto Armijo erected a scaffold in Albuquerque from a design in the *Scientific American*. Armijo called it the "jerk plan" as opposed to the trapdoor method. One historian described it this way:

> Flanking a low platform he erected two fifteen-foot uprights connected by a cross beam. The rope, from its ominous terminal noose, ran upward to a pulley midway on the beam, thence along the beam to another pulley and down to an enclosure where it was tied to a 400-pound weight. A smaller cord held the weight suspended six feet above the ground. When the cord was cut, the weight would fall, and the condemned man at the other end of the rope would jerk suddenly into the air. . . .

In the dark humor of that day, the victim was "Jerked to Jesus." Jerry Ryan, Sheriff of Gila County, Arizona, employed this same method in 1889. He was inexperienced in such techniques and attached a much too heavy weight, causing the head of the victim—an Apache Indian—to be dashed against the crossbar. One observer noted "not a few blanched faces" among the spectators as the Indian's skull was crushed before their eyes. Strong stomachs were necessary for both spectators and executioners.[4]

Sheriffs sought the best hempen rope for the noose and tested it carefully. When the Cochise County board of supervisors ordered the rope for the execution of Frank Spence in 1910, it specified a diameter of one and one-quarter inches. Through preliminary testing and stretching, Sheriff John F. White reduced the rope to only one inch. Perfecto Armijo, the lawman who employed the "jerk plan," soaked the rope to facilitate stretching. Sheriff George Ruffner of Prescott ordered a special "noose rope" from the Runkle and Peacock Company in El Paso, Texas. Ruffner tested it by dropping sacks of sand equal to the weight of the intended victim. Other executioners treated the noose loop with soap so that it would close easily around the victim's neck. The knot also had to be the right size to fit under the man's ear. A quick and painless death by broken neck was preferable to slow suffocation. Sheriff Salome Garcia paid $20.70 for the rope to hang Black Jack Ketchum in Clayton, New Mexico.[5]

To face the hangman's noose was considered the supreme test of masculinity, and the public watched anxiously for signs of loss of nerve. When a deputy sheriff reminded Black Jack Ketchum that his day was approaching, the outlaw betrayed this concern when he replied, "'Yes, but I believe I'll keep my nerve.'" When Manuel Fernandez heard the death sentence in a Yuma courtroom in 1873, he turned to Sheriff Francis H. Goodwin and exclaimed: "'What an idea! Just imagine for a moment me being suspended by the neck! What a beautiful picture I'd make!'" Goodwin inflicted the court's decree upon Fernandez on 3 May 1873. As Goodwin placed the black cap over Fernandez's head, the latter reportedly moaned, "'Ah! What a disgrace this is.'" Some condemned men whiled away their time at cards or read the Bible; Milton Yarberry played the fiddle in the Albuquerque jail. When a reporter asked him if he felt any stress, Yarberry replied, "'Hell, I wouldn't get scared if they walked me out on the scaffold right now.'" "To demonstrate his steely nerves," continued the writer, "he picked up his fiddle and tore through . . . 'Old Zip Coon.'" While in the Santa Fe County jail for safekeeping until execution day, Yarberry admitted privately to Sheriff Romulo Martinez that "'Whiskey is all that keeps me up. . . .'" Martinez permitted him one bottle a day. The editor of the *Tombstone Epitaph* observed "a marked change" in Big Dan Dowd as the reality of execution "forced itself into his mind." From a "devil-may-care, reckless demeanor . . . ," said this observer, Dowd's countenance has "given way to that of a man who hears the rush of Azirel's wings. . . ." He "knows that his eyelids will soon be brushed by them," concluded the editor.[6]

The sheriffs made some efforts to ease the misery of the deathwatch. Sheriff Jerome Ward provided the four Bisbee murderers with a "hearty supper of oysters and other delicacies" on the eve of their day of death and granted them the privilege of marching to the gallows "without handcuffs and shackles." On the morning of the assigned day, 28 March 1884, a barber shaved them, and the sheriff presented them with black suits. As a young Papago Indian faced death in Tucson, he presented Sheriff Matthew F. Shaw with one last request—to be hanged in red-topped boots. Deputy Jeff Milton recalled how he and other sheriff's officers desperately searched the town for this odd apparel. They eventually discovered the elusive footwear in William Zeckendorf's store, and the youthful murderer proudly sported the new boots on the scaffold. Sheriff George Ruffner provided many amenities for Dan Parker as he awaited death in Prescott in 1898. This deathwatch was perhaps doubly difficult for Ruffner, since he and Parker had been acquaintances before the victim embarked on a train-robbing career. Rumor even said they were friends, having traveled together to Arizona. Not only did the sheriff make abundant food and drink available, but he reportedly permitted Parker female companionship. Thomas "Black Jack" Ketchum threw Sheriff Salome Garcia and the county commissioners into consternation with this same request. To fulfill the condemned man's last wish was a hallowed practice in the tradition of the sheriff's office. However, Garcia felt compelled to refuse Ketchum's desire, replying that "There were no public funds available for the purpose."[7]

The prospect of mounting the scaffold so unnerved some doomed men that they made desperate efforts to avoid the noose. Condemned murderer Eugenio Aragon warned Sheriff Charles W. Haynes in Roswell, New Mexico, that he would commit suicide rather than hang. You "will not get the chance to hang me," said Aragon defiantly. "'If you kill yourself,'" Haynes replied, "'I will drop you through the trap anyway. . . .'" The sheriff reportedly admitted that the reason for his determination was the financial expense of the execution. "'We can't afford to lose the fees for hanging you,'" said the lawman. Aragon kept his word and slashed his own throat with a sharpened spoon. Haynes had the lesser satisfaction of executing Antonio Gonzales, Aragon's comrade in crime, on 24 September 1896. When John Conley attempted to cut his own throat in the Taos jail, Sheriff Silviano Lucero persisted with the execution, on 28 February 1906. Lucero had the neck wound bandaged, and deputies carried the unconscious man to the scaffold. In December 1889, Pinal County Sheriff Jere Fryer faced the saddening duty of hanging four Apache Indians. However, two of the inmates hanged themselves with moccasin strings on the 4th. Fryer administered the death penalty to the others two days later. As Zach Booth faced the grim reaper in nearby Globe in 1905, he confessed to Sheriff Edward P. Shanley that he had considered suicide. "'The devil gave me quite a hunch to cheat you . . . Ed,'" said Booth, as he presented the sheriff with a concealed pocketknife, "'but I thought I'd go the route.'"[8]

Maintaining security during the deathwatch proved very difficult, and some untimely escapes embarrassed the sheriffs. Joseph Holmes, who murdered former United States Marshal Milton Duffield, broke out of the Tucson jail and was never recaptured. Augustin Chacon, who killed at least one Graham County deputy sheriff, escaped the Solomonville lockup in 1899. He remained at large for three years. Sheriff Jake Owen had already constructed the scaffold when Rosario Emilio escaped from the Lincoln County carcel in March 1907. He fled to Mexico and was never caught. Billy the Kid's break for liberty in this same village in 1881 became widely publicized. Although two deputies guarded him, the Kid obtained a weapon and killed both men. Garrett's return on the death warrant reads: "I hereby certify that the within warrant was not served owing to the fact that the within named prisoner escaped before the date set for serving said warrant. The sheriff pursued and eventually killed this murderous outlaw."[9]

The stress of carrying out these awful duties became apparent when the sheriff read the death warrant to the condemned man. As Sheriff Jerome L. Ward performed this task before the four Bisbee murderers in March 1884, the lawman obviously regretted the task. "The reading commenced in a clear, firm voice," noted one Tombstone reporter, but the sheriff faltered at the words "to hang until they were dead." "It is no discredit to our sheriff to say," he continued, "that his voice became tremulous and husky with emotion. . . ." James Brent confronted the prospects of three (possibly four) hangings in Lincoln County two years later. "The sheriff's voice quivered," said one observer, who heard Brent read one death warrant, "and his eyes swam in tears. . . ."[10]

Some sheriffs tried to avoid this awesome responsibility and sought willing substitutes to pull the lever. (There is no evidence of professional executioners such as the men dressed in black on the Hollywood screen.) Sheriff James V. Parks offered a man fifty dollars to spring the trap from under Augustin Chacon. When he refused, Parks responded dejectedly, "'Well, I guess it's my job, anyway.'" When Stewart Hunt was elected Cochise County lawman in November 1904, he inherited the duty of executing a young man convicted under the preceding sheriff. When friends chided him about his bad luck, Hunt sought to circumvent this terrible duty.

He instructed his jailer, Mack Axford, to prepare himself for the task. Axford promptly resigned. George C. Ruffner also looked for a surrogate executioner in the Dan Parker case in Prescott in 1898. However, the train robber and murderer adamantly rejected the plan. Parker wanted "a real man" to hang him. Ruffner reluctantly complied with his request. Pinal County Sheriff Peter Gabriel, whom all agreed was as gritty as lawmen came, possessed the same doubts as Ruffner. When he appointed Tom Kerr as special deputy with the duty to spring the trap, the condemned man protested. "'I don't want you [Kerr] to touch me,' he said, 'I want my friend "Don Pedro" to do this job.'" Gabriel reluctantly set the ceremony in motion. Sheriff Gus Livingston was more successful in his search for an alternate executioner. The Yuma County officer reportedly employed Jack Carruth, a part-time lawman, to pull the lever at the hanging of Martin Ubillos in Yuma, in June 1905.[11]

The sheriff could avoid this regrettable task through another means. *The Compiled Laws of the Territory of Arizona* (1871) permitted the peace officer, with the consent of the district judge, to summon a jury "to inquire into the supposed insanity" of a prisoner on death row. If this "inquisition" found him demented, "the sheriff shall suspend the execution of judgment." Frank Murphy, Sheriff of Pima County, Arizona, became convinced that Teodoro Elias was insane. This unfortunate man was due to hang on 26 July 1904. Murphy set the wheels of justice in motion. Acting Governor W. F. Nichols noted that the sheriff "has informed this department that there is a serious question as to the sanity of the said Teodoro Elias. . . ." Nichols appointed a board of physicians to examine Elias. They certified to District Judge George R. Davis and Sheriff Murphy that the condemned man was indeed mentally unstable. He is "a sexual neurotic, and subject to hallucinations and illusions," said their report. The doctors predicted that Elias's condition "will grow steadily worse, and probably end in dementia." The governor wisely commuted the sentence to life imprisonment. While Murphy's act was a humane one, some of the sheriff's constituents believed Elias should hang regardless of his mental condition. He had murdered a Tucson policeman. Murphy may have lost a bid for reelection because he ignored public feeling and revealed a hesitancy to carry out his duties to the final degree.[12]

In New Mexico, a similar procedure existed for the benefit of persons under sentence of death. Harvey Whitehill, longtime sheriff of Grant County, faced the duty of hanging William "Parson" Young on 23 February 1881. Young impressed Whitehill as being insane, and the sheriff held an examination with four physicians present. Jailer P. P. Whitehill, presumably a relative of the sheriff, testified that he had observed the prisoner for nine months. The jailer believed the condemned man weak minded but "with the capacity to judge." The doctors' conclusions agreed with this layman's assessment, and the governor ordered Sheriff Whitehill to proceed with the execution. Even though the *Daily New Mexican* asked, "Should a crazy man be hanged?," Whitehill carried out the sentence on 25 March 1881. In the following year, Governor Lionel Sheldon issued a respite for another of Whitehill's prisoners. This man suffered from a serious head injury and "is various[ly] afflicted," said the sheriff. In the meantime, the prisoner died, much to the relief of the lawman. "I will execute any man . . . if I am required to do so," said Whitehill about this latter case, "but would dislike to be obliged to carry a man to the gallows bodily and swing him up." In the case of Dionicio Sandoval, sentenced to die in Bernalillo County in September 1896, examining doctors could "'find no evidence that . . . he is mentally defective.'" However, they objected to the execution in the name of "justice and public morality." Sheriff Tom Hubbell agreed that Sandoval appeared healthy. The prisoner "sleeps and eats well, and seems to have no fear of death," concluded the lawman. The governor ordered Hubbell to proceed with the hanging on 24 September.[13]

In spite of the rough and ready reputation of frontier lawmen, hangings could unnerve some of them. Deputy Sheriff Billy Breakenridge refused an invitation to witness the execution of the Bisbee murderers. Breakenridge replied curtly that he "did not care to attend." While Buckey O'Neill had a reputation for daring and bravado, he collapsed at the hanging of Dennis Dilda in Prescott. This event took place two years before O'Neill became sheriff; he was serving as part of a militia guard at the scaffold. As the victim plunged through the trapdoor, O'Neill fainted! Later, he relived this awful moment in a fictional account of a lynching for the *San Francisco Chronicle*. In this item, "A Horse of the Hash-Knife Brand," O'Neill describes the end of a horsethief, Jack Stanley. The victim is obviously Dennis Dilda in the author's mind:

A few heavings of the chest, two or three spasmodic bendings of the body at the knees and hips, a turning in of the arms, a blackening of the face, with turgid, protruding eyes and tongue, and then a relaxation of all the muscles of the body. . . .

This vivid description is possibly the only personal description of a hanging from the pen of a Southwestern sheriff.[14]

The sheriffs probably considered some executions less distasteful than others. In their eyes, men who murdered sheriffs or other lawmen deserved death. Cochise County Sheriff Scott White had the satisfaction of seeing Thomas and William Haldiman hang in Tombstone. The two brothers had callously murdered a deputy sheriff and a posseman. Although some doubt existed as to which brother fired the fatal shots, the court found both men guilty in the first degree. Each brother steadfastly refused to implicate the other, and White pulled the lever on 18 November 1900. On 2 April 1897, Sheriff Harry C. Kinsell presided over one of the most celebrated hangings in the Southwest. This case resulted from the murder of former Sheriff Frank Chavez of Santa Fe County. The victims—four members of the Francisco Borrego band—were members of the Hispanic community. Their supporters employed attorney Thomas Benton Catron, who managed to delay the execution for some time. On one occasion, telegraphic word of a presidential reprieve arrived from Washington only thirty minutes before the time of execution! This respite only delayed the final event. Kinsell presided at the execution of the four men on 2 April 1897.[15]

The controversy surrounding the hanging of Milton Yarberry also revealed the doubts that beset the sheriffs during these tragic events. Although he departed Arkansas with a criminal record, Yarberry became a constable and deputy sheriff in Albuquerque. However, he killed a man under questionable circumstances and was sentenced to death. Sheriff Perfecto Armijo doubted the rightness of this decision and was distressed at the prospect of presiding at the execution of a fellow lawman and former subordinate. Such utterances from the sheriff evidently caused the public to doubt his determination to carry out the law. Partisans of Yarberry threatened to help him escape, while enemies talked of lynching him. Governor Lionel Sheldon, who regarded this case as an important test of law and order, directed Armijo to place the prisoner in the more secure Santa Fe County jail until the date of execution, 9 February 1883. Sheriff Armijo resented the implication that he could not protect Yarberry and wrote "a red hot letter" of protest to the governor, swearing to "'hang the first man who attempts to interfere with the execution.'" At the same time, he expressed regret that "'some people'" in Albuquerque "'were determined that he [Yarberry] should swing.'" To the accusation that he would permit Yarberry to escape rather than hang, the sheriff reacted angrily. "'There is no one that feels more than I do that Yarberry should not hang,'" said Armijo, "'but I have a warrant to hang him and I will execute it.'"[16]

Milton Yarberry evidently sensed the discomfiture of his former superior and asked Sheriff Mason Bowman of Colfax County to perform the hanging. Bowman "politely refused," according to one report. Perfecto Armijo did his duty in Albuquerque at the appointed time. Upon the arrival of Yarberry's train from Santa Fe, the sheriff and militia guard led the victim in a solemn procession to the gallows. The realization that the sheriff had carried out the sentence against his personal inclination was cause for some discussion. One Albuquerque journalist observed that Armijo's public remarks had "created much comment here not a little of which is unfavorable to him." His political future was bleak. One student of Armijo's conduct in this matter concluded that he was reluctant to execute Yarberry because he was a former lawman and this duty "infringed upon the peace officer's sensibilities and loyalty to a profession." While law enforcement under American auspices was relatively young, the few sheriffs and other peace officers in New Mexico and Arizona still possessed some consciousness of their profession. The members of this small, select law enforcement fraternity believed that they should stand by each other. This feeling of camaraderie and belonging prevailed even among the amateur lawmen on the remote Southwestern frontier.[17]

Security was often stepped up at these events. When rumors reached Sheriff Francis H. Goodwin that the Spanish-speaking community of Yuma opposed the execution of Manuel Fernandez, he summoned a posse of fifty trustworthy men. On the appointed day, 3 May 1873, this heavily armed body encircled the gallows. A similar state of unrest prevailed in Phoenix in November 1880 as Sheriff Reuben Thomas prepared to hang Demetrio Dominguez. However, Thomas inadvertently contributed to his difficulties. He made the mistake of erecting the scaffold one-half mile from the jail, necessitating a long walk through a hostile crowd. The sheriff employed a fifteen-man posse to escort the official delegation.[18]

A unit of United States soldiers guarded an execution in Tomé on 28 July 1855. James A. Bennett, one of the soldiers, noted this duty in his diary, although he did not mention the presence of the sheriff, presumably Ignacio Gallegos. The prisoner was a Hispano, and it was "feared the prisoner's Mexican friends would endeavor to rescue him . . . ," said Bennett. After standing guard all night, the troops prepared the "dejected" prisoner:

A scaffold was erected in the plaza [of Tomé] and guarded by 12 soldiers with ready arms. I, with the other 13 men, marched the prisoner out [of the jail], accompanied by the Catholic Priest. He walked
upon the stand; confessed to five murders; and was launched into
eternity. . . .[19]

The moment of truth arrived for both victim and executioner as
the official party mounted the platform. The reactions of the prisoners ran the spectrum of emotions at this instant. As Sheriff
Aniceto Valdez escorted Jesus Maria Martinez to the Taos scaffold
in May 1864, an observer noted that "all the bravado he had shown
at his trial seemed to give way." The officers carried him onto the
platform. Sheriff Walter Brown and his staff did the same for Clem-
ent C. Leigh in Kingman, Arizona, in January 1907. Deputies
physically supported his head in order to fit the noose. Antonio
Gonzales slept soundly on the night before his time in Roswell,
New Mexico, "and seemed eager to have the job over." He strode
"firmly" upon the platform and made a brief statement "that he had
forgiven his enemies, hoped they had forgiven him, and . . . asked
forgiveness of his God." Manuel Aviles, reportedly the son of a
revolutionary patriot in Mexico, died stolidly on the scaffold in
Prescott, Arizona, in 1875. Since Aviles's father had died before a
firing squad calmly smoking a cigarette, the junior Aviles asked for a
smoke. Several spectators flipped cigarettes to him, and a Catholic
priest placed one on his lip. Aviles took a puff and then nodded to
Sheriff Edward Bowers "indicating he was ready for the crucial moment." John Henry Anderson, a former slave, met death calmly in
Socorro in May 1887. The Reverend Father Lestra gave him religious instruction. "'I have been kindly treated by Sheriff [Charles]
Russell and his assistants,'" Anderson told the spectators. Russell's
handling of the execution was "a neat piece of work," said one
reporter.[20]

Philip Lashley "exhibited the utmost unconcern" at his hanging
in Tucson, observed a journalist in July 1897. He talked with spectators, sang a song, danced, and then gave a speech "full of pro-
fanity." He refused religious consolation and then abused "all the
officials," including Sheriff R. N. Leatherwood. The doomed man
then assured the lawman that "he would die game." "'Let her go,
Gallagher!,'" shouted Lashley as the trap was sprung. As Sheriff
Jerry Ryan prepared two Apaches for their plunge to eternity in
Globe, one of them broke his calm countenance. As Ryan put the
cap over his head, the condemned man turned to the sheriff and

said, "Boo!" As his last request, Edwin W. Hawkins asked Pima County Sheriff Nabor Pacheco for permission to communicate with his wife in Chicago. He dictated the message on a phonograph record and mailed it. However, the spouse's reply had not arrived by the day of execution. At the last minute, Pacheco delayed the execution for an hour and permitted Hawkins to send a telegram. During this agonizing lull, "he obligingly gave them all firsthand accounts of how it feels waiting to be hung." When the wife's response at last arrived, the cryptic telegram read: "Good-bye, dear. I can't say any more. Bessie." Hawkins went stoically to his death with a final wish that his spouse say the Lord's Prayer at the time of execution.[21]

Southwesterners were no different from other nineteenth-century Americans. They objected to the execution of women. Although the district courts convicted many women of murder in both Arizona and New Mexico territories, the governors almost invariably commuted their sentences. Insanity proceedings were also applied to them. If the sheriff suspected that a condemned woman was pregnant, an Arizona statute authorized him to order a doctor's examination. In January 1869, an Arizona judge sentenced Dolores Moore to hang for the murder of her husband. While she reposed in Sheriff Peter Brady's jail in Tucson, a debate took place about the propriety of hanging a woman. The Tucson *Arizonian* believed the law should be carried out, but the Prescott *Weekly Arizona Miner* concluded that the execution would bring disgrace upon the territory and called for an end to these "insane howlings for the blood of Dolores Moore." The governor agreed and commuted her sentence to life in prison. New Mexican officials drew the same conclusions in such matters. Sheriff Marion Littrell traveled to Santa Fe to confer about the death sentence of Mrs. Eduibigen Valdez de Arellano, while Governor George Curry commuted the sentences of two Sierra County women.[22]

One exception existed to this near uniform policy. On 28 March 1861, Judge Kirby Benedict sentenced Paula Angel to death for the murder of Miguel Martin in Las Vegas, New Mexico. The court documents note that "When asked if she had anything to say—[Angel] said nothing." Benedict then ordered Sheriff Antonio Abad Herrera to keep her "securely by whatever chains and shackles necessary . . . until Friday the 26th day of April. . . ." On that day, the sheriff was ordered "to take the body of Paula Angel to some suitable place . . . one mile from the church in the town of Las Vegas and there to be hung by the neck until dead." Tradition relates that Sheriff Herrera kept her in solitary confinement and deliberately tormented her. He reminded her each day that "'I am going to hang you until you are dead, dead, dead.'" On the appointed day, Herrera placed the unfortunate woman in a wagon and tied the rope to the limb of a tree, a crude scaffold indeed. Had not Militia Colonel Jose D. Sena interfered, the crowd, which apparently experienced last minute pangs of remorse, might have prevented the conclusion of the grisly ordeal. In view of the opposition of frontiersmen to the execution of women, it is difficult to explain this singular event in Las Vegas. Perhaps the authorities in Santa Fe were preoccupied with the growing emergency of the Secession movement. Or possibly the case of Paula Angel slipped through the bureaucratic review procedure unnoticed.[23]

These frontier sheriffs were often inexperienced in the art of hangings and occasionally made some dreadful mistakes. Sheriff Jose L. Lopez failed to set the rope properly about a victim's neck in Las Vegas in August 1892. The unfortunate man, Frederick Falkner, choked for twenty minutes before expiring. An even more tragic blunder occurred at the hanging of William Wilson, in Lincoln. When Sheriff Saturnino Baca set the execution in motion, on 10 December 1875, he carefully left the body suspended for nine and one-half minutes. He then cut down the body and placed it in a coffin. Much to the amazement of all present, someone "discovered that life was not yet extinct" from William Wilson's body! The spectators, who had expressed dissatisfaction with the sheriff's conduct on that day, "drew the inanimate body from the coffin" and suspended it again for an additional twenty minutes. Above all other hangings, Sheriff Salome Garcia's administration of the execution of Black Jack Ketchum acquired the most adverse publicity. Through some miscalculation of the weight of the prisoner or the proper length of the drop, Ketchum was decapitated! By the time of this grisly event, April 1901, newspapers were capable of widespread photographic coverage of such carnage.[24]

Executions were generally public events in the early years of the territories. The sheriffs issued formal invitation cards to select persons who were permitted positions closest to the scaffold, while the public at large viewed from a greater distance. Arizona law specified only that hangings were to occur "within the walls or yard of a jail, or some convenient private place in the county." Apparently, the presiding sheriff had the authority to decide the degree of public exposure to the event. As many as 1,000 persons gathered for the execution of the four Bisbee murderers in Tombstone in March

1884. When he closed off the site, an Arizonan recalled that "A mercenary group leased an adjacent lot on which they erected a grandstand overlooking the courtyard and prepared to sell standing room. . . ." Nellie Cashman, a lady known for charitable work, was aghast at this crass venture. On the morning of the hangings, indignant townspeople—"muttering anathemas on the projectors of the enterprise"—pulled down the stands with "a terrible crash." The *Tombstone Epitaph* praised these righteous citizens for opposing such "means of money making." At a subsequent hanging in the same community, Sheriff Scott White deliberately held the event in a restricted space. Yet, curious persons viewed the proceedings from the second floor windows of the courthouse. In Albuquerque, anxious spectators paid one dollar each for rooftop space overlooking the site of Milton Yarberry's execution. A "carnival-like atmosphere prevailed," according to one observer. With the appearance of railroads, large excursions were possible to hangings. William French encountered a party of Coloradoans returning from the execution of Black Jack Ketchum in Clayton, New Mexico, in April 1901. One exultant person exhibited a relic from Clayton—one of the dead man's ears![25]

Children were always anxious to observe the proceedings. Eight-year-old William Keleher attempted to enter the stockade erected for the hanging of Jose Ruiz in Albuquerque in June 1900. However, "A deputy sheriff refused to allow me to enter," recalled Keleher. The curious youngsters managed to mingle with the crowd and get into Ruiz's funeral services. The sight of "the blue strangulation marks on the throat of the deceased" remained with Keleher. Sheriff Francis H. Goodwin carelessly erected a scaffold opposite the Yuma school in 1873. Mary Post, the teacher, was so dismayed that she dismissed school and carefully instructed the students to go straight home. The children, being children, immediately sought the best vantage points to witness the event.[26]

The sheriffs tended to restrict attendance at hangings and to reduce the number of formal invitations. The scaffolds were often boxed in or erected inside buildings or stockades. Hordes of curious spectators still gathered outside, although they could not see the events. A New Mexico law attempted to narrow the number and types of persons whom the sheriff, and victim, could invite. These included a doctor, the district attorney, "and at least twelve reputable citizens." If the condemned man so desired, two ministers and no more than five relatives and friends could be present. The sheriff was free to invite "such peace officers as he may think expedient." These cards were usually brief, to the point, and appropriately bordered in black. Sheriff Jerome Ward issued 500 cards for the execution of the Bisbee murderers in 1884.[27]

Sheriff Frank Wattron took liberties with the wording of an invitation to the hanging of George Smiley in Holbrook, Arizona, and provoked an incredible outcry. Wattron's card read:

> You are hereby cordially invited to attend the hanging of George Smiley, murderer. His soul will be swung into eternity on December 6, 1899, at 2 o'clock p.m., sharp. The latest improved methods in the art of scientific strangulation will be employed and everything possible will be done to make the surroundings cheerful and the execution a success.

The *Albuquerque Citizen* printed these cards for the sheriff, who intended them for local circulation. However, the Albuquerque printer leaked one to the national press and the entire nation was soon aware of this bizarre and flippantly worded cardboard.[28]

This brief announcement set off a controversy in Arizona Territory and forced many inhabitants to take sides. The prospects of statehood were growing, and such tasteless humor on the part of a responsible official, such as a county sheriff, blemished the reputation of Arizona. The *Arizona Republican* lamented the "coarse" and "unseemly" levity and pointed out that Wattron's invitation had inflicted "a great injury" upon the territory. Persons elsewhere in the United States "have formed their ideas of Arizona from the Arizona Kickers," said the *Republican*, even though this image was erroneous. Governor Nathan O. Murphy agreed and awarded George Smiley a thirty-day respite. In a proclamation of 6 December 1899, Murphy castigated the sheriff for the use of "unseemly and flippant language . . . in terms which have brought reproach upon the good name of this territory." Murphy wanted the American people to realize "that trifling with the dignity and solemnity of justice is not tolerated in Arizona."[29]

In the Navajo County seat, the *Holbrook Argus* admitted that the wording was "weird" but that Wattron composed it as a joke for only "a few intimate friends and brother sheriffs." While the Albuquerque printer indiscreetly released the card, Arizona law failed to specify "the form and language" of such missives. Furthermore, Murphy's proclamation was merely an attempt "to gain a little cheap glory" in the East. Far from "thirsting for blood" as this card might indicate, the sheriff "is a very sober appearing individual" and appears much like an undertaker. Whatever the merits of Wattron's case, he was constrained to issue a new invitation, dated 1 January 1900. While this invitation was more tactfully worded, it contained obvious innuendo and reflected the existence of controversy:

> With feelings of profound sorrow and regret, I hereby invite you to attend and witness the private, decent and humane execution of a human being . . . on January 8, 1900, at 2 o'clock p.m. You are expected to deport yourself in a respectful manner, and any 'flippant' or 'unseemly' language or conduct on your part will not be allowed. Conduct, on anyone's part, bordering on ribaldry and tending to mar the solemnity of the occasion will not be tolerated.

The picqued lawman could not ignore an opportunity to get in a verbal shot at his chief critic, the governor. If anything, this latter invitation could be interpreted as more offensive than the first. In the meantime, Sheriff Wattron carried out the execution of George Smiley on 8 January 1900.[30]

Many officials realized that changes were necessary in the attendance policy at executions. Even Sheriff Wattron recommended that the legislature prescribe uniform wording for future invitations. Governor Murphy agreed and appointed a committee. Arizonans (and New Mexicans) also addressed the larger issue of the public at executions. Arizona journalists lamented "the morbid curiosity of the human race" and pointed out the shortcomings of the usual "high board fence." A few planks did not "obviate the unpleasant situation," argued this writer, who noted that hangings were still occasions for "exhibitions." Maricopa County Sheriff Carl F. Hayden desired to do away with public executions. Not only did he sense a growing public distaste for these public spectacles, but he cringed at the thought of presiding. Hayden mobilized some of his colleagues and lobbied for the option to conduct hangings in the territorial prison. Jack F. White, Cochise County sheriff, strongly supported this effort. The desired legislation took effect at an opportune time, since the new territorial penitentiary had just opened at Florence. Although some sheriffs continued to hold hangings in their county seats, public resistance to such spectacles was growing as statehood approached.[31]

In New Mexico Territory, a similar attitude began to materialize about this same time. In addition to the controversy over Sheriff Wattron's invitation to the George Smiley hanging in Arizona, New Mexicans confronted the macabre decapitation of Black Jack

Ketchum a few months later. In January 1897, the *Daily New Mexican* expressed the opinion that "public executions are brutalizing and barbarous in the extreme. . . ." They should be ended for the improvement of civic morality, the writer declared. Lawmakers in Santa Fe were debating the issue, and several additional journalists joined in the demand for a law to seclude all executions. The New Mexico law that emerged specified private executions and required the sheriff to "erect an inclosure" for such events. However, experience soon showed that makeshift stockades did not completely deny public view. On 17 March 1903, New Mexico solons restricted the number of spectators at hangings to twenty, including officials, clergymen, physicians, and the press. The sheriff and district judge jointly compiled the list of invitees.[32]

Criticism of attendance policy at executions did not mean that frontiersmen objected to capital punishment. Most New Mexicans and Arizonans fully supported the necessity for these brutalizing exhibitions. In such an insecure environment as the Southwestern territories, public hangings may have served as a means—albeit calloused—to reaffirm community solidarity. In March 1873, the *Daily New Mexican* noted the existence of some sentiment against capital punishment as it editorialized against the "Prevailing Sympathy for Criminals" in the territory. Local juries appeared reluctant to impose the death sentence.

> All this is wrong, and the highest duty which a public journal owes to the community compels us to rebuke false humanity which allows it [sympathy]. The [legal] strangulation of a human being is not an agreeable spectacle to contemplate . . . [but] There could be no safety, no sense of security, if those guilty of lawlessness and outrage were not severely punished. . . .

This writer deplored the "maudlin sentimentalism" and "mistaken leniency" among New Mexicans. In an unusual turn of events, Governor George Curry recommended the abolition of capital punishment to the New Mexico Assembly in January 1909. This former sheriff had had firsthand experience in dealing with murderers and concluded that hanging served no purpose. The victims of the death penalty were usually men who had "neither friends nor influence" in the community. They could not muster the financial resources to obtain a good lawyer and a reduction of their sentence. "The deliberate murderer has no fear of death," Curry informed lawmakers in January 1909, and "indeed his execution is often made the occasion

of bravado on his part. . . ." The arguments of an experienced lawman failed to move the legislators, and hangings continued to take
place in New Mexico for some years.[33]

Whatever the merits of legal public executions, Arizona and New
Mexico staged many of them. The total number is difficult to determine since the records are incomplete. In many instances, the Executive Records of the governors of both territories record the issuance
of a death warrant but fail to follow up with confirmation of the
execution. Newspapers supplement many of these notations and enable some confirmations. A preliminary and incomplete compila-
tion indicates that at least ninety-five persons were hanged in New
Mexico and Arizona between 1846 and 1912. Forty-six met death
by hanging in the former territory and forty-nine in the latter. Of
these ninety-five victims, only one was female. While this total is
somewhat alarming, it pales before the record of the vigilantes, who
dispatched some 170 men. Nearly two persons were lynched for
every one person legally executed.[34]

In a recent study of public hangings, *Rites of Execution: Capital
Punishment and the Transformation of American Culture, 1776–1865,*
Louis P. Masur argues that such events were deliberately planned
"as displays of civil and religious authority and order." Representatives of the government and of the clergy in the New Nation used
this opportunity "to bolster order and encourage conformity to a
republican code of social values" and "to remind the crowd of its
own mortality and to demonstrate that God alone could redeem the
sinful. . . ." Many men who became the leaders of New Mexico and
Arizona territories were reared in the midst of this environment in
the eastern states. They continued to subscribe to the efficacy of
hangings, especially since their frontier communities sometimes exhibited an alarming degree of lawlessness and lagged behind the
more mature states in the cultivation of republican virtues. These
considerations might also help to explain the delay of the two territories in accepting the withdrawal of executions from public view,
which many easterners began to regard as damaging to public morality long before the Civil War.[35]

After nearly three-quarters of a century, the sheriffs of Arizona
and New Mexico could reflect upon the duty of imposing capital
punishment and wonder at its effectiveness. This unwanted task no
doubt loomed largest among their many difficult duties. In an age
of coarseness, these county lawmen often demonstrated a surprising
degree of compassion for the plight of condemned men. While few,
if any sheriffs, desired the abolition of capital punishment, many de-

tested the job of administering it. To shift the responsibility to the territorial prisons was a welcome change. The reaction of Sheriff Jim Brent to the job of hanging was commonplace among these frontier lawmen. In 1886, the *Lincoln County Leader* complimented him for steadfastness in the conduct of an execution:

> He dreaded the job in all its parts, but performed its every duty carefully and successfully. When the body had been taken away, Jim turned to other duties with heart unloaded of a great responsibility. . . .

This journalist admitted that he departed the place of execution in Lincoln "feeling that we would prefer the position even of editor, to that of sheriff. . . ." The fact that the President, Grover Cleveland, had been a sheriff in Buffalo, New York, and had presided at a hanging did not make the office of county lawman any more appealing.[36]

The first jails were often abandoned mine shafts. Here unidentified lawmen stand in front of a crude lockup in Miami, Gila County, Arizona. (Courtesy Arizona Historical Society/Tucson.)

Top: The Colfax County Jail in Cimarron, New Mexico, was constructed in the 1870s and represented considerable advance over the prior edifices. Note the masonry wall forming a jail yard. (Courtesy Center for Southwest Research, UNM General Library, 000-147-0058.) *Bottom:* Early county jails were crudely constructed. This is the Yuma County Jail (date unknown). Note the heavy wooden timbers and absence of adequate ventilation. (Courtesy Arizona Historical Society/Tucson.)

Conconino County officials gathered for a photograph in front of the courthouse in Flagstaff, about 1895. *Seated front row far left:* Sheriff Ralph Henry Cameron. (Courtesy Arizona Historical Society, Pioneer Museum.)

Top: Courthouses contained not only trial rooms but the sheriff's office and jail. Shown here is the Doña Ana County, New Mexico, Courthouse in Las Cruces, in 1900. Jose R. Lucero (standing far right) became sheriff in the following year. (Courtesy New Mexico State University Library, Rio Grande Historical Collections.) *Opposite top:* A rare view of the interior of a frontier sheriff's office. Sheriff John Munds (Yavapai County, Arizona, 1899–1902) is seated (right) with Undersheriff A. A. "Tony" Johns (left). Note signs of modern conveniences. (Courtesy Sharlot Hall Historical Society.) *Opposite bottom:* As counties prospered, they constructed "justice complexes." This is the courthouse and jail in Prescott, Arizona, about 1904. (Courtesy Sharlot Hall Historical Society.)

Shown in this grim sequence is Nah Diaz, San Carlos Apache, hanged in Globe, December 1889. Note the weight suspended by chain in upper right corner, which lifted the victim to his doom. (Courtesy Arizona Historical Society/Tucson.)

Those facing capital punishment were expected to act bravely as they went to their death. Zach Booth waves to the crowd in Globe, Arizona, before his death on 15 September 1905. (Courtesy Arizona Historical Society/Tucson.)

Scaffolds were sometimes needed for simultaneous hangings. Here Hilario Hidalgo and Francisco Rentinio await the final drop in Prescott, Arizona, on 31 July 1903. (Courtesy Sharlot Hall Historical Society.)

Doña Ana County Sheriff Jose Lucero (right) escorts convicted murderer Toribion Huerta to execution in Las Cruces, New Mexico, 26 April 1901. (Courtesy New Mexico State University Library, Rio Grande Historical Collections.)

Execution day was an occasion for expressions of community solidarity. Note the presence of women and children, with hearse standing by, at the hanging of George Woods in Arizona Territory (date and place unknown). (Courtesy Arizona Historical Society/Tucson.)

Sheriffs were sometimes the objects of threats. In this letter, accompanied by an outline of a coffin, a fugitive threatens Sheriff George Kimbrell. Kimbrell served out his term unscathed. (Courtesy Lew Wallace Collection, Indiana Historical Society Library.)

SHERIFF'S SALE.

——:o:——

BY VIRTUE OF AN EXECUTION TO ME DIRECTED AND DELIVERED, ISSUED OUT OF the District Court of the First Judicial District of the Territory of New Mexico, sitting in and for the County of Taos, at the April A. D. 1881 Term thereof, upon a judgment obtained in favor of Henry H. Lyon and George W. Thompson and against Alexander M. Greenwood for the sum of ($2,532 45) two thousand five hundred and thirty-two and forty-five one hundredth dollars, damages; and ($21 85) twenty-one and eighty-five one hundredths dollars costs of suit, commanding me that of the goods, chattles, lands and tenements of the said Alexander M. Greenwood, found in the County of Colfax. in the territory of New Mexico, I levy upon, seize, take and sell sufficient thereof to satisfy the same, with interest on said sums, at the rate of ten per cent per annum, from the fifth day of April A. D. 1881, together with the costs of said execution.

Under and by virtue whereof I have levied upon, seized and taken possession of the following described personal property, viz:

1 DOZ. LONG HANDLED SHOVELS   8 PICKS AND HANDLES   6 PICKS   10 HAMMERS   2 ANVILS   1 VISE   1 BELLOWS, Root's Pat.   1 CROW BAR   650 FEET FUSE   50 lbs CARTRIDGE PAPER   10 lbs CARTRIDGE SOAP –   1 RETORT   450 lbs NAILS   ONE IRON WHEELBARROW   21 DRILLS   ONE DOZ. KNIVES AND FORKS   ONE LARGE LOT TIN WARE   FIVE LAMPS   ONE COFFEE MILL   ONE TUB AND WASH BOARD   ONE HEATING STOVE   ONE HAIR MATTRASS   FIVE PAIR BLANKETS   76 lbs COFFEE   36 lbs SUGAR   TWO COLD CHISELS   TWO WOOD RASPS   SIX FILES   TWO PAIRS BLACKSMITH TONGS   ONE PAIR PIPE TONGS   ONE GRIND STONE   FOUR AXES   ONE TAMPING BAR   FIVE KEGS POWDER   SET BLOCK AND TACKLE   ONE ROLL TAR PAPER   TWO CANS POWDER   ONE CAR   15 JOINTS GAS PIPE   ONE No. 8 COOK STOVE   TWO DOZEN SPOONS   ONE MEAT SAW   ONE LIGHTNING SAW   FOUR BUCKETS   TWO BROOMS   HOUSEHOLD FURNITURE   TWO STRAW TICKS   TWO COMFORTERS 106 lbs SALT   57 lbs DRIED PEACHES   FIVE HALF SACKS MEAL   ELEVEN HALF SACKS FLOUR   TWO RUBBER BLANKETS   ONE SHAFT BUCKET   30 FEET OF HOSE   ONE PAIR FAIRBANK SCALES   ONE BENCH SCREW   24 lbs LARD, COFFEE POTS, CAMP KETTLES, DUTCH OVENS, A LOT OF ASSORTED GROCERIES, and many other articles too numerous to mention; and will sell the same at

PUBLIC AUCTION

At the Dwelling House of the said Alexander M. Greenwood, at the AMERICAN or GREENWOOD MINE, situate on the mountain divide between the waters of the Middle and South Forks of the Poñil river on Saturday the

11th DAY OF JUNE, A. D. 1881,

At the hour of 1 o'clock, p. m., on that day FOR CASH TO THE HIGHEST BIDDER.

Dated Cimarron, N. M. May 21st. 1881.

A. C. WALLACE, Sheriff Colfax Co.

(Courtesy Center for Southwest Studies, University of New Mexico, Albuquerque.)

9

Conservator Pacis

In addition to keeping the jail and serving court process, the sheriff had the duty of maintaining the public peace. In 1846, the Kearny Code laid down this charge:

> The sheriff shall be conservator of the peace within his county, shall suppress assaults and batteries, and apprehend and commit to jail, all felons and traitors, and cause all offenders to keep the peace, and to appear at the next term of the court and answer such charges as may be preferred against them.

This was a formidable, sometimes impossible, assignment in the frontier communities of the Southwest. The number and degree of disturbances often exceeded the capacity of the sheriff's personnel to cope with them. Many lawbreakers were comparatively harmless, and one night in jail chastened them. The hardened felons often resisted arrest. A few chose to die rather than submit to the sheriff. Such men made the assignment—"apprehend and commit to jail"— a very dangerous experience.[1]

Like any frontier society, territorial New Mexico and Arizona contained the ingredients conducive to lawlessness. Pioneers were a fractious lot—a peculiar mixture of, at best, equivocal and, at worst, hostile attitudes toward each other. In their grasping for a new material utopia, settlers often collided over property titles. And in their disappointment at failure, personal demoralization often prompted quarrelsome behavior. The presence of disproportionate numbers of men to women and children in mining and cattle towns created volatile situations. These isolated males overindulged in alcohol, narcotics, and gambling and frequented the redlight district. Other footloose elements included large numbers of teamsters and soldiers. Among these individuals, the "bad man" was quick to take offense at slights, real or imagined. James McClintock, an Arizona pioneer, observed the lethal antics of badmen firsthand. He concluded that many possessed "really childish characteristics" and were puffed up with a juvenile conception of "honor." These men were very dangerous and unpredictable when they mixed alcohol with a misguided notion of honor. The clash of cultures—Indian, Hispanic, and Anglo—contributed to the prospects for mayhem. At some point, representatives of each community arose as self-appointed champions against the offenses of the other culture. The gun became the tool of these agents.[2]

The frontier had always attracted various fringe elements, from religious seekers to utopian community builders to veteran evil-doers. Arizona and New Mexico were no exception. Journalists speculated about the sources of criminal behavior. Anglos accused the Hispano community of producing many criminals. Since the Anglos controlled the press in the two territories, the Spanish-speaking community usually lost this battle on the printed page. Both elements could agree on one source of lawlessness: the international boundary. This remote and largely unpoliced region had attracted outlaws since the Mexican War. As the cattle industry spread after the Civil War, town-dwellers accused herders of being a primary source of criminal behavior. Not only did cowboys possess knowledge of guns, horses, and back trails, but their roving trade ran contrary to the best practices of sedentary, civilized life. As this debate raged in the 1880s, livestock men rebutted that villages produced just as many, or more, lawless men. Far from ranches and towns, the railroads probably increased the quotient of criminals more than any other source. The sheriffs certainly witnessed a dramatic increase in public disturbances and crime as thousands of construction workers laid the new rails across Arizona and New Mexico territories.[3]

The practice of carrying deadly weapons added a menacing and often lethal aspect to frontier society. Although the inhabitants of the territories saw no reason to justify this practice, their ancestors had used firearms for hunting food and defending their homes against hostile Indians. If legal justification was needed, frontiersmen could point to the right of self-defense as propounded by the famous eighteenth-century jurist, William Blackstone. In his *Com-*

mentaries on the Laws of England, Blackstone declared that if someone or his family "be forcibly attacked in his person or property, it
is lawful for him to repel force by force. . . ." This Englishman reassured readers that "Self-defense . . . is justly called the primary law
of nature . . . ," and American frontiersmen eagerly agreed. During
the Lincoln County War of the late 1870s, one visitor noted with
dismay how "A murder in an affray where both men have a chance
to fight is regarded as indulgently as a duel in Carolina." After a visit
to western New Mexico, Governor Edmund Ross noted "the loose
interpretation of the law of the code of morals . . . that so generally
prevails on the . . . grounds of self-defense." Although he objected
to the abuse of this law, Ross had to admit that he was "not alto-
gether free from that feeling, familiar as I am with frontier life and
habits of thought."[4]

Peacekeeping duties were possibly the most common of all the
sheriff's concerns. The arrest of persons under the influence of alcoholic beverages was a routine duty, but not to be taken lightly. The
sheriff had to assume that every such disturber of the peace carried a
gun or knife, or both. In an addled and drunken state, such men
were unpredictable and could place the lawman's life in danger. As a
territorial capital, trading community, and host to an army headquarters, Santa Fe presented the sheriffs with many problems. In
February 1856, Sheriff Jesus Salazar attempted to break up a group
of drunks. Someone fired a shot at him. Fortunately, the round
passed harmlessly through the sheriff's coat. During a later term,
this same peace officer again narrowly escaped death when a gang of
toughs lay in wait for him. Although Salazar fought his way clear,
he was forced to wound one assailant. On the following day, deputies rounded up more of the pack. Such encounters continued in
the capital throughout the territorial era. In July 1882, Santa Fe
County Sheriff Romulo Martinez intervened in an argument between two men on San Francisco Street. The pair was so busy
scuffling that they did not recognize the sheriff. In the heat of the
moment they turned on him! One disputant pointed a revolver at
Martinez, but the lawman quickly wrenched the weapon away. Although the sheriff had reason to arrest both men, he let them go. To
make an example of the gunman, Martinez made him "weaken and
beg," according to one observer. On another occasion, Martinez
was observed chasing a troublesome individual down the banks of
the Santa Fe River. Since the sheriff had neglected to carry his revolver on that day, he resorted to throwing rocks at the culprit![5]

The streets of Arizona communities could be just as rowdy. In March 1869, a Prescott justice of the peace noted in his docket book that J. A. Smith resisted Sheriff John Langford Taylor "by drawing a double barreled shot gun upon him while, he, the Sheriff was endeavoring to arrest him." The defendant was bound over to await the action of the grand jury. A drunken soldier took a shot at Taylor a few months later but "the bullet passed through Taylor's coat sleeve," said the *Arizona Miner*. On Tuesday, 27 April 1897, Sheriff Dan R. Williamson and his deputies engaged in the suppression of "a day of disturbances" in Globe, Arizona. Williamson answered calls to a knife fight and several fist fights, one of which resulted in charges of interference with an officer in the performance of his duties. By the end of that day, the sheriff and his subordinates had arrested eight disturbers of the peace. With such dangerous duties facing them, Matthew F. Shaw, Sheriff of Pima County, in the 1880s, was moved to recall that lawmen "couldn't complain of monotony."[6]

Sheriff's personnel often prevented disturbances from growing into more serious crimes. In August 1882, Pima County Deputy Sheriff Martel encountered a hard case named Bain in Calabasas. In the course of a daylong argument with a saloon keeper, Bain disrupted the peace and quiet of a restaurant and endangered the lives of patrons. Martel ejected the troublesome man twice, but he returned for a third time, hurling threats at his intended victim. On this occasion, Bain sat down near a group of women. The exasperated deputy drew his gun "and struck Bain once on the cheek and forehead, felling him to the ground," said one newspaperman. "That he bore with Bain so long," continued this journalist, "and took such desperate chances before resorting to violence, speaks volumes for him as being a most cool and capable officer. . . ." A Yavapai deputy sheriff, one Lacy, forestalled a serious difficulty when a Prescott gunsmith reported that a customer—obviously in an agitated state of mind—had purchased a weapon. The man, a former meat cutter, was distraught at being fired and apparently intended harm to his former employer. Lacy shadowed the gun wielder as he walked directly to the meat shop. The deputy arrested him just as he was pulling his new weapon against the proprietor.[7]

Some frontier communities, such as Cimarron, New Mexico, suffered a prolonged period of public commotion, and the sheriffs were hard pressed to contain the chaos. The influx of miners, cattlemen, and other persons in the 1860s and 1870s created tensions. The dispute between squatters and owners of the Maxwell Land

Grant Company fostered a continuous undercurrent of anger that occasionally led to vigilantism and even the intervention of the United States Army. Many unruly individuals existed among these various elements and created a long series of disturbances in Cimarron and other communities in Colfax County. Among the most troublesome were Robert Clay Allison and his brother, John, David Crockett (a nephew and namesake of the hero of the Alamo), Gus Hefferon, and Francisco (Pancho) Griego. Generally, they fitted James McClintock's characterization of the badman: a person adult in years with a juvenile personality. When not riding the ranges, these men thrived on alcohol and gambling in the St. James Hotel. They frequently rode horses recklessly through the streets, fired their guns indiscriminately, and delighted in other rough mischief. When deeply in their cups, they enjoyed harassing the sheriffs. Allison and Crockett reportedly roped an innocent pedestrian, led him into a general store, outfitted him in expensive clothing, and sent the bill to Sheriff Isaiah Rinehart. When Rinehart protested, the malevolent pair reminded him that they indirectly paid for such goods through the lawman's excessive tax collections. On another occasion, when the sheriff had arrested Allison, this violent man seized Rinehart's hat, filled it with water, and drank from the head gear. While these men have become stock personalities in the iconography of frontier gunmen, they were simply disturbers of the peace to the sheriffs.[8]

In addition to dangerous pranks, these violent men killed— sometimes innocent persons and sometimes their own kind. Sixteen men reportedly died violent deaths in the St. James Hotel bar alone. On 16 January 1875, four Texas cowboys created an uproar in Cimarron and barricaded themselves in a store. Sheriff John Turner and a posse eventually extricated these defiant herders, but only after wounding two of them. When fellow cowboys threatened to burn the county seat, the townspeople, in a public meeting, formally approved the sheriff's action and provided him with an ad hoc defense force. The cowboys wisely abandoned their malevolent intentions. Other saloon incidents followed in rapid succession. On 30 May, Pancho Griego murdered two black soldiers. In March 1876, David Crockett and Gus Hefferon killed three more black soldiers. The last binge of these two desperadoes took place in the following September, whereupon Sheriff Rinehart and a deputy killed Crockett and wounded Hefferon.[9]

While the larger struggle between the squatters and the Maxwell Company went on, the sheriffs continued to wrestle with a remorseless string of public disturbances. Clay Allison killed Pancho Griego in the St. James saloon. Porter Stockton murdered Antonio Archbie in January 1876. In May 1878, Sheriff Peter Burleson was constrained to kill an Indian from the nearby reservation after the man became drunk and resisted arrest. Two years later, this same lawman and a deputy attempted to arrest four mischief-makers at a Cimarron corral. Shooting broke out. The deputy and one gunman were killed; the sheriff and one other man were wounded. Although the evidence is contradictory, Burleson, Deputy Mason Bowman, and a posse reportedly killed four Texans on 4 July 1880. The cowboys had terrorized Cimarron on the previous night. The sheriff was wounded (again) and one posseman was killed in this last incident.[10]

Socorro County sheriffs experienced a series of challenges to public order similar to the difficulties in Cimarron. The problem in Socorro arose from the simultaneous arrival of the Santa Fe Railroad, with its rowdy construction gangs, and large numbers of Texas cowboys. Peter (Pedro) Simpson, sheriff in 1883–84, bore the brunt of these problems. The county seat of Socorro "was lively with saloons and dance halls," recalled cattleman Frank Collinson, and had "everything that went to make up a roaring Western town." The dislike of Texas herders for the Hispanos ("greasers") in Socorro County was no less intense than in Colfax County. The Lone Star interlopers vented much of this spleen upon Sheriff Simpson. That he was the offspring of a mixed marriage probably increased the Texans' dislike of the officer. In January 1883, Simpson's first month in office, he and a deputy attempted to arrest a party of young herders who tried to tree the town. They ignored his command to surrender and defiantly rode away, whereupon the officers opened fire. Two riders fell; one, named Townsend, died from his wounds. Collinson, obviously a partisan, alleged in his recollections that Simpson and the deputy did not seriously attempt the arrest but pursued them on horseback and shot the unwary young herders from their animals. Collinson's memory is faulty when he says that the lawmen killed all three and that "the honest citizens around Socorro were shocked at the crime." By "honest citizens," he is referring to the cattle interests, not the longtime residents, who approved of Simpson's decisiveness. Before Townsend expired, he bitterly castigated his comrades, who fled rather than stay and assist him. Sheriff Simpson's peace-keeping duties continued. Two months later, a drunken bravo pulled a gun on the sheriff. Simpson overpowered the hellion and handcuffed him. A justice of the peace fined the defendant one dollar and costs. A few days later, angry Hispanos mobbed Simpson in nearby San Marcial as he performed some private land surveys. He arrested the ringleader for inciting to riot.[11]

County lawmen such as Pedro Simpson and his Colfax County colleagues learned quickly that they could not afford to take chances when dealing with drunken malefactors. What appeared to be mere abuse of alcohol often masked ethnic or racial hatreds and the desire to commit mayhem. Sheriff Pete Gabriel took no chances with troublemakers in Florence, Arizona. Charles Eastman observed Gabriel use direct action against one disturber. Gabriel had just returned to town and stopped at a saloon, said Eastman.

> We were in Johnny Keating's saloon in Florence. A Mexican boy came in and told the sheriff there was a drunken Mexican at his house, threatening to kill the boy's mother. As Pete and the boy stepping [sic] out of the saloon, this Mexican came galloping down the street on horseback. Pete called to him in Spanish to stop, thinking he had just killed the woman and was fleeing.
>
> As he flashed by, Pete recognized him as a prisoner recently released from Yuma. The man paid no attention to Pete's command, so the sheriff shot at once. . . .

The peace officer's single shot killed both man and animal.[12]

Far from deliberately courting death at the hands of reckless and drunken men, the experienced sheriff always assumed an advantageous position. Premeditated confrontations at high noon on the main street did not take place. That is not to say that peace officers did not engage in gunfights, but such meetings were usually spontaneous. George Smalley, an Arizona newspaperman, observed Gila County Sheriff Ed Shanley attempt to arrest an inebriated horseman in Globe about 1905. While this fight conformed somewhat to the classic Hollywood version of the street duel, the sheriff did not plan it that way. According to Smalley. "The sheriff walked towards his adversary as bullets whizzed past his head." When the badman's fourth round creased Shanley's scalp, continued this eyewitness, "he drew his .45 and the outlaw fell from his horse with a bullet through his heart."[13]

In addition to public tumults, these frontier sheriffs were often called upon to break up domestic disputes. To interfere in family quarrels placed the lawman in more immediate danger than in saloon disputes. Exchanges between husband and wife could explode unpredictably, and the disputants could turn on the lawman. Grant

County Deputy Sheriff Charlie Smith overheard a residential dispute between spouses one Sunday in Silver City shortly after the turn of the century. Robert Bell, who had just been talking with the deputy, recalled the subsequent events. Smith "knocked at the door and told 'em to open up or stop this [quarreling]." At that moment, the angry husband fired blindly through the door. His wild shot hit and killed the unsuspecting peace officer. Smith, a former cowhand for the Diamond A Ranch, had been well liked by all. Sheriff Lindley Orme was forced to intervene in a serious domestic dispute in Phoenix, Arizona. An estranged husband threatened the lives of his wife and her new lover. Orme and a deputy took up positions in the woman's house and awaited a threatening move. It soon came. The outraged husband broke into the spouse's quarters, and the sheriff shot and killed him.[14]

Peacekeeping required the sheriffs to patrol large gatherings. The Hispanos of New Mexico and Arizona enjoyed dances (*bailes*), which took on the atmosphere of festivals. The preceding Mexican regime had looked with grave suspicion upon any large gathering as a potential political threat, and the Anglo conquerors continued to distrust such get-togethers. They tended to promote ethnic solidarity and could serve as centers of treasonous activity. In January 1853, the New Mexico Assembly required that "any person desiring to give a Ball or Fandango, . . . shall apply to the Probate Judge or a Justice of the Peace for a License . . ." to hold such an event. The sheriffs normally collected this fee. As the number of American migrants increased in the Southwest, the fear of large public gatherings among Hispanics declined. The license requirements were rescinded.[15]

Any event that brought people together attracted the vigilant personnel of the sheriff's office. Deputy Sheriff Frank Chavez and Detective Tony Neis were patrolling Santa Fe during the Tertio-Millenial Fair in August 1883, when fire broke out at nearby (abandoned) Fort Marcy. The officers arrested two men who confessed that they had set the blaze to distract policemen from the fair. They apparently planned a robbery. During a Fourth of July celebration in the previous decade, Santa Fe County Sheriff Carlos Conklin was called upon to investigate a tragic event. Whiskey flowed freely and the crowd was in a festive mood. A civilian employee from Fort Marcy fired his revolver wildly into the air. He intended no harm. Unfortunately, a bullet richocheted and killed a teenage girl. Although Conklin arrested the young shootist, the court let him go. He had not fired maliciously.[16]

Southwesterners relished races and other sporting events. The sheriffs always put in an appearance at such contests. Harvey White-hill, sheriff of Grant County, monitored spectators at a unusual local event. On 14 September 1888, promoters sponsored a forty-eight mile race between a velocipede and a horse from Silver City to Deming, New Mexico. The horse won. Horse races posed special problems. Tempers flared easily among gamblers. Sheriff Pat Nugent and his staff patrolled an especially troublesome horse race in Yuma, Arizona, in the 1890s. The chief problem was Frank M. King, a boisterous part-time lawman and race horse owner. King possessed the reputation of a fractious character. When some Hispanos attempted to steal his prize horse, King pulled a weapon and took up pursuit through the crowd. The sheriff and Deputy Burke observed this independent action and feared he might harm bystanders. Although the officers disarmed him, King continued the chase, unsuccessfully. In an attempt to turn King's belligerence against him, friends of the suspected thieves had him arrested for assault! At the sheriff's office, the bellicose King got into a fight with an attorney. A second charge of assault was filed against him. As the eventful day progressed, King continued to make trouble for himself. He engaged in tête-a-têtes with two additional parties who, in turn, filed charges, making a total of four in one day. Four peace bonds were necessary. Fortunately, Deputy Ed Mayes was a relative of this rowdy horse owner and persuaded all concerned parties to settle out of court. King recalled that his temper cost him $2,500 that day. He put his race horse out to pasture for good.[17]

Although the cattle ranges were distant from the county seats, these great grasslands were not free of disturbances. Roundups provided isolated cowhands the opportunity to fraternize, gamble, and let off steam. Since most cowhands owned weapons (though they did not always wear them on the job), gunfights and occasional killings took place. Homicides occurred frequently enough in New Mexico that the stock men took steps to discourage weapons carrying at roundups in the 1880s. The sheriffs also desired to monitor these remote aggregations, in order to spot fugitives from justice. While wanted men were reluctant to put in an appearance in town, they felt less threatened at roundups. The 1890 roundup at Pine Cienaga (just inside the New Mexico border, but adjacent to Graham County, Arizona) aroused the attention of Sheriff Billy Whelan in Solomonville. The lawman's sources reported that the large ranchers intended to use this opportunity to expel small cattle operators, whom the former accused of rustling. Whelan sent Deputy Jim Parks to the scene, recalled sister Jennie Parks Ringgold, "to see that the small ranchers were treated fairly and given a chance to prove their rights [to livestock]." Much to the surprise of the larger ranchers, she continued, "The roundup showed that there was no wholesale stealing. . . ." Needless to say, Sheriff Whelan must have also been relieved.[18]

In addition to keeping the peace, the law required the sheriff to arrest suspected felons and present them to the grand jury for indictment. This task was much more complicated than the law revealed and often required serious investigations and collection of evidence. While these frontier lawmen lacked professional training in criminal detection, many sheriffs and deputies demonstrated common sense and native wit. Gila County Sheriff Tip Lowther solved a particularly grisly murder-robbery near Globe in August 1882. Lowther spotted an unusually small footprint among the highwaymen. Possemen speculated that these tiny impressions belonged to a woman. Lowther measured the prints and began methodical questioning of residents in Globe. He soon found that Lafayette (Fate) Grimes, a dance instructor, possessed diminutive feet. Upon comparison, Lowther definitely placed Lafayette Grimes at the crime scene. (That vigilantes lynched the outlaws did not erase the sheriff's good detective work.) John Henry Thompson, who later occupied Lowther's position, combined a hunch with some deductions and connected Globe badman King Ussery to a stagecoach robbery. While following the tracks of a lone highwayman from the robbery site, the alert officer spotted a piece of wire dangling from a tree limb partly submerged in the Salt River. Upon examination, Thompson found a bar of the stolen bullion affixed. The sheriff also surmised that a red stain on the wire was the blood of the bandit. A Globe doctor confirmed that the stain was human blood and recalled treating King Ussery. The courts convicted Ussery, and Sheriff Thompson had the satisfaction of escorting him to the Yuma prison.[19]

Instances of alert detective work by sheriff's personnel were numerous. In November 1883, highwaymen robbed several stores and murdered a deputy sheriff and three citizens in Bisbee, Arizona. This senseless act, thereafter known as the Bisbee Massacre, outraged Southwesterners. Cochise County Sheriff Jerome Ward and his staff were determined to solve the case. Deputies Fred J. Dodge and Charles Smith found a corral employee who had heard one of the desperadoes speak. This witness also possessed the facility to

imitate voices. When the man mimicked the bandit, bystanders recognized the voice of Big Dan Dowd, a known badman. Deputy Bill
Daniels measured hoof prints left when the outlaws escaped and
presented this evidence at the trial. Sheriff Ward retrieved an in-
criminating hat found in the possession of another suspect taken
into custody in Deming, New Mexico. Ward carefully stored all the
evidence in his office safe in Tombstone. This sound detective work,
added to some determined tracking into Mexico, led to the eventual
arrest of six men. Five were legally executed and one was lynched.[20]

Southwestern highwaymen were not always a shrewd lot and
sometimes left rather obvious telltale signs. During a Southern
Pacific train heist near Maricopa, Arizona, in 1887, two outlaws
sported new, black handles on their six-shooters. Lawmen easily
traced the grips to the merchant who sold them. Another member
of the band, Oscar Rogers, left his poll tax receipt at their campsite!
In November 1883, a murderous aggregation robbed a train at
Gage Station, near Deming, New Mexico, and killed the engineer.
Former Sheriff Harvey Whitehill, who was anxious for the reward
and reelection, found a current Kansas newspaper at the robbers'
campsite. He found a Silver City storekeeper to whom the newspaper belonged. It was his hometown journal. He used well-read
copies for wrapping packages. This knowledge led the former lawman to a customer, George Cleaveland, a black man who worked at
a local restaurant.[21]

A mere hunch could lead sheriff's men to a fugitive. When two
men robbed a bank in Las Cruces, New Mexico, in 1901, Sheriff
Pat Garrett and his staff followed all trails to dead ends. Garrett, a
veteran officer, allegedly employed the third degree on one suspected cowhand, until lawyer Albert Fall intervened. Finally, a
cattleman informed Chief Deputy Ben Williams that an old friend,
Oscar J. Wilber, had unexplainably avoided him when passing on
the range. While Wilber was not a known badman—and the sheriff
knew most potential troublemakers—he had recently kept company with a tough, Billy Wilson. A search for Wilber led Deputy
Williams to San Antonio, Texas. Williams disguised himself, rented
a room across the street from Wilber's new quarters, and awaited
the suspect's return. Wilber soon appeared in company with Billy
Wilson. Williams arrested both men.[22]

Common sense and a shrewd comprehension of the conspicuous
absences of things led veteran lawman Henry (Enrique) Garfias to
an equally clever highwayman. This lone bandit robbed three stage-
coaches within walking distance of Gillette, Maricopa County, Ari-

zona, in 1882. Mine owners, who lost valuable payrolls, complained to Sheriff Lindley Orme. Orme concluded that probably two men were involved, that they were wanderers, and that they had departed the region. Henry Garfias, Orme's Gillette deputy, disagreed with his superior. Garfias sensed a local job. He observed that a bandit could, by walking cross-country from the site of the robbery, reach Gillette before the victimized stagecoach could negotiate the twisting approach road into town. The cagey deputy questioned children who played in the area. They informed him that Henry Seymour, a blacksmith, had recently hunted quail in the vicinity. Upon closer examination, Garfias concluded that Seymour's hunting excursions—on foot—coincidentally took place on the days of the robberies. When Garfias asked the children to describe Seymour's weapon, they described a rifle, a gun inappropriate for bird hunting. The shotgun was the standard weapon. Garfias arrested the blacksmith. In April 1882, the highwayman received a ten-year prison sentence. The loot, reportedly $67,000, was never found.[23]

The subjects of the sheriff's arrest warrants were not always hardened criminals. In May 1861, the sheriff of Doña Ana County faced an embarrassing assignment—the arrest of a Catholic priest. The occasion was a dispute between communicants of Mesilla and Las Cruces over possession of the image of San Ysidro, patron saint of bountiful crops. After the residents of Mesilla carried the santo to the head of their *acequia* (irrigation canal), the faithful of the neighboring community demanded their turn. When the holy father refused, the disappointed Las Crucans seized the image. Mesillans obtained a writ of replevin and reclaimed San Ysidro. At this point, the priest "became much excited," said the *Mesilla Times,* "and a warrant is issued for his arrest." With tongue in cheek, the writer continues:

> The High Sheriff [Samuel G. Bean?] of the County is finally called on who arrests his Reverence and takes him to [the village of] Doña Ana, escorted by devoted women and armed men, all afoot through mud and rain. The Padre walks into the jaws of the law with an expressed decision to have everything his own way, as a Mexican Padre should, to revolutionize the earth, but finally gives security for his reappearance [in court].

This incident caused much chagrin in Doña Ana County. The *Times* remarked that "We trust that the civil courts will not again be invoked to settle ecclesiastical questions on the right of property in

Saint Ysidro." If the sheriff was Samuel Bean, he no doubt agreed with this desire. This may have been one of Bean's last official acts for the Union. The Confederate Army marched into his bailiwick a few weeks later, and Bean assumed another office under these new auspices.[24]

In addition to the holy father, these county lawmen were called upon to arrest rowdy women. Such a task could be disconcerting, as Silver City deputy sheriffs Al Card and C. D. Cantly learned. In February 1889, Ada Humes, a member of the demi-world, killed a man in a saloon brawl. She then sought refuge in the quarters of Savannah Randall, described as "a golden-toothed siren." When the officers forced the door, they encountered a ferocious Ada at bay. "She came forth swinging her arms and yelling like a hyena, . ." said the *Silver City Enterprise,* although the lawmen eventually overpowered her. Deputy Sheriff Mack Axford prepared for the worst when his superior, Cochise County Sheriff Del Lewis, sent him to arrest a female cook at a mine in Hereford. She allegedly shot at her boss when he fired her. This assignment unnerved Axford at first, and he feared she might be insane. Much to his surprise, the deputy never met "a more pleasant woman." The arrest proceeded without incident. A Santa Fe deputy sheriff created a stir when he boarded a train in Cerrillos with "a respectable woman" in tow. She had gotten drunk and attempted to "take the town," said one journalist. Because the inebriated woman was a member of a prominent family, her name was suppressed.[25]

In spite of the fact that some danger existed in most arrests, stories persist that some sheriffs refused to carry arms. Such tales are difficult to document. If an officer persisted in going unarmed, he probably knew that his quarry was relatively inoffensive. John Lorenzo Hubbell, sheriff of Apache County, Arizona, in 1885–86, reportedly avoided the use of guns. Hubbell allegedly approached felons "in his usual calm and quiet way" and persuaded them to surrender. Sheriff George Ruffner employed this same procedure to arrest "Bugger" Bennett, who shot a Prescott physician. Bennett fled, thinking he had killed the doctor. He had only wounded the victim. Ruffner knew Bugger as the harmless town character and set off in pursuit without a gun. When Ruffner overtook Bennett, the officer persuaded him to surrender. Only then did the sheriff inform Bennett that the doctor's gold watch had deflected the bullet. Carl Hayden, chief lawman of Maricopa County, also deplored guns.[26]

On rare occasions, a wanted man sought out the sheriff. Such an unusual event took place in Springer, New Mexico, one day in

1891. An elderly stranger strolled into Sheriff Thike Stockton's office and confessed to a murder committed in Colfax County in 1866. This mysterious person introduced himself as Service, and said that he had killed a man near Lucien Maxwell's ranch and had fled to Montana. Stockton was an old resident and had some recollection of this homicide, but he went on to say that public opinion had applauded Service's act at the time. The victim was a noted badman. Service "had served the country well," added the sheriff in a droll bit of humor. The penitent man persisted in confessing even though Stockton urged him to forget the matter. "You are too old . . ." for prison, advised the sheriff. But the guilt-ridden fugitive insisted that Stockton find a lawyer for him and pursue the case to a conclusion. Although the district attorney refused to prosecute this long-forgotten case, the minimal formalities satisfied Service. Upon receiving his freedom, Service became a changed man. "Service shaved and became a white man and free citizen . . ." for the first time since 1866, according to one account.[27]

As in the arrest of drunken disturbers of the peace, the experienced sheriff sought the advantage against hardened criminals. When Sheriff Henry Denney and Deputy Ben Wooten undertook the arrest of William Mitchell, wanted for murder, they made careful plans. As they took the long carriage ride from Alamogordo to Estey City in March 1907, Denney decided that they would pose as mining speculators. When they approached the suspect in this guise, Mitchell, whose alias was "Baldy Russell," took the bait. He offered to walk with the two men to a promising mining site.

> They started out [says Russell's biographer], Denny [sic] on one side and Wooten on the other. When they got far enough from the house to make their play without interference, each one of them grabbed an arm, and the battle was on. Baldly put up the best fight he could, and his best was pretty good. He kicked their shins and struggled, and told them what sort of people they were. In the course of the scuffle his pistol fell out of his waistband, and they had him. They put the handcuffs on him and took him back to the hack. . . .

Sheriff Denney gave Russell a moment to say goodbye to his wife and children and drove away.[28]

If the lawmen were not in a position to employ such a ruse, other means were required to avoid danger. As Dee Harkey observed, "the best time to arrest a criminal and avoid a fight is at daybreak. . . ." The fugitive's guard was down, his body sluggish and eyes heavy with sleep. This disorientation gave the arresting officer an edge. When Sheriff Pat Garrett of Doña Ana County attempted to arrest Oliver Lee and Jim Gililland at Wildy Well in 1898, he surprised the wanted men at daybreak. Garrett also chose an elevated spot above the sleeping fugitives with the sun at his back. Oliver Lee recalled this attempted arrest many years later.

> The first thing I knew, just about daybreak the Garrett posse was shooting at us from the top of the shed. Garrett so placed his posse that when they shot at us they got the benefit of the morning sun at daybreak, shooting from east to west. . . .

Unfortunately, the first shots of the lawmen missed their mark— Lee alleged that Garrett fired without warning—and the fugitives killed one posseman and forced Garrett to withdraw. The distance between Garrett and his quarry was later measured at only thirty-seven feet, a poor reflection upon the marksmanship of the noted lawman.[29]

The prospect of having to kill a person during an arrest always loomed large. John Slaughter, sheriff of Cochise County, Arizona, cautioned his deputies about arresting a "bad sort." "I'd advise you to fire first and then yell, 'throw up your hands,'" said this noted manhunter. Dee Harkey, a longtime deputy sheriff, recalled the advice of his elder brother Joe, a sheriff in Texas in the 1880s. When he deputized his younger sibling, the sheriff enjoined him to be "'Damned sure you don't get killed, but don't kill anybody unless you have to.'" "I could never bring myself to kill a man just because I had the drop on him," confessed Dee Harkey, "or when he didn't have a chance to defend himself. . . ." While Harkey's memory is suspect at times, he was probably sincere in this regard. One historian asserts that Western lawmen did not worry about public censure when they killed a suspect. Frontier juries "almost invariably" ruled in favor of them or accepted the lawman's plea of justifiable homicide. While juries were not always uniformly lenient in trials of peace officers, there is some truth in this conclusion as well.[30]

A Cochise County coroner's jury accorded Sheriff John Slaughter a clean bill in the death of two train robbers. Slaughter, Deputy Burt Alvord, and two possemen caught them asleep in the Whetstone Mountains on the morning of 7 June 1888. In frank, if colorful, language, Slaughter related this engagement to the jury:

> This morning, after daylight, I crawled up to within fifty yards of [the band and] . . . asked them if they would surrender. They answered with their guns. . . . Just at this time, one of the men fired a

shot, and knocked the bark off the tree close to my ear. Just about that time I shot him. About a second afterwards [a second man] . . . jumped with a six-shooter in his hand and I said, 'Burt [Deputy Alvord], there is another Son-of-a-bitch,' and I shot him. Just after that this man Manuel [Robles] ran down the Canyon, . . and I said, 'Burt, there is another Son-of-a-bitch. Shoot him!' and I shot him. . . .

The latter fugitive, the third, was only wounded and escaped. In such confrontations, the county lawman could not be too careful. Slaughter's biographer notes that the sheriff "seldom waited for the other party to make the first move."[31]

It was not always possible to plan for an arrest. The alert sheriff had to be prepared to move quickly, as Pedro Simpson demonstrated in December 1883. This Socorro County lawman had delivered two suspected train robbers to Sheriff James B. Woods in Silver City and was returning to his county seat by train. While en route to Socorro, Simpson learned to his surprise that two more suspects in this same robbery were on his train. A journalist happened to be aboard and observed the Socorro lawman go into action. Fortunately, District Attorney William Rynerson and Territorial Attorney General William Breeden were aboard and agreed to assist Simpson. Said the newspaperman:

It was just fun to see the activity of that sheriff; that black satchell [sic] came open, nippers and shackles were out in almost no time. The big ivory handled carbine, that knife, that shot gun, were put in condition for effective service, in less time than I am writing it.

The three officials, accompanied by the newsman, moved quickly to the adjacent car where the suspects were seated:

On entering the car, the men were looking out in the dark, but how sudden their heads turned, inside, when, 'click,' 'click,' and 'hold up' was demanded of them by the sheriff. . . . The men, who were facing each other in the double seat, . . could look down the muzzle of an ugly looking carbine, and . . . a double barrell [sic] shot gun. . . .

The rough-looking desperadoes were completely surprised, and "up went four hands, as if their owners were about to invoke a devine [sic] blessing. . . ." The. elated sheriff left the train with his prisoners and escorted them to Silver City.[32]

Any arrest could take an unsuspected turn and end in violence. This was another unexpected dimension of the frontier shrievalty.

Commodore Perry Owens, newly elected sheriff of Apache County, Arizona, learned this fact in an attempt to arrest a wanted stock thief, Andy L. Blevins, alias Cooper, in Holbrook. Although Owens knew of Cooper's reputation as a hard man, the sheriff had no reason to anticipate a major shootout. On 6 September 1887, the sheriff walked up to the family residence and asked to speak to Cooper. Within the blinking of an eye, a gunfight erupted and Owens killed Cooper, Samuel Blevins, the outlaw's younger brother, and Mose Roberts, a visitor. John Blevins, another brother, was wounded but eventually recovered. The large number of casualties hardly conformed to the expectations of an arrest of a cattle thief, although Cooper had recently killed men in the Pleasant Valley War. The facts of this gunfight remain controversial, although Owens was probably unaware of the number of persons in the Blevins house. (Mrs. Eva Blevins—Cooper's mother—and a sister-in-law were also in the structure.) According to the sheriff, Cooper refused to submit to arrest, pointed a revolver at the officer's midriff, and closed the front door in Owens's face. At that moment, the sheriff fired his rifle through the door. The shot inflicted a mortal wound. The two half brothers, John and Samuel Blevins, entered the fray, although Owens did not carry warrants for them. The lawman killed Samuel, who was only sixteen, and wounded the other man. Mose Roberts, the unsuspecting guest, took flight through a window, whereupon the sheriff shot him to death.[33]

Although Commodore Owens acted in the name of the law, the consequences of his acts gave reason for pause. W. H. Burbage, a local journalist, visited the scene moments later. "The sight within the house was horrible," he wrote, and "Blood was everywhere." Andy Cooper, in his death throes, was "cursing and imploring anyone to put him out of pain." The Blevins women were screaming hysterically and, at the same time, attempting to care for their dying and wounded men. "Most pitiful was the sight of the mother mourning her slain sons," recalled Burbage. The anguished mother continued to live in this same house, although it must have evoked agonizing memories. Although the coroner's jury ruled that the sheriff was justified, Eva Blevins maintained for the remainder of her life that Owens had murdered her men.[34]

This unfortunate confrontation went further than either side intended. The rustling warrant had been outstanding on Andy Cooper for a year. He was aware of it and had moved warily. Cooper had recently participated in shootings in the Pleasant Valley War. He probably feared that Owens would turn him over to

Yavapai County Sheriff William Mulvenon on a graver charge. The sheriff was also guilty of indiscretion as he went about this arrest. He turned down offers of assistance from druggist Frank Wattron and other men just before the shooting. Had a posse confronted Cooper, this force might have dissuaded the outlaw from resisting. In his haste or foolhardiness, Sheriff Owens neglected to scout out the Blevins house adequately. When he stumbled into greater danger than anticipated, he reacted—possibly overreacted—decisively. The killing of Samuel Blevins was questionable, and the killing of Mose Roberts was unjustifiable. Had Owens known the number of occupants in the house, he might have acted more circumspectly. On the other hand, Owens was under much public pressure to serve the warrant on Andy Cooper. It was reportedly a part of his campaign promise in the previous November elections. Certainly, the cost in lives was incongruous with a mere arrest warrant for rustling. The sheriff reportedly experienced nightmares about the gunfight, and the death of the youngest Blevins haunted him. Owens's political fortunes faded, although he continued in law enforcement. He was appointed sheriff of newly formed Navajo County in 1895 and held a commission as a deputy United States marshal.[35]

Rarely did a sheriff who had killed in the line of duty reveal his inner thoughts about this regrettable experience. The public assumed that such men as Commodore Owens "knew no fear." Sheriff Pat Garrett spoke out shortly after he killed Billy the Kid. Garrett was so moved after dime novelists began to twist the circumstances of the shooting against the lawman and to transform the youthful murderer into a hero. Garrett deeply resented the assertion of a San Francisco newspaper that he should be arrested and tried for the murder of the Kid. This journal went so far as to accuse the sheriff of hiding behind Pete Maxwell's bed and shooting the desperado from ambush. Said Garrett in his defense, the outlaw "took me by surprise—gave me no chance on earth to hide." However, the officer admitted that "The Kid got a very much better show [opportunity] than I had intended to give him." Garrett went on to say that he was terribly frightened as he hunted the outlaw. "Scared, Cap? Well, I should say so . . ," he confessed. "I went out [in pursuit] contemplating the probability of being hurt, perhaps killed . . ." he concluded. Such a frank admission from one of the frontier's most famous sheriffs probably echoed the misgivings of many lawmen who were called upon to chase vicious desperadoes.[36]

One of the most persistent myths about frontier lawmen is that some sheriffs went outside the law to protect their constituents.

Presumably, this legend arose in the post-Civil War Southwest when the public often resorted to vigilante tactics against evildoers. Residents of Cochise County, Arizona, asserted that John Horton Slaughter killed fugitives and neglected to report the deaths. Since the sheriff carried out these acts alone, such reports cannot be proven or disproven. James Wolf, an occasional deputy sheriff, recalled one visit of Sheriff Slaughter to Wolf's ranch while in pursuit of an outlaw. Two days later, the well-travelled official returned with the wanted man's horse, but no prisoner. According to Wolf, Slaughter had "insisted on fighting it out" with the badman rather than run the risk of the fugitive escaping on the return trip to Tombstone. Wolf then went on to generalize from this episode and grant Sheriff Slaughter a larger number of "judicial murders":

> Slaughter was killing these bad men just as they had killed so many poor victims, but on more even terms. . . . At all times they had an even break [from the sheriff]. It saved the County excessive witness and court fees and the expense of feeding this element in jail, to say nothing of the possibility of some freak of the law or shyster lawyer getting them freedom.[37]

In addition to James Wolf's numerous rationales for John Slaughter's vigilante-like behavior, popular writers alleged the existence of an overwhelming crime wave in Cochise County in the late 1880s. Just what brought on this descent into lawlessness is difficult to determine. Such writers as Walter Noble Burns praised Wyatt Earp and his brothers for "cleaning up" Tombstone earlier in the decade. The Gunfight at OK Corral was presumably the Earps's crowning law enforcement achievement. In his widely read *Tombstone: An Iliad of the Southwest*, Burns declared that a sort of law enforcement "decadence" set in after the departure of the Wyatt Earp posse:

> This decadent period was notable for a lax administration of law and the absence of strong men at the helm of public affairs. Crime flourished as never before. . . . The criminals were pestiferously active. It was an age of thieves rather than bandits. . . . Though they operated on a small scale, they kept eternally at it. . . . Criminals were showing a disposition to organize. Tombstone was their headquarters, and the town was gradually passing under their domination.

In such adversity, says Burns, Cochise countians sought "a man with the force and courage to handle a serious situation . . ," even if he had to adopt extralegal measures. This man was Sheriff John H. Slaughter.[38]

In the absence of firm evidence, only opinion is left for an assessment of the popular Sheriff Slaughter. Viola Slaughter, wife of the lawman, naturally refused to believe such stories about her husband. In a 1934 interview, she (rightly) maintained that her spouse "killed fewer men than some sheriffs who were almost unknown." However, Allen Erwin, Slaughter's biographer, asserts that Slaughter "never discussed his work with his wife." "Affairs like that [killings] the sheriff would keep to himself," continued Erwin, "at least as far as the ladies were concerned." After John Slaughter's death in 1922, an unnamed friend denied that the famous law officer was "the sort of man we used to call a 'killer.'" "He didn't like to shoot people," continued this anonymous person, but "He did it simply because it was in the day's work, [and] was his duty. . . ." Nor did newspaper reports of the sheriff's daily activities betray hints of official "hits." In April 1887, one Tombstone journalist noted that Slaughter "is doing good work in rounding up horsethieves." Such lawbreakers were allegedly his most common victims on his wilderness rides. Although written evidence is lacking, one gets the impression from the frequency of such reports that Slaughter did not kill indiscriminately, but just as often brought his subjects to the Tombstone jail. It is tempting to conclude that the legend about this lethal sheriff arose from Anglo prejudice. The only victim whom the legend named was Juan Soto, a Mexican or Spaniard. Other infamous desperadoes whom Slaughter pursued were the train-robbing bands of Geronimo and Frederico. Anglo opinion easily sanctioned summary acts of justice against Hispanos and Mexican citizens. Whatever the truth of this matter, Allen Erwin concludes that Slaughter "put the final period to a whole book of violence . . ." in Cochise County.[39]

In spite of some laxity in county government, frontier sheriffs were never absolutely free to kill indiscriminately. Even the Earps were subject to legal charges after the shootout in Tombstone in 1881. There were many counterweights to such wanton acts by lawmen. The threat of lawsuits, grand jury investigations, reelection bids, the Christian ethic, and public opinion acted as restraining forces. When Deputy Sheriff Peter Burleson and Deputy Joseph Holbrook killed two cowboys in Cimarron, New Mexico, friends of the dead men obtained an indictment against Holbrook. The court exonerated the deputy. A short time later, Las Vegas Policeman James Joshua Webb fell prey to the courts after he killed a man who resisted arrest. The jury sentenced Webb to hang. Even though Webb successfully appealed his case, the *Daily New Mexican* opined that this lawman's "fate will carry a lesson" to other lawmen who used their weapons carelessly. "No officer of the law is justified in killing a man," declared this journalist, "when his arrest could be [peacefully] effected. . . ." The writer concluded that the evidence indicated that the Las Vegas officer's use of his weapon "was unnecessary and murderous." When John Henry Thompson, who had occupied the Gila County shrievalty for some eleven years, killed a drinking partner in a Globe saloon, a grand jury indicted him for murder. Thompson was forced to resign from office.[40]

Accidents and injuries were more common than deaths in and around the shrievalty. Since these lawmen handled weapons daily, carelessness and misadventures were frequent. In March 1881, Sheriff Harvey Whitehill's pistol accidentally fell from his coat pocket and discharged upon impact. The bullet struck a bystander and inflicted a serious facial wound. Billy Breakenridge recalled a potentially serious incident in the Cochise County sheriff's office. While leaning against the wall in a chair, he recalled, "a shot was fired so close to me that a grain of powder struck my temple and set the blood running freely." The deputy instantly ran to the office door, thinking that friends of a prisoner were attempting to deliver the inmate. Far from it—"[Sheriff] Behan's pistol had . . . fallen on the floor and accidentally discharged," added Breakenridge. This near-fatal experience taught him a lesson. "I took a cartridge from my pistol and placed the hammer on an empty chamber," he wrote, "and never carried but five shots in it from that time [on]. . . ."[41]

Accidents involving horseback riding and buggies were even more common. Cochise County Sheriff Carlton Kelton experienced an unnerving and bruising experience one day in 1891. While watering his carriage horse in a stream, the animal's hoof became entangled in the dangling harness. The horse panicked, kicked the sheriff on the leg, and ran away. Kelton eventually retrieved the runaway, hooked up the buggy, and resumed the trip, only to have the carriage shafts come loose (evidently weakened in the original accident). The horse broke free again and bolted with the sheriff still grasping the reins. "The horse dragged him about a half mile," said the *Tombstone Epitaph,* before the lawman was able to disengage himself. Mariano Barela, Kelton's counterpart in Doña Ana County, New Mexico, suffered a similar mishap while crossing a canal, or acequia, in January of the same year. His buggy overturned, and the sheriff's foot became entangled in the spokes of a wheel. Barela, who was a hefty man, managed to grasp the reins and restrain the frightened horses until help came along. While riding down a snow-filled street in Prescott in February 1898, Sheriff George Ruffner's horse suddenly "commenced to buck," reported the *Journal-Miner*. The embarrassed officer landed "at full length, life size, back view being obtained, as he lit face upwards." Ruffner's colleague in neighboring Flagstaff had the misfortune to be "bruised up pretty badly" in a train wreck a few months later.[42]

In addition to accidental injuries, the sheriffs sometimes experienced serious wounds at the hands of wanted men. In December 1879, the elderly sheriff of Santa Fe County, Jose D. Sena, ran afoul of a pair of brothers who owned a saloon in Glorieta. "They immediately set upon him," said the *Daily New Mexican*, "beating him unmercifully over the head and other parts of the body and breaking his arm. . . ." After holding Sena prisoner overnight, these brutal siblings released him and fled the county. The *New Mexican* deplored this "unlawful attack upon an officer in [the] discharge of sworn duty" and hoped that the saloon keepers would "be caged" soon. In August 1877, two Lincoln County toughs, Charles Bowdre and Frank Freeman, viciously beat up Sheriff William Brady. Had not bystanders rescued the officer, these bullies would have killed him. James Lowry, chief lawman of Yavapai County, Arizona, received a serious bullet wound in the shoulder. Some weeks were required to recover. John Hixenbaugh, Colfax County sheriff, took a bullet in the leg. Amputation was eventually required.[43]

In spite of the dangerous nature of the shrievalty, surprisingly few occupants died in the line of duty in New Mexico and Arizona territories. It was true that the office did not begin under good auspices. The first sheriff of Taos County, Stephen Lee, was killed by rebels in January 1847. However, the death rate declined dramatically. In September 1871, Yuma County Sheriff James Dana was killed in an attempt to arrest an Indian fugitive. The most notable death in the Southwestern sheriffalty was that of William Brady, whom feudists assassinated on the main street of Lincoln, New Mexico, on 1 April 1878. His death evidently took place not far from where two bravos had beaten him up the year before. Among victimized Arizona sheriffs, the murder of Glenn Reynolds, sheriff of Gila County, caused widespread anger. He was killed by Indians. One of the most calculated murders of a sheriff took place in Eddy County, New Mexico, in January 1897. David Kemp, former chief county lawman, callously shot and killed James Leslie Dow, who had taken the oath of office a few days earlier. Luciano Trujillo, Sheriff of Taos County, became a needless casualty in December 1898. The lawman became drunk during a religious festival and opened fire upon a group of Anglo bar patrons, whom he accused of being disrespectful toward local religious customs. The saloon crowd returned the fire, mortally wounding the sheriff. Other sheriffs died in office, but through suicide or natural death.[44] Information about the motives for suicide is difficult to obtain.

Given the dangers to the sheriffs, it is surprising that more were not killed or injured. These peace officers ran a gamut of malevolent men, and women, throughout the territorial era. As county peace officers, the sheriffs confronted rowdy miners, teamsters, soldiers, and cowhands. While the lawmen generally made arrests without resistance and lodged the culprits in jail for the night, much violence and death resulted as well. In fact, many of the gunmen who later won fame in dime novels, such as the gallery of toughs in Colfax County, New Mexico, earned their spurs in encounters with sheriffs in that region. The task of peace officer was just one aspect of the larger duty of arresting felons and holding them for trial. In spite of the amateurish nature of this frontier office, incumbents demonstrated common sense and surprising imagination in the detection of criminals. If an occasional sheriff refused to carry firearms, this was the exception that proved the rule. The job could be extremely threatening. Few, if any, sheriffs deliberately faced a badman in the classic "duel in the street" so widely publicized in Western fiction. The existence of "killer" sheriffs is also difficult to document, although such men might occasionally occupy the sheriffalty. The vast majority seem to have trudged that conventional middle road. They accepted the realities of lawlessness, and they employed the tried and tested methods of their predecessors. Furthermore, the public maintained certain restraints and safeguards against such evils. In the cases of John Slaughter and Commodore Owens, about whom so much lore exists, the truth may be impossible to uncover. In defense of the use of caution and even callousness in making arrests, it should be remembered that some sheriffs were wounded, and a few died, in the line of duty.

10

Fugitives from Justice

 Arizona and New Mexico territories attracted an unusual number of desperate outlaw bands in the post-Civil War era. This unsavory element had always accompanied the westward movement of productive Americans, but Arizona and New Mexico territories were peculiarly susceptible to roving outlaw bands. The dislocations of the Mexican War and Civil War created a violent element in the Hispanic and Anglo communities. The exaltation of force as a means to settle personal disputes and the proximity of the international boundary also contributed to this lawless condition. Counties were thinly populated and many were enormous—many of them larger than Eastern states—which made it easy for outlaws to congregate in isolated areas. The fact that Arizona and New Mexico offered the last sanctuaries—the ultima Thule of the lawless frontier—for westward drifting fugitives made the confrontation with lawmen even more deadly. As new communities sprang up after the Civil War, they restricted in number and size the havens open to outlaw bands and forced a confrontation between sheriffs and these frontier outcasts. To pursue and arrest or exterminate these toughs—many were prepared to fight—often required more resources than the sheriff could muster and exposed fundamental weaknesses in this ancient office.

The free-ranging outlaws flourished in the wide open spaces of New Mexico and Arizona territories. Since they moved from county to county with ease, the sheriffs were often unable to fix their location. In a message to the New Mexico Assembly in January 1882, Governor Lionel Sheldon remarked about the perplexing nature of outlawry. "Desperadoes and 'rustlers' are migratory in their operations," said Sheldon, and "They seek places where they can best apply their practices." In a letter to Secretary of Interior Henry M. Teller in the following year, the governor attempted to explain the gathering of desperadoes in the counties along the international boundary. Not only were there few villages, but "the physical characteristics of the country render . . . pursuit . . . a matter of great labor and expense." The "Sheriffs and constables live a great distance from the line. . . ," said Sheldon in conclusion. An Arizona newsman added the observation that these roving criminals were men "without a country" and answered only to their own code. In describing the hermit-like habits of Thomas "Black Jack" Ketchum and his comrades, one observer noted that they "rarely go into a town, and spend all their time in the bush on ranches, where they are not likely to be found." They were "known to the officers as bushmen," concluded the writer. In describing one member of this band, Will Carver, the *San Angelo Standard* (Texas) noted that he was very shy and "preferred to dwell in the solitudes of the great southwestern plains, with a few choice spirits." Aside from an occasional visit to a saloon or redlight district (which often compromised them), these nomadic highwaymen sought the remotest mountain or desert fastness.[1]

Such badmen were uncommon in the highly concentrated communities of the East. In June 1892, a Santa Fe journalist editorialized upon the attraction of the frontier to this lawless element:

> In one form or another crime is to be expected on the frontier outposts of all countries, for usually the bad men of the land, unable to rest in anything like peace elsewhere, take refuge in these sparsely settled districts. . . . In a measure this is true of many sections of the west to-day. In the thinly populated communities of western Texas; in the newly opened sections of the Indian Territory; in the new northwestern states and in the budding, booming mining towns of Colorado, and elsewhere in the west, this is true, and New Mexico is no exception to the rule. . . . There are men in every community [in New Mexico], men who think little more of taking human life than they do of taking their breakfast. . . .

In an ironic turn of events, highway robbers and other parasitical persons thrived to a greater degree as the population and material wealth of New Mexico and Arizona increased after the Civil War. There was just more to steal.[2]

These desperadoes brazenly defied the sheriffs and even sent them taunting messages. Bill Brazleton, one of the most vicious lone wolf bandits in southern Arizona, threatened Sheriff Charles Shibell, while Lincoln County outlaws conveyed a similar note to George Kimbrell. "You son of a bitch," wrote an anonymous desperado, "you had as well pass in your checks for you have not got many days before you will git one of these boxes. . . ." The outlaw affixed an outline drawing of a coffin. "God dam[n] you why don't you send your Heel Flys [militia] out after men," the bandit continued, "and see how fast they will bring them [highwaymen] in." When Socorro County Deputy Sheriff Joel Fowler pursued a band of cattle thieves in 1883, these audacious pilferers wrote him an intimidating letter. Deputy Sheriff R. P. Gaddis, who informed Governor Sheldon of this unusual event, said the rustlers promised "not to interfere with his [Fowler's] cattle but . . . that they have 'softer snaps' . . ." to steal. Just after the turn of the century, Henry Hawkins and the "Mesa Hawks" bluntly informed Otero County Sheriff James Hunter that they were prepared to kill or be killed should he interfere with their movements.[3]

Veteran bandits carefully planned their movements. Matt Warner, a Utah outlaw who conducted forays into Arizona, recalled that he and his comrades "never thought of venturing into a flight from the law . . . without a pack animal, light camp outfit, provisions, and [extra] saddle horses. . . ." Warner and his friends "laughed at officers that didn't know enough to come prepared for a long journey." These criminals knew the trails, sanctuaries, and watering places along their escape routes. Access to water was especially important to both pursuer and pursued. Joe Pearce, a veteran deputy sheriff and Arizona Ranger, learned this through experience. "If the trailer is familiar with the country," said Pearce, "he knows the location of the various watering places. . . ." In the parched mountains and desertlands, continued this manhunter, the man on the run "has to make for a water hole." In June 1900, the Phoenix *Arizona Republican* criticized sheriffs in the southern counties of New Mexico and Arizona for failing to use their knowledge of the desert's few springs as a means to corral roving outlaws. "Water holes are few and far between," he pointed out, and "pursuers and pursued alike know where they are and it is absolutely known where the fugitives must stop." This knowledge should enable lawmen to employ the element of surprise against the desperadoes. In New Mexico, Governor Sheldon had similar thoughts about the use of water holes to curb rustler bands along the border with Mexico.[4]

Like the cagey outlaw, the experienced sheriff refused to dash unprepared into wilderness. In August 1892, residents of Phoenix criticized Sheriff John Montgomery for hesitating to bolt into the desert after suspected murderer Ed Tewksbury. The *Daily Herald* reminded readers that Montgomery "knows the climate and country too well to rush out pell mell into the desert." Furthermore, the accused killer was prepared "for a long chase into his own mountain fastness and among his friends and supporters." As a local justice of the peace pointed out, Tewksbury had staked out "blooded horses" along his escape route. These animals "will go 100 miles where our alfalfa fed horses will not go 25. . . ." When Texas ranchers dispatched a posse to assist the Lincoln County sheriff in the hunt for Billy the Kid in late 1880, these manhunters were well outfitted for a prolonged stay. They took extra horses, a cook, and "a chuck wagon with four good mules to pull it," recalled member Charles Siringo. Lawmen in Tucumcari County, New Mexico, did likewise in February 1902. Before going into the dangerous Redondo Mesa country, the posse obtained the latest Winchester rifles and steel-jacketed cartridges as well as "a four-mule 'grub' wagon."[5]

To track fugitive outlaw bands into remote hideaways required much skill, and the sheriffs employed many different methods. While horses left very obvious hoofprints and men left "signs," the more clever and artful fugitives took measures to throw off pursuers. Tom Rynning, Captain of the Arizona Rangers, described the art of trailing:

> Say you're following a trail across country. You dasn't keep your eyes on the ground all the time or some bad man you're tracking will get the drop on you and blow your head off. The trail, say, is heading in a certain direction. You take a long slant along that way without losing time looking at tracks, for you know as a rule a man trying to get away don't make many sudden turns. Then there's such things as passes ahead that you know he'll have to head for, and lot of [other] things to consider.

If the manhunter lost the trail, "then you begin quartering . . ." or "cutting sign." That is, continued Rynning, the tracker rides "in circles till you pick it [the trail] up again." In addition to hard work and common sense, Rynning also believed that "There's a lot of hunch or clairvoyance, . . . to a real tracker's mental layout." Many lawmen accorded Indian and Hispano trackers top honors. Juan Elias, who was Mexican and Indian, won applause for an "unexplained instinct" to trail outlaws, according to John P. Gray, a Cochise County deputy sheriff. Caesario Lucero, who served as a deputy sheriff in the same county in the 1880s, won equal commendation for tracking several vicious outlaw bands. Vindictive badmen finally assassinated Lucero for his successful efforts.[6]

The sheriffs also employed informants as a means to trace criminal movements, although with uneven success. Pat Garrett assigned Deputy Barney Mason the task of infiltrating the Billy the Kid aggregation. Mason was acquainted with this rustler group. In summer 1885, Nathan Appel, veteran Pima County deputy, hired a member of the Chinese community "to ferret out the whereabouts of one Wong Jey Gee." When the culprit was located, Appel and his informant made the arrest. "The whole affair was quietly and nicely done . . ." concluded a local journalist. John Slaughter planted a Hispano, Victoriano Sandoval, in the band of Geronimo, a vicious Mexican train robber (not to be confused with the Apache chief). However, Geronimo kept such a close vigil over his subordinates that Sandoval was unable to communicate with the sheriff. A deputy sheriff's posse eventually killed Geronimo and liberated the informant. A similar plan by Valencia County sheriff Carlos Baca ended tragically. Although Baca succeeded in planting a mole in a group that planned a robbery in Grants, in neighboring McKinley County, the lawman failed to alert McKinley law officers as to the informant's identity. When these officers ambushed the highwaymen, they killed Sheriff Baca's spy![7]

Bloodhounds were another device, although their record was not impressive. Given the Southwesterners' love of big-game hunting, their affinity for dogs came naturally. Montague Stevens, a transplanted Englishman, became a noted canine aficionado in New Mexico. In a discussion of his bear-hunting exploits, *Meet Mister Grizzly,* Stevens noted that a human being leaves two trails, physical footprints and body scent. Therefore, manhunter and dog complimented each other, since the former followed the footprints by sight, while the bloodhound followed the scent. The dogs had their limitations, as a Santa Fe newspaperman pointed out. They could follow a trail only up to thirty-six hours old and then only over ordinary ground. The animals were ineffectual in sandy or desert regions. After an outbreak of robbery in Arizona in 1898, one observer concluded that the sheriffs had reduced the manhunting qualities of bloodhounds by taking them on rabbit hunts. The writer could not resist this opportunity for a jab at the lawmen, who had failed to capture the outlaws. "Wonder if the officers have been rabbit hunting too?" he asked. Elsewhere, when dogs were set on the trail of badmen, they were unsuccessful or poorly managed. Sheriff Holm O. Bursum's possee placed bloodhounds on the wrong

trail in a chase after Bronco Bill Walters and others escaped the Socorro jail in 1896.[8]

Sheriff's personnel selected armaments with care and presented
an imposing figure in full panoply. Weaponry included a handgun,
shotgun, and rifle with the latter weapon holding a central place in
this arsenal. Outlaws avoided close-in engagements when possible.
The Winchester Arms Manufacturing Company produced a widely
used rifle, although more powerful European-made varieties became available about the turn of the century. High velocity, smokeless powder cartridges also made both lawman and badman much
more lethal. In 1898, Prescott sportsmen tested a new bullet that
penetrated a thirty-four inch pine tree at forty yards. Shotguns were
effective at shorter range, but created a much wider pattern on the
target than the rifle. Personnel of the Yavapai County sheriff's office
used one particular shotgun to kill one felon at 115 yards and on
another occasion to wound a fugitive at 95 yards. Deputy Sheriff
J. J. Rascoe of Roswell, New Mexico, appeared very intimidating in
full equipage:

> He had [wrote one observer] scabbards strapped to either side of his
> saddle. In one he carried a sawed-off double-barreled 12-gauge shot-
> gun; in the other he had a Winchester 30-30 repeating rifle, known
> to old-timers as a 'saddle gun' because it had a shorter barrel than the
> ordinary high-powered hunting rifle. On his left hip . . . he wore a
> regulation double-action Colt 45.

While an occasional sheriff might sport a pair of revolvers, the
"two-gun sheriff" was largely myth.[9]

The choice of a weapon appropriate to the situation gave the
sheriff a definite advantage in gun battles. Inexperience or haste to
take up the pursuit could lead to tragic circumstances. On man-
hunts, the long-ranged rifle was regarded as superior to the pistol.
An especially tragic example of rifle-over-revolver took place in Valencia County, New Mexico, in 1898. When Bronco Bill Walters,
Daniel "Red" Pipkin, and William "Kid" Johnson robbed a train
near Belen, deputy sheriffs Francisco Vigil, Dan Bustamente, and
two Indian trailers took up immediate chase. In his haste to get the
pursuit underway, Vigil had armed his men only with revolvers.
This was an incredible oversight and possibly a sign of inexperience.
The Walters band was as hard a lot as any in the territories and
would take double delight in ambushing Hispano and Indian pursuers. When Deputy Vigil came upon the outlaws at daybreak and

ordered them to surrender, he made the mistake of issuing this command while still out of effective pistol range. Bronco Bill and his companions opened up a withering rifle fire which killed Vigil, Bustamente, and one trailer. A dispatch to the Denver *Rocky Mountain News* praised Vigil's bravery but concluded that he "took too many chances." "There was not a single Winchester [rifle] in his posse . . . ," observed this writer, while the outlaws "were fully armed with improved rifles." When Sheriff Jesus Sanches, Vigil's superior, arrived at the site of the shooting—still known today as the "shooting ground"—the bodies of his men were already decomposing. The saddened sheriff buried them on the spot.[10]

On other occasions, the sheriffs possessed the best weaponry for a fight with highwaymen. In 1889, Yavapai County Sheriff Buckey O'Neill and posse chased a band of train robbers into Utah before overtaking them. The lawmen's rifles quickly overawed the bandits, who only carried pistols. Years later, Dan Harvick, one of the robbers, recalled his one and only essay into banditry and the reason they were so poorly armed. They "did not want to excite suspicion" when they gathered at Canyon Diablo, Arizona, the robbery site. When men sported rifles, the public regarded them with suspicion. "We had made a mistake," admitted the chastened outlaw. In May of the previous year, a Duncan, Arizona, peace officer reaffirmed this rule in armaments. A prisoner had broken out of the local jail, armed himself with a revolver, and fled down the street. In reporting the incident, the *Silver City Enterprise* pointed out that the escapee's revolver was inferior in range to the lawman's Winchester rifle. This longer ranged shoulder weapon permitted the officer to fire at the felon "without exposing him [the sheriff] to danger." The escapee was killed in the exchange.[11]

Some of the most difficult criminal elements to detect in the remote hideaways of Arizona and New Mexico were cattle rustlers and sheep thieves. These livestock pilferers knew the land intimately, and the sheriff's meager resources in manpower severely limited his ability to patrol ranches that were often 50 or 100 miles away. To assist the cattlemen, the lawman deputized ranchers whom rustlers had just victimized. This gave them official color in the particular chase. The sheriff also commissioned employees—sometimes the range foreman—of larger ranches. Even though these officers could serve only part time, the presence of such official representatives in cattle country enabled the chief county lawman "to show the flag" of office at roundups. These deputies paid off when outlaws put in appearances at remote chuckwagons for food and companionship. Grant County Sheriff James Lockhart assigned a deputy, Victor Culberson, to the roundup in the Black Range in August 1891. Culberson spotted James Gould, a prison escapee wanted for robbery and cattle theft. The deputy earned a $125 reward for this arrest.[12]

Not until cattlemen organized associations in the 1880s did the rustlers begin to feel some pressure. The cattlemen's associations required registration of brands and membership fees. They employed stock detectives who were devoted full time to the study of the stock thieves' modus operandi. The stockmen also persuaded the territorial assemblies to enact tougher laws to protect brands and to require record keeping for the sale and purchase of livestock. Butcher shops and slaughter houses were required to document their business transactions and to retain hides for fixed periods of time. The sheriffs usually welcomed these associations and cooperated fully by deputizing stock detectives. These cattlemen's organizations also provided posses for sheriffs to invade the domains of the thieves. Such incursions usually took place when the big companies became sufficiently aroused to action against dens of thieves. Stockmen continued to complain about cattle and horse theft throughout the territorial era even though some sheriffs were able to assign permanent "range deputies" to troubled districts.[13]

In many wilderness chases, the sheriffs depended heavily upon the support of the citizenry in the form of the *posse comitatus* ("the power of the county"). Usually referred to as the "posse," this force consisted of all able-bodied adult males of the county. The codes of both New Mexico and Arizona territories required such service. The latter territory's law provided that:

> any sheriff, deputy-sheriff, coroner, or constable may require suitable aid in the service of process [of court] in civil or criminal cases, in preserving the peace, or in apprehending or securing any person for felony or breach of the peace when such officer may have power to perform such a duty.

The law provided for a fine for noncompliance. Sheriffs employed citizen possemen in all the areas referred to in the statutes, although the lawmen did so knowing the shortcomings of these amateur policemen. In spite of today's exalted notions about the superior qualities of the typical frontiersmen, the average man could not always be counted upon in confrontations with hardened criminals. Many did not possess durable horses and weapons appropriate to long-distance pursuits. Not everyone agreed to serve, in spite of the posse statutes. Deputy Sheriff Billy Breakenridge recalled that posses were often hastily formed from saloon hangers-on. He scoffed at these "pick-up" posses. Tom Horn, a veteran army packer and Gila County deputy sheriff, was equally contemptuous of the typical Arizona posse. In 1896, Horn counseled United States Marshal William Kidder Meade against the use of such a posse in a search for bandits in southern Arizona. "Any posse you could get . . . ," wrote Horn, "could not accomplish any thing. . . ."[14]

Regardless of such misgivings, sheriffs continued to call citizens to posse duty. Some responded with enthusiasm. Many residents of these pioneer communities were accustomed to civic services in tightly knit villages in the Eastern states or in Europe. In 1889, bandits ambushed the paymaster of the Vulture Mine near Wickenburg, Arizona. They needlessly murdered him and two guards. In Phoenix, Sheriff Bud Gray quickly organized a posse. D. J. W. Huntington happened to be walking downtown at the time. He recalled hearing the town crier summon the men whom Gray desired "to join a posse being formed at the Sheriff's office. . . ." Three days later, he watched as this force returned "with a wagon carrying the corpse of a Mexican [robber] and the stolen bullion. . . ." Citizens of Globe, in neighboring Gila County, sprang into action when highwaymen held up the Wells Fargo pack train in 1882. "Three taps of the bell of the Methodist Church, repeated at intervals," said one writer, "brought the citizens of Globe together. . . ." Such expressions of local patriotism were not uncommon, especially in isolated mining camps. While the reasons for calls to posse duty were often to be deplored, they did give the inhabitants an opportunity to express community solidarity in a very insecure frontier world.[15]

Whatever doubts the sheriff harbored about the reliability of citizen possemen, the casualty rate among them indicated a high degree of devotion to service. An especially tragic loss took place in Apache County, Arizona. On 27 March 1900, outlaws ambushed and killed Gus Gibbons and Frank Lesueur. The young men were riding cross-country to join Sheriff Edward Beeler's posse but inadvertently stumbled into the desperadoes' camp. Dick Gibbons, uncle of one of the victims, described finding the bodies in the rugged badlands of eastern Arizona:

I saw an object on the steep hillside that startled me. It looked like the body of a man, but I would not admit it to myself. . . . I saw another object that looked like a quilt had been thrown away by the outlaws and had been rolled up by the wind and lodged in the wash where it now laid, but as we drew nearer, I saw that it was the body of a man, and upon closer inspection, I recognized it as the body of my nephew, Gus Gibbons. It was lying in the bottom of a little draw with head down hill and face upwards, with three ghastly bullet holes through the head. . . . In addition to these he had several wounds in the body. . . .

Gibbons could not erase this horrific experience from his mind. "They were just in the pink of manhood and for them to be ambushed and shot down like dogs," continued this anguished uncle, "made me sick." Although Sheriff Beeler made an extensive search for the murderers, he failed to capture them. There were many other instances of deaths among possemen in both territories. In the period 1896–1901 alone, at least twelve men died performing posse service. Aside from a eulogy in the newspaper, neither the county nor the territory provided assistance to stricken families of deceased possemen.[16]

A cooperative spirit did not always prevail, and some elements obstructed the lawmen's pursuit of badmen. Society in Arizona and New Mexico consisted of a patchwork of insecure and often mutually hostile communities. Whether American citizens or Mexican aliens, the Hispanics resented Anglo peace officers. As Deputy Sheriff Pat Garrett tracked the Billy the Kid band through the Spanish-speaking communities of northern Lincoln and southern San Miguel counties in late 1880, he had great difficulty. The inhabitants regarded the young outlaw as something of a hero. Even after the outlaw's death in 1881, the residents of this region continued to shield other badmen, Mariano Leyba and Manuel Aragon. Sheriff John Poe had great difficulty in the hunt for Aragon, who had murdered two of his deputies. Likewise, Augustin Chacon eluded Graham County sheriffs for three years, in part because the Mexican immigrant community of Clifton-Morenci protected the convicted murderer.[17]

On the cattle ranges, the largely Anglo herders often refused to divulge information. While otherwise law-abiding, they feared retribution. Les Dow, Sheriff-elect of Eddy County, New Mexico, led a posse in pursuit of train robbers into Grant County in November 1896. Dow later informed the *El Paso Daily Times* that the desperadoes "have more friends out there than the officers." Such hostility toward posses was motivated not only by fear of the bandits but contained a political ingredient as well. In the late 1880s and 1890s, lawmen frequently complained about a general reluctance of small farmers and ranchers—of all ethnic groups—to provide information. Such public hostility was a result of political alienation from the "establishment." Common people deeply resented the excessive profits and political power of big economic institutions—railroads, and mining and cattle companies—and demonstrated their discontent by providing bandits with sanctuary. As a Southern Pacific Railroad detective, Billy Breakenridge recalled how the company "was rather unpopular with the people" of southern Arizona in the 1890s and that "whenever a train was held up a great many sympathized with the robbers."[18]

Many other forces worked against an effective penetration of bandit lairs. The organization and financing of the sheriffalties combined to hinder such activities. The new and sparsely populated counties lacked a solid tax base, which translated into a poorly financed local government. A wide gulf separated the sheriff from the county board in the matter of pursuit of fugitives from justice. The absence of a "line item" marked "expenses of pursuit" in the board's annual allowance to the sheriff explained much of the lawman's problem. To him, the presence of roving fugitives was rather routine, a common occurrence. To the county commissioners, outlawry was an exceptional event, and they preferred to deal with the expenses of a posse on a case-by-case basis. When the need arose, the sheriff had to appeal to the board for funds, if they existed. The sheriff assumed responsibility—under the law, he was perhaps obligated to mount pursuit immediately—and then informed the county commissioners of his action. However, he had no assurances that the county officials would approve this expense. If the sheriff had personal or political enemies on the board, they might delight in embarrassing him with a rejection. Or, the county treasury might be empty. The board also required receipts for posse expenses, even in the field, where gathering them was difficult, if not impossible. In August 1897, the Yavapai County supervisors passed a resolution to this effect as a means to control the expense account of Sheriff George Ruffner. In May 1900, the *Lordsburg Liberal* summed up the attitude of county boards toward posse expenses. Experience had demonstrated the inability of the sheriffs to run down bands of outlaws in southern New Mexico and Arizona. The reason for this, said the writer, was that the county paid the sheriff only for successful pursuit and not for failure. This journalist recommended the creation of territorial ranger forces for anti-outlaw operations.[19]

In the absence of a permanent "pursuit" expense account, the sheriffs combatted free-ranging, nomadic outlaws under the traditional fee system. The law provided a fixed sum (eventually one dollar), plus mileage, for the service of a warrant upon a fugitive from justice. The lawman earned this same amount for presentation to a single, inoffensive suspect or a violent band of hardened criminals. Obviously, this system of remuneration failed to take into consideration the peculiar circumstances of horseback outlaws in the frontier territories of the United States. To look forward to the prospects of one dollar, plus mileage, for each attempt to serve a warrant on a murderous fugitive—Bronco Bill Walters, for instance—was insufficient incentive. What the sheriff needed was a permanent fund for the purposes of supporting not only his personnel but posses. While public discussions of such shortcomings in the shrievalty did not arise, newspapers occasionally hinted at these problems. During Governor Lionel Sheldon's militia campaign against rustlers in southern New Mexico, some newspapers criticized the sheriffs for failure to run down the thieves. In May 1883, a Grant County rancher defended the sheriffs through the *Silver City Enterprise*. While this anonymous writer approved of Sheldon's use of the territorial soldiers, he pointed out that "neither county nor territory allows mileage, or pay enough for a sheriff or constable to go over a few miles from his residence to serve a writ of any kind. . . ." The inadequacy of this funding process also extended to support for the sheriff's retrieval of fugitives from neighboring states and foreign lands.[20]

To a frustrated sheriff, the immediate shortcomings of the budgeting process were most apparent. However, an ancient heritage and the prejudices of the American founders provided a more long-term explanation for the lawman's problems. The hardheaded revolutionaries who formulated (or merely retained) the English ideals of law enforcement assumed that most citizens were law-abiding and that the county sheriffs did not require any additional resources beyond those inherited from their ancestors. Furthermore, malcontents who broke the law in the Atlantic coast states could not (or would not) flee any distance from the crime scene. The close-knit society of the East Coast, like ancestral England, imposed strong moral restraints upon passions that were likely to lead to lawbreaking. The existence of the Indian frontier west of the Appalachian Mountains at the end of the eighteenth century also discouraged flight. Only the most incorrigible wrongdoers would flee to the frontier. The Indians could have them. The founders of this country obviously did not envision a republic encompassing the continent and including the vast desert Southwest. They could not have imagined how ill prepared the shrievalty was for the vast and thinly populated territories of the future century.[21]

In the late 1890s, Socorro County Sheriff Holm Olaf Bursum reached the point of distraction in his efforts to fund posses. In July 1897, the sheriff explained to rancher William S. French that he had exhausted all resources in the pursuit of the Black Jack Christian band:

> I am sure that I can get every man of them [outlaws] if there was only some means to pay the expenses of keeping the search up, but the county has no available means that could be used for this purpose and I cannot personally afford to stand the expense any longer, in as much as the county is unable to do anything towards defraying the expenses. . . .

In a subsequent letter, Bursum asked for private contributions:

> It has been suggested that money might be raised by subscription, and I thought perhaps you might feel disposed to do something regarding paying the expenses of keeping a posse after the [Black Jack] outfit until I get them. I dislike very much to have to call on citizens in this way . . . , but conditions are such that if the expense of continuing the case is not raised in this way it will be impossible to successfully accomplish anything.

Evidently, French and other cattlemen in the western precincts rejected Bursum's request. In an ironic twist, French was unwittingly employing members of one of the most active train-robbing aggregations in the West, Butch Cassidy's Wild Bunch.[22]

The presence of such lawless bands embarrassed the citizens of New Mexico and Arizona territories, but the cost of eradicating them was very high. The burden of financing pursuit fell primarily upon the counties, since support from the territorial legislatures was sporadic and minimal. The sheriffs obtained funds occasionally through relief legislation, to include repayment for private expenses and rewards. When Sheriff Buckey O'Neill became involved in a dispute with Yavapai County and the Arizona territorial authorities over a claim for posse expenses in 1889, this controversy aired the many shortcomings in law enforcement funding. A Tucson journalist pointed out that the costs of effective enforcement of the laws might be excessive. In a new country such as Arizona, explained this writer, the sheriffs often tracked outlaws hundreds of miles. "The cost of maintaining order and peace come very high . . . ," he continued, but "it [is] worth the price." New Mexico Governor Lionel Sheldon pointed out to lawmakers that the territory paid a big price for failure to provide lawmen with a "right and proper" remuneration—outbreaks of vigilante justice.

> The officers of justice in this territory have been generally [poorly?] recompensed and too often Judge Lynch has been called to its aid. Encourage and support [with funds] our officers of the law and confidence in them will exist; their work will be well done, and people will cease to look to lawless courts for vengeance upon criminals. . . .[23]

The reward system offered some hope as a means to remunerate lawmen in the hunt for badmen. William Blackstone, the famous eighteenth-century English jurist, believed the purpose of rewards was "to encourage further the apprehending of certain felons." America's founders regarded rewards as means "to induce *private citizens* to observe the law," by encouraging good people to divulge information about law breakers. While authorities did not admit it, rewards also appealed to greedy instincts and brought out unscrupulous natures. The territorial assemblies of Arizona and New Mexico made regular appropriations for rewards. The governors, who managed these funds, normally announced rewards of $25 to $500, depending upon the gravity of the crime. They occasionally offered more. In 1891, Governor L. Bradford Prince posted a $2500 bounty for the assassins of ex-Sheriff Frank Chavez in Santa Fe. The legislature posted even greater sums for the murderers of lawyer Albert J. Fountain in Doña Ana County five years later. Other sources of rewards included United States agencies, cities and counties, private citizens, fraternal orders, and private businesses.[24]

The sheriffs may have been strong believers in the effectiveness of rewards, but there were many problems associated with them. In January 1888, Pinal County Sheriff Jere Fryer remarked to the governor of Arizona that "a suitable reward" for a fugitive murderer would "undoubtedly make officers along the [international] line more vigilant." In July 1889, Deputy Sheriff James Speedy informed Pima County Sheriff Matthew Shaw that an informant "will deliver him [a fugitive] up for pay of $300 cash or no [arrest] . . ." will be made. Delays in payments were common, as three claimants in Doña Ana County learned in March 1853. In response to their appeal, Governor William Carr Lane attempted to reassure them. "I promise you," said Lane, "that I will 'leave no stone unturned,' to get you the money." Rival claimants for the same reward often confused the distribution process. Wells Fargo Detective Fred Dodge became angry with a colleague, Charles Thacker, who unjustly steered a company reward to an undeserving man in 1887. Dodge deplored Thacker's reputation for "Manipulations of Reward Money." Chancery court settlements were sometimes necessary in contested reward cases. The Southern Pacific Railroad arranged for former Grant County Sheriff Harvey Whitehill to file suit against the company as a means to persuade other claimants to come forward in one reward case.[25]

While a few sheriffs earned some reward money, very few profitted from such bounties. Donald Moorman, who studied the shrievalty of Holm O. Bursum in Socorro County, New Mexico, concluded that his reward earnings added only $50 to $100 to his annual income. Such a paltry sum dissuaded most lawmen from devoting an excessive amount of time to the search for head money. There is little, if any, evidence that lawmen became professional "bounty hunters." In one instance, Jim Herron, who was wanted for murder in Oklahoma Territory, was surprised to learn that the $2,000 reward for him did not bring out the greed of an Arizona sheriff. John Henry Thompson, longtime sheriff of Gila County, said to Herron and his brother, "'I'm not interested in blood money.'" Such an attitude of restraint belied charges of critics, such as the *Daily New Mexican,* that the sheriffs deliberately delayed manhunts until rewards were posted, or even more, until they were inflated to an attractive amount. In 1895, the same paper commented favorably upon a Denver *Field and Farm* article which blamed sheriffs of the Rocky Mountain states and territories for an increase in stock thievery. When Governor William T. Thornton joined in this hostile chorus in May 1896, the Las Vegas *Daily Optic* took an extreme step and accused New Mexico sheriffs of lacking the esprit de corps so common in the states. This editor declared that when the governor refused the request of a sheriff that a reward be increased, the officer "is humiliated." "There is a pride of office . . ." among sheriffs in the East, said the *Optic,* which causes them "to endure every possible hardship." Such a spirit did not prevail in New Mexico, according to this writer. He hoped that the sheriffs would arouse themselves and do their duty.[26]

The sheriffs played a key part in pursuit of fugitive bands, but these lawmen were not alone. Other agencies provided valuable assistance. The territorial governor held a unique place in the network of law enforcement agencies and provided many services. He proclaimed rewards and served as a clearinghouse for information about the movements of desperadoes. With the arrival of the telegraph (and later railroad and telephone) network, he was able to step up this process measurably. When Miguel A. Otero, newly appointed governor of New Mexico, received information that the Black Jack Ketchum band had established a camp near Cimarron in the summer of 1897, he immediately "notified the sheriffs of Colfax and Taos counties." The outlaws were probably planning a train robbery. Unfortunately, the county officers failed to maintain a close surveillance, and the desperadoes stopped a train near Clayton in the following September. Governor Edmund Ross, who preceded Otero by a few years, was not above using the prestige of his office to cajole Don Jesus Luna, sheriff of Valencia County, into the pursuit of a suspected murderer. In this instance, the suspect was Hispanic and Ross hinted that Luna might be hesitating out of sympathy for one of his own community. Whereas the governor had used his influence to prod Anglo sheriffs to do their duty where sheepmen—that is, Hispanos—were the victims, Ross reminded Don Jesus Luna that "it is your duty, to thoroughly investigate this case. . . ." The territorial executive also played a critical part in facilitating the extradition process, although the vast distances, poor communications, and petty jealousies between states and territories and with the Republic of Mexico made the retrieval of fugitives very difficult.[27]

The relations between New Mexico Territory and her neighbors in extradition matters were very uneven, although they improved with time. Colorado authorities sometimes haughtily ignored proper procedure and at other times cooperated fully. In July 1867, an official in Denver denied a New Mexico extradition request on very suspicious grounds. In the next line of the letter, this official inquired about the reward in the case. The Rocky Mountain Detective Agency of Denver kidnapped four accused murderers from New Mexico in 1875. Thereafter, the agency abided by the extradition law, but operatives complained that the paperwork "consumed a greater part of the night." This process could be swift. On 20 August 1876, the sheriff of Conejos County, Colorado, telegraphed Governor Samuel Axtell in Santa Fe that he had arrested Porter Stockton, wanted for murder in Colfax County, New Mexico. On the following day, Sheriff Isaiah Rinehart wired Axtell: "Send Requisition on Governor of Colorado for Porter Stockton . . . to deliver him to me or a deputy. . . ." Territorial Secretary William G. Ritch mailed the document seven days later. Within ten days, Rinehart presented the fugitive in person to district court in Taos where he was to be tried. "The prompt action of the Colorado authorities, and of Sheriff Rinehart," the *Daily New Mexican* applauded, "is highly commendable."[28]

The long, very remote border between New Mexico and Arizona became infamous as a stronghold for outlaw bands and the location of a segment of the "Outlaw Trail," a corridor that reportedly extended from Canada to Mexico. Yet, the presence of the legitimate cattle, sheep, and mining companies along this line imposed responsibilities upon the affected territories to attempt to extradite fugitives. T. S. Bunch, District Attorney of Apache County, Arizona, sought to explain the border problem to Governor John Irwin in February 1891. "The trouble we have here in many [criminal] cases," said the frustrated lawyer, "is we are near the New Mexico line. . . ." When outlaws "get into New Mexico," he continued, it "is almost impossible to [return] them here . . ." for trial. Bunch noted that Apache County Sheriff O. B. Little was "actively engaged in locating [fugitive] parties" in neighboring New Mexico, and he went on to ask that Irwin provide Little with the necessary assistance to retrieve wanted men. Financial problems also beset the authorities in this border county. When Little's predecessor, St. George Creaghe, desired to extradite a felon from New Mexico, the Apache County Board of Supervisors refused to pay expenses. "If there is no pay for running down criminals that cross the territorial line," he grumbled, "the criminal is in luck."[29]

Some extradition cases transcended mere violations of the law, and the sheriffs found themselves embroiled in complicated political problems. Pedro Simpson, who presided over the Socorro County shrievalty during the intrusion of big cattle companies, encountered forces beyond his control as he attempted to extradite Timothy "Longhair Jim" Courtright and James McIntire from Texas in 1884. Although both men were former Socorro County deputy sheriffs and deputy United States marshals, they were accused of murdering two homesteaders. The two men flaunted their freedom, and Courtright even opened a detective agency. When a Simpson deputy traveled to Fort Worth to arrest Courtright in April 1884, a mob prevented the extradition. The Texans protested that the New Mexicans would lynch the accused man. Not until January 1886 did the new Socorro County sheriff, Charles Russell, reclaim the fugitive. By that time, critical witnesses had wandered away, and the jury exonerated Longhair Jim. Jim McIntire was never tried. Many people suspected that powerful political forces were at work behind the scenes in this, and another, controversial extradition case. The attempt of Pima County Sheriff Robert H. Paul to persuade Colorado authorities to reclaim Wyatt Earp and John H. "Doc" Holliday for trial in Arizona met the cold shoulder. These two men, former deputy sheriffs and deputy United States marshals, in Cochise County, Arizona, were indicted for the murder of Frank Stillwell, also a former deputy sheriff. In Denver, Governor Frederick Pitkin expressed the fear that a lynch mob awaited the fugitives. As a means to prevent the extradition of Doc Holliday, friends of the fugitive trumped up a minor charge against him in Colorado. Although rumor alleged that much influence was brought to bear upon Pitkin, this incident has never been fully explained. Sheriff Paul returned to Tucson emptyhanded.[30]

If the Arizona-New Mexico border presented difficulties in the pursuit of fugitives, the boundary with the Republic of Mexico was an even greater aggravation. Even though the United States Government had the primary responsibility for security between the two countries, the New Mexico and Arizona sheriffs whose counties rested upon the line still encountered many perplexing problems. The process of extraditing wanted men from Mexico ranged from very difficult to impossible throughout the territorial era, depending upon the status of relations between the two republics. Not until 1862 did the United States succeed in persuading Mexico City to sign an extradition treaty. Even then, this much desired document failed to require either side to submit its nationals to extradition. In spite of this handicap, the two countries managed periods of cordiality and cooperation along the international boundary.[31]

The sheriffs were often perplexed by lawbreakers who made their escape into the neighboring Mexican states of Sonora or Chihuahua. Such flights were facilitated by towns such as Mesilla, Las Cruces, Silver City, Tucson, and Yuma being within easy horseback rides of the border. John Spring, who served as a deputy sheriff in Tucson in the 1870s, recalled that a well-mounted felon could ride the eighty miles from the Pima County seat into Mexico in only twelve hours. Badmen planned their getaways with this fact in mind. When Howard Chenoweth killed a policeman in Silver City, New Mexico, in 1904, friends of the shootist set up a relay of horses to enable him to make the seventy-mile sprint to the border so speedily that Grant County Sheriff James K. Blair's pursuit was completely out-distanced. Chenoweth was never brought to justice.[32]

The officials of both countries were often frustrated by the protracted and tedious extradition process. While the hindrances were not always insuperable, and many fugitives were so retrieved, the bureaucratic requirements were time consuming. In March 1902, Sheriff John L. Munds of Yavapai County, Arizona, spent two weeks in the southern republic in an effort to extradite a stagecoach robber, William Royal Curtis. When Munds eventually learned that as much as sixty days would be required, he returned home without his prey. When Arizona authorities encountered another such delay in the following year, one journalist lamented the absence of Colonel Emilio Kosterlitzky, commander of Mexican *rurales* (rural police) from Sonora. This legendary officer, who often assisted Arizona sheriffs in the circumvention of such delays, was temporarily away from his post.[33]

The sheriffs sometimes permitted their impatience to get the best of them and entered Mexico without the proper authority. Officials in the sister republic could not permit such indiscretions to go unnoticed. In February 1873, a Chihuahuan judge refused to turn over two Mexican citizens wanted by Grant County Sheriff James J. Crittenden for robbery. Crittenden had followed them into Mexico without proper permission. In the following year, Charles McIntosh, Crittenden's successor, suffered an even greater humiliation at the hands of a *jefe político* (political chief) in Casas Grande, Chihuahua. When the *jefe* learned that McIntosh also lacked the proper admission papers, this angry officer placed the sheriff in jail! The sheriff was naturally indignant at such treatment. "Not wishing to die of dry rot in that tumble down [jail]," said the Santa Fe *Daily New Mexican,* McIntosh made his escape and returned to his homeland, but without prisoners. The *New Mexican* writer was outraged at this insult. Characterizing the *jefe político* as "The sapient alcalde" and the "Mexican dogberry," this journalist expressed the opinion that such disregard of Sheriff McIntosh, or any American lawman, "will embolden thieves" to commit more crimes. Furthermore, added this writer, it "conveys the idea that it is only necessary for freebooothers [sic] to make a successful run . . ." across the boundary and find permanent security. Mexican authorities also imprisoned an Arizona posse led by United States Marshal William Kidder Meade in February 1888. This party, which included Pima County Sheriff Matthew F. Shaw, had made an unannounced entry into Chihuahua in hot pursuit of train robbers. When the lawmen introduced themselves to customs officials at Janos, Chihuahua, the surprised Mexicans subjected the possemen to a two-week stay in jail while diplomats worked out their release.[34]

Such unhappy incidents did not preclude instances of cooperation against desperadoes who attempted to hide away in this border nether world. In the 1870s, desperadoes of both nations became very active in southern Arizona and northern Sonora. The affected governors, including Ignacio Pesquiera of Sonora, and John C. Fremont of Arizona, made some efforts to cooperate in the suppression of these freebooters. A large party of American rustlers and highwaymen, often called the "Cowboys," created serious concern. In December 1879, Fremont honored a Mexican requisition for four Sonorans who had taken refuge in Arizona. In turn, Mexico City assisted Cochise County Sheriff Jerome Ward in the chase after five American highwaymen and murderers who raided several Bisbee businesses in December 1883. However, American newspapermen were skeptical about the real motive for this sudden burst of official energy south of the border. One journalist accused the Mexicans of a desire for the reward money. They were "suddenly afflicted with the complete loss of eyesight and memory," said one newspaper, and quietly permitted the Americans to smuggle William Delaney, one of the suspects, out of Sonora without benefit of official protocol.[35]

This tendency toward closer cooperation at the local level became more apparent as the century waned. Emilio Kosterlitzky and his Gendarmería Fiscal, or *rurales*, began to police the Sonoran border in 1885. For more than a quarter-century, this energetic and sometimes ruthless lawman actively cooperated with his Arizona counterparts to suppress crime along this troublesome boundary. The two sides worked out an informal agreement to avoid the time-consuming extradition procedure. James Wolf, a Cochise County deputy in the early 1900s, recalled that Kosterlitzky routinely "flushed" fugitives wanted in Arizona back into that territory "where a sheriff was waiting." "In accordance with this gentlemen's agreement," continued Wolf, the Cochise County officers always returned "the favor." Although this procedure may have stretched the letter of the law, the former deputy asserted that it "added a lot of safety on both sides of the border" and avoided the "long winded" extradition process. This cordial relationship continued for many years. Harry Saxon, Sheriff of Santa Cruz County, which was carved from the border precincts of Pima County in 1899, recalled that he "stood well" with his counterparts in Nogales, Sonora.

"They would just turn [wanted] men over to us," he declared, and he "didn't need to extradite, or go through all this red tape."[36]

There is little doubt that violations of international law took place. Even Emilio Kosterlitzky's biographer admits that the rurales chieftain may have crossed the Arizona border, but only "in isolated cases." He goes on to add that Kosterlitzky turned his head the other way when Arizona lawmen transgressed the line. Deputy Sheriff James Wolf witnessed an instance of the colonel's determined tracking of a Mexican citizen into Cochise County. Kosterlitzky informed Sheriff Del Lewis, who, with Deputy Wolf, met the rurales and surrounded the fugitive in a grassy area. When the killer refused to surrender, Kosterlitzky ordered his men to set the field afire. The fugitive burned to death. Wolf justified this incineration by saying that the murderer was as dangerous "as a rattlesnake." When the charred remains were located, the colonel "cooly prodded the body with his toe," recalled Wolf, and "made sure his man was thoroughly dead." In 1902, Arizona Ranger Captain Burt Mossman slipped into Sonora and effected the capture of Augustino Chacon, who had been sentenced in Graham County for murder. Mexico City raised no protest.[37]

As American and Mexican communities arose upon the the international boundary, the difficulties attending the arrest of fugitives were exacerbated by the clashes between lawmen of the two nations. Nogales, in southernmost Pima County, Arizona, was a case in point. A companion village of the same name grew up opposite it, in Sonora. A thirty-foot-wide street, astride the border, separated the two communities. Clashes between lawmen became common in the 1880s. Deputy Sheriff James Speedy, a testy frontiersman, engaged in a gunfight with Mexican soldiers on 3 March 1887. Speedy accused them of violating American territory as they attempted to bring a fleeing prostitute back into Sonora. In turn, the angry Sonorans laid a trap for Speedy, but the wily deputy suspected foul play and eluded them. In July 1893, the Mexican consul in Nogales, Arizona, accused Deputy Sheriff John Roberts, who succeeded Speedy, of kidnapping and imprisoning Jesus Garcia, a Mexican citizen. When Garcia filed a $2,000 damage suit against the Territory of Arizona, the American State Department felt compelled to investigate the complaint. Roberts was exonerated. However, Mexico City rejected these findings and demanded a second investigation. This one also absolved Roberts of any wrongdoing.[38]

The international boundary provided these border sheriffs with a continuous diet of problems. From the unsuccessful filibustering escapade of "Colonel" Henry A. Crabb against Sonora in 1857 to the Mexican Revolution in 1911, a steady procession of restless persons employed this borderland for various political purposes. In 1879, and again in 1896, the sheriffs in Arizona and New Mexico were alerted to influxes of rebels who were fleeing Mexican forces. In 1907, Arizona Governor Joseph H. Kibbey instructed the sheriffs of Yuma, Pima, Santa Cruz, and Cochise counties to be alert to the efforts of Yaquis, who had rebelled in Sonora, and were purchasing guns and ammunition in southern Arizona. "I will do all in my power to detect and prevent the sale of firearms . . . ," wrote Sheriffs James E. McGee of Tucson, while John F. White of Cochise County declared that "I will notify all [arms] dealers, and will also direct my deputies to cooperate. . . . " While this Indian scare failed to materialize, the border flared into a major problem only four years later, and the sheriffs were again called upon to cooperate with federal officials in policing this troublesome region.[39]

The extradition system was merely one technique in the complex of means to an end—the trackdown of bands of freebooters. It is difficult to assess fairly the success rate of these hardworking sheriffs. Some of them scored notable victories and won public applause. Yavapai County, Arizona, boasted several able manhunters. William J. Mulvenon traced a pair of murderers to Idaho before making the arrests. Buckey O'Neill and posse rode 500 miles on horseback before capturing train robbers in Utah. When J. J. Smith, the leader of the bandits, escaped to Texas, the sheriff took the trail again and eventually placed him in the Yavapai County jail. Mulvenon and O'Neill rode the same horse, "Sandy," on many pursuits. This noble animal was reportedly "pensioned off" to permanent and honorable pasture for these services. George Ruffner won accolades for chasing down train robber Dan Parker in February 1897. Although Parker sought sanctuary in the rough Grand Canyon country, Ruffner persisted. One Prescott journalist praised the sheriff for "a pretty piece of criminal [detection] work," while he "received an ovation at the depot" when he returned with the prisoner. When this desperate bandit escaped jail in May, Ruffner had to run down Parker a second time. The lawman presided at the execution of Dan Parker in 1898. John L. Munds, Yavapai County sheriff from 1899–1902, won praise for his search for the murderer of two Camp Verde merchants. Munds stayed on the trail of clues across New Mexico and finally found the suspect, Thomas "Black Jack" Ketchum, in the Clayton jail for attempted train robbery. Munds failed to obtain custody but had the satisfaction of knowing that Ketchum was hanged in April 1901. Many more examples of successful sheriffs could be cited in both territories.[40]

Of all the professional duties of the sheriffs, the task of manhunting presented the greatest frustrations. While they had at their disposal a comprehensive network of law enforcement agencies, this mechanism was ill suited for the purpose of penetrating the remote hideways of desperadoes and bringing them to justice. In the absence of a standing, professional force in the sheriff's office, the chief county lawman had to call upon the amateurish *posse comitatus*. While lacking experience and training, these public-spirited people inflicted enough casualties upon outlaw bands to dampen their lawless spirits. Perhaps the most glaring weakness in the sheriff's pursuit apparatus was the omission of a permanent budget for such purposes. The absence of this "line item" forced the lawmen to attempt various desperate measures, many of which failed. The wonder is that the sheriffs won as many battles as they did with these tough and resourceful outlaw bands. Several things may have spurred them on in this uphill effort. They desired reelection, and a success in the field against highwaymen won many votes. The prospects of an occasional bonus in the form of reward money probably contributed to a burst of professional energy as well.

11

Sheriffs in Times of Crisis

 If long-range manhunts taxed the resources of the sheriffs, feuds and other larger scale disturbances often exceeded their capabilities and forced the county lawmen to call upon outside assistance. The post-Civil War years were troubled times in New Mexico and Arizona territories. Political, economic, and ethnic forces jostled for position and sometimes provoked explosive situations. In several New Mexico counties—Colfax, Rio Arriba, Lincoln, and Doña Ana—conditions were ripe for bloody confrontations. Although Arizona lacked some of the more compelling ingredients for violence, there were enough to provoke troublesome situations there as well. The agencies that the sheriffs could call upon for help had their own problems. Territorial governors lacked the confidence of the people. Militias were composed of rival ethnic groups, and United States soldiers detested the duties of a civil constabulary. Washington, D.C., which governed the territories, was very distant and its appointees were often at odds with the locally elected officials. The two sides sometimes worked at cross purposes. Sheriffs and other law enforcement personnel were sometimes guilty of partisan behavior in the feuds. These crisis situations often taxed not only the frontier shrievalty but the entire governing apparatus.

Arizona and New Mexico experienced several disturbances that neutralized, or engulfed, the sheriffs and rendered them ineffective. Several such incidents were actually called "wars." In Arizona, the Pleasant Valley War (Tewksbury-Graham Feud), and the uprising of the Cowboys (Earp-Clanton vendetta) claimed numerous lives. The list of similar events in New Mexico is longer and includes the Colfax County War (various flare-ups), the San Juan County War, and the Rustler War in Doña Ana County. Two of the costliest feuds took place in Lincoln County: the Horrell War and the Lincoln County War.[1]

The eruption of such serious disturbances in the various counties was symptomatic of larger cleavages in the fabric of the territories. These divisions cut many ways and reduced society to a welter of factions and interest groups. Ex-Confederates and sympathizers concentrated in the southern counties of both territories. They clung to the Democratic Party and bitterly resented the federal patronage system directed by Republican presidents. Many of the former Confederates were also ex-Texans who detested the Hispanic majority in New Mexico. These former Rebels manifested their hostility in various ways, one of them being a cynical tolerance of desperadoes so long as they ravaged the other side. New Mexico Governor Lionel Sheldon publicly accused "a large element" in the southern counties of being "opposed to law and order" in 1883. Some of the most active border outlaws in both territories, including John Kinney, the alleged "king of the rustlers," were Democrats. Newman H. Clanton, reportedly the kingpin of rustlers and stagecoach robbers in southern Arizona, was likewise a Democrat.[2]

The existence of narrow and exclusionary political factions, or "rings," contributed to the incidence of emergency situations. In Arizona, new arrivals complained of an Indian Ring through which a few wealthy men monopolized federal contracts. In New Mexico, the Santa Fe Ring manipulated the territorial government for the personal gain of a small clique, allegedly directed by lawyer Thomas Benton Catron. Catron and his fellow grafters sought to purchase controlling interest in Spanish and Mexican land grants. These disputed claims bound up vast acreages in protracted court battles and rendered property titles extremely insecure. Claimants often resorted to the gun to protect their property, hoping that the federal government would eventually resolve the titles in their favor. The establishment of stakes or groups of congregations of the Church of Jesus Christ of Latter Day Saints (Mormons) in eastern Arizona in the late 1870s added another uncertainty and fostered a three-way rivalry between Mormons, Hispanos, and the remainder of the white population. In an ironic twist, the railroads—the supposed harbingers of progress—formed a new interest group and contributed to instability in both territories. A flood of migrants followed. While these new arrivals were law-abiding, some time was required to accommodate them. A few came for criminal ends. By the 1890s, the cosmopolitan influence of the railroads and other modern means of communication had begun to integrate New Mexico and Arizona into the national community. The appearance of violent secret societies, labor agitators, and the White Cap Movement (a Southwestern counterpart to Populism) caused much concern.[3]

Although it was a less visible cause of instability, the premature creation of counties contributed heavily to the outbreak of violence. The occupants of the shrievalty were often victimized. Southwestern frontiersmen desired immediate signs of the success of civilization, and the formation of a new unit of local government provided immediate gratification. Property owners, who resented the drain of local tax revenue to a distant county seat, and budding politicians who sought government office united to push new county bills through the territorial legislatures. Unfortunately, lawmakers often consented long before the region possessed the wealth, population, and political maturity to support a local government. Small, grasping factions took command. Some counties were established upon land entangled in disputed land grants, and the sheriffs' offices became ensnared in these rivalries. The perpetual wrangling over the Maxwell Land Grant in Colfax County was a good example. Indian hostilities, which continued into the 1880s, also handicapped many counties. The sheriffs were constrained to devote valuable time to leading posses or militia units after hostiles. The "war zone" nature of many counties persisted for years. Even after the Indians were confined to reservations, these lands were off-limits to sheriffs.[4]

The inhabitants of new counties exhibited a spirit of independence—indeed, of defiance—toward outsiders, including officials in the capitals. The sheriffs imbibed this provincialism as well. Parochial attitudes flourished especially in counties where a faction or interest group attempted to monopolize local government and exclude new arrivals. Such regimes arose more easily in counties where one activity—mining, cattle, sheep—dominated the region. The control of Lincoln County by the mercantile firm of Lawrence Murphy in the 1870s was one of the more notorious instances. A similar pattern was apparent in counties where persons of Mexican descent predominated. The one-family governance of the dons was traditional in such counties as Valencia. Newspapers referred to the "Kingdom of Valencia" because the Luna family controlled government offices, including the shrievalty, for many decades. In Cochise County, Arizona, the first set of appointees to office—the so-called Two Percent Ring—alienated many new arrivals, especially Republicans from the northern counties.[5]

Such isolation at the county level severely restricted the possibil-

Map 3. County Boundaries of New Mexico, c. 1880

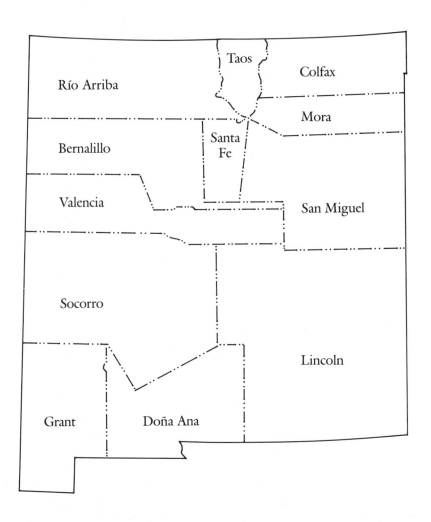

Source: loc. cit. maps 1 and 2

Map 3. County Boundaries of Arizona, c. 1880

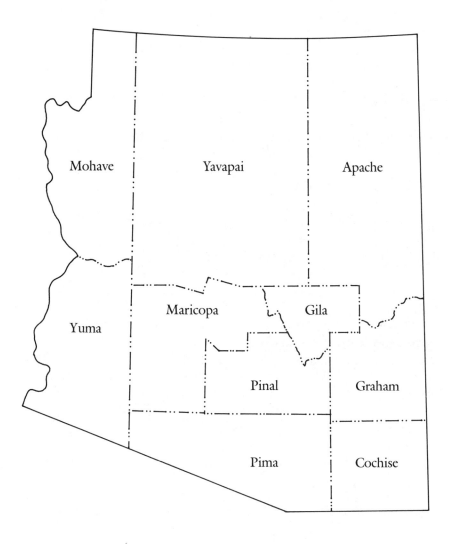

Mohave

Yavapai

Apache

Yuma

Maricopa

Gila

Pinal

Graham

Pima

Cochise

ities for cooperation between the sheriffs during this era of crises. Lew Wallace, who entered the New Mexico governorship in the midst of the Lincoln County War, quickly learned about the inability, or unwillingness, of these lawmen to resolve or suppress the conflicts. After a visit to the stricken county in February and March 1879, Wallace concluded that the criminal by-products of this vendetta had spread far beyond Lincoln County and even into neighboring Texas. When the governor returned to Santa Fe, he determined to bring together the sheriffs of those counties that were especially troubled by lawlessness. He circularized the officers in counties that were experiencing "white outlaws and troublesome Indians" and asked them (he could not order them) to confer with him in Santa Fe. Wallace's call may have been the first such attempt to mobilize the sheriffs against a common enemy. If so, he was sadly disappointed. Not one officer, not even the sheriff in Santa Fe, responded. When one journalist in the capital learned this news, he asked rhetorically, "Did they come? No! Not a mother's son came near. . . ." "Like foolish virgins," he continued, these errant sheriffs "sent in their excuses . . ." and continued their defiantly independent ways.[6]

This unfortunate attitude among the sheriffs continued for some years and became especially grievous in the southern counties of New Mexico and Arizona that were carved from the Gadsden Purchase. Lionel Sheldon, who succeeded Lew Wallace in spring 1881, hoped to overcome the provincialism of county lawmen by on-the-spot visits to the south. When the *Silver City Mining Chronicle* praised Sheldon's support of sheriffs in southern New Mexico, the *Tombstone Epitaph,* in neighboring Cochise County, Arizona, took up the cudgels against similarly unresponsive sheriffs in that territory. In a pointed editorial, this Tombstone newspaperman was very critical of the failure of Governor John C. Fremont to affect the crime-fighting posture of his colleague in New Mexico. However, the journalist went on to propose:

> would the sheriffs of Pima, Pinal, Graham and Cochise counties consult among themselves, and co-operate with the sheriffs of New Mexico, they could soon rid this country of the cow-boy [outlaw] nuisance and earn the everlasting gratitude of those who contribute to their support.

The southern tier of counties that lay along the international boundary had served as an outlaw corridor since the 1850s and would continue to attract desperadoes until the sheriffs learned to work together.[7]

The failure of the county peace officers to collude against the desperate element left other avenues open to these bad men. Since the 1860s, a regular flow of Texas cattle had been driven up the Pecos River Valley to stock the ranges of eastern New Mexico and Colorado. New Mexicans sometimes found it difficult to distinguish between legitimate Texas stockmen and the desperado class. Both were heavily armed and capable of much ruthlessness. During the Lincoln County War, this wilderness avenue flourished more than ever. Feudists marched and counter-marched this road and sought recruits in Texas. By fall 1878, the authorities in western Texas had become alarmed at the raids of Lincoln County badmen as far south as the Big Bend Country. In October 1878, District Judge Allen Blacker of Fort Concho appealed to William Steele, Adjutant General of Texas, for the help of the Rangers. Blacker informed him that pillagers from Lincoln County had been at work since 1875, or three years before the Lincoln County War broke out. On one of these rustler escapades, said Blacker, a Lincoln County sheriff was present. Presumably Blacker referred to Sheriff Ham Mills or a deputy. G.M. Frazer, a Pecos County judge and possibly subordinate to District Judge Blacker, reiterated the dangers of these Lincoln County criminals. Frazer believed that there were "immediate prospects" that these freebooters would spill over permanently into his area. They traveled in the guise of legitimate cattlemen. They not only drove stolen New Mexico cattle into western Texas but, added Frazer, "have made repeated incursions into For Stockton [Texas], and have shot into houses, and through the town and [military] garrison." The lawmen in Fort Stockton and other communities were overawed, concluded Judge Frazer.[8]

These alarmed frontier jurists hardly exaggerated. Western Texas was an alluring place to enterprising badmen and very difficult to police. Judge Blacker included a revealing piece of outlaw correspondence in his report to Adjutant General Steele. In September 1878, a Lincoln County outlaw signing his name "S. Z." wrote his girlfriend from the Guadalupe Mountains of western Texas. S. Z. and his comrades were on "an independent scout" and expected to make a big haul.

In the following February, Texas Ranger Pat Dolan informed a superior that "There is a band of New Mexico outlaws on the Pecos [River] with 600 head of stolen cattle. . . ." Dolan asked for reinforcements. While Governor Lew Wallace corresponded with the governor of Texas about the possibility of mutual action in the Pecos River corridor, neither executive possessed the necessary resources at that time. George Kimbrell, Lincoln County sheriff in 1879–80, opened communications with his counterparts in the nearest Texas counties but was also unsuccessful. Nonetheless, these overtures registered the desire to cooperate at the shrievalty level and set the stage for more tangible results in the future.[9]

In addition to the difficulties caused by lack of collaboration among sheriffs, these county lawmen sometimes lost the confidence of sizable sectors of their constituencies. An explosive situation developed in Socorro, New Mexico, when the Anglo community accused Sheriff Jesus Maria Garcia of permitting personal and family loyalties to interfere with enforcement of the law. The crisis arose on Christmas Eve 1880 when Onofre and Abran Baca, sons (or nephews) of Don Antonio Baca, murdered Anthony M. Conklin, editor of the *Socorro Sun*. The Anglos, led by merchant Ethan W. Eaton, demanded the arrest of the villains, who had taken refuge with their father and other relatives. The killing, which was apparently provoked by ethnic hatred in the first place, seriously compromised the sheriff. He was related by blood to the murderers, and Don Antonio Baca was his patron. In aristocratic custom, the hidalgo sat at the pinnacle of society and served as the community "father." To Sheriff Garcia, the idea of arresting the sons of his patron was unthinkable. Furthermore, Garcia was a lame duck sheriff whose term would expire at midnight on the 31st. He would probably have preferred to leave this dilemma to his successor, Andres Montoya. The Las Vegas *Daily Optic* spoke contemptuously of this "Mexican sheriff" who placed family ties before his oath of office. With Ethan Eaton in the lead, the Anglos formed a vigilante committee and "arrested" the sheriff, Don Antonio, and Antonio Jaramillo Baca, a relative and third suspect in the Conklin murder. Onofre and Abran Baca escaped to Mexico. Antonio Jaramillo Baca shot and killed a jail guard during an escape attempt. In turn, he was shot to death.[10]

Juan Jose Baca, evidently another relative of the accused men, appealed for the help of Governor Lew Wallace. "Sheriff and four other citizens arrested . . . ," he telegraphed frantically, "without any warrant and authority of law." "All citizens arrested kept without allowing communication with anybody," he continued, "and belong to the first families in [the] co[unty]." Wallace was much concerned, since the disturbance in neighboring Lincoln County had not been completely quieted and a similar quarrel appeared to be brewing in the far northwest, in Rio Arriba County. Wallace referred the case to District Attorney J. Francisco Chavez, who administered a sharp rebuff to Sheriff Garcia. "Your duty [is] to preserve the peace . . . ," said Chavez's telegram, and "to summon such posse . . . as may be necessary, and to arrest all persons guilty of unlawful violence." When it became apparent that the sheriff was in no position to comply, Wallace dispatched federal troops to Socorro. Although the authority of the bluecoats was severely limited by law in civil policing, Wallace hoped that by "showing the flag" they might have a calming influence. Unfortunately, a Texas Ranger kidnapped the Baca brothers from Mexico and returned them to New Mexico. The Socorro vigilantes defied the new Hispano Sheriff, Andres Montoya, and lynched Onofre Baca in March 1881. Abran was tried and exonerated. The New Mexico press, largely in the hands of the Anglos, pointed an accusing finger at Sheriff Garcia and blamed him for all these problems. "The troubles at Socorro," said the *Albuquerque Daily Journal* on 30 December 1880, were "caused by the sheriff's refusing to act. . . ." Formal charges were filed against the former lawman and his deputies but the court presumably threw out the case. When Juan Garcia died five years later, his obituary made no mention of this embarrassing episode.[11]

The employment of United States troops was by no means uncommon in New Mexico and Arizona territories. When the sheriff and his civilian forces were overwhelmed, federal troops became a standby *posse comitatus*. The process by which sheriffs and other lawmen obtained bluecoated assistants varied. Until 1878, United States marshals and sheriffs could apply directly to the nearest garrison commander and avoid much bureaucratic paperwork. This was a boon to law officers in the territories, especially when emergencies arose. In June 1878, Congress passed the Posse Comitatus Act, which revoked this liberal policy and imposed serious restrictions upon the use of troops in civil matters. Frontier commanders lost their discretionary power to release troops to civil lawmen except in the most threatening situations. This sudden policy change took place at a time when highly disturbed conditions prevailed in the Southwest. However, access to United States forces was not completely lost. The sheriffs and United States marshals merely reverted to an earlier procedure in which they applied through channels to the President. A district judge informed the governor or legislature that lawless persons had overpowered the constituted lawmen and prevented the courts from functioning. Upon appeal to the President, the latter issued a proclamation in which he urged the lawless element to "retire peaceably to your abodes" by a certain date. If they refused, the Chief Executive placed military forces at the disposal of the governor who, in turn, made them available to the sheriff or marshal. These forces did not technically serve as a *posse comitatus* but merely assisted the peace officer to serve court process. The President took pains to avoid the next logical step in the use of troops, martial law. This extreme measure called for the usurpation of the sheriff and suspension of the writ of habeas corpus.[12]

The incapacitation of the sheriff usually played an important part in the decision to call upon federal troops. In fall 1878, Judge Warren Bristol decided against a session of court in Lincoln, New Mexico. The vicious feud that raged in that area had already cost the life of one sheriff, William Brady. In a letter to United States Marshal John E. Sherman, Bristol declared that the present county lawman, George Peppin, "has either abandoned or been driven from his office. . . ." Other reasons included the absence of the district attorney and the fact that "the better class" of citizens who normally served on juries had fled the county. The feuding factions had employed hired killers to intimidate persons who remained. Local officials were clearly partisan and would thus make the court "a mockery," concluded the judge. No term was held that autumn. The authorities in Washington did not require such an elaborate argument to persuade them but employed a simpler formula for assignment of troops to lawmen. In May 1890, Secretary of Interior John W. Noble explained to Governor L. Bradford Prince that the President would not commit troops "until it is demonstrated that the Sheriff or United States Marshal, . . . is unable to preserve the peace or to serve [court] process because of [violent] resistance. . . ." To document this inability, continued the secretary, "The civil authorities must first act to the extent of their ability. . . ." Only when the sheriff had exhausted his resources—deputies and the *posse comitatus*—could the military arm be requested. This same procedure was used when the sheriff asked the governor for territorial militia.[13]

United States forces provided the sheriffs with various services. They patrolled feuding communities in an effort to keep the warring parties apart and to protect innocent citizens. Fort Union troops did this for Cimarron in November 1875, in the wake of the Parson Tolby assassination. They repeated this duty ten years later when deputy sheriffs killed outlaw-vigilante Dick Rogers in Springer. Bluecoats secured the gallows during hangings in Los

Lunas, New Mexico, in 1854, and in Yuma, Arizona, in 1871. They kept the peace in various court sessions when rowdies threatened to disrupt proceedings. They protected the United States mails, both on stagecoach and railroad routes. They accompanied deputy United States marshals in the pursuit of illegal traders in Indian country and expelled white intruders from reservations. In 1882, they guarded the Santa Fe County jail against lynchers. They accompanied sheriffs in the search for stolen livestock. They assisted sheriffs (and deputy United States marshals) in the arrest of feudists in the Lincoln County War. They "showed the flag" along the international boundary as a means to deter Mexican, and Anglo, bandits. Military guardhouses substituted in the absence of, or insecurity of, county jails. In spite of these many constabulary duties on behalf of county sheriffs, the bluecoats seldom killed or even wounded culprits.[14]

Many problems attended the employment of United States soldiers in constabulary situations. The Posse Comitatus Act of June 1878 caused the lawmen some dismay. The governors of New Mexico, Arizona, and other Rocky Mountain states and territories regarded their frontier region as an exceptional case. They quickly appealed to Washington for special dispensation from the provisions of this controversial law. In January 1881, Governor Lew Wallace testified before the Senate Committee on the Territories to this effect. Wallace informed the *Washington Star* that he did not believe the lawmakers intended the Posse Comitatus Act to apply to territories. The Democratic majority in Congress, which inspired this statute, desired to prevent the use of troops to protect the voting polls in the Reconstruction South. These politicians gave no thought to the problems of lawlessness on the frontier. Wallace added that residents of the territories were not permitted to vote in presidential elections and therefore had no stake in such political maneuverings in Congress. Wallace did not ask the national lawmakers to repeal the restrictive legislation, only to amend it to omit the territories. Arizona Governor John C. Fremont endorsed Wallace's mission. "I trust he may be successful," wrote Fremont to Secretary of Interior Carl Schurz. Fremont faced the gloomy prospect of a complete breakdown in cooperation between the sheriff and deputy United States marshals, and a consequent increase in lawlessness, in Cochise County. He believed that only army-assisted lawmen could "terminate all such raids and tranquilize the [Mexican] frontier." While many officials in Washington sympathized with these frontier lobbyists, and President Chester Arthur endorsed their recommendations, Congress rejected the appeal. If frontier authorities truly desired military aid, they would have to use the protracted proclamation procedure or find an alternative military force.[15]

Other problems accompanied federal military assistance. The professional soldiers regarded themselves as Indian fighters and disliked civil constabulary duties. Governor Lew Wallace complained to the Secretary of Interior in March 1879 that troops at Fort Stanton "do not enter heartily into the [constabulary] work . . ." in Lincoln County. The garrison regarded such tasks as "distasteful," continued Wallace, and resented "acting under direction of civilians." He also pointed out that citizens sometimes brought suit against soldiers for real or imagined transgressions of the constitutional separation of military and civilian spheres. The dilemma of Colonel Nathan A.M. Dudley, whom Mrs. Alexander McSween sued for his part in the death of her husband, was only the most notable such instance. As a consequence, post commanders gave their subordinates strict orders to fulfill only the most minimal instructions in service to civil lawmen.[16]

Many people questioned the effectiveness of federal troops against lawless whites. The cavalry moved at a plodding rate, and well-mounted armed desperadoes laughed at such pursuers. When the *New York Daily Mail & Express* applauded the peacekeeping services of the army, the Tombstone *Weekly Epitaph* objected and declared that the troops "have proven a miserable failure." "All the troops now in Arizona could not catch a sick squaw if she had five minutes the start of them, much less a live cowboy [outlaw] . . . ," concluded this writer. The fact that the outlaws were better armed, as Governor Lew Wallace informed the secretary of interior, may have also discouraged the soldiers. Nor were federal military forces always impartial in civil disturbances. The sheriffs appreciated them for an assumed nonaligned position, especially in such vendetta situations as the Lincoln County War. In the first weeks of this bitter feud, a deputy United States marshal vied with Sheriff William Brady for control of military posses and actually employed them in partisan fashion. Post Commander Nathan Dudley soon received orders to assist only the sheriff. As events transpired, this decision became decisive in the eventual defeat of the Alexander McSween forces. During the climactic engagement, "the five days battle," in July 1878, Dudley so situated his troops between the warring parties in Lincoln that he gave the decisive advantage to Sheriff George Peppin's posse.[17]

As restrictions upon United States forces increased, territorial officials substituted militia men for bluecoats in sheriffs' posses. When the relatively poor territories were able to support militias, Indian fighting had been their primary purpose. Neither New Mexico nor Arizona had done much more than to maintain paper organizations. However, the alarming increase in lawlessness in the late 1870s prompted New Mexico Territory to action. Governor Lew Wallace began the conscious rebuilding of the militia with the formation of the Lincoln County Rifles in March 1879. He assigned this unit the specific duty of assisting Sheriff George Kimbrell in the mop-up of the remnants of the feuding factions. Wallace did the same in April 1881 when he authorized a new company in northwestern Rio Arriba County. A potentially dangerous clash loomed between settlers and rustlers from Colorado. Governor Lionel Sheldon, Wallace's successor, made the first concerted use of territorial soldiers in the so-called Rustlers War of 1882–83. In this campaign, the New Mexico militia alone (rather than the United States Army) served as possemen under the sheriffs. In Grant and Doña Ana counties, livestock theft reached alarming proportions as new mining camps and railroad construction gangs created a boom atmosphere in the beef market. Butchers asked no questions. In response to a petition by Doña Ana County ranchers, Sheldon ordered the militia into action. By 1883, the territory supported thirty militia companies. Arizona Territory lacked such resources, but Governor Frederick Tritle managed the formation of militia companies in Cochise, Pima, Gila, and Graham counties to combat white outlaws and Indians.[18]

The flurry of militia building in New Mexico was clearly aimed at assisting the sheriffs in the suppression of domestic disturbances. In General Orders No. 1, dated 1 September 1881, Governor Sheldon decreed that:

> Upon proper requisitions of sheriffs of different counties, commanding officers will furnish such posse comitatti [sic] from their commands, as such sheriffs may require in their respective counties, to preserve the peace, guard jails and prisoners and make arrests. . . .

In a subsequent order, Sheldon extended to city officials the power to summon militia. He also gave militia officers authority to arrest white outlaws without warrants in emergency cases. These arresting officers in uniform were required to turn over the culprits to the nearest sheriff. When a militia unit in Lake Valley, in Doña Ana

County, complained about the sheriff's demand that they assist in the recovery of stolen sheep, Sheldon admitted that "Sheriffs may misjudge and call militia forces when not necessary, but it is better to misjudge on the side of caution than on the other in this wild country. . . ." In Cochise County, Arizona, Governor Frederick Tritle placed a newly recruited company under a deputy United States marshal but also made this unit "subject to the call of the sheriff . . . when needed by him in the service of legal process."[19]

The frequent use of the militia in sheriffs' posses soon provoked public complaints of abuse of power and even accusations of "martial law." Even some sheriffs regarded the militia as a threat to their offices and rejected offers of aid. When a Las Vegas mob threatened to lynch a prisoner of Sheriff Jose Esquibel in April 1884, the local militia commander offered assistance. Esquibel turned down this offer, an act that the editor of the *Weekly New Mexican* considered "incomprehensible to all law-abiding citizens." The Las Vegas soldiers persisted and placed a guard at the jail in defiance of the sheriff. Sheriff Santiago Ascarate of Doña Ana County expressed anger at the intrusions of Colonel Albert Jennings Fountain's militia during the Rustler War and insisted that he was capable of arresting rustler kingpin John Kinney and his followers. When Fountain continued the campaign in defiance of the Doña Ana sheriff, killing some outlaws and capturing others, the offended lawman accused the militia officer of acting without authority. Governor Sheldon was sensitive to the various political issues raised by these militia posses. Anglos despised the all Hispano units, the so-called greaser militia. This was one source of the charges that he was imposing martial law. In his annual message to the New Mexico legislature in 1884, Sheldon attempted to reassure the lawmakers that "In no cases, with a single exception, has the militia been employed except on the application of citizens and in the aid of the civil authorities. . . ."[20]

The militia campaign against the rustlers in New Mexico was merely a part of a larger problem. In Arizona, stock thieves and other criminals were (erroneously) called the Cowboys. The extent of their activities is difficult to determine, although they focused upon the boomtown of Tombstone and smaller camps in the vicinity of the Mexican border. In February 1881, the Arizona Assembly created the County of Cochise to bring political order to this region, and Governor John C. Fremont appointed the first cadre of officers. Fremont, a longtime Republican, inexplicably appointed Democrats to all offices, among them a veteran Arizona Democrat,

John H. Behan, as first sheriff. This remarkable action has never been fully explained and alienated the Republicans from the outset. Republicans in the new county resented this betrayal of party discipline. Ordinarily, the first appointees to new county regimes held office for only a few weeks or months until elections. The legislature neglected to give Cochise County voters the privilege to choose their public servants, that is, until the regular territory-wide elections in November 1882. This oversight gave Fremont's appointees, including Sheriff Behan, practically a full two-year term. Many new citizens concluded that this was too long for the voters to be deprived of a voice.[21]

The Fremont appointments set off a chain of events that led to violence and an aggravation of the outlaw problem. Wyatt Earp, a Republican, professional gambler, and part-time lawman, had desired the shrievalty. He charged Behan with reneging on a promise to make Earp the first undersheriff if he withdrew his candidacy. Earp set his sights on the November 1882 elections and concocted a plan to kill or capture a band of stagecoach robbers. To gain entre into the ranks of the highwaymen, Earp approached Isaac Clanton, an alleged rustler leader. When Clanton divulged this plan during a drunken binge, a rift occurred between Earp and the rustlers. On 26 October 1881, Earp and his brothers, Virgil and Morgan, and gambler John H. "Doc" Holliday met Ike Clanton and three more suspected outlaws in a bloody confrontation in Tombstone. Although the Earp party was covered officially by the city marshal's badge of Virgil Earp, many people considered the shooting unwarranted. The Cowboys vowed vengeance and permanently maimed Virgil Earp and murdered Morgan Earp. In turn, Wyatt Earp, by now a deputy United States marshal, led a federal posse in pursuit of the suspected assassins. This posse killed two, possibly three, suspects under very questionable circumstances. In April 1882, Earp and his party fled the territory to avoid murder warrants in the hands of the sheriffs of Cochise and Pima counties.[22]

This regrettable feud and related outlawry exposed many shortcomings within the law enforcement machinery of Arizona Territory. From the governor's mansion to Sheriff John H. Behan's office in Tombstone, every echelon appeared helpless or unwilling to cooperate with the other. In the absence of John C. Fremont, Acting Governor John J. Gosper reported to Washington that the Cochise County sheriff and City Marshal Virgil Earp were at odds and that political factions, with respective newspapers, had taken sides. The Earps and John Clum, editor of the *Tombstone Epitaph*, publicly accused Sheriff Behan of being either in league or sympathy with the outlaws. As the vendetta between the Earps and Cowboys went its remorseless way, a new governor, Frederick Tritle, assumed the helm of Arizona Territory. Like Lew Wallace in New Mexico, Tritle felt compelled to ask President Chester Arthur for federal troops to assist lawmen in Cochise County. In May 1882, Arthur issued the necessary proclamation and ordered lawless elements to return to their homes.[23]

The place of Sheriff John H. Behan in this vendetta—more particularly his equivocal role—caused a storm of controversy. Even before the shootout at the OK Corral, the Republican opposition accused him of deliberately ignoring the rampages of the Cowboys. He fielded posses separate from the federal posses of Deputy United States Marshal (and concurrent City Marshal) Virgil Earp. Earp suspected that one of Behan's deputies, Frank Stillwell, was a stagecoach robber. On the day of the OK Corral shootout between the Earps and Clantons, Sheriff Behan was present and attempted to prevent the two sides from colliding. The two justice of the peace investigations of this gunfight exposed his ineptitude or ineffectiveness. Nonetheless, Behan's fellow Democrats were embarrassed at his failure and ignored him at the nominating convention in August 1882. During the Earp-Clanton vendetta in late 1881, Acting Governor John J. Gosper contemplated removing Behan, only to learn that he lacked the authority. When Gosper proposed measures to supress this lawlessness, the Arizonan recommended that Congress enact the necessary removal legislation. (An amendment to the Posse Comitatus Act was also a part of this package.) Secretary of Interior Samuel Kirkwood complied, and President Chester Arthur presented this request in a special message to Congress. The national legislators rejected the proposal, and the Chief Executive issued the proclamation, preparatory to assigning troops to Cochise County lawmen. As events transpired, these measures were not necessary. The lawless elements either killed each other or departed the county. Sheriff John H. Behan served out his term, somehow surviving one of the most humiliating tenures of any frontier sheriff.[24]

Arizona was the victim of another vicious vendetta, the Pleasant Valley War in 1887–88, which presented the affected sheriffs much difficulty. While the brunt of the feuding took place in the easternmost precinct of Yavapai County, the bloodshed spilled over into neighboring Apache and Gila counties. This vendetta resembled the Lincoln County War in some ways. Both cost many lives; at least twenty-eight person died in the Arizona conflict and possibly forty in Lincoln County. Both episodes presented extraordinary challenges to the sheriffs. However, the comparisons end here. Whereas the United States Army and New Mexico Militia played some part in restoring some order in Lincoln County, Arizona Governor C. Meyer Zulick hesitated to ask for army assistance in the Pleasant Valley War. He may have considered this possibility, since a news report declared that Zulick had asked for the help of the Fort Verde garrison. This did not materialize, although two companies of regulars rode through the valley in the summer of 1888. The worst was over, and the bluecoats made no contribution to the restoration of order. Nor did Zulick summon militia units, although Arizona did maintain a few companies.[25]

Evidently, Governor Zulick concluded that the sheriffs of the victimized counties could be relied upon to suppress the feudists. This was an unusual assumption, since the county lawmen involved in similar violent episodes had either been killed or compromised by one of the factions. In the instance of the sheriff of Yavapai County, William Mulvenon, the governor's confidence was not misplaced. Mulvenon's difficulties were great. Pleasant Valley lay astride the common border of Yavapai and Apache counties, well over 100 miles from either county seat. The problem of the typical hyperextended counties could not have been greater. In addition, two other counties, Maricopa and Gila, were located on the southern margin of Pleasant Valley. The fact that neither Mulvenon nor Commodore P. Owens, chief lawman of Apache County, were partisans of one of the factions also added weight to the governor's determination to rely upon these peace officers. (In the Lincoln County War, the sheriff's office became totally compromised.) On 7 September 1887, Governor Zulick held a conference with Sheriff Mulvenon and the district attorney. They determined that a large posse should intrude on Pleasant Valley. Two separate incursions were necessary. The second sheriff's *posse comitatus*, which included some citizens of Apache County, succeeded in killing two members of the Graham faction and arresting some of the opposition.[26]

That Sheriff Owens deliberately concerted his movements with Yavapai County officials is by no means certain. While William Mulvenon's raid was in progress, Sheriff Owens killed three feudists in Holbrook in an attempt to serve a warrant for rustling against Andrew L. Cooper. The five deaths at the hands of the two sheriffs represented only a few of the twenty-eight deaths in the Pleasant Valley War. Yet, Mulvenon and Owens could boast that they contributed measurably to the reduction of the trouble. When compared with the abject and partisan role of the Lincoln County sher-iffalty, the performance of the Arizona lawmen stood out. In neither vendetta did the county lawmen succeed in stamping out the bitter conflicts. Vigilantes—the Committee of Fifty—arose after the Mulvenon raids and reportedly lynched or expelled some troublemakers. In both vendettas, only the mutual extermination of the most fervent participants finally ended the blood lust. The in-ability of sheriffs and district courts to decisively suppress such san-guinary goings-on served to highlight the shortcomings of county law enforcement in the frontier territories.[27]

The gravest crisis to beset and undermine the shrievalty in the Southwest took place in Lincoln County in 1878–80. Although a decade old, the county experienced political, ethnic, and economic factionalism of the most remorseless kind. Sheriff William Brady (1877–78), an Irish immigrant and army veteran, lost the confi-dence of one faction, that of lawyer Alexander McSween and ranchers John H. Tunstall and John Chisum. This element included both Anglos and Hispanos. The Tunstall-McSween group accused Brady of many shortcomings, including the failure to arrest rustlers, permitting notorious outlaws to escape jail, and irregularities in tax collections. Although it was not a violation of office, Brady was ac-cused of being indebted (figuratively and literally) to merchant Lawrence Murphy and his partner, James J. Dolan. The sheriff's gravest offense was to allow Jesse Evans, a known badman, to ac-company a posse that served a writ of attachment upon horses be-longing to John H. Tunstall. While in the company of this Brady force, Evans and his comrades callously murdered Tunstall in Feb-ruary 1878. The fact that Tunstall was an English citizen compli-cated the affair. Although Brady was not present at the killing and denied any knowledge of Evans's participation in his posse, the McSweens refused to believe him. Open warfare erupted. On 1 April 1878, several hotheads in McSween's camp assassinated Brady and a deputy in Lincoln. Among the assassins was William Bonney, alias Billy the Kid, who had begun to earn a man-killing reputation.[28]

While McSween reportedly refused to countenance the murder of the sheriff, this singular assassination drove formerly neutral resi-dents into the warring camps or out of the county. Local govern-ment, which had never been very effective, quickly dissolved. Rival elements sought to place their nominee in the shrievalty, the office most critical to the control of law enforcement. The McSween party won this struggle initially when District Judge Warren Bristol rec-ommended John Copeland for the sheriffalty. Governor Samuel Axtell confirmed him, and Copeland took office in early May. The new lawman soon revealed dissolute habits, going so far as to be drunk in public and to associate with the accused murderers of Sheriff Brady. Fort Stanton army officers, who served as a posse for Copeland, exposed his gross misconduct in an official report, the "Conduct of John N. Copeland, Sheriff of Lincoln, Lincoln County, New Mexico." Furthermore, Copeland's deputies, among them McSween partisan Josiah "Doc" Skurlock, used his powers to harass the Murphy-Dolans. Governor Axtell removed Copeland after only one month in office. The governor used the technicality that Copeland failed to obtain adequate sureties for his bond. (Axtell was able to use this removal power in a similar circumstance in the Colfax County War as well.)[29]

Axtell's next choice, George Peppin, flung the Lincoln County shrievalty back to the Murphy-Dolan faction. This equally incautious act convinced the McSweens that justice was not possible and erased any hope of a peaceful settlement. Before his appointment, Peppin had been a prisoner of Sheriff Copeland. Alexander McSween refused to recognize Peppin and characterized him as the "quasi-sheriff." Apparently he continued to regard John Copeland as the legal sheriff. One report circulated that the McSween partisans held a separate election and selected their leader as the new sheriff! Nonetheless, the Axtel appointee, George Peppin, assembled a large posse and prepared to crush the opposition. This force included residents of the Seven Rivers area in southern Lincoln County and a contingent from Doña Ana County. This latter element included the infamous rustler John Kinney, who later helped provoke the Rustler War. Sheriff Peppin, with the passive intervention of troops from Fort Stanton, routed the McSween party in a bloody battle in Lincoln in July 1878. Alexander McSween was killed and his following was permanently crippled. Sheriff Peppin had the doubtful distinction of leading his posse in the largest pitched battle in the history of shrievalty in New Mexico and Arizona territories.[30]

Although the victor, George Peppin quickly became disillusioned with his position. Congress had passed the Posse Comitatus Act a few weeks before the gun battle in Lincoln, imposing restrictions upon military assistance to lawmen. Furthermore, a change occurred in the governorship in September 1878. Lew Wallace, the new territorial executive, had the duty to resolve the disturbance in Lincoln County and other areas as well. By the time of Wallace's arrival, Peppin's posse had dissolved and he had withdrawn to the

sanctuary of Fort Stanton. (He did manage to arrest John Copeland, his predecessor, on an assault charge.) The governor concluded that sources other than the sheriff's office would be needed
to suppress the lawlessness. He obtained a presidential proclamation against the feudists in October 1878 and followed it with an
offer of amnesty for all participants not under murder indictments.
George Peppin left office on 31 December 1878 content to merely
fill out William Brady's term.[31]

In the previous November, Lincoln County voters had elected a
new sheriff, George Kimbrell, who professed nonaligned status.
Kimbrell made a sincere effort to enforce the laws impartially but
soon convinced the remnants of the Murphy-Dolan faction that he
was a closet McSween. Nonetheless, he served out a complete term,
no mean feat when three men were required to fill out the preceding one. Kimbrell brought representatives of both factions to a
peace conference in Lincoln in February 1879. When this failed and
another killing ensued, Governor Wallace visited Lincoln (for the
first and only time) and personally placed the Fort Stanton garrison
at Kimbrell's disposal. Wallace also broke new ground in the war
upon the lawless throughout New Mexico by mustering a militia
company to serve as the sheriff's right hand. For the first time in
a year, the district court met in Lincoln, although many people
thought that even its proceedings were again partisan.[32]

In spite of such accusations, George Kimbrell wisely exhibited a
degree of circumspection and enabled tempers to cool. The rank
and file of both factions began to reach an accommodation. George
Coe, a McSween warrior, recalled how former Sheriff Peppin and
Deputy Johnny Hurley paid him visits in an attempt to bury the
hatchet. Only the hardcore fighters of both armies refused to return
to peaceful pursuits and sank into outright outlawry. At the November 1880 elections, Lincoln County voters selected an outsider,
Patrick Garrett, for the sheriffalty. With the backing of the growing
cattle interests and the new mining camp of White Oaks, Garrett
managed to hold the office securely and to kill or capture the most
notorious refuse of the Lincoln County War, the Billy the Kid
band. In spring 1881, the Kid was convicted of participating in the
assassination of Sheriff William Brady. Although other assassins
were still living, they had the good sense to leave the territory. Bonney had stubbornly remained in the county. Although sentenced
to hang in Lincoln, this wily sheriff-killer escaped jail, killing two
deputies in the process. Sheriff Garrett ended the Kid's rampage in
July 1881. It was perhaps fitting that Garrett, an occupant of the

office that Billy the Kid and his comrades had victimized in 1878, should have ended the murderer's life.[33]

To persons in the grip of the violent disturbances in New Mexico and Arizona, it was probably difficult to detect an end to this era of emergencies. The year 1887 might be arbitrarily selected. In that year, the worst of the Pleasant Valley War passed and the age of large-scale vendettas went with it. As early as September 1883, Governor Lionel Sheldon could assure the Secretary of Interior that the outlaw element in New Mexico had

> substantially disappeared, and nothing more is heard of vigilantes or lynch law. . . . The courts are able and efficient, officers generally perform their duties well, criminals are usually captured, and convictions . . . are quite certain. . . . Thirty militia companies are organized. . . .

While the governor was apt to applaud himself too much, the prospects of excessive bloodshed had indeed been reduced. Those rifts within counties that caused great loss of life began to heal, largely through attrition, exhaustion, and accommodation. The men who presided over the shrievalties during these harsh times could not claim the role of peacemakers. Newly elected sheriffs, who were so critical to the prevention of future bloodlettings, attempted to rise above partisan behavior. Others, such as Pat Garrett, Commodore Owens, and William Mulvenon, used violent means to help end vendettas and outlawry. In the end, the sheriffs failed to accomplish this alone. Only the introduction of organized military forces— both regulars and militia—helped stamp out the spirit of mayhem. Perhaps the demonstration of impotency in this chief county law enforcement post was no better illustrated than in these post-Civil War decades in New Mexico and Arizona. The ability to enforce the laws depended almost completely upon the goodwill and public-spiritedness of the frontier citizenry. The observation of a Tucson journalist was well taken when he noted that the people of Cochise County were bent upon acquiring wealth and ignored the good of society. The result of this abdication of responsibility were bloody wars.[34]

12

Ex-Officio Collector

 Besides their law enforcement duties, the sheriffs of New Mexico and Arizona territories performed an additional task—tax collecting. Although seemingly unrelated to their primary responsibility, the lawmen had gathered public revenues for centuries in England and, later, in the eastern states. They carried out this duty in an *ex-officio* ("by virtue of office") capacity. In both territories, the sheriffs also collected license fees of businesses. In a property conscious society such as that of the American frontier, these tasks were often very sensitive and could occasionally involve physical danger. The main hindrances lawmen faced in collecting taxes were evasion of payment, a widely scattered and wandering population, and hostile ethnic and religious groups, to name only a few obstacles. Since the sheriff-collectors managed large sums of public monies, citizens often accused them of dishonesty. The territorial assemblies attempted to tighten oversight of the sheriffs, but such accusations continued to follow the collectors. Toward the end of the territorial era, Arizona and New Mexico sought to resolve such controversies by divesting the sheriff of tax collecting duties, at least in counties that could afford the luxury of an additional public servant. The emancipation of the sheriff from this double duty improved the law enforcement efficiency of the sheriffs, although they were dismayed at the loss of extra income.[1]

Frontiersmen commonly held multiple offices. Not only did the territories lack the wealth necessary to support many public officials, but the essential offices seldom yielded the income necessary to support a family. The combination of sheriff and collector also came naturally to Arizonans and New Mexicans. In the course of serving warrants and other court papers, the chief county lawman and his deputies routinely traveled to the farthest corners of the bailiwick and knew the country better than any other official. Who better to gather the revenue than the sheriff? These wide-ranging officials collected an array of monies, including poll taxes, school taxes, and property taxes, as well as fees for business and other licenses. In Arizona, the sheriffs also performed the additional task of tax assessment, although this combination of duties could lead to conflicts of office. New Mexicans seem to have normally combined the office of assessor with that of county clerk. The collector received as his fee a percentage—perhaps five percent—of all taxes gathered.[2]

When tax time arrived, the sheriff's office became the center of feverish activity. In September 1873, the Santa Fe *Daily New Mexican* advised readers that Sheriff Carlos Conklin would soon make his collection rounds. "Parties owing taxes should be collecting their loose change," the writer noted. To inform all his constituents, Conklin carefully published notices in both English and Spanish. Three years later, Sheriff Conklin—a veteran lawman by now—urged all late taxpayers to visit his office in the probate court room and pay up and thus "save costs." The collector in Yavapai County, Arizona, was equally busy in this important period. "There will be a great deal of work to be done in and out of [the collector's] office from now until fall," said a Prescott journalist on behalf of Sheriff Andrew J. Moore in April 1868, since he will be "assessing the property of the county, and collecting the taxes. . . ." Knowing that citizens were generally unhappy about such official activities, this journalist jokingly reminded taxpayers that they should be prepared "to pungle," that is, shrink or shrivel, before the almighty sheriff-collector. Some cautious sheriffs, such as Santiago Baca of Bernalillo County, New Mexico, preferred to avoid face to face confrontations with reluctant taxpayers and attempted to work through the mails.[3]

The collectors traveled extensively to assess and gather taxes. To ease the tedium, they sometimes traveled with their wives or children. Lincoln County Sheriff John Poe permitted his wife, Sophie, to go along after the Indian threat had diminished in the mid-1880s. Peter Brady, Jr., recalled that his father took the son along on official trips through Pima County, Arizona, as early as the 1870s. The *Prescott Courier* had some fun at the expense of Deputy Collector Orick Jackson, a subordinate of the notable Sheriff, Buckey O'Neill, in the following decade. Jackson apparently tended to become disoriented in the sprawling wilderness of Yavapai County and wander aimlessly for days. When the *Courier* observed Jackson departing on an assessing tour of the Agua Fria region this writer remarked humorously that O'Neill was holding a search party in readiness, since the deputy "never fails to lose himself when he gets a few miles away from Prescott." Jackson evidently made his way back to the county seat in this instance.[4]

The assessment of property, which Arizona sheriffs were called upon to perform, often presented more problems than that of collection. The frontiersmen were anxious to make improvements to their homesteads, mines, and other endeavors, but were understandably reluctant to submit to a new assessment. Such a visit by the sheriff would almost certainly result in an increase of taxes. Furthermore, this hardworking citizen might regard the lawman-assessor as unsympathetic to his economic situation or as a political enemy. In either instance, the taxpayer naturally was wary of the assessor when this official placed a value on the property at variance with that assigned by the owner.

The wise assessors moved cautiously. Corydon Cooley, a deputy assessor in the isolated eastern precincts of Yavapai County, Arizona, in the 1870s, later admitted that he relied upon the property owner's judgment to assign value to their real estate. Cooley did not desire to court trouble with his neighbors. Although he, as well as all assessors, were instructed to inquire about the number of cattle or sheep on each ranch, they could not physically count the vast herds or flocks in such large counties. This discreet assessor sometimes distributed assessment forms in advance of a personal visit and permitted property owners to estimate the value of their land and goods. Sheriff Frank Wattron began his duties as assessor and collector in Navajo County, Arizona, in this manner, according to the *Holbrook Argus,* in March 1900. While Wattron and his deputies tended to accept the owners' valuations in good faith, many of them naturally underestimated their property values. Some even failed to register conspicuous items. One of Wattron's deputies enumerated 257 bicycles, but could find no owners! If any taxpayer felt aggrieved in any assessment, he could appeal to the local board of equalization. The board of county commissioner usually doubled in this capacity.[5]

The common border between New Mexico and Arizona presented many difficulties for assessors and collectors. Cattle and sheep men moved herds between the territories at will. When the tax men charged that the ranchers were attempting to avoid assessments, the stockmen replied indignantly that they were merely searching for the best grass and water. Sometimes, they owned property in both territories. New Mexico sheepmen, who began to move flocks into the Little Colorado Valley of Arizona as early as the 1870s, were especially a problem for local sheriffs. While these roving stockmen grazed their sheep in Arizona, they then withdrew their animals into New Mexico each year for shearing. This was necessary, they alleged, to place their crop of wool closer to market.[6]

Sheriffs on both sides of the state line were alert to roving stockmen. In March 1876, Deputy Sheriff James Stimson, who resided in St. Johns—then Yavapai County—wrote Sheriff Edward F. Bowers, his superior in Prescott. "Send me the proper papers so that I can assess these sheep men early . . . ," Stimson urged. Otherwise, continued the deputy, "they will start for New Mexico early to avoid paying tax." Even these precautions were sometimes unsuccessful. When a resident of the Little Colorado criticized Sheriff Bowers of failing to collect from the sheepmen, the collector tried to assure this grumbler that "every reasonable effort has been made to catch these roving bands of sheep. . . ." A similar, but perhaps less aggravated, problem existed along New Mexico's border with Texas. When a Sweetwater, Texas, cattleman received an assessment notice from the sheriff of Lincoln County, New Mexico, the stockman promptly mailed the collector a copy of his Texas tax receipt. This angry Texan expressed the hope that the New Mexico collector would "giv [sic] me no more truble [sic]."[7]

While New Mexico sheriffs were spared the duty of assessment, the lawmen of both territories shared many common problems in the collection of taxes. In the early 1880s, Deputy Sheriff Billy Breakenridge faced the delicate problem of collecting taxes among the rough and independently spirited cattle and rustling element in eastern Cochise County, Arizona. The deputy shrewdly made the friendship of William "Curly Bill" Brocius, an outlaw with a keen sense of humor, and asked him to assist with the collection of taxes. Brocius sensed the irony in such a game and entered it enthusiastically. When the deputy collector described this ploy to his superior, Sheriff John H. Behan, the latter thought it "a good joke." Behan "thought it over for a few moments," recalled Breakenridge, "and then, laughing, said 'Yes, and we will make every one of those blank blank cow thieves pay his taxes'. . . ."[8]

Large corporate organizations often presented the most serious collection problems. This was especially true in New Mexico, where disputes persisted for many years over the titles to Spanish and Mexican land grants. In some counties, such as Colfax, the collectors were at a complete loss as to which citizens were taxable. Many long-time settlers were technically squatters on Maxwell Land Grant land. Furthermore, this great company, which enveloped Colfax County and parts of the neighboring counties of New Mexico and Colorado, was owned by absentee Dutch capitalists. The investors in many concerns—whether mining, cattle, or railroad—in either territory resented any form of taxation. They argued that without their risk capital the frontier would have remained a wilderness. Excessive taxation, continued these financial barons, would merely discourage future investments. They naturally neglected to acknowledge the incentives provided by the United States, as well as the territorial governments. Such disregard for the public good outraged many inhabitants of New Mexico and Arizona and helped to spawn political protest movements in the Southwest. These antagonisms were related to the larger national Populist (People's) Party movement in the 1880s and 1890s.[9]

At the same time, the inhabitants of Arizona and New Mexico realized that the tax revenue derived from the railroads and other large companies was critical to the support of county government. Frontier counties were usually desperate for funds with which to build new buildings and make improvements. Such a problem beset Mohave County, Arizona, whose jail had fallen into disrepair. One journalist noted, in December 1881, that the citizens expected to be able to build a new facility with the first installment of taxes due from the Atlantic & Pacific Railroad, then entering Mohave County. While the sums paid by railroads into the treasuries of these frontier counties were modest by modern standards, such revenues loomed large in the territories. In November 1884, the *Las Vegas Daily Optic* reported that the Maxwell Land Grant Company had just paid its annual assessment—$8,000—and that the Prairie Cattle Company, another corporate entity, turned over $7,000 to Colfax County Collector Matthias Stockton. The Atlantic & Pacific did even better. This enterprise paid $14,964.82 to Bernalillo County in 1891, on its machinery, depots, and rolling stock. This same company paid an additional $1,520.73 on its lands, while the company trustees paid another $2,000 in taxes. The Santa Fe Railroad paid $8,410.41 into the county treasury. Of course, the county was not permitted to retain this entire amount, since a portion was designated to the territorial treasury.[10]

In both territories, the railroad companies adopted the delaying tactic of costly court litigation against the tax collectors. Since the sheriffs in Arizona were assessors, as well as collectors, they earned the double enmity of the railroad barons. As the Southern Pacific Railroad advanced across Arizona in the early 1880s, clashes with the tax collectors became commonplace. In February 1882, the company filed for a restraining order against Sheriff John H. Behan of Cochise County to prevent the lawman from collecting the assigned levy. "This act does not take any person by surprise," said the *Tombstone Epitaph*, "as it was expected . . . that the company would fight it [the assessment] out in the courts." The Southern Pacific took similar legal action against the sheriffs of Maricopa and Yuma counties.[11]

Similar minor dramas were acted out between collectors and companies in the neighboring territory to the east. In December 1886, the *Weekly New Mexican* of Santa Fe reported legal clashes between the sheriffs of the Counties of San Miguel, Valencia, and Grant on the one hand and the Pullman Palace Car Company on the other. This company, which leased passenger cars to the railroads serving Arizona and New Mexico, claimed exemption from local taxes. Company attorneys argued that Pullman paid taxes in Illinois, headquarters of the firm. Yet, the sheriffs of these three New Mexico counties persisted with efforts to collect the necessary levy. They "were the only collectors in the territory who attempted to collect taxes from the Pullman company," according to this Santa Fe journal. On 8 December, Territorial Chief Justice Elisha Long granted a temporary writ of injunction at the request of the Pullman Company enjoining the sheriffs from further collection. These three lawmen were instructed to reappear in court in the following month and show cause why the injunction should not become permanent. The outcome of this litigation is unclear, although most such cases were settled eventually out of court. While southwesterners did not agree that these giant economic empires should be exempt from taxation, the citizenry usually consented to compromises. Even after significant reductions of assessments, railroad taxes often constituted the largest single contribution to the county coffers.[12]

During the course of these tax collecting controversies with the railroad companies, some sheriffs won considerable popular applause for resisting these economic giants. Sheriff Buckey O'Neill of Yavapai County, Arizona, went farther than most collectors to compel the Atlantic & Pacific Railroad to pay its fair share. In 1889 O'Neill attempted to assess all of the property of the railroad within his county. This included 614,000 acres of federal land grants, much of which company officials declared was undeveloped and therefore should not be assessed. When O'Neill assessed this land at the rate of $1.25 per acre, Yavapai County levied the A & P for the spectacular sum of $892,260.38.[13]

When the county board of equalization obligingly reduced the company's assessment to thirty cents per acre—even though private citizens were required to pay more personal taxes on similar land— Collector O'Neill expressed much disgust at this affront to the popular will. In a widely publicized letter, O'Neill pointed out that he had actually assessed only the improved railroad lands and ignored the company's four million unimproved acres. O'Neill had little hope of winning such a battle. He was only one man against this far-flung economic empire. Furthermore, Arizona Governor Nathan O. Murphy feared the Atlantic & Pacific executives would make political trouble for him and might not pay any 1889 taxes at all. O'Neill's radical position against the company, which had attempted to prevent his election, cost him any hope of returning to office. He soon openly joined the Populist Party.[14]

Sheriff Santiago Baca of Bernalillo County, New Mexico, stunned the Santa Fe Railroad officials in January 1886, when he served an attachment upon an entire freight train in Albuquerque. The lawman was prompted to take this action when he disagreed with the district attorney's compromise tax settlement with the company. The *Albuquerque Journal* reported that Collector Baca had presented the Santa Fe with a tax bill for $18,732.65, "but despite his patient waiting and repeated applications . . . , the company has taken not the least notice of his demand. . . ." "Sheriff Baca is a very good natured officer . . . ," this writer protested, "but there is a time when forbearance ceases to be a virtue. . . ." The company "defied his authority" and the lawman lost "all patience at the lack of common courtesy." Hence, his attachment of the freight train. Baca forbade the engineer from taking his locomotive and cars out of the yard until the interested parties resolved the suit. The precise nature of this settlement is not clear, although many New Mexicans expressed admiration for "Bold Baca," as the territorial press described the Bernalillo County lawman.[15]

In such confrontations between private interests and public officials, compromise was the most common solution. The boards of county supervisors usually consulted with railroad management and arrived at some mutually satisfactory tax rate. In September 1899, an Arizona journal noted such a settlement when the Navajo County supervisors approved an agreement which compromised the taxes of the Santa Fe Pacific (formerly the Atlantic & Pacific) for several years.[16]

Of the many duties of the sheriff-collector, the management of public tax monies caused him the most concern. The system of accounting for such revenues was often rudimentary in the early days of the territories and exposed him to much public criticism. The dual offices of collector and sheriff retained a private character that dated from medieval England, in which the office holder held his position(s) as a personal, unsalaried trust of the Crown. The incumbent was then expected to conduct the office largely unsupervised, charge fees to recipients for services rendered, manage all monies collected, and retain a percentage as personal income. While the frontier sheriffs were far from their ancestral English counterparts—the shrievalty was sometimes hereditary in Britain—these Southwestern lawmen still enjoyed considerable independence in the conduct of office.[17]

Such a system prevailed in the United States in the nineteenth century, and the Territories of New Mexico and Arizona were no exception. However, the negative aspects of this aristocratic practice of office holding emerged more fully in the tax collector's office in these frontier districts. The collector incurred sizable debts when he assumed the duty of gathering revenues. Not only did he assume responsibility for the debts of his predecessor, who invariably left a list of delinquent tax payers, but the new official had to begin his term without official financial support. In addition to filing a bond (equal to the amount of tax monies that would accrue in his first levy) the collector was constrained to begin formal duties with personal monies. These obligations were duplicated, to some degree, as he initiated his shrieval duties. However, the monetary outlay required to begin tax collecting was probably greater than in beginning those of sheriff.

The *Roswell Record* attempted to explain these procedures to its readership in April 1896:

> When the sheriff and collector gives bond and takes charge [of his office], the tax rolls are turned over to him and he is charged with the full amount of the taxes due the county. At stated intervals [each month] he makes settlements [with the territory], and at the end of his term all his receipts from treasurers are taken into account, and the tax rolls are examined and all taxes not collected are placed on the 'delinquent' list, and credited to the out-going sheriff and charged to his successor in office. . . .

In this way the sheriff-collector and his bondsmen entered office with debts. He could only hope that political enemies refrained from demanding a settlement of the collector's entire debt at the end of his term. A mutual understanding seems to have prevailed between political interests that each collector could pass his delinquent tax list and other uncollectable debts to his successor or until the county government agreed to erase the debt.[18]

Perhaps the most nettlesome aspect of the *ex-officio* collector's duties concerned delinquencies. The law required the sheriffs to make some additional efforts to collect this overdue revenue. Each year the lawman published the delinquent list in county newspapers. His success in this endeavor was a measure of the collector's mettle and could win votes at the next election. In January 1885, the Tucson *Arizona Daily Citizen* asked through its pages what Sheriff Robert H. Paul intended to do about the back taxes list, but went on to add, "We don't pretend to know what action Paul will take. . . ."[19]

The collectors preferred to resolve delinquencies with a minimum of effort. Communications by mail could prevent tempers from flaring. In January 1876, Alexander McSween, a lawyer and banker in Lincoln County, New Mexico, informed Joseph Blazer, a sawmill owner, that his taxes were past due. "The matter may cause you trouble . . . ," cautioned McSween, since Sheriff William Brady was contemplating a personal visit. McSween tried to reassure Blazer that the lawman had "deferred his trip upon my promise to communicate with you." Apparently, this sawmiller continued to neglect the collector's call. Some years later, in December 1891, after Blazer's precinct was annexed to Dona Ana County, Sheriff Mariano Barela had similar problems with him. "Unless you . . . make immediate settlement," cautioned the lawman, "I shall be compelled to seize and sell sufficient property to satisfy said [overdue] tax." A short time later, Lincoln County Sheriff George Curry informed John Y. Hewitt, President of the Old Abe Mining Company, in White Oaks, that his firm's taxes were in arrears and that "Interest at the rate of 25 per cent per annum from Nov. 1st of each year [is assigned] until paid. . . ." "If you do not call and settle . . . before July 1st," continued Curry, "I will be compelled to proceed against your property as the law directs."[20]

The seizure and sale of personal property for back taxes took place frequently, as the economic promise of this new land was not always forthcoming. The collectors had no recourse but to enforce the law, no matter how unpopular this unpleasant duty might make them. In February 1893, Eddy County Sheriff David Kemp announced that he would seize "without deviation or discrimination" all goods necessary to satisfy back taxes. In January 1888, Neill B. Field, outgoing president of the New Mexico Bar Association, called the attention of his fellow barristers to the extraordinary increase in sheriffs' suits against delinquent taxpayers. In the Second Judicial District, "a most flagrant abuse . . . has oppressed the people . . . ," said Field. The collectors had entered 984 suits against citizens whose taxes were in arrears, in some instances only by two to four dollars. In the other districts, the collectors had also entered suits, but in lesser numbers. To add to the discomfort of these citizens, added this attorney, "large amounts of [court] costs were taxed against the unfortunate and impoverished people for fees . . ." of the court clerks, sheriffs, and district attorneys. Such tactics, whatever their justification, could only harm the relations of county lawmen with their constituents and may have contributed to the growing Populist sentiment in New Mexico.[21]

Sheriff Tomas Perez of Apache County, Arizona, experienced a embarrassing moment in December 1883, when the supervisors reversed him in a delinquency case. Some citizens were already unhappy with Perez and accused him of "heaping a heavy tax upon the people" through unjust assessments. When the collector accused two ranchers, Benjamin and Edward Brown, of failing to declare all of their livestock for tax purposes, the lawman soon appeared with a posse and announced that he intended to seize the animals in question. However, upon closer examination of the assessment form— and much to the consternation of the collector—the brothers demonstrated that they had actually assessed themselves more horses than in their herd! Sheriff Perez was forced to withdraw empty handed, and Benjamin Brown noted joyfully in his diary, "This little exploit cost the County $400.00." The Browns probably took some delight in the failure of Tomas Perez, a wealthy Hispano, to win reelection. Benjamin Brown went to the trouble to mention in his diary that the posse consisted of Spanish-Americans, whom the Anglo brothers detested.[22]

The duties of tax collecting could occasionally lead to violence, as Deputy Sheriff Frank Nichols learned in May 1883. While engaged in a card game with a citizen named Scott in Colfax County, New Mexico, the two men quarreled. The source of the argument was reportedly the deputy's assessment of the property of Scott and others at the table. They declared that Nichols's valuation was too high. The exchange of heated words quickly led to violence, as the players ganged up on Nichols and gave him a beating. However, the officer was eventually able to reach his revolver and to kill Scott, the ringleader. Although the deputy sheriff pleaded self-defense at his trial, the district judge in Springer sentenced him to seven years in prison.[23]

In addition to collecting taxes, the sheriff also gathered the proceeds from licenses. From the outset of New Mexico Territory, all businesses were required to purchase an operator's license. On 13 November 1847, Santa Fe County Sheriff Ennis J. Vaughn published such a notice in the *Santa Fe Republican:*

> All merchants, grocers, or dram shop keepers are hereby notined [sic] that they must come forward and obtain Licenses or I shall report them for selling without a License. I can always be found at my store on the west side of the Plaza, next door to Mr. McNight's No. 76 [Saloon ?].

In addition, persons who sponsored dances (*bailes*) were also required to purchase a permit.

Just as the public resented paying taxes, many businessmen disliked buying operator's licenses. In February 1886, Cochise County Sheriff Robert S. Hatch chided his hesitant constituents:

> If some of the members of the grand jury, who are so loud-mouthed in their talk about license tax collecting, will call at the sheriff's office and settle their accounts with the county, as the law directs, they will have a better right to talk.

In January 1903, a saloon owner in Wickenburg, Arizona, informed a lawyer friend that "the sheriff keeps writing me . . ." for the operator's fee. "Say Joe," he wrote, "I wish you would call at the sheriff's office and pay my saloon license for me." "I am hard up," admitted the saloon man.[24]

Arizona Territory generally increased license fees, especially on sporting men. In 1879, the Assembly provided for a $300 fee each quarter on each gambling hall. Twelve years later, the lawmakers removed this requirement but substituted a thirty dollar fee for each table within such establishments. John Cady, a Tucson saloon owner, recalled his experiences with licensing. He paid several fees: for the privilege of selling liquor in his dancehall; a daily $5 dancehall license fee; and a $1.50 collector's fee. Failure to pay each morning, Cady recalled, "would have threatened my business." At first, Cady considered these license fees reasonable. But a sudden increase of the dancehall license to $25 angered him. He believed that his competitors conspired with the officials of local government to raise the fee, in an effort to squeeze him out of business. However, it is more likely that Cady ran afoul of a general reform movement that desired to remove all vices.[25]

The sheriffs fitted license collecting into their daily routines. In Phoenix, Arizona, the sheriffs set aside Saturday afternoon for a jaunt through the saloons and gambling houses. The lawmen bought rounds of drinks for everyone and, in turn, the houses responded with drinks for the collectors. When Carl Hayden entered this shrievalty in 1907, he surprised these sporting men by changing this routine. While perhaps not a teetotaler, Hayden held the saloon crowd at arm's length. He made his rounds on Saturday morning, much to the dismay of the bar men. They were accustomed to sleeping late on Saturday morning and could no longer court his favor with free drinks. Billy McGinty, a deputy to Sheriff James Parks in Solomonville about this time, recalled that the job of collecting licenses on gaming tables could be time consuming and that "They came due at all times during the month. . . . A person could start any game at any time by paying a month's fee," said McGinty. The fee was thirty dollars on each table—roulette, poker, dice, and others—"and there were plenty of them" in the county seat.[26]

By the early twentieth century, reformers had begun to whittle away at the once politically powerful "sporting crowd." The collectors were instrumental in this effort, since one means to harass the gamblers out of business was through dramatic increases in the cost of licenses. When New Mexico Territory initiated a "high license law" in 1891, this proscriptive legislation had an immediate effect. According to the *Denver News*, the sixty liquor businesses in Santa Fe County, New Mexico, alone were quickly reduced to sixteen, and "all of the low dives have been closed." Sheriff James R. Lowry became involved in a similar action in Jerome, Arizona, in 1906. The territorial assembly had imposed similarly high license fees and authorized the sheriffs to close gambling establishments if they failed to pay. Although a resident of Prescott, Lowry's jurisdiction included the bustling mining camp of Jerome. The gamblers declared that this proscriptive ordinance was illegal. Even the district attorney agreed, but in the absence of a court restraining order, the sheriff began to issue the new and very costly gambling licenses to saloons on 1 January 1906. Opponents of these exorbitant ordinances continued to grumble until the following year, when the Arizona Assembly abruptly ended legal gambling. The lawmakers also barred women from dancehalls.[27]

The public maintained close watch upon the collectors in New Mexico and Arizona territories. Of the two duties that the sheriffs commonly performed, collecting and "lawing", the former was potentially the most sensitive. Tax collecting required the officer to be custodian of large amounts of public revenues. Any hint of irregularities resulted in an immediate public outcry. Loss of revenues could mean the loss of important resources for construction of schools, roads, bridges, and other improvements. In January 1869, the Yuma County Board of Supervisors met with the sheriff, apparently Marcus Dobbins, to make a settlement for his past year's tax collections. The collector was short $1,500. When the board threatened to sue, Dobbins resigned. One of Dobbins's successors, George Tyng, also fell under similar suspicion in 1873, although he avoid his predecessor's fate and soon became United States marshal.[28]

In New Mexico, several sheriffs also felt the weight of the guardians of public monies. Taos County Sheriff Caesario Baron, who had a large following among the commoners in his bailiwick, fought a long battle in the courts to retain his post in 1892–93. His county board filed charges against him for "persistently" refusing to hand over tax receipts. "It is about time that it were demonstrated," said the *Daily New Mexican* about Baron, "that public funds are public funds and not a private snap." Baron apparently retained his position, but only after a protracted court battle and threatening demonstrations of his followers, in the form of the feared semi-secret White Cap organization. In Bernalillo County, the board of commissioners succeeded in removing Perfecto Armijo, a popular and veteran lawman, for failing to turn in some $14,000 in taxes. The *Weekly New Mexican* called this episode an appropriate "Lesson for Sheriffs."[29]

In every county in the two territories, some collectors were subjects of charges of embezzlement or mismanagement of tax revenues. The collectors of Lincoln County, New Mexico, came under heavy fire in the 1870s. In 1875 the governor informed the assembly that this county had failed to turn in tax revenues for the years 1873 and 1874. It fell to Probate Judge Lawrence Murphy to explain this delinquency. Murphy alleged that Sheriff Lewis G. (Jack) Gylam had neglected to collect any revenues in 1873 at all. Murphy hinted that the lawman's negligence was due to his political partisanship, but would only add by way of explanation that Gylam was a Radical Republican. If there was any truth in this charge, the lawman was unavailable for prosecution. He had been killed in the Horrell War in December 1873. Murphy blamed the absence of 1874 tax revenues on the hostile Mescalero Apaches, who, said the judge, prevented the new sheriff, Alexander Hamilton (Ham) Mills, from traveling his county.[30]

Judge Murphy's explanation failed to impress the authorities in Santa Fe. The *Daily New Mexican,* which passed for the official newspaper, sided with the territorial auditor and took some delight in pointing out that the politics of Sheriff Gylam had nothing to do with the obligation of Lincoln County taxpayers to obey the law. Nor did political allegiance bear directly upon the collector's duty to collect the taxes. The *New Mexican* added that Lawrence Murphy, "the democratic mogul" of Lincoln County, had urged Lewis Gylam to run for sheriff in 1871. After Gylam won, Murphy became a bondsman, a clear indication that the new lawman's Radical Republican political faith had not deterred the judge originally. This writer also expressed doubts about the seriousness of Indian hostility as a means to discourage Sheriff Mills. There had been no reported outbreaks, and the Mescaleros had resided upon their reservation for some time. This writer ended his commentary upon the state of Lincoln County's tax problems with the observation that Judge Murphy had the duty of prosecuting delinquent tax collectors and their bondsmen. While Murphy did reluctantly and half-heartedly bring suit against the bondsmen of the former Sheriff Mills, nothing came of it. Controversy continued to surround the Lincoln County tax collectors. In 1878, Sheriff William Brady came under severe criticism for irregularities in his management of public monies. This dispute helped to set off the vicious feud known as the Lincoln County War.[31]

Such problems persisted in the stricken county and beset Chaves County, an offspring of Lincoln. The collectors were unfortunately in the middle of this dispute. On 1 January 1891, two new counties, Eddy and Chaves, were separated from Lincoln. Sheriff Campbell C. Fountain of Chaves, and David L. Kemp of the sister county, inherited old delinquent lists from the parent county but for their appropriate spheres. In turn, these collectors "dunned" the appropriate property owners, now a part of the new counties. An immediate outcry arose when some of these affected tax payers presented the new sheriffs with official receipts showing that they had paid the previous sheriff of Lincoln County, Dan Nowlin. The revelation of such inconsistencies in Nowlin's term was a great surprise. Not only was he a former Texas Ranger, but many citizens of Lincoln County believed him a man of fine "business habits." The *Roswell Record* began to assemble telltale signs of suspicious behavior in Sheriff Nowlin's conduct after the expose. The fact that he departed the county one day after his term expired, that is, on 1 January 1891, should have been a tip off. Not only did he leave "the jurisdiction of . . . New Mexico," said this newspaperman, but the former collector "kept his whereabouts unknown for a long time."[32]

A subsequent investigation revealed that Sheriff Dan Nowlin hit upon a clever scheme to defraud his constituents of tax money. He quietly, but energetically, collected longstanding delinquencies and did not credit them to his accounts. Nowlin counted upon the county board's loss of interest in these old taxes. The county fathers regarded them as uncollectable and had "written them off." While the sheriff may have possessed "business habits," they were of the extortionate type. Just what pressure he used to cajole delinquent taxpayers into paying these debts to the county was not recorded. Chaves Countians were equally embarrassed only five years later, when Sheriff Charles C. Perry absconded to South Africa with more than $7,000 in tax receipts.[33]

The success or failure of the sheriffs to collect the revenues and turn them into the territorial auditor had a direct bearing upon the efficiency of the district courts and other public institutions. The absence of strict laws governing the conduct of the collectors was a constant source of concern. In a message to the New Mexico Assembly in December 1868, Governor R. B. Mitchell complained that collectors failed to turn in the proper amount of revenues and went on to connect such inadequacies with the efficiency of the justice system. He was especially concerned about the territorial paper (currency), which had continued to depreciate and left the government seriously in debt. Mitchell associated a grave deficiency in the ability of the court system to enforce the laws with the absence of revenues:

> In consequence of the want of [financial] means to prosecute criminals, our laws are daily violated with impunity; murderers, run riot throughout the Territory with impunity, for want of public means [revenues] to bring them to justice.

Mitchell admitted that he even lacked revenues with which to requisition three murderers from foreign countries. The embarrassed governor's successors, William A. Pile and Marsh Giddings, continued to express similar regrets about the nonchalant and careless behavior of the sheriff-collectors in the gathering of revenues.[34]

A vicious cycle had arisen in New Mexico, and the sheriffs as collectors were at the center of it. When the sheriffs made little or no effort to collect taxes, their failure had a direct bearing upon the financial welfare of all public institutions. In the absence of revenue flowing into the treasury, New Mexico substituted script to pay salaries and government debts. The script soon lost value because of the insolvent treasury. This worthless paper money—worth twenty-five cents on the dollar about 1870—passed into the hands of taxpayers who, in turn, paid taxes, purchased licenses, and paid fines, with this poor paper. Through their neglect, the sheriffs contributed to their own discomfiture and the wrecking of the judiciary. Public and private morale went into serious decline in this post-war malaise.[35]

On 5 October 1869, Governor William Pile informed Secretary of State Hamilton Fish, the chief administrator of the territories, of this abject breakdown of tax collecting in New Mexico. The county collectors were turning in such negligible amounts of taxes that the absence of revenues was having a deplorable "effect . . . upon the administration of civil law and justice." Only one sheriff, Jose D. Sena of Santa Fe County, turned in an adequate collection for 1869. However, Sena's collections alone enabled the territorial government to limp along.[36]

This black picture persisted for several years in the 1870s. Each governor presented negative tax collecting statistics in his annual message. In January 1878, Governor Samuel B. Axtell reported that the counties collectively owed $76,000 in back revenues. Among the counties with the greatest deficients were Colfax ($33,000) and San Miguel ($21,000). Axtell predicted that the present year, 1878, appeared to continue this trend. Sheriff Desiderio Romero of San Miguel had failed to turn in any monies for the present year, and Lincoln County Sheriff William Brady had not turned in any funds since his term began, on 1 January 1877.[37]

The angry governor lamented this "unfortunate condition" in the tax collectors' offices and proposed a radical solution. Since these arrearages were probably not recoverable, he recommended a special territorial law to permit an out-of-court settlement with each sheriff. In some counties, a complete "write off" of the collector's indebtedness would be necessary, although the governor did not specify the reason. The collectors would be permitted to make new starts. Axtell urged stronger measures to prosecute delinquent sheriffs and to "remodel" the revenue structure, in order to maintain closer bureaucratic controls upon the collectors. He also desired to "make the [district] courts as near self-sustaining as possible," and thus remove them from dependency upon the sagging territorial revenues. The government paid for the support of the justice system, but in the future, if Axtell's recommendations were accepted, "litigants [would have] to pay . . . fees in civil cases. . . ." In criminal cases, the fees of witnesses and jurors would be reduced for the purposes of economizing. It was a poor commentary upon the ineffectiveness of the collectors when the governor proposed to constrain the taxpayers to pay a second time for the upkeep of the justice system.[38]

With the appearance of the railroads and a fresh wave of settlers in the 1880s, the revenues increased measurably in Arizona and New Mexico. However, many problems associated with the tax collectors continued. The assemblies of both territories tightened controls over the sheriff-collectors, requiring them to keep detailed records and to make quarterly—eventually, more frequent—reports to the territorial auditor. Newspapers printed these collection reports. Bonds of collectors were increased to one hundred percent of the taxes to be gathered. Governors became more watchful. In January 1884, Governor Lionel Sheldon summoned all district attorneys to meet in Santa Fe in conjunction with the Assembly to discuss ways to prosecute the sheriffs and county boards when they failed to fulfill the revenue laws. Governor L. Bradford Prince addressed this subject in amazement at the "serene indifference" of collectors who neglected to turn over revenues due the territory and then were shielded through the connivance of county boards. Although these county fathers possessed authority to prosecute delinquent sheriffs, added Prince, the boards refused. "And no doubt [local] political reasons often cause this . . . ," concluded the angry governor. Such regrettable conduct constituted defalcation in fact, but the delinquent sheriff did not feel compelled to flee his county. Presumably, Prince referred to the common practice of the county boards and sheriffs to retain a disproportionate amount of revenues collected, or to make compromise settlements when the collectors failed to take in the assessed amount. In 1894 Prince's successor, William Thornton, reiterated the need to break up "any fraudulent contract and arrangement entered into by the county commissioners and the several sheriffs and collectors. . . ."[39]

In subsequent messages, Governor Prince joined a growing public sentiment in support of the separation of the sheriff's office from the collectorship. This movement became very pronounced in the 1890s as the related subject of removing sheriffs and other officials from the fees system and placing them on salaries grew. In a special address to the New Mexico Assembly in January 1891, Prince recalled the origins of this wedding between the sheriff and collector.

When Gen. Stephen Watts Kearny made this arrangement in 1846, said the governor, it "answered the purpose well enough." The territory was young and economically poor. Such concurrent office holding was no longer an effective answer to the problems of revenue collecting, concluded Prince. He returned to this subject in the following year and expressed some contempt for the lawmen's claim that tax collecting required special skills, presumably that only the sheriffs possessed. "Any honest man who can keep accounts," said the executive, "can perform all the duties satisfactorily."[40]

Prince also objected to "the enormous amounts of fees" earned by collectors, who (he believed) did not devote "one-quarter of his time" to this task. While he did not believe that a separate collector should necessarily receive a salary, Governor Prince recommended a significant reduction of this official's fee, from five to one percent. Such a modest income would remove the temptation to corrupt county politics in order to acquire this lucrative joint position— "these gilded prizes." While the sheriffs would naturally resent the loss of fees from tax collecting, their income from law enforcement duties alone in the larger counties would provide a comfortable living. By 1900 Arizona and New Mexico had begun to implement this highly desirable division of law enforcement and tax collecting responsibilities. In New Mexico, the county treasurer acquired the revenue collecting responsibilities. In both territories, the less wealthy counties were constrained to continue the traditional method of concurrent office holding begun by the military authorities in 1846.[41]

Whatever the merits of combining the tasks of sheriff with tax assessment and gathering, the chief county law officers of New Mexico and Arizona territories shouldered this burden for much of the frontier era. Although the fees of the collectorship were much appreciated, this duty placed the sheriffs in a very "high profile" position. The propertied element—that part of the public with large assessments—maintained a keen interest in the elections to the collectorship. Since this office was combined with that of sheriff, the incumbents in this joint-office were probably not always the best suited persons for the very demanding tasks of county law enforcement. Instead, they were chosen because they, too, were property owners, whom the corporations and other vested interests trusted. That is not to say that the office of collector did not sometimes require a brave occupant. The duty of tax collecting often provoked the public and could arouse the anger of the citizenry.

Perhaps, in this regard, the combination of the two offices—sheriff and collector—made some sense on the Southwestern frontier. However, the decision of the assemblies of New Mexico and Arizona territories to permit the sheriff's office to go its own way—at least in the more prosperous counties—represented a significant step foward for the efficiency of county law enforcement.

13

Handyman

 In addition to the dangerous duties of arresting badmen and pursuing highwaymen, the sheriffs of New Mexico and Arizona territories performed many tasks which appeared unrelated to their official position. The sheriff might be called the local public "handyman," a characterization that also applied to his federal counterpart, the United States marshal. Among county officials, the chief lawman was better placed and perhaps more capable of countering the many and diverse problems that threatened the public welfare. These challenges—public health issues, juvenile problems, supervision of roads and bridges, to name only a few—often fell to the sheriff by default. To attend to such chores required that the lawman possess many qualities not usually associated with the image of the gunfighting sheriff.

The residents of New Mexico and Arizona were very concerned about sanitation and public health and required the sheriffs to assist in efforts to ward off epidemics. When the prefect instituted police regulations for Santa Fe County in February 1856, this code provided that the sheriff and constables use prisoners to clean the streets of all deceased animals and offal every twenty-four hours. The Assembly also took an interest in public health at the territorial level, although its laws were not always well enforced. One 1891 statute required the county commissioners, who had replaced the prefects, to serve as a board of health and each justice of the peace to be a "health officer." During an epidemic, the board of health was to isolate persons in a separate building, the pesthouse. The justice of the peace was empowered to place a warrant in the hands of any sheriff, deputy sheriff, or constable, directing him "to remove any person infected" to this place of quarantine. If the county lacked such a place, the sheriff possessed authority "to take possession of [a] convenient house" for this purpose. Apparently, this law was not well enforced, since the *Daily New Mexican* remarked some years later that it was "a dead letter." The fact that the public health officer served without pay may have contributed to this weakness. Arizona also enacted a health law, authorizing quarantine against smallpox, bubonic plague, and other infectious diseases. Each county contracted the services of a doctor in the capacity of county physician to care for prisoners, conduct autopsies, and advise officials about public health matters.[1]

Southwesterners dreaded outbreaks of smallpox. The sheriff was constantly alert to any signs of this infection. His network of regular and special deputies formed a web across the county and made the chief county lawman the most likely official to be first alerted to the disease. In October 1887, Deputy Sheriff James Speedy informed the Pima County Board of Supervisors that "smallpox [is] very bad" in Nogales and vicinity. He recommended that Tubac and environs "ought to be quarranteened [sic]" and that travelers be forbidden to pass through that village. When rumors circulated to the effect that the disease had returned a few years later, Sheriff R. N. Leatherwood tried to reassure citizens that no new cases of smallpox had been reported. However, smallpox did appear in neighboring Graham County. Sheriff Ben Clark reported six new cases in Clifton. Lorenzo Hubbell, sheriff of Apache County, Arizona, in 1885–86, went far beyond the call of duty during a smallpox epidemic among the Navajos. Having survived the malady as a child, his immunity made it possible for him to personally care for ailing Indians. He vaccinated many victims. He also buried their dead. The grateful Indians accorded him superhuman powers since he succeeded where the medicine men failed.[2]

A successful quarantine required officials to strictly enforce the public health laws. Two cowboys inadvertently wandered into a smallpox cordon in Fort Sumner, New Mexico, in 1882. Jesse James Benton and a friend rode their horses casually into this community late one evening. He recalled:

> We rode . . . right into town never noticing the little yellow flags until we got into the middle of the town. . . . We asked what they were put up for and found out that there was about twenty-five cases of black smallpox. Before we knew it we was quarantined.

Even though Benton and his comrade had had the disease as children, quarantine officers required them to remain in Fort Sumner at their own expense for twenty-one days.[3]

The pesthouse was the most visible sign of the presence of an epidemic and was often the responsibility of the sheriff. A Silver City newsman observed Sheriff Harvey Whitehill escorting a traveler who had contracted smallpox to a designated house outside the town in January 1877. Even known outlaws were not spared the stigma of residence in the pesthouse. In 1899, Bruce "Red" Weaver, a suspected member of the Black Jack Ketchum band, was ordered to this house of the diseased in Springer, New Mexico. Tragedy was always possible in such places. Deputy Sheriff Warren H. Mooers had the unwelcome duty of arresting Joseph Macha, the attendant at the quarantine house in Wallace, New Mexico. Evidently, Macha was acting erratically. The sheriff directed Mooers to send Macha away. When the attendant refused to go, a gunfight erupted. The deputy was killed. Citizens liked the deputy, who had been a Civil War veteran. The *Daily Optic* of Las Vegas, which reported this tragic incident, added that the murderer was lynched by "parties unknown."[4]

Outbreaks of epidemic diseases and other contagions also took place along the international boundary. The constant ebb and flow of people—both Americans and aliens—promoted such unfortunate circumstances. Among the diseases to appear was leprosy. Cochise County, Arizona, maintained a leper colony near Tombstone. In November 1896, a resident of San Miguel County, New Mexico, also contracted leprosy. However, the *Daily New Mexican* noted that in view of the very weak public health law, the victim was not likely to receive any attention.[5]

While caring for the sick was not a part of the sheriff's duties, the lawman often assisted the ill or injured in other ways. In August 1896, Santa Fe County Sheriff William Cunningham received word that a man had been accidentally shot near Glorieta. The message asked Cunningham to bring a doctor at once. The sheriff, who had a reputation as a very tough and unfeeling man, immediately obtained a physician. The two men made the twenty-seven mile journey in a little over three hours. Sheriff John Munds performed a similar service for an ailing citizen in Yavapai County, Arizona. When Munds received a report of a sick man on a local ranch with no one to care for him, the officer took him to a Prescott hospital. A deputy sheriff in Phoenix received an unusual request to come to a residence one night in August 1897. Upon arrival, the deputy found a man, apparently in a daze, sitting naked on the banks of a canal. The man, Carl Smith, was very ill and had wandered from his sick bed in a half-conscious state.[6]

Custody of the insane became a routine part of the sheriff's duties. A noticeable number of mentally disturbed persons were present in Arizona and New Mexico, and the territories built insane asylums as quickly as they erected penitentiaries. The hostile desert environment imposed many stresses upon the pioneers. The mental depression that followed the failure to find El Dorado, and the abuse of alcoholic beverages—quantity and no quality—combined against many fragile personalities. One New Mexican rancher observed that sheepherders were very susceptible to mental derangement. He speculated that the "thirst and loneliness" inherent in their tasks brought on this condition. He could have extended this diagnosis to many other occupations on the lonely Southwestern frontier, to include cowboys and miners. The lives of women on isolated farms and ranches were especially demanding. Many of the insane whom the sheriffs detained were itinerants who drifted along the stagecoach trails and railroad lines. Journalists blamed the new steel rails for an increase in the incidence of insane cases in New Mexico and Arizona. The ease of travel now made it possible for communities to shunt these unwanted persons on to the next village. Like any community, frontier villages were reluctant to admit that insanity took place among long-time residents. Journalists in Prescott, Arizona, often reported sightings of persons exhibiting strange behavior in the surrounding mining camps or on the nearby desert. While not necessarily dangerous, the demented people were often unable to care for themselves. Many died from exposure.[7]

The earliest sheriffs in New Mexico acquired custody of insane persons. In the 1840s, the governor ordered the Santa Fe County sheriff to admit an insane member of the Conklin family to jail. This same family later produced a prominent sheriff of this county. In 1884, the *Weekly New Mexican* reported thirteen such cases in Santa Fe County. Six of them, five women and one man, were in such poor condition that they were placed in the county jail. One year later, Sheriff Eugene Van Patten of Doña Ana County reported that three of his twenty-five prisoners were insane. He urged the territorial authorities to construct an asylum to provide proper care for them. The *Daily New Mexican* observed later that there was "Not a village or town . . . but has from half a dozen to as high as twenty insane persons running at large." Mentally deficient persons resided in "nearly every county jail amidst filth and without comfort or medical care," he added. When New Mexico opened an asylum in Las Vegas in 1892, seventy persons were registered immediately. By April 1884, Arizona maintained fifty-three insane patients in a contract asylum in Stockton, California. The annual cost was exorbitant by territorial standards, about $20,000. The territory constructed a facility near Phoenix in 1885. The incidence of insanity continued to alarm Arizonans. A Prescott paper noted in late 1898 that "The insanity business" had assumed "huge proportions." Sheriff George Ruffner had to assign one deputy exclusively to detain and escort the growing number of cases to the asylum. James Rosborough, Ruffner's colleague in neighboring Mohave County, experienced a similar flurry of cases of dementia about the same time.[8]

Both territories demanded court confirmation of insanity before the sheriffs acquired custody. In New Mexico, legal procedure required affidavits setting forth the subject's mental condition. These documents were filed with a justice of the peace who, if documentation was convincing, presented the case to the district judge. This official summoned two witnesses to affirm the judgment. A physician then examined the patient. The doctor's opinion carried critical weight, although psychiatric medicine was very backward. "Softening of the brain" was one common diagnosis. Arizona Territory required a similar procedure.[9]

The sheriffs were hard-pressed to provide minimal care for insane charges. As many lawmen pointed out, the county jail was not an insane asylum and could hardly accommodate healthy prisoners. One New Mexico journalist rightly condemned the practice of confining lunatics in county jails as "a very dark and ugly blot" upon the territory. When a citizen accused Sheriff Carlos P. Conklin of mismanaging insane prisoners in the Santa Fe County jail in June 1892, he replied that "The insane people are as well taken care of as the circumstances will permit. . . ." The lawman asserted correctly that "The jail is not a proper place for them . . ." and added that the insane "should be where they can have proper medical attendance. . . ." Conklin requested a grand jury investigation of these accusations, but his explanation apparently sufficed. Healthy inmates also objected to residing with these psychiatric cases. In February 1884, Sheriff Robert Paul was constrained to incarcerate a demented traveler in the Pima County jail, only to have the poor man attempt suicide. Paul put "mufflers"—apparently heavy gloves—and handcuffs on the ailing prisoner and even assigned a trusty to sleep in the demented man's cell. However, his self-destructive behavior continued and seriously unnerved other inmates. According to the *Arizona Weekly Star*, the prisoners have "peculiar superstitions" about the presence of lunatics in their cells.[10]

In addition to fits of despondency, insane prisoners were prone to irrational and murderous acts. A Globe newspaper expressed sympathy for a deputy sheriff who had the duty of escorting a "very violent" man to the Stockton mental hospital, in November 1883. The writer predicted that the escort "will have his hands full." Sheriff George Ruffner of Prescott acquired a stubborn demented prisoner, Nick Koko. When Koko refused to put on his clothes for the trip to the asylum in Phoenix, the jailer forcibly dressed the prisoner. The guards carried him down the stairs, where "He then lay on the floor singing to himself. . . ." The staff had to carry him to the carriage. Sheriff John Slaughter had embarrassing moments while caring for the insane in Tombstone, Arizona. One mentally imbalanced woman bit the sheriff as he escorted her to a sanity hearing, while another demented Mexican whom Slaughter lodged in jail poured a bucket of water on the unsuspecting officer.[11]

Misfortune dogged the heels of these mentally deranged persons, and the sheriffs could not escape complicity. In June 1891, fire broke out in the San Miguel County jail in Las Vegas. The conflagration set off panic among several insane prisoners. One struck another mental patient and killed him. A local editor surmised that this tragedy should be good and sufficient reason to speedily complete the asylum, then under construction. A demented man in the Santa Fe County jail assaulted and dangerously wounded a prisoner in December 1892. The victim was a schoolteacher serving a brief sentence for a misdemeanor. Probably the most regrettable event associated with the insane took place on a short buggy ride from the Phoenix railway depot to the Arizona asylum. Undersheriff H. J. Bargman of Navajo County was transporting an insane prisoner to the facility when the prisoner suddenly bolted and fled the carriage. Bargman drew his pistol and fired into the ground. He hoped to frighten the fleeing man and to persuade him to stop. The bullet apparently struck a rock, ricocheted, and struck the patient. One newspaper reported that the unfortunate man might die, although his ultimate fate is unknown.[12]

The frontiersmen were a peripatetic lot. Wandering strangers were a common sight in remote Southwestern communities. While most were probably honest and hardworking, their presence gave cause for public uneasiness. The sheriffs monitored the movements of these anonymous persons. One odious duty associated with vagrants was to bury them. Although the expense of such burials was supposed to be a county responsibility, some local governments refused to assist the sheriff. In January 1867, Sheriff Jose D. Sena of Santa Fe applied to the territorial assembly for special relief for expenses he incurred in such a task. On 18 January, the lawmakers approved his request. The text of this law pointed out that in the absence of a county provision for the burial of unclaimed bodies, the territory was liable. Sena received seventy-five dollars to cover "several such cases" of deceased vagrants.[13]

While few Southwesterners could claim native status, the townspeople were always suspicious of persons with no visible means of support. The public assumed that thieves and other wrongdoers used this roving element as a cover for their criminal acts. This assumption made the enforcement of the vagrancy laws an important part of the sheriff's duties. After the citizens of Phoenix, Arizona, lynched two desperadoes in August 1879, Sheriff Reuben Thomas posted a notice warning all unemployed persons to leave town:

> NOTICE: All idle persons who not having any visible means to maintain themselves, live without employment and not having a good account of themselves, will be arrested in two days after the publication of this notice and dealt with according to law.

A local journalist remarked approvingly that "This town is becoming very unhealthy for hoodlums. . . ."[14]

The vagrancy problem increased when railroads entered the territories. Not only did more outsiders travel through the Southwest, but companies laid off many construction workers upon completion of the railroad. Many unemployed workers remained in the vicinity, while others became vagrants and hoboes. Their numbers increased during economic hard times. The Panic of 1894, the first nationwide crisis to reach Arizona and New Mexico after the entry of the railroads, brought home this problem to lawmen. Cochise County Sheriff Scott White was called to Bowie, Arizona, in the mid-1890s to round up vagrants attracted by a railroad construction project to Globe. The construction company was unable to employ all available workers. A Chinese restaurant owner in Peach Springs, on the Atlantic and Pacific Railroad, had trouble with nine unemployed wanderers on one occasion. After serving food to them, the hoboes refused to pay. In the process of ejecting them, the angry proprietor shot and wounded one man. The justice of the peace fined the cafeman one dollar and costs. Sheriff William

Lake of nearby Kingman, Arizona, informed United States Marshal Robert Paul in June 1892, that "There is a rich harvest of cases here of tramps and hobos. . . ." They were selling whiskey to the Indians, a practice calculated to arouse the public. "We round them up and give them about 50 days on the chain gang," added Lake, "and we have from 3 to [a] dozen [in jail] nearly all the time. . . ."[15]

In addition to vagrants, the sheriffs became involved in many cases involving the custody and care of children. In March 1885, the Maricopa County board of supervisors directed Sheriff Noah Broadway to place Edith Samples, a young orphan, in "the care of Mrs. E. Gardiner and that ten dollars per month is appropriated from the poor house fund . . ." to clothe the young lady. In neighboring Yavapai County, lawmen encountered several similar cases. Sheriff George Ruffner and his wife temporarily took in six-year-old Charles Thompson, whose father had been arrested for train robbery in 1897. One journalist noted that the boy arrived in Prescott "with a tag attached to him, directed to Sheriff Ruffner." Mohave County authorities, who had assumed responsibility for young Thompson when the father was arrested, no longer desired this public charge now that the suspected bandit resided in Ruffner's jail. The ultimate fate of this unfortunate boy is not known. John Munds, Ruffner's successor, assumed responsibility for a parentless Hispanic youth who simply turned up at the Yavapai County jail. The jail staff "adopted him" and named the boy Eduardo Ruffnero (after Jailer Edward Ruffner). Undersheriff John Johns assisted an anxious mother in a child custody case a few weeks later. The estranged husband kidnapped his thirteen-month-old daughter and fled Prescott. Johns and the mother successfully retrieved the child, but the court placed her in the custody of Sheriff Munds until the courts determined the proper parent.[16]

Tempers ran high where homeless children were concerned, as Graham County Sheriff James V. Parks and his staff learned in October 1904. Several residents of the mining camps of Clifton and Morenci had arranged with the New York Foundling Hospital to adopt children and looked forward to their arrival. These anxious foster parents were laboring people from the Hispanic community. When the Anglos (from the wealthier class) learned of this arrangement, they raised a remarkably shrill protest. They objected to the assignment of presumably Anglo children to persons of Latin background. These haughty protesters accused the Catholic hospital administrators of being insensitive to the children's health. Racist hackles were obviously up. Although Sheriff Parks assigned deputies to keep the contending parties apart, the well-to-do Anglo families forcibly took possession of the foundlings. In an incredibly muddled decision, the territorial supreme court sanctioned this forcible seizure and granted the kidnappers legal custody of the children![17]

The sheriffs also monitored the activities of older children who thrived upon roughhousing and mischief-making that sometimes endangered themselves and persons around them. In May 1883, a Santa Fe policeman complained to the *Daily New Mexican* about lenient parents who permitted children to play in the streets. He urged parents to keep them home. Instead of counselling children against fighting, Deputy Sheriff Henry Lovin encouraged Lane Cornwall, a Kingman schoolboy, to defend himself. Irene Cornwall Cofer, sister of the boy, recalled that the school bully regularly picked on her brother. One day Deputy Lovin "came along just as the fight was at its best and pulling off his hat he laughed and shouted in his booming voice, 'Whip him Cornwall.'" Instead, Irene watched helplessly as her brother received another beating. After school was dismissed, the deputy had a bag of candy waiting for the dejected youth. Even though young Cofer lost the fight, the deputy sheriff had taught him to try to defend himself.[18]

Many community activities centered upon the county sheriff's office even though they did not necessarily relate to the official duties of the lawman. His office served as a clearinghouse for information about many miscellaneous subjects. His bulletin board contained messages and information about varied things. The alert and heady county lawman made it his business to know everything happening in his bailiwick. This included noncriminal activities as well as the doings of the underworld. C. B. Genung, who grew to manhood in the vicinity of Prescott, Arizona, recalled that his mother sent him to Sheriff Buckey O'Neill's office for information about the whereabouts of the senior Genung. The father was working away from home in 1889, and the wife became alarmed when she learned that stagecoach robbers were running loose in the county. She feared her husband might have run afoul of the bandits. "We went to Bucky's office first," recalled Genung, "because he knew everything that was going on. . . ." Sure enough, the sheriff knew the location of the elder Genung. In 1886, John P. Clum, former editor of the *Tombstone Epitaph,* announced his desire to be appointed Apache Indian agent. Sheriff Robert Hatch obliged Clum by permitting the candidate to leave a petition for signatures in the lawman's office.[19]

When governmental agencies desired any information, the sheriffs were the logical choice to gather the data. They often took local censuses and served as assistant census marshals in the national enumerations. The auditor of Arizona Territory called upon these county officers for information gathering on another occasion. The auditor distributed blank forms to the sheriffs and asked them to collect economic statistics and other information for use in promotional literature. In March 1884, the auditor complained that the county lawmen had neglected this duty. Many sheriffs had failed to return any forms at all. The *Weekly Citizen* of Tucson scolded them and expressed the desire "that the sheriffs . . . will recognize the value such information will be to the territory. . . ." This writer urged each chief county lawman to "insist on their subordinates paying special attention to obtaining and compiling" the requested information. Sheriff Robert Paul of Pima County replied in his defense that he "had never received such blanks." Nonetheless, the sheriffs were considered an important element in efforts to publicize the territory and to attract settlers. These county officers were closest to the sources of valuable information about crops and other economic activities in the hinterland, since they routinely traveled to the farthest corners of their jurisdictions. Newspapers tapped them regularly for a wide variety of news from across the county.[20]

The sheriff's office often became a missing persons bureau. Robert Hatch, Sheriff of Cochise County during the days of declining mining in Tombstone, often received requests for information about missing men. In March 1886, he had two such inquiries: one from a mother who was anxious about her son, and a second query about a man reportedly killed in a mining accident five years earlier. In March 1882, Harvey H. Whitehill, Hatch's colleague in neighboring Grant County, New Mexico, received a request from an anxious mother in faraway Russia. She had last heard from her son, Woldemar Tethenborn, when he wrote her from Silver City about one year earlier. This inquiry placed the sheriff in an awkward position. Whitehill knew of the whereabouts of Tethenborn. The wayward son desired to be a tough frontier badman and had adopted the sobriquet "Russian Bill." He joined a band of rustlers who apparently used the Russian as the brunt of their jokes. In October 1881, vigilantes in the Shakespeare mining camp put an end to their forays by hanging the leader, Sandy King, and Russian Bill. In his reply to this anxious mother, Sheriff Whitehill tried to let her down gently. He informed her that her son had committed suicide. While not the most tactful way to break the news, this information was technically correct. The coroner's jury had so ruled in order to spare the sheriff the embarrassment of trying to arrest his own constituents, the vigilantes.[21]

The sheriff was also expected to observe the conduct of foreign nationals who resided in his county. This was especially difficult and sensitive when Mexican nationals were involved. When this republic to the south experienced revolutionary movements, many political refugees took sanctuary in Arizona and New Mexico. In August 1907, Augustin Pina, Mexican consul in Phoenix, Arizona, directed an inquiry to Sheriff Carl Hayden. Several Mexican citizens resided in Maricopa County. Pina's superiors desired the lawman's evaluation of the "personal character and standing" of each Mexican citizen. Apparently, Mexico City planned to request their repatriation if the sheriff found them engaging in politically subversive activities against their homeland.[22]

Natural disasters were an ever-present menace in the Southwest, and the sheriffs were often called upon in such emergencies. Fires and floods constituted the biggest hazards. When heavy rains caused a dam to break on Walnut Creek, in Yavapai County, in February 1889, Sheriff Buckey O'Neill went into action. The flood swept through the mining camp of the same name. O'Neill kept relief teams working day and night to assist survivors and to recover the dead. Only 56 bodies were recovered, out of 150 missing persons. Some months later the sheriff arrested Daniel Burke in connection with the disaster. Burke had been dispatched to warn the residents of Walnut Creek camp when the rains began. He became drunk along the way and failed to spread the alarm.[23]

Fires were a common hazard in the hastily constructed towns of the West. Buildings were jammed closely together, and streets were narrow. Most communities lacked any firefighting equipment other than the usual shovel and bucket brigades. A serious fire broke out in a Prescott hotel on Saturday night, 14 July 1900, just as Sheriff John Munds was making his rounds. Although the village boasted the oldest firefighting department in Arizona, the water source failed at this critical moment. Munds quickly organized a bucket brigade and dynamited buildings in the path of the flames. The fire burned itself out about 3:30 A.M. When another fire erupted in this same community a short time later, proprietors of shops and gambling houses moved merchandise and equipment into the streets and continued to function. Sheriff John Munds served as treasurer to safeguard cash receipts in the "open air" marketplace.[24]

Looting was always a problem in such circumstances. The piles of merchandise and other materials in the streets were a constant temptation to thieves. Sheriff Desiderio Romero organized a posse in Las Vegas, New Mexico, to guard property after a fire in September 1880. Even the militia came into play. Romero "did everything in his power to preserve order and arrest the scoundrels who . . . were stealing goods . . . ," said one newspaperman. Sheriff John Henry Thompson provided the same service when flames gutted downtown Globe, Arizona, in June 1894. He surprised many citizens when he ordered the famous hanging tree cut down. The fire had killed this old landmark, and the sheriff feared it might fall on an unsuspecting passer-by. A Tombstone journal commended Sheriff John H. Behan and his posse which fought "manfully" to break up a massive blaze in this mining camp in May 1882. Deputy Billy Breakenridge had discovered and extinguished a fire in the county treasurer's office in the previous month. He believed a careless smoker had left a burning cigarette in an ashtray. The *Tombstone Epitaph* speculated that this second fire began the same way.[25]

Since animals played such an important part in the lives of frontiersmen, it was only natural that the sheriffs' duties should include them. Yavapai County Sheriff George Ruffner was a lover of fine horseflesh. He owned race horses and rode them in competition. Ruffner had the duty of interceding on behalf of a team of horses in March 1897. The owner had frightfully abused the animals. By the time the sheriff arrested the man, the horses were so terribly mangled that they were not expected to recover. The sheriffs acquired a new connection with animal life near the end of the territorial era. In 1895, the New Mexico Assembly passed a game law which provided for hunting seasons and forbade killing certain wildlife—deer, elk, fawn, and antelope—except in designated months. While this law created the position of game wardens, they served without pay. With this fact in mind, the law also called upon sheriffs and constables "to file complaints when they have knowledge of violation of the game laws," said the *Daily New Mexican*.[26]

It was not uncommon for personnel in the sheriff's office to perform many unusual tasks in one day. They were troubleshooters, in the modern sense of the word. On 19 January 1905, the *Arizona Republican* reported that Sheriff John Elliott Walker of Phoenix, along with his men, removed one dead calf from a woman's yard, performed relief work among victims of a local flood, and searched for a lost woman. Rabid dogs were also a part of the sheriff's problems. William C. Truman, chief county lawman in Florence, Arizona, encountered an infected animal. The animal bit him. The sheriff had to travel to a Chicago hospital for the painful anti-rabies treatments.[27]

These county handymen performed many tasks not necessarily a part of their official routines, yet for the public good. The *Socorro Chieftain* reported that Sheriff Holm O. Bursum was absent from his office in September 1896. Bursum was far away in the western precincts supervising the construction of a wagon road between Magdalena and Mogollon. Oscar F. Townsend, chief lawman of Yuma County, Arizona, moved the county records from La Paz to the new county seat, Arizona City (Yuma) in 1871. Andrew J. Doran, sheriff of Pinal County, performed a similar service some years later. Some public debate was stimulated in March 1898 when the *Prescott Courier* accused a competitor of insulting former Sheriff Buckey O'Neill. In an effort to beautify downtown Prescott, this energetic lawman had planted many trees. Since O'Neill's departure from office nearly ten years earlier, his successors had ignored the trees. Apparently, subsequent sheriffs found no "pleasure" in such gratuitous undertakings for the public good. "There is no place in the statute[s]," said the *Courier,* "where this duty is imposed on that official [the sheriff]. . . ."[28]

The hardworking officers received many requests for assistance, some rather exotic. Perhaps Sheriff John Poe was called upon to perform the most bizarre duty of all—to search for a ghost in Lincoln, New Mexico. The sheriff and his wife resided in a building that had formerly belonged to the local business baron, Lawrence Murphy, leader of one of the feuding factions in the Lincoln County War. Many legends circulated about him, although he died early in the vendetta of complications arising from alcoholism. Colonel Mickey Cronin, a retired soldier, rented a room in the old Murphy building. His quarters were on the floor above the Poes. Cronin also enjoyed his whiskey. When in his cups, this old veteran began to suspect the presence of Lawrence Murphy's ghost. On several occasions, Cronin raised the alarm in the middle of the night and pleaded for the sheriff's protection from this ghostly apparition. On each occasion, the lawman could find no evidence of the unearthly shade. In another connection, a New Yorker, acting on the notion that the sheriff knew all things about his bailiwick, asked a Maricopa County lawman to help him find a wife. This spouse-seeker desired the "perfect woman," he reminded the officer. The anxious Easterner approached the Phoenix lawman, he added, because he must be a "big-hearted man, else you could not be sheriff . . . in that big western country."[29]

Marriage counselling was not outside the many-sided sheriff's competency. In 1905, Socorro County Sheriff Leandro Baca was surprised when two young newly married couples visited his office. They had just gotten married in San Marcial, but the girls were anxious about their father's reaction. This patriarch was William (Baldy) Russell, a standoffish rancher who was reportedly hiding from a Texas murder indictment. While there was no easy solution to this predicament, Baca made the best of the situation. He obligingly escorted the newlyweds to a neighboring ranch for their honeymoon and then accompanied them to the Russell ranch. To the relief of all concerned, both parents were absent. Sophie Poe, wife of the Lincoln County sheriff, recalled that his Hispano constituents held mistaken notions about her husband's official powers. They confused him with the Mexican predecessor to the sheriff, the *alguacil mayor,* as well as with the *alcalde.* One couple came to Sheriff Poe with the plea that he divorce them. They wanted a "'separate,'" recalled the sheriff's wife.[30]

This wide range of miscellaneous duties added a dimension to the activities of the frontier sheriffs not normally associated with the image of the fighting lawman. These many jobs indicated that they possessed a keen sense of responsibility and civic-mindedness. They demonstrated compassion when they assumed responsibility for homeless children and the insane. They revealed resourcefulness during natural disasters and discretion when dealing with family problems among constituents. They showed much courage as they carried out public health duties during epidemics. They served the public in innumerable ways, especially as the sheriff's county-wide network of subordinates doubled as a public information system. When these many services are considered together, it is clear that the inhabitants of New Mexico and Arizona territories expected much from their sheriffs.

The Shrievalty Enters
the Twentieth Century

 The office of the county sheriff somehow endured the turbulent territorial era and began to experience significant positive changes as statehood approached in 1912. This is not to imply that a mood of optimism was always apparent, as many problems still existed in law enforcement. But considerable change had taken place in organization and procedures as a result of professionalism. Facilities were much improved and new technology was employed. More counties were created and, hence, more sheriffs existed in both territories. Society was much more stable as the inhabitants of the region outgrew their wanderlust. Communications were vastly improved, giving the sheriffs the jump on badmen. Unfortunately, criminals were no less adept. On the contrary, they were generally one step ahead of the sheriffs in sophistication. Nonetheless, the years between 1880 and statehood were important ones in the development and maturity of the sheriff's office.

Many changes in the territories indirectly benefitted the sheriffs. The flow of immigration increased with the introduction of the railroads. Whereas New Mexico contained only twelve counties in 1880, this figure climbed to eighteen in 1895 and twenty-six in 1910. This growth affected the sheriff's office in two important ways. First, the number of county sheriffs more than doubled. And second, with the formation of each new unit of government, the size of the parent county declined. Oftentimes, the absurd, hyperextended configuration of counties was also simplified and borders more precisely surveyed and delimited. Never again would a sheriff be called upon to police a district stretching from the Texas border to the Colorado River, as Samuel G. Bean had attempted in the 1850s.[1]

The growth of Arizona Territory took place at a more moderate rate but was nonetheless significant. In 1880, this territory contained only seven counties. By 1895, the number had increased to twelve; by the end of the territorial era, Arizona contained fourteen counties. Unlike the configuration of New Mexico's later counties, which were more rectangular and therefore easier to administer, many of Arizona's basic units of government remained elongated and less manageable. This incongruency can be exaggerated, since there were far fewer people in Arizona. The duties of the sheriffs in some counties continued to be demanding, especially along the international boundary and in the northern counties which lapped over the Grand Canyon of the Colorado River. This inaccessible "Arizona Strip" remained a problem.[2]

While the inhabitants of both territories continued to urge the premature creation of new counties after 1880, Congress and the territorial governors monitored the process more closely and urged restraint. This was especially true in New Mexico where more vocal county movements took place. In the 1880s, Congress forbade territories from passing special legislation. New county bills sometimes fell into this category. In February 1887, Governor Edmund Ross vetoed a proposal to create a new county from part of Grant. It constituted special legislation and gave the county commissioners excessive power. Ross's successors continued this vigilant attitude. In a message to the New Mexico Assembly in January 1905, Governor Miguel A. Otero reminded the lawmakers that new counties should "answer a real need and wish of the taxpayers." He observed that any region to become a separate unit of government should also "possess sufficient assessed valuation" to support the county. Governor Herbert J. Hagerman agreed. In January 1907, he reminded lawmakers that the results of hasty county building were "grievous, often resulting in a great degree of lawlessness and disorder." Hagerman added that the formation of two counties—with attendant public buildings and officials—caused additional tax burdens, "where one would have been sufficient." With such vigilance exercised over the establishment of new counties, more stability was assured. When the first sheriff assumed his duties in a new area, he was much better assured of a solid beginning.[3]

The sheriffs of both territories also demonstrated a greater professional awareness. This enlightened attitude was apparent through the formation of sheriffs associations. Provincialism, isolation of county seats, and slowness of communications discouraged the possibility of cooperation in the early days. Although the telegraph had permitted county lawmen some opportunity to concert their efforts against lawless persons, the railroads had a near revolutionary effect. As statehood approached, the automobile loomed as an even greater innovation in law enforcement. The formation of professional associations was an important sign of this growing self-awareness. The sheriffs of Texas and Colorado formed professional groups well before their colleagues in the neighboring territories. As the sheriffs in New Mexico and Arizona were constrained to unite against growing lawlessness in the post-Civil War years, they began to see the desirability of some permanent and enduring organization. Public opinion also held county officials to greater accountability. As tax collectors, the sheriffs managed an ever-increasing amount of public revenue. Scandals within the collectors' offices brought home the need for stronger laws to discourage malfeasance and absconding. This aroused public opinion came to bear in the territorial assemblies, where bills that incorporated new standards of conduct in the shrievality were passed. When the territorial solons began to entertain such legislation, the sheriffs felt constrained to take some defensive measures. They believed (and perhaps rightly) that the legislators did not always fully perceive the true circumstances and problems of these officials, either in law enforcement duties or tax collecting.[4]

The county lawmen responded to this legislative challenge with sheriff's associations. As early as February 1884, New Mexico sheriffs gathered in Santa Fe for this purpose. Sheriff Pedro A. Simpson of Socorro County, chairman of the new association, issued the call:

> All sheriffs . . . are respectfully requested to meet in Santa Fe, February 25, for the purpose of having a general consultation in regard to some needed legislation pertaining to the duties of the office of sheriff. . . .

Simpson added to his letter the names of several colleagues who had already professed a desire to participate: James B. Woods (Grant), Perfecto Armijo (Bernalillo), Guadalupe Ascarate (Doña Ana), Romulo Martinez (Santa Fe), and Patrocinio Luna (Valencia). It was probably no accident that these first participants presided over counties located along the newly constructed railroads. These ar-

Map 4. County Boundaries of New Mexico, c. 1910

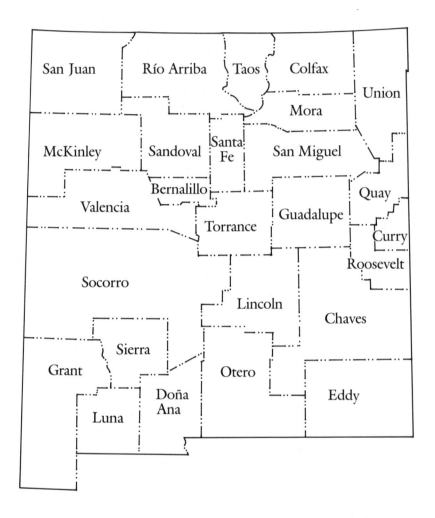

Source: loc. cit. maps 1 and 2

Map 4. County Boundaries of Arizona, c. 1910

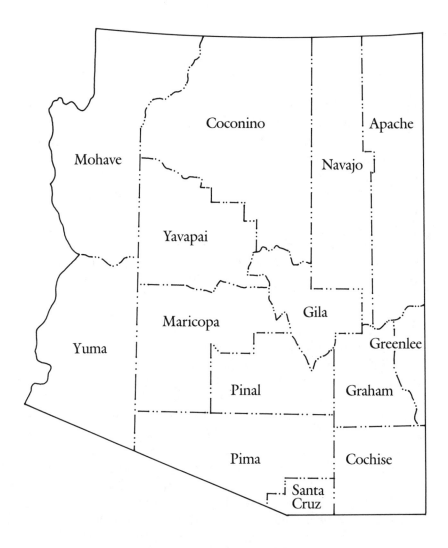

Mohave

Coconino

Apache

Navajo

Yavapai

Gila

Greenlee

Maricopa

Yuma

Pinal

Graham

Pima

Cochise

Santa
Cruz

teries of communication exposed the sheriff to new and more inten-
sive criminal activity and prompted the peace officers to cooperate
in official matters.[5]

This meeting in February 1884 was preliminary to the formation
of a New Mexico Sheriff's Association on 10 August 1885. The announced purpose of the organization was "to facilitate the capture
of criminals." It "will enjoy all the advantages of a detective agency,"
said the *Silver City Enterprise*. However, the invitation to the meeting in the following year, 1886, bluntly admitted that its purpose
was to obtain "additional legislation to aid the sheriffs . . . in the
exercise of their office." This letter, signed by Sheriffs Eugene Van
Patten (Doña Ana), Santiago Baca (Bernalillo), and Charles T. Russell (Socorro), also extended the invitation to chief deputies. The
longevity of this professional organization is difficult to determine,
although it continued to meet in conjunction with legislative sessions as late as 1893. In January 1891, a Santa Fe journal noted that
"sheriffs and assessors held a secret conclave to-day concerning proposed . . . legislation. . . ." "When these gentlemen get together,
regardless of politics," continued this writer, "they are a very and
right powerful set of men. . . ." This effort at professionalism seems
to have fallen into disuse by the turn of the century, although the
sheriffs continued to lobby at legislative sessions.[6]

An Arizona counterpart to the New Mexico sheriff's organization appeared some years later. Although the date of creation is
unclear, the sheriffs gathered in Phoenix as early as February 1899.
This meeting was prompted out of concern about proposed legislation. In October 1902, the *Arizona Republican* reported that several
sheriffs were again in town with questions for legislators who were
considering new law enforcement legislation. Was this "A sheriffs
convention?" asked the editor. He went on to add, perhaps half in
jest, that Sheriff Adalbert (Del) Lewis of Cochise County, Deputy
Sheriff R. J. Walker of Coconino, and other colleagues, were discussing a strike for higher wages. Three years later, five sheriffs, led
by Pinal County Sheriff Tom Wills, gathered in the territorial capital to express opposition to a proposed salary bill for county lawmen. The outcome of their lobbying is not known. Like their New
Mexico counterparts, the Arizona sheriffs did not maintain a permanent association until the 1930s, although such failures did not
preclude professional expression. In July 1900, sheriffs of both territories attended a meeting of the Texas Sheriffs Association in El
Paso. Their purpose was to discuss the need for territory-wide police forces on the order of the Texas Rangers. The sheriffs associa-

tion continued in Colorado, although it is not clear that New Mexico's county lawmen attended. Other peace officers, including chiefs of police, were also organizing elsewhere in the nation.[7]

That the sheriffs should express concern about income was not surprising. The public did not always agree, especially in regard to the annual income of county sheriffs. By about 1890, many citizens had concluded that these officers earned an excessive amount. This penurious sentiment did not extend to deputy sheriffs and other lawmen, who earned much less. Arizona Governor Louis C. Hughes became involved in a dispute over a pay increase for prison guards in 1894. While not always an example of consistency, Hughes admitted that "the average compensation paid throughout the Territory for police service is less than $80 per month. . . ." This testy executive may have believed that the modest sum was sufficient, since he had recommended earlier that the pay of public officials, including local ones, actually be reduced.[8]

The fee system of income lay at the heart of this growing controversy, and the sheriffs could not remain immune. This ancient practice provided remuneration for services actually performed and may have been beneficial for a time. It helped to moderate the cost of government and was especially appropriate to the spartan budgets of frontier territories. The duties of the sheriffs and other county officials often demanded only part-time attention. They were able to maintain a full-time occupation while in office. By the late 1880s, opposition to the fee system had grown considerably across the nation. Critics charged that the meager incomes of lawmen under the fee system exposed them to corruption, bribery, and especially "fee making." This expression referred to malicious arrests in order to earn fees.[9]

When Congress placed the United States marshals on salary in 1896, Southwesterners proposed to extend this reform to lesser officials. The *El Paso Daily Times* discussed the pros and cons of the fee system in March 1896:

> Public officers should be allowed a reasonable compensation but the fees should be turned into the public treasury. The idea that some one else than the state is paying the salaries of officials when the money comes from fees is very delusive. It is . . . also a delusion to suppose that officers are more earnest in the prosecution of their duties when a fee is the inducement. The truth is that while the official is always eager for his fee he may sometimes permit his rapacity to lead him away from the ends of justice in the satisfaction of avarice. When a [court] case which has put the state to some, perhaps considerable,

expense is dismissed on payment of costs the officials feather their nests, but the state is the loser. When an officer [voluntarily] remits his costs it is not always so much in the interest of justice and humanity as in the hope of a return to his personal benefit in a primary or general election to occur thereafter. When the office has a fixed salary, without fees or perquisites, the tax payer knows what the public servant receives in the way of compensation for the services performed and can form a pretty good idea as to whether he earns it.

This journalist pointed out that under the fee system "a thousand dollar man" sometimes undeservedly receives "a ten thousand dollar income." Furthermore, the money for remunerating public servants ultimately comes from the taxpayers' pockets, concluded the *Times* writer.[10]

That a salary system could fit the needs of the territories had been obvious to many persons for some time. As early as 1876, Governor Samuel B. Axtell urged the New Mexico Assembly to assign salaries to sheriffs and other officials. When outcries occurred against the "fee making" practices of United States marshals a decade later, proponents of the salary procedure extended their recommendations to county sheriffs as well. An editorial in the *Las Vegas Daily Optic* characterized the fee system as "a monster political evil" and demanded that county public servants be given fixed incomes.[11]

While New Mexicans talked about placing sheriffs on salary, Arizonans actually implemented such a plan. The 1884–85 session of the assembly made an effort to place all county lawmen on salary as part of a larger effort to separate the office of tax assessor and collector from the shrievalty. While the advocates of these far-reaching measures did not obtain all that they desired, they made considerable strides. Instead of a blanket law that applied to every county sheriff, the lawmakers passed a separate law for each county. Yuma alone refused to place its sheriff on salary. The reason is unclear. Under this new legislation, each county sheriff earned a salary but was also permitted to keep the income of a few fees. For instance, Sheriff John Lorenzo Hubbell of Apache County was paid $5,000 annually. Other incomes varied according to the size of the bailiwick. This new system did not please the officials of every county, and the Arizona Assembly modified the law in piecemeal fashion over the years. For instance, Yavapai County apparently withdrew its sheriff from the salary plan altogether.[12]

The territorial governments also initiated efforts to monitor the sheriff's management of official funds. Careless recordkeeping, mismanagement, and even occasional absconding took place in the 1890s. This was especially true in the New Mexico shrievalties. Scandals took place in the Santa Fe, Mora, and Chaves offices. Perhaps the most notable instance—the outright flight of a sheriff—took place in the latter county in 1896. Sheriff Charles C. Perry, who had earned a notable reputation as a manhunter and whom some touted as a successor to Pat Garrett, was known to have a grudge against the Roswell bank where he deposited his tax collections. Perry also felt cheated when he failed to receive rewards for the capture of outlaws. He enjoyed gambling and carousing with known underworld figures, and had deserted his wife and child and taken up with a member of the demi-world. Suddenly, in summer 1896, Perry disappeared with more than $7,000 of tax receipts. Eventually, he turned up in the goldfields of South Africa! The public monies that he had stolen were never recovered. Under the law, Perry's bondsmen were constrained to make up the deficit.[13]

Several instances of such reprehensible conduct finally persuaded the New Mexico and Arizona legislatures to send traveling auditors to each county. In January 1905, Governor Miguel A. Otero noted considerable improvement in the efficiency of local government since the New Mexico auditor had begun his circuit. The first report of Arizona's new auditor for 1905–06 was comprehensive and outlined many shortcomings in every county. Not only did Public Examiner N. V. Foster recommend "a uniform system of accounting between county officers" but he detected many "evils" in county administration, including the sheriffs. In Coconino County, Sheriff Harry Henderson illegally claimed "double mileage" in one case; in Graham, James V. Parks wrongly claimed fees for a deputy; in Mohave, Walter Brown claimed income from six different salary funds (not fully explained); in Navajo, Chester I. Houck neglected to reside in the county seat; in Santa Cruz, Charles Fowler performed tax assessing duties in a "careless manner"; in Yuma, the auditor found no regularized administrative procedures. Sheriff Gus Livingston, he noted, demonstrated an "Apparent indifference . . . in making an [tax] assessment."[14]

Foster's comprehensive report constituted the first searching examination of county government in Arizona and had a direct bearing upon the conduct of the sheriffs. He admitted that "I have been strict, but . . . fair in my treatment of county officials. . . ." Sometimes, he continued, the work was "unpleasant," since local officers resented two visits annually. He found an:

almost total lack of system in some counties, with the attendant irregularities that had crept in through long years of carelessness, inat-
tention and misinterpretation of the laws,—which in consequence
became established custom and were considered lawful—together
with the further duty, of perfecting and introducing a uniform system of accounting between county officials. . . .

While he was not completely satisfied, Foster concluded that a
foundation had been laid. He presented the sheriffs with new forms
for monthly and quarterly reports of tax collections and for criminal
and civil dockets and the jail register, all to begin 1 January 1906.
Foster admitted that his "uniform system of accounting" might of-
fend county officials. They would resent "an extra amount of labor,"
but they should remember that this new mass of paperwork ultimately descended upon Foster's office.[15]

Of the many problems in Arizona's county government, Foster
concluded that permitting the sheriffs and others to draw salaries
and fees simultaneously was "the cause of more contention." Not
only did county officials deliberately create "a new duty for which
they charge and claim a fee," but, he continued,

> The sheriffs, constables, justice[s] of the peace, and sometimes the
> police and [Arizona] rangers, will stand in together for the making of
> as many fees for each other as it is possible to charge for. None of
> these officers, outside of a few rare exceptions, will hesitate to charge
> an irregular fee and fight for its payment.

The dismayed auditor recommended the abolition of all the fees
that the Legislature had continued in the reforms of 1885 and
urged the implementation of strict salaries. He also urged that the
task of tax assessing be taken from the sheriff. "The system is
wrong," he said, "as the sheriff values the office [of assessor] only so
far as it will aid him to a re-election. . . ." This lawman "is indif-
ferent to the assessment and collection of any portion of county
taxes that may have an influence in opposition to his [election]
return."[16]

The reports of Public Examiner Foster represented a new and
critical challenge to the traditional autonomy of the county sheriffs.
The era of free-wheeling county lawmen was coming to an end.
However, neither the reformers nor the stalwarts won a complete
victory. A compromise system emerged in both Arizona and New
Mexico. In Arizona, the counties were divided into five classes ac-

cording to population and taxable wealth. In each county, the sheriff received a salary and fees accordingly. In first-class counties, the law officer lost all connection with tax collecting. Lawmakers concluded that the tasks of serving the courts had become full time in the heavily populated counties. The sheriff continued to wear the hats of lawman, tax assessor, and collector in the smaller counties. New Mexico adopted the lesser tactic of separating the offices of collector and shrievalty in March 1897. The county treasurer took up the collecting duties. While it was still an imperfect system, these various reforms measurably improved the efficiency of the shrievalty.[17]

The governors demonstrated a greater determination to intervene in the affairs of sheriffs after the crises of the 1880s. Governor Miguel A. Otero created a stir in Bernalillo County political circles when he abruptly removed Sheriff Thomas S. Hubbell in 1905. This action, which appeared arbitrary to some observers, must have awakened many county lawmen to a growing vulnerability. In the past, some sheriffs had acted as though they were "lords" of their domains (counties), insulated from outside interference. The Hubbell family exercised great political influence. Since the patriarch, James Lorenzo Hubbell, became the first sheriff of Valencia County in September 1846, his descendants had occupied numerous law enforcement positions. Thomas became sheriff of Bernalillo County in 1895. A brother, Frank, served as county treasurer and directed the local Republican Party. A brother-in-law, Eslavio Vigil, served as school superintendent.[18]

When reports of mismanagement reached Otero, he quickly dispatched an investigator, W. W. Safford, to Albuquerque and scheduled a public inquiry into the conduct of all three men. Safford began his mission in Bernalillo County late in 1904. Although Safford anticipated problems with the powerful Hubbell family, the sheriff and other accused men cooperated from the outset. On 31 December 1904, Safford informed the governor that he had demanded the official papers of the three accused men and that "I will not have any trouble getting everything. . . ." "I Told Tom Hubbell that I wanted to go through his jail records," added Safford, "and he said 'alright.'" The nervy investigator promised to act quickly and "send you [Otero] all statements by the time you wish to start work [on the public hearings]." The hearings were held in the Alvarado Hotel on 28–29 June and 15 August 1905.[19]

In addition to an examination into the activities of Treasurer Frank Hubbell and School Superintendent Eslavio Vigil, Governor

Otero exposed Sheriff Thomas Hubbell's alleged offenses. Melquiades Martin, a deputy sheriff in Alameda, admitted that Sheriff Hubbell had bestowed many favors upon him in return for political support. The sheriff obtained for Martin a liquor license, the offices of road supervisor, and majordomo of acequias, and his deputy commission. Hubbell quietly ignored the failure of this political henchman to pay for the liquor license. Other persons testified that Sheriff Hubbell failed to collect on liquor licenses (presumably as a part of political deals). One illegal liquor dealer allegedly said in public when questioned about this illicit vending, "'As long as Hubbell helps us, what do we care about it.'" Additional testimony revealed that the lawman permitted eight or ten illegal gambling operations at the territorial fair. Another person charged that he quietly permitted jail inmates to depart before the expiry of their terms, but he continued to keep their names on his jail book in order to collect their upkeep from the county. On 31 August 1905, the governor removed the two Hubbells from office. "I do hereby vacate the commission of the said Thomas S. Hubbell . . . ," concluded Otero. As a replacement, Otero passed over younger prospects and appointed an aging Perfecto Armijo. Armijo had held the Bernalillo County shrievalty more than twenty years earlier. Some tense days passed before the former sheriff would relinquish his suite of offices to Armijo.[20]

In spite of such embarrassments, there were obvious signs of vigor in this important office. New "justice complexes" began to spring up on the former sites of dilapidated public buildings. These facilities always included office space for the sheriff as well as a new jail. In January 1882, an Arizona journalist observed this "March of progress" in Tucson, as a new courthouse neared completion. This writer's enthusiasm soared as he speculated upon the meaning of this and other improvements such as railroads and gas works. Such modern innovations persuaded the citizens of the county seat to realize, he surmised, that "their destiny is indissolubly linked to that of all nations upon the earth. . . ." The new justice complex exceeded in size and furnishings all preceding courthouses in Pima County. "It is of soft graystone, laid in regular courses of rustic masonry," said the newspaperman, "and makes a fine appearance." Gila County erected a four-storied courthouse in Globe about this time. The sheriff's office and jail were on the ground floor. The supervisors of Mohave County issued $30,000 in bonds for a similar facility in 1905. This fine stone structure contained a jail fitted with nine cells and was valued at $6,000. Not everyone approved of such costly buildings. When a $20,000 bond issue was proposed for Lincoln County in 1891, businessman John Y. Hewitt organized the opposition and asked taxpayers if "there is an urgent demand" for a new courthouse. The outcome of this debate is not clear. A general improvement took place in the physical facilities of sheriffs in both territories. Dee R. Harkey, an Eddy County officer, expressed surprise at the spaciousness of Sheriff Tom Hubbell's office in Albuquerque at the turn of this century.[21]

Although Southwesterners seldom expressed serious interest in the wave of judicial and penal reform movements that swept the nation at the turn of the century, they were not without feelings. In October 1908, the *Albuquerque Morning Journal* noted that the Society for the Friendless had begun work among prisoners in the territory. The Reverend Earl Ward Pierce sought jobs for newly released persons under the society's auspices. While progress was slow, some mention was made as early as 1907 about establishing a separate juvenile jail in Albuquerque. Such sentiments were probably a result of the reforms of Progressive Denver jurist, Judge Ben Lindsay. The sheriffs of New Mexico and Arizona had long recognized the deplorable consequences of housing youthful offenders with hardened criminals. After all, young Henry McCarty, alias Bonney, alias Billy the Kid, had escaped from the Grant County Jail in 1876 through the leniency of Sheriff Harvey Whitehill. The lawman had permitted him the run of the hallway, in order to isolate the impressionable boy from veteran badmen. Although uninformed about the latest reform practices, Cochise County Jailer Mack Axford noted that his prisoners "had no way of amusing themselves" or of improving morale. Axford permitted his eighty-five prisoners to have cards and checker games, musical instruments, boxing gloves, and even haircuts. This resourceful jail tender believed that unkempt persons had no reason to take pride in personal appearance. Furthermore, as Axford recalled, "The more active one could keep the prisoners the less time they would have to think of means to break out. . . ."[22]

The admission of women into the sheriff's office loomed as the territorial era drew to a close, although it appears that few, if any, actually served in office before 1912. The movement of females into law enforcement was a half-century old before reaching the Southwestern territories. As early as 1845, the American Female Reform Society in New York brought about the appointment of matrons to supervise female prisoners. No doubt sheriffs in New Mexico and Arizona had used women informally to assist in the care of female prisoners, but few chief lawmen issued badges to them. In 1893, Yuma County Sheriff Mel Greenleaf reportedly deputized his wife to take charge of women inmates. Joe Pearce, an Arizona lawman, recalled that James Scott, Sheriff of Apache County in 1895–96, disliked his position and permitted his wife, Linda, to act in his stead. James Scott resigned before completion of his term.[23]

The admission of women to the hallowed ranks of male-dominated law enforcement gained momentum during the transition to statehood. The need was obvious. In October 1915, the *Tombstone Epitaph* noted the tragic death of an insane female prisoner who jumped from a moving train to escape from a Pima County deputy sheriff. The *Epitaph* remarked that "such accidents can be avoided by sending women deputies on such trips. . . ." This writer reminded readers that one Tucson woman, Minnie Estabrook, an Indian field matron "holds a deputy sheriff's commission, and has already accompanied women prisoners on trips. . . ." "A movement for women deputies" might result from the unfortunate death of the insane lady, concluded the Tombstone journalist. Ambitious women were making inroads elsewhere in Arizona. In June 1914, the *Arizona Gazette* of Phoenix declared that "For several years the Civic League has been after the city to put in a police matron and a woman on the regular [city police] force. . . ." This reform organization, which desired to fight the growing crime rate among women and young girls, greeted the appointment of Ora Mathews to the concurrent positions of policewoman and deputy sheriff with much applause. Her jobs were "to censor moving pictures and repress unseemly conduct in public places. . . ." Cochise County acquired its first female deputy sheriff, Viva C. Villman, in 1917. Lucretia Roberts probably gained the most notoriety among these pioneer women. She was elected constable in Santa Cruz County in 1914, and Sheriff William McNight deputized her in December. She spoke to a women's suffrage organization in New York two years later while wearing Western garb and a six-shooter. Her son, Richard Roberts, wrote a novel about his famous mother, *Star in the West*.[24]

Advancements in communications promoted the efficiency of the sheriffs and other law enforcers. The telephone possessed much potential. The United States Army introduced the first Bell devices into Arizona in 1878, while Prescott began a civilian line in the following year. These first systems were merely intra-city and did little to help sheriffs communicate with the hinterland. By the turn of the century, conversations were possible between the larger towns of

Arizona. In March 1900, plans were announced to connect Tucson, Phoenix, and Florence. Wires were strung between Las Vegas, New Mexico, and the nearby Hot Springs in 1881. Within two years, the Bell Telephone Company employed a general manager in New Mexico. Many short lines were strung in both territories in the following two decades, although some were restricted to private business firms. Albuquerque had 263 phones in 1896. By this time, calls were possible between Las Vegas and El Paso, Texas. Long distance connections outside the territories were approaching by the time of statehood. In August 1907, residents of Albuquerque acquired connections with the East by way of Kansas City, Missouri.[25]

The sheriffs of both territories were quick to take advantage of telephone connections. As early as 1881, Sheriff Robert Paul communicated by telephone with John H. Behan, his counterpart in Tombstone. Probably neither officer possessed an office phone. Cochise County Sheriff Carlton B. Kelton had a telephone in his office by 1891. In this same year, citizens petitioned Pima County authorities "to have the sheriff's office, the treasurer's office, and the clerk of the Board of Supervisor's office connected with the Tucson Telephone Exchange. . . ." As early as 1900, Yavapai County Sheriff John Munds had access to a comprehensive, if local, telephone network to many nearby mining camps. In November, Undersheriff A. A. Johns received an early morning telephone report of a crime at nearby Mayer. In turn, Johns rang his deputy in that camp. Since the evildoers were from Phoenix, Johns then telephoned Sheriff David L. Murray in that community for more information. Only a year later, telephones in the border towns of Douglas and Naco were employed to coordinate with Mexican police in the pursuit of the Burt Alvord band of train robbers. The telephone also facilitated the administrative needs of the shrievalty. Shortly after the turn of this century, Colfax County Sheriff Marion Littrell commissioned Fred Lambert of Cimarron over the phone.[26]

Among communications innovations, the automobile proved invaluable to the sheriffs. As early as July 1899, the *Phoenix Herald* announced the arrival of the first horseless carriage. Someone proposed a bus line from Flagstaff to the Grand Canyon in the following year. "Autos are taking over the wild west," said the *Weekly Republican*. The humorous story circulated that a faithful horse fell over dead in Douglas when his master drove up in a new automobile. A mining tycoon purchased a new car for $20,000 in order to make the long trip from Cananea, Sonora, to San Francisco, California, in November 1903. The first automobile arrived in

Santa Fe on 5 May 1903, traveling the 450 miles from Colorado Springs, Colorado, in about six days. An enterprising Roswellian opened a bus line to Torrance and Artesia two years later. The *Roswell Record* concluded that this new company could, with the help of railroads, "knit the interests of the prosperous lower Pecos Valley with those of central New Mexico to the profit of the business men of both sections. . . ." The same could be said for law enforcement interests as well. In July 1907, a Silver City writer noted the appearance of an automobile line between that place and surrounding mining camps. "That the good old stage coach which has monopolized the field for scores of years is doomed . . . is becoming more apparent every day . . . ," concluded this dispatch.[27]

That the gasoline-powered vehicles possessed potential for law enforcers and other public officials went without saying. In 1904, Governor Miguel A. Otero purchased the first automobile for New Mexico Territory. In March 1907, Sheriff Charles Ballard of Chaves County transported a prisoner by bus. Three years later, he employed the automobile to retrieve a prisoner from Plainview, Texas. Ballard's colleague in Tucumcari, James Street, recaptured an escaping prisoner by the same means in 1908. Arizona lawmen quickly took to this novel means of travel. By 1910, Sheriff Carl Hayden substituted the auto for horses in the pursuit of train robbers near Phoenix, while John Henry Thompson borrowed a four-cylindered Cadillac to chase murderers across the San Carlos Indian Reservation. Thompson was constrained to deputize the owner, Tom (Red) Brewer, since he was the only person capable of operating the machine. The outlaws "struck out for a territory [north of San Carlos] which no car had yet penetrated . . . ," said Thompson's biographer, and the auto soon burned out a bearing. However, the resourceful owner fashioned a new one over a campfire. The sheriff soon captured the killers near Holbrook.[28]

In the absence of good roads, this newfangled contraption had to be used in combination with the horse. When Sheriff John Nelson pursued a wanted rapist in Pima County in August 1910, he drove his gasoline buggy until it broke down. He and a deputy then obtained horses to complete the chase. Bernalillo County Undersheriff Fred Heyn employed his own motorcycle until he wrecked it in Albuquerque in August 1907. When Harry Wheeler became sheriff of Cochise County, Arizona, in 1912, he gained access to the single official county automobile. This was too restrictive, and he soon obtained permission to purchase a sheriff's car. In 1916, he added four motorcycles to the official fleet. In something of a come-down,

Sheriff Miles C. Stewart and Deputy Dee Harkey conducted a "high speed" chase of a badman on bicycles in Eddy, New Mexico. However, the wanted man, who was on horseback, rode over the sheriff and wrecked Stewart's two-wheeler. The two lawmen then obtained horses and concluded the chase successfully.[29]

By the end of the territorial era, New Mexico and Arizona contained enough automobiles to present the sheriffs with new official duties. On 3 June 1910, the Rantz Motor Car Company of Bridgeport, Connecticut, sent the New Mexico secretary of state the description of "a Speedwell car which was stolen." In neighboring Arizona the territorial government began to register all automobiles in the following year. By December 1911 some 1,200 were licensed, and the territory saddled the sheriffs with a new responsibility, to notify delinquent tag purchasers. For instance, on 23 October 1912, the secretary instructed Sheriff John Nelson of Pima County to arrest anyone who refused to buy the required tag. In the following year, all sheriffs were required to maintain a record of all motor vehicles registered in their bailiwicks.[30] The criminal element was quick to take advantage of new innovations such as railroads and automobiles. By 1880, the entry of the railroad into the Southwest made possible swift and secretive movements of the more sophisticated criminals. This was especially true of the counterfeiters, forgers, and confidence men. Nighttime crooks such as safecrackers could enter a town by train, break open a safe, and depart on the next train. In May 1902, the Phoenix *Arizona Republican* carried a *Scientific American* story which noted the arrival of a new breed of criminal, the "scientific" crook. This story prophesied the employment of modern explosives such as nitroglycerin and lamented the passing of dynamite. A rumor even circulated in Albuquerque shortly after the turn of the century that the Mafia, a manifestation of modern "organized crime," was then active in the city. If true, the frontier sheriffs could look forward to a new and more devilish criminal enemy. In spite of such events, the portrait of the typical criminal in the Southwest changed very little from the heyday of the horseback outlaw of 1880. As late as the advent of statehood, the train and stagecoach robber still flourished in Arizona and New Mexico.[31]

The sheriffs demonstrated some awareness of modern detection techniques. For many years, they had collected photographs of known offenders, although it is not clear when the first mug book was compiled in the territories. Railroad companies and Wells Fargo probably maintained the first files in Arizona and New Mexico. In June 1890, the *Arizona Daily Star* reprinted a *Youth's Companion* story that explained M. Bertillion's "thumb autographs." However, it is not clear how quickly Southwestern sheriffs adopted such innovative procedures. In August 1909, H. Parliman of the Yawman and Erbe Manufacturing Company of Rochester, New York, wrote Sheriff Carl Hayden of Phoenix to describe a criminal identification kit. Parliman explained that his equipment not only measured and photographed criminals but provided an accurate filing system. He urged Hayden to attend a nationwide convention of sheriffs in Seattle later that month.[32]

Modern forensic practices were slow to reach the territories, although sheriffs employed them in isolated cases. In 1888, Doña Ana County Deputy Sheriff Rucker sent soil samples of a supposed grave to the post surgeon at Fort Stanton to determine if the grave contained human remains. Holm Bursum, Sheriff of Socorro County in 1896, sent blood samples in a murder case to the Zoology Department at the University of New Mexico. In Arizona, the stomach of a murdered man was removed at an autopsy on the order of Sheriff Lyman Wakefield and the contents were analyzed. Poison was found in the excised organ. A dentist also identified the body through fillings in the teeth. Sheriff Nabor Pacheco, the only Hispano to hold that office in Pima County during the territorial era, cleverly planned to use ice to preserve the bodies of two accused rustlers whom Arizona Rangers killed in the desert in June 1907. Unfortunately, the bodies decomposed before the sheriff could deliver the ice.[33]

New Mexico and Arizona took decided steps to improve law enforcement at the turn of the century. Since the crisis years of the early 1880s, Southwesterners had called for the creation of territorial police agencies to complement the jurisdictions of the sheriffs. These new policemen appeared belatedly: In 1901, the Arizona Rangers; and in 1905, the New Mexico Mounted Police. These lawmen answered to the governors rather than the counties. Both forces were small and, like the sheriffs, lacked formal law enforcement training. Amateurism continued to flourish in the tradition of frontier peacekeeping. Burton Mossman, superintendent of the Hashknife Ranch, became first captain of the Rangers; Fred Fornoff, a deputy United States marshal and former Rough Rider, headed the Mounted Police. In his message to the Arizona Assembly in 1907, Governor Joseph Kibbey emphasized that the special task of the Rangers was to patrol "the favorite haunts of the criminals of the most desperate class" in "remote sections in which the county peace officers do not ordinarily travel. . . ." In this way, added Kibbey, "the Rangers to a large extent perform functions that can not well be performed at all by sheriffs or their deputies. . . ." The *Solomonville Bulletin* concluded that the Arizona Rangers would assume "much of the expense of hunting down criminals." Mounted Police Captain Fornoff reflected this same desire to go where the sheriffs seldom ventured. He would not assign his subordinates to the county seats, said Fornoff, since "The work and duty of enforcing the law is properly that of the sheriffs at such points."[34]

Like a stormy marriage between incompatible mates, the sheriffs and these new policemen entered into a decade of uneasy relationships. The sheriffs resented these interloping policemen who possessed the power to make arrests within each county and thus rob them of fees and mileage. The *Arizona Republican* sensed another, unspoken reason for the sheriff's hostility. As long as this peace officer was unchallenged within his sphere, the sheriff possessed discretionary power, to arrest or not arrest resident wrongdoers. The county lawmen disliked the Rangers, these "new men," said the *Republican*, because they arrested local boys who had "gone wrong." The sheriffs looked upon many minor troublemakers, especially rustlers, with "fatherly" tolerance. Like any long-term resident of one community, the sheriff had many ties with the inhabitants of his county. These people also comprised his voting population. The sheriffs evidently detested Thomas Rynning, the second captain of the Arizona Rangers. To judge from Rynning's reminiscences, he feuded with many county lawmen. He denied that Ranger arrests intruded upon the sheriffs' income and asserted that the fugitives whom his subordinates took into custody were the most hardened and least likely to be arrested by county officers. Rynning even accused (unnamed) Arizona sheriffs of complicity—"playing in with their game"—in crimes of the outlaws. He especially despised the typical deputy sheriff whom the Ranger captain regarded as a flashy, gun-toting ne'er-do-well and little better than the drunks he rolled. Rynning believed one sheriff plotted to assassinate him, although this is unlikely.[35]

There was another reason for resentment of these new territorial policemen. They served as monitors of the sheriffs and reported the activities of county lawmen to the governors. In February 1906, Mounted Police Captain John Fullerton urged Governor H. J. Hagerman to examine reports of cattlemen that Quay County Sheriff James Alexander Street "fails to perform the duties of his office." If Street was incapable, added Fullerton, the sheriff "should be removed and a good man appointed." While Street attempted to explain away such complaints, the Mounted Police captain informed Will C. Barnes, Secretary of the New Mexico Cattle Sanitary Board and former Arizona livestock official, that the policemen would proceed in the investigation of cattle thieves "as if the sheriff cannot be trusted." Fullerton expressed the opinion that other New Mexico sheriffs were equally inattentive to duty. Later in the year, the Mounted Police investigated accusations against Manuel S. Sanchez, Sheriff of Torrance County. Among the charges were extortion. The governor removed the errant lawman in February 1907.[36] Whatever the contributions of the Rangers and Mounted Police, the legislators of both territories were keenly aware of the controversial status of these agencies. Some sheriffs still resented them, and the policemen represented a considerable expense. By the end of the territorial era, both assemblies had withdrawn the funding necessary for the Rangers and Mounted Police to operate and they ceased to function.

Many instances of cooperation took place between policemen and sheriffs. Burt Mossman, first captain of the Arizona Rangers, and Sheriff James V. Parks, of Graham County, combined forces to run down Augustino Chacon, one of the most notorious outlaws on the border. Harry C. Wheeler, who became captain some years later, applauded Cochise County Sheriff Jack White. White joined with Sonoran officials to break up the George Arnett rustler band in 1908. Wheeler also praised Nabor Pacheco, chief lawman in Pima County, who worked with Rangers in the arrest of Papago Indian fugitives about this same time. "There are no peace officers in the World," said Wheeler, "to compare with our Arizona sheriffs. . . ." With the support of the Rangers, he continued, the work of county lawmen "can only result in perpetuating the peaceful conditions of our State." Pacheco returned the praise and asserted that the Rangers "brought law to Arizona and wiped out the bad men."

As the prospects of statehood approached after 1900, Arizonans and New Mexicans desired to convince Easterners that the Southwest had discarded the evils of the frontier era. One means to this end was to rid their communities of vice. Redlight districts had always been conspicuous. Gambling, drinking, and prostitution flourished. In October 1905, the Presbyterian Synod of New Mexico asked Congress to prohibit gambling in the territories. The Women's Christian Temperance Union in New Mexico mounted a crusade against the vices attendant on saloons. The Anti-Saloon League of New Mexico and Arizona mounted a crusade in the following year. In 1907, the Arizona Assembly forbade gambling, banned females from saloons, and imposed a much higher—$300—saloon license. About this same time, New Mexico Governor Herbert J. Hagerman proposed an anti-gambling law and averred that public opinion was overwhelmingly supportive. On 21 March 1907, such a law was passed as well as a statute forbidding saloon liquor licenses in towns of under 300 people. Newspapermen could not restrain expressions of nostalgia as these frontier institutions passed by. When women were banned from Arizona saloons, the *Albuquerque Morning Journal* lamented the demise of "another old custom" and reminded readers that the painted ladies did more than entertain customers. They were "nightingales." The gamblers were formerly "leading citizens," added the *Journal,* and "discussed the ethics of the frontier with the authority of an unanswerable philosopher." Now, the sporting fraternity "has become an object for ingenuous pity . . ." concluded this journalist, and has "sullenly gone to work."[37]

The sheriffs played an important part in the enforcement of these controversial anti-vice laws. Before these laws took effect in New Mexico, the lawmen were required to report the present status of saloons and gambling in their counties. In July 1907, Don Johnson filed a "Sheriff's Report as to Liquor and Gaming Houses" for Luna County. He found nine liquor and thirteen gaming establishments. Based upon this and reports from other counties, the New Mexico Anti-Gambling law went into effect on 1 January 1908. Whatever the personal preference of the sheriffs, they were required to come down on the side of higher morality. When Sheriff Leandro Baca closed the saloons in the remote mining camp of Ketner, in western Valencia County, he reportedly expressed satisfaction at the closures. Baca believed that many of the public disturbances in such isolated villages resulted from drunkenness. Harry Wheeler, Captain of the Arizona Rangers, agreed that the new legislation helped reduce crime. In his report to the governor in July 1908, Wheeler noted an eighteen percent decline in arrests over the previous fiscal year and attributed this fact to the anti-gambling legislation. Yet, these laws were difficult to enforce. As a young lawyer in Gallup, Arthur Hannett recalled that "The attitude toward gambling . . . was liberal" and that enforcement was troublesome.[38]

The purpose of these reform laws was to impress upon the United States Government the ability of Arizona and New Mexico to enter the communty of states. The territories acquired this coveted status in 1912. The duties of the chief county lawman changed very little under statehood because county level governance did not change from territory to statehood. Some administrative changes took place as the territorial district courts passed away. Two separate sets of courts emerged. Each new state acquired a federal district court, which the United States marshals served. The sheriffs served the now separate state district courts, although their duties in support of them did not change.[39]

In the three decades prior to statehood, the county lawmen of New Mexico and Arizona experienced many changes. By 1880, the sheriff's public esteem had fallen to low ebb. These peace officers appeared incapable of carrying out their duties. Yet, they persevered. Through a set of happy circumstances, not all of their own doing, order was restored. The railroads and telephones enabled them to join forces against the lawless element. The formation of professional associations helped them to reach a consensus among themselves and to communicate their problems to the territorial assemblies. No doubt the divestiture of tax-collecting duties did more than anything else to emancipate this lawman and to permit him to direct all of his energy toward law enforcement tasks. (Unfortunately, in counties with more modest populations, the sheriff continued to perform tax-collecting chores.) In other ways, this important office changed. Physical facilities were improved, and jail security with it. The decline of lynchings and large-scale jail deliveries was noticeable. Nonetheless, these county lawmen were still largely in the byways of national trends in law enforcement techniques. Criminal activities were still largely confined to traditional horseback outlawry. The appearance of new trends, such as the employment of women, was very tentative but still loomed on the horizon. While the sheriffs provided valuable services through the enforcement of anti-vice laws in preparation for statehood, the transition to this much cherished status brought about very little change in the day-to-day activities of the shrievalties of Arizona and New Mexico.

15

Conclusion

 In March 1908, former Sheriff Patrick Floyd Garrett was shot and killed near Las Cruces, New Mexico. His death took place under very tragic circumstances and caused many pioneers to pause and reflect upon the contributions of the sheriffs to law and order on the Southwestern frontier. The editor of the *Carrizozo Outlook* captured in a few words the sharp contrast between the world in which Garrett thrived and the world in which he died. This aging lawman, wrote the journalist, was "One of those characters who are as inevitably linked with the conditions which existed here during those early days of American settlement of the territory as the stars are linked with the shades of night." The writer applauded Garrett's spirit of sacrifice in his earlier years, when he placed his life in jeopardy in order to run down the Billy the Kid outlaw band. The sheriff placed more value upon the welfare of the citizenry than upon his own life. But "The story of his violent death in an area where there is now talk of irrigation, schools, [and] settlement all point up the contrast of old passing for new," concluded the observer.[1]

The years 1846–1912 were momentous for the ancient office of sheriff. From the seven original appointees under the Provisional Military Government, the number grew to forty in 1912 (with Arizona Territory included). While this number was still inadequate to police the vast territories, these pioneer officers made great strides in carrying out the duties traditionally assigned to them: peacekeeping, service of court process, maintenance of the jail, and collection of taxes. Although this latter task was not strictly a part of the shrievalty, the lawman performed it ex officio. In addition, the public expected a multitude of unofficial services as the county handyman. He did all this, to some degree, on a part-time basis. Most often, the sheriff continued a private occupation—a ranch, store, or other business. The second in command—the undersheriff in Arizona or chief deputy in New Mexico—often served as immediate supervisor of the office, field deputies, and jailer.

Although the shrievalty in the territories was a carbon copy of its counterpart in the Eastern states, the frontier presented the county lawman with serious obstacles not present in the East. The chief hindrance was the vast, rural, often unpopulated, arid and mountainous lands of Arizona and New Mexico. Whereas a sheriff in an Eastern state policed a county of only a few hundred square miles, the typical Southwestern lawman had the responsibility for one of thousands. This predominantly rural society is revealed in population figures. New Mexico Territory changed very little in the territorial era. Of the 61,547 persons residing in this territory in 1850, only 4,539 were classified as urban dwellers, or 7.4 percent. The majority of these residents lived in villages of 500–1,000. Little change took place in the subsequent six decades. Of the 327,301 in New Mexico in 1910, only 46,571 lived in towns, or 14.2 percent. Arizona was even more rural. In 1870, this territory of approximately 10,000 contained only 9 towns, ranging in size from about 150 to Tucson's 3,224. Fifty years later, Arizona's numbers had increased to about 204,000. There were twenty towns with populations from about 150 to Tucson's 13,000. As the territorial period drew to a close, the sheriffs could still look forward to enforcing the laws among a primarily rural constituency.[2]

In New Mexico Territory, the presence of a large Hispanic population affected the history of the shrievalty. Even at statehood, in 1912, the community of Spanish-speakers outnumbered the Anglos, mostly recent arrivals since 1880 and the appearance of the railroads. Although the native element resented the presence of these interlopers, the Hispanos demonstrated a keen understanding of American institutions—including the sheriff's office—and dominated the election process. Hispanos virtually monopolized the sheriffalty, with the exception of counties created late in the territorial era. Arizona presented the opposite spectacle, in that the Hispanic population remained a minority. Only in one or two counties—chiefly Apache and Navajo—did they control the vote and hence the sheriff's office.

Twentieth-century Americans associate the task of peacekeeping on the frontier with the sheriff. He is most often portrayed in popular literature, Hollywood movies, and television programs as a gunfighting hero who possesses more dexterity with guns than the bad-man. In a deliberate and calculated move, the two men meet in the streets and shoot it out. Of course, this is far from reality. Indeed, sheriff and outlaw did confront each other in the streets, but this encounter was more often governed by chance than calculation. The shootings that took place were generally spontaneous, with the sheriff seldom exposing himself to the prospects of injury or death from the gun of a drunken hellion. In fact, the typical sheriff hardly resembled the hard-eyed gunfighter of the Hollywood variety, al-though the voters of a county might occasionally feel the need to elect someone who possessed a reputation for nerve. Instead of electing the stereotypical "fast gun" (that is, someone who could draw a gun swiftly), the public chose a man who was noted as a "quick gun." By this term, the voter meant a person who resorted to the use of a weapon in a more peremptory fashion than the preced-ing sheriff. Pat Garrett earned this reputation. He and his posse fired their weapons at outlaws much more readily than had any pre-ceding Lincoln County sheriff.

One underlying condition dictated the tenor of the sheriff's office in Arizona and New Mexico territories—the fact that sheriffs were popularly elected. In each new county, the initial appointment was made by the governor. After that, the people (meaning eligible males) elected the county lawman. In the large and settled popula-tion in the East, this process worked acceptably. This was not al-ways true in the territories. Factionalism, ethnicity, and economic rivalry sometimes intervened to render the electoral system ineffec-tual. That the sheriff often did not adequately represent the public of a certain county sometimes had the ironic effect of contributing to public disturbances rather than moderating them.

Just who was the typical sheriff? A profile of this officer is very difficult to create. Some 504 men held this important office in the two territories combined; 349 held office in New Mexico and 155 in Arizona. Of the incumbent sheriffs of New Mexico, 206 were Hispano and 143 were Anglo, judging from the names. This His-panic domination of the office was especially marked in the years from the American Conquest to 1880. Of the approximately 153 men who held this office from 1846 through 1880, 113 were His-panos. As more Easterners migrated into the Southwest later in the century, the proportion of Anglo incumbents increased. Generally, the new counties created in both territories after 1880 represented the efforts of new Anglo arrivals to achieve political equality in the legislatures.[3]

Considering that the Spanish-speaking community was the conquered population, their domination of the shrievalty indicated a rapid adjustment to the constitutional practices of the conqueror at the local level. In Arizona, no such discrepancy existed. Of the 155 men who held the sheriffalty, only four were Hispanos. John Gregory Bourke, a professional soldier in the Southwest shortly after the Civil War, noted this strong contrast in the racial composition of the shrievalty. Whereas "all officers of the law were Americans" in Arizona, he wrote, "they were almost without exception Mexicans . . ." in New Mexico. While Bourke exaggerated, and men of diverse backgrounds occupied the sheriff's office, much truth lay in his remarks. Where Anglos dominated the county lawman's position, these men were astute enough to recognize the Hispanic community with permanent deputyships. By the last decade of the nineteenth century, the Mormons had begun to enter the mainstream of frontier society. As early as 1896, William Wiley Berry, a Mormon, held the shrievalty of Apache County, Arizona. The Indians, who preceded the whites in the Southwest, still remained largely within their reservation boundaries and somewhat insulated from the civilian law enforcement arm.[4]

In spite of ethnic or religious divisions among the people of New Mexico and Arizona, some common bonds existed between the sheriffs. The typical chief county lawman owned property. Both territories imposed minimal property qualifications of at least $500. In Hispano dominated counties, the sheriff was apt to be one of the biggest property holders. Even in Anglo-dominated counties, where the sheriff was likely to be a recent arrival, ownership of land or other real estate was normally expected. That the property holder had a greater reverence for others' holdings went without saying. Within the scope of the sheriff's duties, the service of civil process (usually against property) was regarded as a very sensitive duty. Likewise, this official's additional duty of tax assessing and collecting gave him much say in property rights. The taxpaying population of each county, whether Hispanic or Anglo, naturally paid close attention to the property background of the candidates for the sheriffalty. One reason such sheriffs as Buckey O'Neill became so controversial during the Populist Party's agitations was that they used their office to tinker with property rights.

These men engaged in a wide variety of occupations in order to gather their property. Using personal data gathered on 168 of these 504 sheriffs, several facts emerge about the primary occupations of these men. The majority owned cattle ranches (47), mines (23), mercantile houses (22), sheep ranches (13), farms (13), hotels (9), or saloons (6). A wide variety of additional undertakings were represented, including real estate, ferry operator, lawyer, sawyer, photographer, schoolteacher, freighter, banker, machinist, journalist, stagecoach operator, restauranteur, soldier, government contractor, livery operator, and even an owner of a house of prostitution. Although the precise nature of property ownership is difficult to determine, only a few sheriffs seem to have been men of lesser means. Frontier citizens were generally insistent that the sheriffs own property. Occasionally, a ranch foreman or manager or mine superintendent held this office. Many of the above officers also invested in additional economic endeavors while concentrating on their primary occupation. Of the 168 men for whom some evidence is available, at least 101 carried on supplemental activities. A not unusual pattern would be for a man to arrive in the territories as a teamster or soldier and then engage in ranching, mining, farming, or a combination of these. Eventually, he concentrated upon the occupation that earned him the greatest profits.[5]

Other characteristics emerge from the data about these (168) men who became sheriffs. Many (42) possessed a military service record, either in the United States Army during the war with Mexico, the Civil War, or the Spanish-American War. Others served in the Confederate Army. Just as many of the Southwest's future economic and political leaders arrived with General James Henry Carleton's California Column during the Civil War, so did several men who became sheriffs. While many obviously possessed only the rudiments of formal education, they were fortunate to have been born during or just after the Jacksonian Era, when an elementary public school education was made available. Thirteen of the 168 specifically had some public schooling, five private schooling, and a surprising eighteen had some college work. Several of the Hispanos who held the sheriffalty were trained in Catholic colleges either in Santa Fe or St. Louis.

Many men held the shrievalty as part of a "career" in public service. The "professional" politician was common on the frontier and often had "busted" in his efforts to find a cornucopia in the West. Fifty-two of the 168 men sampled held at least one public post before entering the sheriff's office. These persons normally continued to serve in government office afterward. The frontier voter had a healthy skepticism about the motives of aspirants to the shrievalty and obviously desired that candidates have some prior law enforcement experience. In the pool of 168 incumbents, thirty-nine had

had some form of previous record as peace officers. These men also participated in benevolent and secret rite societies such as the Masonic Lodge, International Order of Odd Fellows, Knights of Pytheas, Elks, or, for Hispanic sheriffs, the Spanish-American Alliance.

Many of the men who held the shrievalty were not native to New Mexico and Arizona territories. Of the 168 in the pool, 104 were born in one of the states in the Union or Washington, D.C. This figure includes Hispanos born in New Mexico after the Conquest. Some states contributed a larger number; New York provided seven, Kentucky eight, Missouri nine, and Texas eleven. A sizable number were natives of foreign countries: three were born in Ireland, two in England, two in Germany, two in Canada, and fourteen in the Republic of Mexico.

Frontier lawmen had an ideal to aspire to—the equal enforcement of the laws for all constituents. The sheriffs of New Mexico and Arizona were no exceptions, although it is doubtful they achieved this exalted goal. As historian Frank Richard Prassel has observed, the legends about frontier peace officers have become so confused with the facts that we can hardly separate them. The twentieth-century reader identifies the frontier sheriffs collectively with the exploits of a few individuals such as John Slaughter and Commodore Perry Owens. Prassel concludes that this "rampant individualism" has tended to mislead the American people into the erroneous belief that the "personal will" of today's law enforcement officers will suffice. There is no need for an efficient system. This same attitude prevailed to some degree in the Southwestern territories in the last century. Voters in Arizona and New Mexico tended to starve the shrievalties with minimal financial support and to elect a "law and order" sheriff only when the degree of lawlessness reached alarming proportions. This tendency has had the unfortunate result of clouding our perspective upon the county law enforcement system—the web of sheriffs and other lawmen—across New Mexico and Arizona territories. The office of sheriff was much more important than the occasional "quick gun" occupant. Indeed, the efforts of hundreds of average and largely unknown men in this important office contributed decisively to the establishment of some order in the two territories. Yet, they too, failed to impose law and order absolutely. As Prassel has observed, "Frontier lawmen did not bring peace and order to the American West." That is not to say that the sheriffs did not strive for this end. At best, however, they only approximated the ideals of this hallowed calling.[6]

In an ironic turn of events, the sheriffs, who had just survived the turbulent territorial era in New Mexico and Arizona, were becoming the subject of criticism across the United States. This aging office, which had served as the rallying point for law abiding people for centuries in England and the United States, fell prey to charges of inadequacy in the emerging urban-industrial society. Although the sheriff—an amateur lawman in a world of emerging professionalism—continued to police the rural areas, many observers opined that his days were numbered.

In an article appropriately entitled, "Goodbye to the Sheriff," one critic, R. E. Heiges, argued that the various functions of the sheriff could be better managed by more efficient agencies. The state police should assume criminal duties of the county lawman, while court clerks should take over his civil tasks. The states should maintain district jails and thus remove this job from the counties. As for the detection of crime, Heiges observed that the sheriffs were not trained for this fulltime undertaking. Indeed, "The sheriff never was constrained by law to ferret out crime and criminals," he continued, "but was ordered to arrest any persons for unlawful acts . . ." after the fact. Such criticism, coming from observers in distant cities, made little impact upon the inhabitants of the southwestern states in the early decades of the twentieth century. For the time being, the sheriffs appeared to be secure in the traditional scheme of law enforcement, the framework that had brought Arizona and New Mexico through the lawlessness of the territorial era.[7]

Notes

CHAPTER 1

1. Many works exist about the early sheriff's office, but see: William Alfred Morris, *The Medieval English Sheriff to 1300* (New York: Barnes and Noble, 1968); *Encyclopedia of the Social Sciences*, ed. Edwin R. A. Seligman, 15 vols. (New York: Macmillan, 1930–34), 14: 20–22, s.v. "Sheriff"; Cyrus Harreld Karraker, *The Seventeenth-Century Sheriff: A Comparative Study of the Sheriff in England and the Chesapeake Colonies, 1607–1689* (Chapel Hill: University of North Carolina, 1930); Julius Goebel, Jr., and T. Raymond Naughton, *Law Enforcement in Colonial New York: A Study in Criminal Procedure, 1664–1776* (Montclair, N.J.: Patterson Smith, 1970); Robert M. Ireland, *The County Courts in Antebellum Kentucky* (Lexington: University of Kentucky, 1972).

2. Howard Roberts Lamar, *The Far Southwest, 1846–1912: A Territorial History* (New York: W. W. Norton, 1970), Chap. 3; James Madison Cutts, *The Conquest of California and New Mexico by the Forces of the United States in the Year 1846 and 1847* (Philadelphia: Carey and Hart, 1847), p. 220; U.S., Cong., House, 29th Cong., 2d Sess., *Occupation of Mexican Territory*, Serial 499, Exec. Doc. 19, pp. 27–73, for Kearny's report, which included a copy of his code.

3. Warren A. Beck and Ynez D. Haase, *Historical Atlas of New Mexico* (Norman: University of Oklahoma, 1969), maps 40, 41; Aurora Hunt, *Kirby Benedict, Frontier Federal Judge, An Account of Legal and Judicial Development in the Southwest, 1853–1874* (Glendale, Calif.: Arthur H. Clark, 1961), pp. 50–53.

4. *The Kearny Code* [Laws of the Territory of New Mexico], ed. Nolie Mumey (Denver, Colo.: n.p., 1970; orig. pub. Santa Fe, October 7, 1846), p. 5.

5. F. Stanley (Stanley Crocchiola), *Giant in Lilliput: The Story of Donaciano Vigil* (Pampa, Tex.: Pampa Print Shop, 1963), pp. 156–58.

6. Ralph Emerson Twitchell, *Old Santa Fe: The Story of New Mexico's Ancient Capital* (Chicago: Rio Grande Press, 1963), p. 286; for James Lawrence Hubbell, see *Weekly New Mexican* (Santa Fe), 15 January 1885 (hereafter cited as *WNM*); Jay J. Wagoner, *Early Arizona: Prehistory to the Civil War* (Tucson: University of Arizona, 1975), pp. 385–87; Carey McWilliams, *North From Mexico: The Spanish-Speaking People of the United States* (New York: Greenwood, 1968), p. 165.

7. Sister Mary Loyola, "The American Occupation of New Mexico, 1821–1852," *New Mexico Historical Review*, 14 (January 1939): 34–75, pt. 1.

8. First Judicial District, Criminal Cases, Santa Fe County, 1846–51, New Mexico State Records Center and Archives (hereafter cited as NMSRCA), for a return of Sheriff Francis

Redman, dated 5 December 1846, in the case of Territory of New Mexico *vs.* Corrilio Chavis [sic Chavez].

9. See Appendix A. Seventh Census of the United States, 1850, New Mexico, National Archives micro. M432, roll 467, p. 502, for Antonio Aragon, p. 177, for Lopez.

10. Marc Simmons, *Spanish Government in New Mexico* (Albuquerque: University of New Mexico Press, 1968), pp. 160–99; Brantz Mayer, *Mexico: Aztec, Spanish and Republican,* 2 vols. in 1 (Hartford, Conn.: S. Drake, 1851), 2:146–47; Lansing B. Bloom, "Beginnings of Representative Government in New Mexico," *El Palacio* 12 (15 March 1922): 74–78; Robert J. Rosenbaum, *Mexicano Resistance in the Southwest: 'The Sacred Right of Self-Protection'* (Austin: University of Texas, 1981), p. 25.

11. Benjamin F. Taylor, *Short Ravelings From a Long Yarn, or Camp March Sketches of the Santa Fe Trail,* from notes of Richard L. Wilson (Santa Rosa, Calif.: Fine Arts Press, 1936; orig. pub. 1847), p. 152; Hunt, *Kirby Benedict,* p. 52.

12. Rosenbaum, *Mexicano Resistance,* pp. 25–26. This same process took place in Hispanic areas of American Texas; see *The Handbook of Texas,* ed. in chief Walter Prescott Webb, 3 vols. (Austin: Texas State Historical Association, 1952), 2:603, s.v. "Sheriffs."

13. Edward D. Tittmann, "By Order of Richard Campbell," *New Mexico Historical Review* 3 (1928): 390–98; *idem.* "The Last Legal Frontier," 2 (July 1927): 219–27; Hunt, *Kirby Benedict,* p. 138.

14. Tittmann, "The Last Legal Frontier," 219–27; William W. H. Davis, *El Gringo: Or, New Mexico and Her People* (Santa Fe: Rydal, 1938; orig. pub. 1856), pp. 103–104.

15. *The Kearny Code,* p. 70.

16. *Daily National Intelligencer* (Washington, D.C.), 19 April 1851.

17. *Santa Fe Republican,* 15 January, 12 February, 1848; Larry D. Ball, *The United States Marshals of New Mexico and Arizona Territories, 1846–1912* (Albuquerque: University of New Mexico Press, 1978), p. 22; Ralph Emerson Twitchell, *The History of the Military Occupation of the Territory of New Mexico* (New York: Arno Press, 1976; orig. pub. 1909), p. 152.

18. Lamar, *Far Southwest,* pp. 73–82.

19. *Daily Picayune* (New Orleans), 12 April 1851, reporting news from Santa Fe; Ralph Emerson Twitchell, *Leading Facts of New Mexican History,* 2 vols. (Albuquerque: Horn & Wallace, 1963; orig. pub. 1917), 2:282–85.

20. Loomis Morton Ganaway, *New Mexico and the Sectional Controversy, 1846–1861* (Philadelphia: Porcupine Press, 1976), Chap. 2; Beck and Haase, *Historical Atlas of New Mexico,* maps 42–43. The date and engineers of the creation of Socorro County are something of a mystery; see Appendix A.

21. Beck and Haase, *Historical Atlas of New Mexico,* maps 42–43. The precise beginnings of Doña Ana County are also vague.

22. Wilma Loy Shelton, comp., *Checklist of New Mexico Publications, 1850–1953* (Albuquerque: University of New Mexico Press, 1954), p. 155; Hunt, *Kirby Benedict,* pp. 59–60; Katherine Stoes, et al. "Doña Ana County History," (Las Cruces, N. Mex.: Aztec Lodge No. 3, n.d.) p. 142, copy in Rio Grande Collection, New Mexico State University, Las Cruces.

23. Arie W. Poldervaart, *Black-Robed Justice: A History of Justice in New Mexico From the American Occupation in 1846 Until Statehood in 1912,* Historical Society of New Mexico Publications in History, vol. 13 (Santa Fe: Historical Society of New Mexico, 1948), pp. 1–2.

24. See Bean's recollections, *Silver City Enterprise,* 29 March 1889; and Maude Elizabeth McFie Bloom, "History of Mesilla Valley" (Master's thesis, New Mexico College of Agriculture and Mechanic Arts, June 1903), p. 35, for another interview with Samuel G. Bean.

25. *Silver City Enterprise,* 29 March 1889; Wagoner, *Early Arizona,* pp. 347–49, 393.

26. Charles Leland Sonnichsen, *Roy Bean: Law West of the Pecos* (New York: Macmillan, 1944), pp. 13–26, 40–42. Samuel Bean's life paralleled that of his brother Roy in the early years.

27. *Weekly Arizonian* (Tucson), 7 July, 15 September 1859; Ball, *United States Marshals,* pp. 27–29.

28. George Wythe Baylor, *John Robert Baylor: Confederate Governor of Arizona,* ed. Odie

B. Faulk (Tucson: Arizona Pioneers Historical Society, 1966), p. 8; Message of Acting Governor William F. M. Arny to the New Mexico Legislature, 2 December 1862, State Department Territorial Papers, New Mexico, 1851–72, National Archives Microcopy T-17, roll 2, 26 pp. (hereafter cited as State Dept. Terr. Pap., NM, etc.); Benedict to Edward Bates, United States Attorney General, 5 October 1861 and 12 June 1862, quoted in Hunt, *Kirby Benedict*, pp. 153–61.

29. Aurora Hunt, *Major General James Henry Carleton, 1814–1873: Western Frontier Dragoon* (Glendale, Calif.: Arthur H. Clark, 1958), p. 220. See copy of the proclamation of martial law in Arizona, Tucson, 8 June 1862, in B[enjamin F.] Sacks Collection, Arizona Historical Foundation, Hayden Library, Arizona State University, Tempe.

30. *The Santa Fe Weekly Gazette*, 22 July 1865, recalled the necessity for martial law. Arny to William H. Seward, Secretary of State, 1 May 1863, State Dept. Terr. Pap., NM, roll 2; Proclamation of William F. M. Arny, 26 March 1863, ibid.; *Santa Fe Weekly Gazette*, 12 and 19 March, 30 April 1864, for the controversy. General Orders No. 17, 4 July 1865, lifted martial law; see reprint in ibid., 22 July 1865.

31. Jay J. Wagoner, *Arizona Territory, 1863–1912: A Political History* (Tucson: University of Arizona, 1970), p. 36; Frank C. Lockwood, *Pioneer Days in Arizona: From Spanish Occupation to Statehood* (New York: Macmillan, 1932), pp. 261–62; John Nicolson, ed., *The Arizona of Joseph Pratt Allyn, Letters from a Pioneer Judge: Observations and Travels, 1863–1866* (Tucson: University of Arizona, 1974), pp. 153–54, for Allyn's description of the first session of court at Prescott in September 1864.

32. For Van Ness Smith, see ibid., pp. 77, 153–54, and n. 14; recollections of W. H. Hardy, *Arizona Weekly Journal-Miner* (Prescott, hereafter cited as *Weekly J-M*), 3 February 1897, for some memories of Smith and the first session of court; biographical sketch of Jerome B. Calkins, Hayden Biographical Files, Arizona Historical Society, Tucson (hereafter cited as AHS). Calkins was elected to succeed Van Ness Smith, 18 July 1864. Van Ness Smith was one of three land commissioners appointed to sell town lots on the site of Prescott; see Wagoner, *Arizona Territory*, p. 38. See Appendix A, this volume, for terms of other sheriffs.

33. See Giddings's remarks in *First Annual Message of Governor Marsh Giddings to the Legislative Assembly of the Territory of New Mexico, December 7, 1871* (Santa Fe: A. P. Sullivan, 1871), 54 pp.: Twitchell, *Leading Facts*, 2:419, for abolition of prefect.

34. See Appendix A; *Silver City Enterprise*, 30 November 1888.

35. See Appendix A.

36. Beck and Haase, *Historical Atlas of New Mexico*, maps 42–45; Twitchell, *Leading Facts*, 2:414 n. 340, 426.

37. Table compiled from Hubert Howe Bancroft, *History of Arizona and New Mexico, 1530–1888*, vol. 17, *Works of Hubert Howe Bancroft*, 39 vols. (New York: Arno, n.d.; orig. pub. 1889), Chap. 31, pp. 779–801.

38. Henry P. Walker and Don Bufkin, *Historical Atlas of Arizona* (Norman: University of Oklahoma, 1979), maps 29–31.

39. Rosenbaum, *Mexicano Resistance*, pp. 25–26.

CHAPTER 2

1. District Court: Misc. Papers and Transcripts of Cases, 1867–1900, Pima County, Original Documents, Vol. 36, n.p., Special Collections Dept., University of Arizona, Tucson; for Samuel Bean's oath, see Doña Ana County Records, 1844, NMSRCA; William S. Harlow, comp., *Duties of Sheriffs and Constables, Particularly under the Practice in California and the Pacific States and Territories, with Practical Forms for Official Use*, 3d ed. (San Francisco: Bancroft-Whitney, 1907; orig. pub. 1894), for an example of a handbook.

2. *The Revised Statutes of Arizona, 1913, Civil Code,* Comp. Samuel L. Pattee (Phoenix: McNeil, 1913), Chap. VI, pp. 874–78, citing a 1901 law.

3. Pima County, Original Documents, Vol. 36, Special Collections Dept., University of Arizona; *Daily New Mexican* (Santa Fe, hereafter cited as *DNM*), 4 January 1895, reporting the alleged squabble between Lohman and Ascarate.

4. For the removal of Sheriff Thomas Hubbell, see W. W. Safford [Examiner?] to Miguel A. Otero, Governor, 31 December 1904, and "Testimony Given at the Hearing in the Case of Frank A. Hubbell [County Treasurer] and Eslavio Vigil [Superintendent of Schools] of Bernalillo County, 28 June–29 June 1905, before Gov. Otero in the Alvarado Hotel," Miguel A. Otero Papers, Special Collections Dept., University of New Mexico, Albuquerque, box 4; John F. Fullerton, Captain, New Mexico Mounted Police, to Cipriano Baca, 12 September 1905, and Fullerton to W. E. Dudley, 12 September 1905, Letters Sent, 1905–1911, Territorial Archives of New Mexico, NMSRCA, roll 92.

5. *Weekly Arizona Miner* (Prescott), 25 July 1865, for Moore's bond; *DNM,* 22 December 1892, for Laird's bond; George Curry, *George Curry, 1861–1947: An Autobiography,* ed. H. B. Hening (Albuquerque: University of New Mexico Press, 1958), p. 74.

6. Samuel Axtell, Governor, to Edward Hatch, Brigadier General, 30 May 1878, copy in Maurice G. Fulton Collection, Special Collections Dept., University of Arizona, Tucson; William A. Keleher, *Violence in Lincoln County, 1869–1881: A New Mexico Item* (Albuquerque: University of New Mexico Press, 1957), p. 135 n. 5.

7. "From Whence It Came: Title and Badge," *The Sheriff* [Arizona] 25 (February 1971): 25–28; Ron Donoho, "Lore of the 'Tin Star,'" *Collector's World* (July–August 1970): 6–9.

8. Ibid.; *Weekly Arizona Miner,* 9 January 1889; for the Hassayampa badge, see Dale L. Walker, *Death Was the Black Horse: The Story of Rough Rider Buckey O'Neill* (Austin, Tex.: Madrona Press, 1975), pp. 67–68; *Argus* (Holbrook, Arizona), 16 January 1897, 15 April 1899, quoted in Lloyd C. Henning, "Sheriff, Scholar and Gentleman [Frank Wattron]," address at Snowflake, Arizona, 25 July 1941, amplified into a monograph (Holbrook, Ariz.: pvt. ptd., 1941).

9. Curry, *Autobiography,* p. 111; Frazier Hunt, *The Tragic Days of Billy the Kid* (New York: Hastings House, 1956), p. 212; Sierra County District Court Records, NMSRCA.

10. William Breakenridge, *Helldorado: Bringing the Law to the Mesquite* (Boston: Houghton Mifflin, 1928), pp. 127–28.

11. *St. Johns Herald* (Arizona), 29 November 1895; *The Compiled Laws of the Territory of Arizona, Including the Howell Code and the Session Laws, from 1864 to 1871, Inclusive,* comp. Coles Bashford (Albany, N.Y.: Weed, Parsons, 1871), p. 39, sec. 15; "An Act Requiring County Officers in This Territory to Establish and Maintain Their Offices in the County Seat of Their Respective Counties," 12 March 1903, in *Acts of the Legislative Assembly of the Territory of New Mexico, Thirty-fifth Session, 19 January 1903–19 March 1903* (Santa Fe: New Mexican, 1903), Chap. 38, p. 10; "An Act to Amend Chapter 38 of the Acts of the 35th Legislative Assembly of New Mexico," 21 March 1907, in *Acts of the 35th Legislative Assembly of the Territory of New Mexico, Thirty-seventh Session, 21 January 1907–21 March 1907* (Santa Fe: New Mexican, 1907), Chap. 87, p. 195.

12. Delbert Littrell Hughes, *Give Me Room! [Marion Littrell] 1855–1910* (El Paso, Tex.: Hughes Pub., 1971), p. 157.

13. Mike Anderson, "Posses and Politics in Pima County: The Administration of Sheriff Charlie Shibell," *Journal of Arizona History* 27 (Autumn 1986): 253–82. New Mexico sheriffs also appointed city policemen in unincorporated county seats; see "An Act Creating a Police Force in the County Seats of Each County, and for the Protection of Citizens and Their Property in the Territory of New Mexico," 11 February 1887, in *Acts of the Legislative Assembly of the Territory of New Mexico, Twenty-seventh Session, 27 December 1886–24 February 1887* (Las Vegas: J. A. Carruth, 1887), Chap. 57, pp. 208–211.

14. "Alexander McSween's Testimony," given to Judge Frank Angel, 1878, copy in R. N. Mullin Collection, Nita Stewart Haley Library, Midland, Texas; John P. Wilson, *Merchants, Guns & Money: The Story of Lincoln County and Its Wars* (Santa Fe: Museum of New Mexico, 1987), p. 89; *Rio Grande Republican* (Las Cruces), 14 October 1892.

15. For Harley Cartter, see *Prescott Courier,* 1 December 1890, in the William O'Neill Scrapbooks, Vol. 1, p. 36, Sharlot Hall Museum, Prescott, Arizona; for Ward's appointment, see *Weekly Epitaph* 18 November 1882; see *DNM,* 9 March 1886, 1 August 1889, for Morrison Jr.

16. For Pease's remark, see Henning, "Sheriff, Scholar"; William A. Keleher, *The Fabulous Frontier: Twelve New Mexico Items,* rev. ed. (Albuquerque: University of New Mexico Press, 1962), p. 215; Arthur Thomas Hannett, *Sagebrush Lawyer* (New York: Pageant Press, 1964), p. 10.

17. For Buckey O'Neill's education, see Walker, *Death Was the Black Horse,* pp. 10−11; William Brent, *The Complete and Factual Life of Billy the Kid* (New York: Frederick Fell, 1964); Jeff C. Dykes, *Law on a Wild Frontier: Four Sheriffs of Lincoln County* (Washington, D.C.: Potomac Corral of Westerners, n.d.), pp. 10−11; Pat F. Garrett, *The Authentic Life of Billy, the Kid: The Noted Desperado of the Southwest, Whose Deeds of Daring and Blood Made His Name a Terror in New Mexico, Arizona and Northern Mexico,* Intro. J. C. Dykes (Norman: University of Oklahoma, 1954; orig. pub. 1882); John W. Poe, As Told to E. A. Brininstool, *The True Story of the Killing of Billy the Kid* (Houston, Texas: Frontier Press, 1958; orig. pub. 1922); Curry, *Autobiography.*

18. See note 17; George Herbert Smalley, "Arizona's Gay and Gun Nineties," ms., 1946, p. 170, Smalley Collection, AHS, published in part, as *My Adventures in Arizona: Leaves From a Reporter's Notebook,* ed. Yndia Smalley Moore (Tucson: Arizona Historical Society, 1966).

19. John Alexander Carroll, ed., *Pioneering in Arizona: The Reminiscences of Emerson Oliver Stratton and Edith Stratton Kitt* (Tucson: Arizona Pioneers Historical Society, 1964), pp. 27−29; Interview, W. Orme-Johnson, 6 April 1947, Charles Leland Sonnichsen Papers, Special Collections Dept., University of Texas, El Paso; Frank M. King, *Wranglin' the Past: The Reminiscences of Frank M. King* (Pasadena, Calif.: Trail's End, 1946), pp. 196−97.

20. *Compiled Laws of the Territory of Arizona,* p. 38, sec. 3; For laws concerning justices of the peace, see *The General Laws of New Mexico; Including All the Unrepealed Laws, from the Promulgation of the 'Kearny Code' in 1846, to the End of the Legislative Session of 1880, with Supplement, Including the Session Laws of 1882,* L. Bradford Prince, comp. (Albany, N.Y.: W. C. Little, 1882), Chap. XXII, pp. 81−115. Jim East, "Memoirs" (unpub. ms., Haley Library, Midland, Texas, n.d.), pp. 20−21.

21. Crawford to William Griffith, U.S. Marshal, 10 December 1897, General Correspondence of the United States Marshals of Arizona, United States Marshals' Records, 1882−1927, AHS; Wallace to Max Frost, Adjutant General of New Mexico, 27 March 1881, Interior Department Territorial Papers, New Mexico, National Archives Microcopy M-364, roll 8 (hereafter cited as Int. Dept. Terr. Pap., NM, etc.); Dan R. Williamson, "Personal Reminiscences of Dan R. Williamson," AHS; and Soto to Charles Overlock, U.S. Marshal, September 1909, General Correspondence of the United States Marshals, AHS; *DNM,* 10 January 1893.

22. Frank D. Reeve, ed., *Albert Franklin Banta: Arizona Pioneer,* Historical Society of New Mexico Publications in History, vol. 24 (September 1953), pp. 78−79. As an example, two deputy sheriffs in Raton, New Mexico, in 1882 were saloon men; see Chuck Hornung, "The Lynching of Gus Mentzer," *Real West,* special ed. (Spring 1986): 31−37.

23. Curry, *Autobiography,* p. 74; for DeVane, see George B. Gross, "Tom Hart Stole an Iron Horse," *Sheriff Magazine* (June 1948), xerox copy in Sharlot Hall Museum, Prescott; for Giles, see *Weekly Arizona Miner,* 25 May, 27 July, 3 August 1877.

24. Pima County, Original Documents, Special Collections Dept., University of Arizona.

25. For Baca's commission, see Napoleon Laughlin Papers, NMSRCA.

26. William Swilling Wallace, intro. and ed., *A Journey Through New Mexico's First Judicial District in 1864: Letters to the Editor of the Santa Fe Weekly New Mexican* (Los Angeles: Westernlore Press, 1956), pp. 31−32; *DNM,* 18 May 1891. At least one sheriff was caught napping by the 1891 amendment. On 23 May, Sheriff Frank Chavez of Santa Fe County placed the following notice in the *Daily New Mexican:*

Notice is hereby given that in compliance with Section 4 Chapter LXII of the laws of 1891, which allows me the appointment of only five deputies, all commissions held by parties other than Francisco Delgado, Z. M. Crutchfield, Romulo Valles, Henry Metzar and W. H. Soehn . . . are this day revoked.

27. For Olinger's appointment, see Donald Cline, *Alias Billy the Kid: The Man Behind the Legend* (Santa Fe: Sunstone Press, 1986), p. 108; Jim East, "Memoirs," Haley Library, Midland, Texas.

28. Tom Horn, *Life of Tom Horn: Government Scout and Interpreter, Written by Himself: A Vindication* (Norman: University of Oklahoma, 1964; orig. pub. 1904), p. 213; unidentified newspaper clipping, June 1946, Law Enforcement Collection, AHS.

29. Mary Hudson Brothers, *Billy the Kid: The Most Hated, the Most Loved Outlaw New Mexico Ever Produced*, story by Bell Hudson (Farmington, N. Mex.: Hustler Press, 1949), pp. 18–22; Hervey E. Chesley, *Adventuring With the Old-Timers: Trails Traveled—Tales Told*, ed. B. Byron Price (Midland, Tex.: Nita Stewart Haley Memorial Library, 1979), p. 64, interview with Charles L. Ballard; Brent, *The Complete and Factual Life*, pp. 171–72; Allen A. Erwin, *The Southwest of John H. Slaughter, 1841–1922: Pioneer Cattleman and Trail-Driver of Texas, the Pecos, and Arizona and Sheriff of Tombstone* (Glendale, Calif.: Arthur H. Clark, 1965), pp. 228–29; for Blevins, see *Holbrook Argus*, 29 October 1901, Law Enforcement Collection, AHS; "Reminiscences of Leonard Alverson," AHS.

30. Roscoe G. Willson, "Broncho Bill Holdups Recalled by Pioneer," unidentified clipping, 25 June 1950, Law Enforcement Collection, AHS.

31. For a list of sheriffs of Pima County, Arizona, see Appendix A. For the Chinese "deputy," see *Arizona Weekly Star* (Tucson), 2 September 1886; for Nathan Appel, see biographical files, AHS; Ball, *United States Marshals*, p. 184; Jennie Parks Ringgold, *Frontier Days in the Southwest: Pioneer Days in Old Arizona* (San Antonio: Naylor, 1952), p. 166.

32. See *Albuquerque Evening Democrat*, 8 May 1885, for Jilson's appointment; William French, *Some Recollections of a Western Ranchman: New Mexico, 1883–1899* (London: Methuen, 1927), pp. 43–52.

33. *Clayton Enterprise*, 1 August 1891, quoted in F. Stanley (Stanley Crocchiola), *No Tears for Black Jack Ketchum* (Denver: World Press, 1958), pp. 125–28; Bursum to C[ipriano] Baca, Deputy Sheriff, Mogollon, 2 August 1895, quoted in Donald R. Moorman, "Holm O. Bursum, Sheriff, 1894," *New Mexico Historical Review* 39 (October 1964): 333–44.

34. For the coal company's request, see Hornung, "The Lynching of Gus Mentzer," pp. 31–37; *El Paso Lone Star*, [n.d.], quoted in *DNM*, 25 May 1882; interview, Harry Saxon, [n.d.], Haley Library, Midland, Texas.

35. For Tom Kane, see John H. (Jack) Culley, *Cattle, Horses and Men of the Western Range* (Tucson: University of Arizona, 1967), pp. 35–36.

36. For Slaughter's family appointments, see Erwin, *John Slaughter*, pp. 218–19, n. 6.

37. *Compiled Laws of the Territory of Arizona*, p. 40, sec. 18, for sheriff as collector; Message of Gov. John N. Goodwin to the Arizona Assembly, September 1864, State Dept. Terr. Pap., Arizona, National Archives Microcopy M-342, 1 roll.

38. Sherman to Charles Devens, United States Attorney General, 19 July 1877, Department of Justice, Letters Received, New Mexico, National Archives, Record Group 60, box 545. *DNM*, 28 February 1877, noted that Sheriff Martin Quintana of Santa Fe County had been serving as deputy marshal at district court.

39. Dee R. Harkey, *Mean As Hell* (Albuquerque: University of New Mexico, 1948), pp. 72–73; J. George Hilzinger, *Treasure Land: A Story* (Tucson: Arizona Advancement Co., 1897; reprint ed., Rio Grande Press, 1969), pp. 153, 156.

40. Harkey, *Mean As Hell*, p. 61.

41. John P. Meadows, "Billy the Kid As I Knew Him," with Maurice G. Fulton, copy in Philip Rasch Papers, Lincoln County Courthouse Museum, Lincoln, New Mexico. The writer is indebted to John P. Wilson, Las Cruces, New Mexico, for arranging access to these

papers. Michael M. Rice, "Pete Gabriel," from a ms. by Mrs. George F. Kitt, "Pinal County," Law Enforcement Collection, AHS; Chuck Parsons, *Clay Allison: Portrait of a Shootist* (Seagraves, Tex.: Pioneer Book Pub., 1983), pp. 71–72.

42. *Apache County Critic,* 31 March 1887, quoted in Henning, "Sheriff, Scholar," p. 1; Joe T. McKinney, "Reminiscences of J. T. McKinney," *Arizona Historical Review* 5 (April 1932): 33–54 and (October 1932): 195–204; J. Evetts Haley, *Jeff Milton: A Good Man With a Gun* (Norman: University of Oklahoma, 1948), pp. 144–45; clipping, *Arizona Republican* (Phoenix), 19 January 1975, in "Outlaws and Badmen," Special Collections, Hayden Library, Arizona State University, Tempe.

43. Anderson, "Posses and Politics in Pima County," pp. 253–82; *Arizona Republican,* 23 June 1904. That deputy sheriffs did not consider their positions of much importance was reflected in their entries in the censuses. Professor Dennis Rousey of Arkansas State University enumerated the entries of all lawmen in New Mexico Territory in the 1870 and 1880 censuses. Only four men listed themselves as deputy sheriffs (1870) and seven in 1880. The remainder presumably listed their occupations, such as farmer, clerk, and so forth. The author wishes to thank Professor Rousey for this information.

CHAPTER 3

1. For one set of laws concerning justices of the peace, see *The General Laws of New Mexico,* L. Bradford Prince, comp., Chap. 21, pp. 81–115.

2. Jess G. Hayes, *Boots and Bullets: The Life and Times of John W. Wentworth* (Tucson: University of Arizona, 1967), p. 49.

3. Address of Benjamin M. Read, *Proceedings of the New Mexico Bar Association, Fourth Annual Session* (Santa Fe: New Mexican, 1889).

4. Grand Jury Report, April 1859, Bernalillo County District Court Records, NMSRCA; Grand Jury Report, May 1878, ibid.; Grand Jury Report, May 1885, reprinted in *Albuquerque Evening Democrat,* 26 May 1885; *Newman's Thirty-Four* (Las Cruces), 23 February 1881; French, *Some Recollections,* pp. 149–50; for Wilson, see *DNM,* 23 December 1876.

5. Frank C. Lockwood, *Pioneer Days in Arizona: From Spanish Occupation to Statehood* (New York: Macmillan, 1932), pp. 266–27; F. Stanley (Stanley Crocchiola), *Dave Rudabaugh: Border Ruffian* (Denver: World Press, 1961), pp. 84–102, passim; for Redfield, see the recollections of W. C. Davis, who, as chairman of the board of county supervisors, appointed the outlaw, *Arizona Weekly Republican* (Phoenix), 17 July 1902; Petition of N. H. Clanton et al., 12 June 1874, Pima County Original Records, Special Collections Dept., University of Arizona, Tucson.

6. Lockwood, *Pioneer Days in Arizona,* pp. 263–66; John R. Wunder, *Inferior Courts, Superior Justice: A History of the Justice of the Peace on the Northwest Frontier, 1853–1889* (Westport, Conn.: Greenwood, 1979), p. 167.

7. John Myers Myers, *I, Jack Swilling: Founder of Phoenix, Arizona* (New York: Hastings House, 1961), pp. 260–62; for the death of Flake, see *DNM,* 28 November, 10 December 1892, and Snowflake Centennial Committee, *The Life and Times of Snowflake, 1878–1978: A History in Stories* (Snowflake, Ariz. 1978), p. 22; John B. Anderson, Justice of the Peace, Greaterville, Pima County, Arizona, to Fred Hughes, Chairman of the Board of Supervisors, [5 December?] 1895, Pima County Original Documents, Special Collections Dept., University of Arizona, Tucson; Louis I. Marshall, Justice of the Peace, [11th?] Precinct, Grant County, New Mexico, to Bursum, 18 February 1899, Holm O. Bursum Papers, Special Collections Dept., University of New Mexico, Albuquerque.

8. For some official acts of Justice of the Peace John Wilson, see Keleher, *Violence in Lincoln County,* esp. pp. 81–82, 87, 92–93, 97, 116, 143–45; French, *Some Recollections,* pp. 42–52.

9. F. Stanley (Stanley Crocchiola), *Desperadoes of New Mexico* (Denver: World Press, 1953), pp. 213–20; Hayes, *Boots and Bullets*, pp. 54–55. A subsequent Gila County sheriff, John Henry Thompson, had difficulties with another justice of the peace. See *Silver Belt* (Globe), [?] January 1908, reprinted in Joseph Miller, ed., *The Arizona Rangers* (New York: Hastings House, 1972), pp. 179–80.

10. For some laws of constables, see *Compiled Laws of the Territory of Arizona*, Chap. 10; see p. 511 for fees.

11. This incident involving Sheriff Hyler Ott is recounted in William F. Hogan, "John Miller: Pioneer Lawman," *Arizoniana* (now *Journal of Arizona History*) 4 (Summer 1963): 41–45; Miller was simultaneously constable and city marshal; Rosenbaum, *Mexicano Resistance*, pp. 134–37.

12. Bernts Rube, "A Yuma Tragedy," *Quarterly of the National Association of Outlaw and Lawman History* (NOLA) 5 (October 1979): 16–18.

13. *Laws of the Territory of New Mexico, Passed by the Legislative Assembly Session of 1866–67* (Santa Fe: Manderfield and Tucker, 1867), pp. 130–35; *Compiled Laws of the Territory of Arizona*, Chap. 4; Ed. Bartholomew, *Wyatt Earp: The Man and the Myth* (Toyahvale, Tex.: Frontier Book Company, 1964), pp. 137–38.

14. *DNM*, 20 July 1894; V. H. Whitlock (Ol' Waddy), *Cowboy Life on the Llano Estacado* (Norman: University of Oklahoma, 1970), pp. 200–207.

15. *Weekly Arizona Miner*, 14 August 1869.

16. *Arizona Weekly Star* (Tucson), 27 October 1867.

17. For incorporation of Santa Fe, see State Dept. Terr. Pap., NM, 1851–72, National Archives Microcopy T-17, roll 1; *Town Ordinances of Albuquerque, New Mexico, 1863* (Albuquerque: Vinegar Tom Press, 1970); Act of 19 January 1856, *General Laws of New Mexico*, Chap. 85, pp. 421–22; *Laws of the Territory of New Mexico*, pp. 18–21, Act of 26 January 1866 (for Santa Fe), pp. 116–24, Act of 1 February 1866, for Las Vegas; *Weekly New Mexican*, 10 February 1881; See Eric H. Monkonnen, *Police in Urban America, 1860–1920* (Cambridge: Cambridge University Press, 1981), pp. 53–55 & App. A, pp. 164–68, for uniforms. The nearest city to adopt uniforms—Denver in 1873—could possibly have encouraged Santa Feans in this direction. Whether the spread of uniformed police in New Mexico and Arizona best illustrated the process of contagious diffusion or constant source diffusion, as outlined by Monkonnen, is not clear.

18. For early Tucson policemen, see *Weekly Arizona Miner*, 3 October 1868; Dick Hall, "Jesus Comacho, the Mayor of Meyer Street," *Journal of Arizona History* 20 (Winter 1979): 445–66. Hall may be confused, since the *Weekly Epitaph* (Tombstone), 7 October 1882, reported that the Tucson police force consisted of four regulars, two specials, one chief and one nightwatchman at the jail; see unidentified clipping, 15 April 1909, James H. McClintock Collection, Phoenix Public Library, for police force of that time.

19. Ibid.; Philip D. Jordan, "The Town Marshal: Local Arm of the Law," *Arizona and the West* 16 (Winter 1974): 321–42; *Silver City Enterprise*, 6 April 1883.

20. Jordan, "The Town Marshal," pp. 321–42; George Hochderffer, *Flagstaff Whoa! The Autobiography of a Western Pioneer* (Flagstaff: Museum of Northern Arizona, 1965), pp. 121–22.

21. For Santiago Baca, see *Silver City Enterprise*, 24 September 1886; *Santa Fe New Mexican Review*, 25 January 1884; *DNM*, 14 February 1893; Hochderffer, *Flagstaff*, p. 122.

22. Quoted in Ball, *United States Marshals*, pp. 202–203.

23. Ibid.

24. Clipping, *Las Cruces Sun-News*, Centennial Edition, 9 October 1949, provided by John P. Wilson.

25. Ball, *United States Marshals*, pp. 110–11, 128.

26. Paul Joseph Vanderwood, "The Rurales: Mexico's Rural Police Force, 1861–1914," (Ph.D. Diss., University of Texas, Austin, 1970).

27. For some observations about railroad detectives, see Richard Patterson, *Train Robbery, The Birth, Flowering, and Decline of a Notorious Western Enterprise* (Boulder, Colo.:

Johnson Books, 1981), pp. 32–34, 140. For a thoughtful and informative study of the Pinkertons, see Frank Morn, *'The Eye That Never Sleeps': A History of the Pinkerton National Detective Agency* (Bloomington: Indiana University, 1982). Charles A. Siringo, *Riata and Spurs: The Story of a Lifetime Spent in the Saddle as Cowboy and Detective* (Boston: Houghton, Mifflin, 1927); see also Siringo's *Two Evil Isms: Pinkertonism and Anarchism* (orig. pub. 1915; facs. ed., Austin, Tex.: Steck-Vaughn, 1967).

28. D. J. Cook, *Hands Up: Or, Twenty Years of Detective Life in the Mountains and on the Plains* (1882; reprint ed., Norman: University of Oklahoma, 1958); William Ross Collier and Edwin Victor Westrate, *Dave Cook of the Rockies: Frontier General, Fighting Sheriff and Leader of Men* (New York: Rufus Rockwell Wilson, 1936).

29. William A. Keleher, *New Mexicans I Knew: Memoirs, 1892–1969,* intro. Lawrence R. Murphy (Albuquerque: University of New Mexico Press, 1983), Chap. 10, pp. 153–64, "About Elfego Baca"; *Arizona Republican,* 22 March 1901.

30. Leon C. Metz, *Pat Garrett: The Story of a Western Lawman* (Norman: University of Oklahoma, 1974), Chap. 4, pp. 58–66; *DNM,* 9 January 1881; clipping, *Arizona Citizen* (Tucson), 23 June 1877, Hayden Biographical Files, AHS; *Weekly Arizona Miner,* 7 December 1877.

31. *Silver City Enterprise,* 16 September 1887; *Rio Grande Republican* (Las Cruces), 15 July 1892.

32. Larry D. Ball, "Lawman in Disgrace: Sheriff Charles C. Perry of Chaves County, New Mexico," *New Mexico Historical Review* 61 (April 1986): 125–36; William Pinkerton, "Highwaymen," *North American Review* 157 (November 1893): 530–40; Morris F. Taylor, *O. P. McMains and the Maxwell Land Grant Conflict* (Tucson: University of Arizona, 1979), pp. 212–13; Siringo, *Riata and Spurs,* pp. 153–57.

33. Calvin Horn, *New Mexico's Troubled Years: The Story of the Early Territorial Governors* (Albuquerque: Horn & Wallace, 1963), Chap. 10 for Wallace. For Sheldon, see Philip J. Rasch, "The Rustler War," *New Mexico Historical Review* 39 (October 1964): 257–73. For Thornton, see Ball, *United States Marshals,* pp. 153–55; Curry, *Autobiography,* pp. 216–18. For Safford, see Safford to Hamilton Fish, Secretary of State, 29 December 1871, State Dept. Terr. Pap., Arizona, National Archives Microcopy M-342, 1 roll. For Gosper, see Gosper to Samuel Kirkwood, Secretary of Interior, 29 November 1881, Int. Dept. Terr. Pap., Arizona, National Archives Microcopy M-429, roll 3. For Zulick, see Don Dedera, *A Little War of Our Own: The Pleasant Valley War Revisited* (Flagstaff, Ariz., Northland Press, 1988), pp. 158–59.

34. "Instructions in Relation to Applications for the Extradition of Fugitive Criminals," May 1876, in Carl Schurz, Secretary of Interior, to Wallace, 30 November 1878, box 7, Lew Wallace Papers, Indiana Historical Society, Indianapolis.

35. Stuart H. Traub, "Rewards, Bounty Hunting, and Criminal Justice in the West, 1865–1900," *Western Historical Quarterly* 19 (August 1988): 287–302, concludes that the bounty hunter "did not exist."

CHAPTER 4

1. Moorman, "Holm O. Bursum," 333–44; Curry, *Autobiography,* p. 94.

2. *Rio Abajo Weekly Press* (Albuquerque), 8 September 1863.

3. Wagoner, *Arizona Territory,* p. 361, for photocopy of clipping, *Coconino Sun,* 3 November 1900; *Lincoln County Leader* (White Oaks), 21 October 1882; *DNM,* 3 March 1892; clipping, *Tombstone Prospector,* 2 November 1892, in William D. Monmonier Family Papers, Special Collections Dept., University of Arizona, Tucson, box 1; clipping, *Tucson Citizen,* 20 October 1890, Law Enforcement Collection, "Pinal County," AHS; clipping, *Arizona Enterprise,* 24 August 1878, Biographical Files, Edward F. Bowers, AHS; *WNM,* 23 October 1884.

4. *Lincoln County Leader*, 21 October 1882; Mrs. Kurt Schmidt, "Vignettes of Arizona Pioneers: Commodore Perry Owens," *Arizoniana* 1 (Fall 1960): 6–8; For Pat Garrett's election campaign, see Leon C. Metz, *Pat Garrett: The Story of a Western Lawman* (Norman: University of Oklahoma, 1974), pp. 52–57; *Lincoln County Leader*, 21 October 1882.

5. Breakenridge, *Helldorado*, pp. 180–85; New Mexico Pioneers Foundation Interviews, Robert and Ollie Bell, 24 August 1952, Special Collections Dept., University of New Mexico, Albuquerque; *Arizona Republican*, 13 August 1900.

6. William Eugene Brooks to Anna P. Brooks (mother), 4 October 1906, Brooks Collection, Arizona State University Library, Tempe, box 3; Upson to "sister," 9 September 1890, Maurice Garland Fulton Collection, Special Collections Dept., University of Arizona, Tucson, box 11.

7. Clipping, *Arizona Daily Miner*, 11 October 1878, Biographical Files, Edward F. Bowers, AHS; New Mexico Pioneers Foundation Interviews, Robert and Ollie Bell, 25 August 1953, Special Collections Dept., University of New Mexico, Albuquerque; for Blackington, see Keleher, *The Fabulous Frontier*, pp. 261–62.

8. Carroll, ed., *Pioneering in Arizona*, p. 57 and note; Hayes, *Boots and Bullets*, p. 70; unidentified clipping, 7 August 1947, Buckey O'Neill Scrapbooks, no. 1, p. 9, Sharlot Hall Museum, Prescott, Arizona; Miguel A. Otero, *My Life on the Frontier*, 2 vols., *1864–1882*, vol. 1 (New York: Press of the Pioneers, 1935); *1882–1897*, vol. 2 (Albuquerque: University of New Mexico Press, 1939), 2:222–30; Curry, *Autobiography*, pp. 18–20.

9. Clipping, *Arizona Weekly Star* (Tucson), 17 October 1878, Biographical Files, Edward F. Bowers, AHS; Otero, *My Life*, 2:18–20; *WNM*, 28 October 1886.

10. *Arizona Weekly Republican*, 25 September 1902; Breakenridge, *Helldorado*, pp. 189–90.

11. Ringgold, *Frontier Days*, p. 166; *Daily Optic* (Las Vegas, New Mexico), 1, 4, 5, 6 November 1884.

12. *Arizona Weekly Republican*, 25 September 1902; J. Evetts Haley, *Jeff Milton: A Good Man With a Gun* (Norman: University of Oklahoma, 1948), p. 195.

13. Wagoner, *Arizona Territory*, pp. 96–98; Haley, *Jeff Milton*, p. 152; W. P. B. Field to Frank E. Murphy, Silver Bell, Arizona, 23 August 1900, Biographical Files, Frank E. Murphy, AHS.

14. Walker, *Death Was the Black Horse*, pp. 61–66; *Weekly J-M*, 28 September, 5, 12, 19, 26 October, 1, 9, 16, 23, 30 November 1898.

15. Haley, *Jeff Milton*, p. 122; New Mexico Pioneers Foundation Interviews, Henry Brock and John Cox, 8 October 1953, Special Collections Dept., University of New Mexico, Albuquerque; Curry, *Autobiography*, pp. 74, 79.

16. As early as 1878, Don Dionicio Baca reportedly controlled the Hispano votes in and around Springerville, *Arizona Weekly Star*, 17 October 1878. The *Albuquerque Evening Democrat*, 31 October 1884, noted the intimate ties of Apache County, Arizona, with Albuquerque and declared that the election of John Lorenzo Hubbell "is absolutely necessary if the people of Apache [County] want to see the county prosper." Frank C. Lockwood, "John Lorenzo Hubbell, Navajo Indian Trader," University of Arizona Bulletin, No. 6, 8 (1 July 1942): 64–66; John Lorenzo Hubbell, as told to John Edwin Hogg, "Fifty Years an Indian Trader," *Touring Topics* (Westways), 22 (December 1930): 24–29, 51; J. L. Hubbell folder, James McClintock Collection, Phoenix Public Library.

17. Kearney Egerton, "Buffs Still Debate Holbrook Killings," clipping, *Arizona Republican*, 19 January 1975, Outlaw and Badman file, Special Collections Dept., Arizona State University; Clara T. Woody and Milton L. Schwartz, *Globe, Arizona* (Tucson: Arizona Historical Society, 1977), p. 144; McKinney, "Reminiscences," (April 1932): 33–54, (October): 195–204. Jim Schmitz, "The Sheriff and the Desperado," *Scottsdale Progress* (Arizona), 8 August 1987, copy courtesy John P. Wilson, Las Cruces, New Mexico. *St. Johns Herald*, 21 October 1886, quoted in Schmidt, "Commodore Perry Owens," pp. 6–8; Charles Sharon Peterson, *Settlement on the Little Colorado, 1873–1900: A Study of the Processes and Institutions of Mormon Expansion* (Ph.D. diss., University of Utah, August 1967), pp. 402–403.

18. *St. Johns Herald*, 28 October 1886, quoted in Schmidt, "Commodore Perry Owens," pp. 6–8.

19. Metz, *Pat Garrett*, pp. 54–57; Curry, *Autobiography*, pp. 18–20, 40; Erwin, *The Southwest of John H. Slaughter*, pp. 210–12; C. L. Sonnichsen, *Billy King's Tombstone: The Private Life of an Arizona Boom Town* (Tucson: University of Arizona, 1972), pp. 224–25; James G. Wolf, "Story of James G. Wolf, Cochise County Guide," 6 parts, 4 September 1937, Small Collection, AHS; Andrew James Doran, "Interesting Reminiscences," *Arizona Historical Review* 1 (October 1928): 54–62.

20. See handbill against W. S. Oury, dated Tucson [September 1874], signed by James H. Toole, J. E. McCaffry, George Cooler, and L. W. Carr, Biographical Files, William S. Oury, AHS; Cornelius C. Smith, Jr., *William Sanders Oury: History-Maker of the Southwest* (Tucson: University of Arizona, 1967), pp. 208–10.

21. Bob D. Blair, "The Murder of William Joe Giles," *Journal of Arizona History* 7 (Spring 1966): 27–34; see Chapter 10 for Sheriff Beeler; *Arizona Weekly Star*, 2 November 1882; *Weekly Epitaph* (Tombstone), 28 October 1882, for Bob Paul; clipping, *St. Johns Herald*, 1 November 1888, Law Enforcement Collection, "Apache County," AHS; Carolyn Lake, ed., *Under Cover for Wells Fargo: The Unvarnished Recollections of Fred Dodge* (Boston: Houghton Mifflin, 1969), p. 55; Carroll, *Pioneering in Arizona*, pp. 75–77, 87.

22. Clipping, *Arizona Enterprise* (Florence), 2 June 1888, Biographical Files, Pete Gabriel, AHS; Rice, "Pete Gabriel," AHS; "The First Election in Maricopa County," *The Sheriff* (Arizona) 7 (February 1948): 5–11.

23. Marc Simmons, *Albuquerque: A Narrative History* (Albuquerque: University of New Mexico Press, 1982), p. 288; for the Armijo-Baca campaigns, see *Albuquerque Evening Democrat*, 28, 29, 30 October, 1, 3 November 1884, *WNM*, 21, 28 October 1886; for the Mesilla riots, see George Griggs, *History of Mesilla Valley, or the Gadsden Purchase, Known in Mexico as the Treaty of Mesilla* (Mesilla, N. Mex.: n. pub., 1930), pp. 90–93.

24. Whitehill to Joseph Collier, 23 December 1881, John J. Cockrell and William T. Thornton Correspondence, in Lincoln County Collection, box 265, folder 2, Museum of New Mexico History Library, Santa Fe; *Rocky Mountain News* (Denver, hereafter cited as *RMN*), 9 September 1900.

25. Harkey, *Mean as Hell*, pp. 59–62; Moorman, "Holm O. Bursum," pp. 333–44; *DNM*, 17 November 1882, reported seventy-five deputy sheriffs sworn in to guard Santa Fe County polls; the issue of 13 August 1890 reported "half-drunk" deputies at the polls.

26. Bob Paul's election troubles attracted much attention; see James M. Barney "Bob Paul—Early Arizona Sheriff," *The Sheriff* (Arizona) 8 (February 1949): 3, 8–10; Barney, "Who Was Elected Sheriff," ibid., 11; "When All Roads Led to Tombstone," John Pleasant Gray Papers, AHS, 1 box; Mike Anderson, "Posses and Politics in Pima County: The Administration of Sheriff Charlie Shibell," *Journal of Arizona History* 27 (Autumn 1986): 253–82.

27. John Pleasant Gray Papers, AHS.

28. J. C. Hancock Papers, AHS.

29. *Arizona Weekly Star*, 18 April 1881.

30. See *Daily Epitaph*, 24 February 1886, for a summary of this case and the Pima County Grand Jury report on the burglary.

31. *Arizona Weekly Star*, 15 April 1886.

32. Mike Rice ms., Sharlot Hall Museum, Prescott, xerox copy of original in AHS; New Mexico Pioneers Foundation Interviews, Miles Cicero Stewart, 1954, Special Collections Dept., University of New Mexico, Albuquerque; Philip J. Rasch and Lee Myers, "Les Dow, Sheriff of Eddy County," *New Mexico Historical Review* 49 (July 1974): 241–52; Harkey, *Mean as Hell*, pp. 57–60.

33. *WNM*, 13 January 1887.

34. For Behan's recollections, see unidentified clipping [after 1900?], McClintock Collection, Phoenix Public Library; Glenn G. Boyer, "Johnny Behan: Assistant Folk Hero," *Real West* annual ed. (Spring 1983): 6, 8, 10–17, 70, 72–73; Ed Bartholomew, *Wyatt Earp, 1848 to 1880: The Untold Story*, vol. 1, and *Wyatt Earp, 1879–1882: The Man and the Myth*, vol. 2 (Toyahvale, Tex.: Frontier Book Co., 1963–64), for background.

35. For coverage of the debate over Cochise County in the assembly, see *Arizona Weekly Star*, 10, 17 February 1881. The proceedings were very stormy, according to one observer;

see Angie Mitchell (Brown) Notebook, 1880–1881, Angie Brown Collection, Sharlot Hall Museum, Prescott, entries for 17, 20 January, 10 February 1881. Brown was legislative clerk. Glenn Boyer, ed., *I Married Wyatt Earp: The Recollections of Josephine Sarah Marcus Earp* (Tucson: University of Arizona, 1976), pp. 26–27; William M. Breakenridge, *Helldorado: Bringing the Law to the Mesquite* (Boston: Houghton, 1928), pp. 101–2.

36. Alford E. Turner, ed., *The O.K. Corral Inquest* (College Station, Tex.: Creative Pub., 1981), pp. 136–55 for Behan's testimony, pp. 155–73 for Wyatt Earp.

37. *Arizona Weekly Star*, 17 February 1881, announced the appointment of Gila County officers; *Silver Belt* (Globe), [February?] 1881, quoted in George H. Kelly, comp., *Legislative History: Arizona, 1864–1912* (Phoenix: Manufacturing Stationers, 1926), pp. 102–103.

38. Pat Savage, *One Last Frontier: A Story of Indians, Early Settlers and Old Ranches of Northern Arizona* (New York: Exposition, 1964), p. 39, for Van Ness Smith deal; *Weekly New Mexican Review,* 9 June 1883, for appointment of Matthias Stockton; *WNM,* 7 January 1886, for Jim Brent; W. T. Thornton to John J. Cockrell, 16 January 1886, R. N. Mullin Collection, Nita Stewart Haley Library, Midland, Texas; Sophie Poe, *Buckboard Days,* ed. Eugene Cunningham (Caldwell, Idaho: Caxton, 1936), pp. 253–54.

CHAPTER 5

1. *The Kearny Code,* sec. 2; *Compiled Laws of the Territory of Arizona,* Chap. 467, pp. 382–87.

2. *General Laws of New Mexico,* Art. 30, Chap. 68, pp. 362–67; Leonard Alverson, "Reminiscences of Leonard Alverson," as told to Mrs. George F. Kitt, typescript, AHS; The *Weekly Star* (Tucson), 30 January 1879, noted that "The sheriff, probate judge and clerk of the district court . . . drew a list of grand jurors for the February term of the district court."

3. *Compiled Laws of the Territory of Arizona,* Chap. 46, pp. 380–81; *New Mexico Statutes Annotated; Containing the Codification Passed at the Second Session of the Legislature of the State of New Mexico,* comps. Stephen B. Davis, Jr., & Merritt C. Mechem (Denver: W. H. Courtright, 1915), Sec. 1357, p. 471, for earlier laws on clerks.

4. *Santa Fe Weekly Gazette,* 20 October, 10, 24 November 1855; *Arizona Citizen* (Tucson), 30 May, 13 June 1879.

5. *Santa Fe Weekly Gazette,* 5 January 1856; Franz Huning, *Trader on the Santa Fe Trail,* with notes by Lina Fergusson Browne (Albuquerque: University of Albuquerque, in collab. with Calvin Horn, 1973), pp. 58–59; Arny to Lincoln, 19 December 1863, in Hunt, *Kirby Benedict,* p. 165; for the removal of McMillan, see *Capitan Press,* 26 June 1903. The author is indebted to John P. Wilson for a copy of the McMillan news item; for Judge Richard Sloan, see *Weekly J-M,* 20 December 1899.

6. For Palen, see *DNM,* 28 September 1872; for the Waldo story, see William G. Ritch Collection, originals in the Huntington Library, San Marino, California, microfilm copy in Special Collections Dept., University of New Mexico, Albuquerque, reel 5, frame 1709; Walter John Donlon, "Lebaron Bradford Prince: Chief Justice and Governor of New Mexico Territory, 1879–1893," (Ph.D. diss., University of New Mexico, 1967), p. 76; *DNM,* 3 January 1895, for Thomas Smith.

7. Jean M. Burroughs, ed., *On the Trail: The Life and Tales of 'Lead Steer' Potter* (Santa Fe: Museum of New Mexico, 1980), p. 40; Evans Coleman, "The Jury Strike at Solomonville," *Journal of Arizona History* 16 (Winter 1975): 323–34.

8. For Peter Brady, Jr., see undated clipping, James H. McClintock Collection, Phoenix Public Library; *Arizona Weekly Star* (Tucson), 27 December 1883; *Argus* (Holbrook), 3 December 1898, quoted in Henning, "Sheriff, Scholar"; *DNM,* 20 July 1876; *Daily Record-Epitaph* (Tombstone), 7 June 1885.

9. Richard E. Sloan, *Memories of an Arizona Judge* (Stanford: Stanford University, 1932), pp. 173–74.

10. *Revised Statutes of Arizona* (Prescott: Prescott Courier, 1887), Para. 510, p. 144; *Arizona Weekly Star*, 19 June 1884, for Fitzgerald.

11. *Silver City Enterprise*, 3 April 1885; for Lincoln County's first session of district court, see exhibit, Lincoln Museum, Lincoln, New Mexico; for first court in Prescott, Arizona, see W. H. Hardy, "Early Reminiscences," *Weekly J-M*, 3 February 1897; Judge William Howell's charge to grand jury, *Arizona Semi-Monthly Miner*, 20 April 1864.

12. George H. Kelly, "First Term District Court Held in Graham County," *Arizona Historical Review* 1 (October 1928): 63–67; Edward D. Tuttle, "Journal and Letters of Edward D. Tuttle," 2 vols., Special Collections Dept., University of Arizona, Tucson (photostat reproduction in Huntington Library, San Marino, California).

13. Robert N. Mullin, "An Item from Old Mesilla," *Password* 15 (Winter 1970): 128–29; French, *Some Recollections*, pp. 151–52.

14. For the Beveridge Committee's observations about multiple languages in New Mexico courts, see Ellen Lloyd Trover, *Chronology and Documentary Handbook of the State of Arizona* (New York: Oceana Pub., 1972), p. 97; Jose D. Sena, longtime sheriff of Santa Fe County, served as a court translator (*DNM*, 28 January 1868).

15. French, *Some Recollections*, pp. 151–52; "A Drunken Atty. Gen. with an Important *case pending*, As Related by Those Who Were There," Ritch Collection, Special Collections Dept., University of New Mexico, roll 5, frame 1658.

16. Poldervaart, *Black-Robed Justice*, p. 126; B[enjamin] Sacks, *Arizona's Angry Man: United States Marshal Milton B. Duffield*, Arizona Monographs, No. 1 (Tempe, Ariz.: Arizona Historical Foundation, 1970), pp. 43–48; A. M. Gustafson, ed., *John Spring's Arizona* (Tucson: University of Arizona, 1966), pp. 265–66; Harkey, *Mean as Hell*, p. 125.

17. Lake, ed., *Under Cover*, pp. 73–74.

18. Clipping, *Arizona Daily Gazette* (Phoenix), 10 August 1892, Hayden Biographical Files, John Britt Montgomery, AHS.

19. Hayes, *Boots and Bullets*, pp. 84–85; *RMN*, 30 September 1902.

20. Curry, *George Curry*, p. 114.

21. Woody and Schwartz, *Globe*, p. 166; McKinney, "Reminiscences," 5 (April 1932): 33–54, (October 1932): 195–204.

22. *DNM*, 21 April 1892; Hannett, *Sagebrush Lawyer*, pp. 9–11.

23. Lake, ed., *Under Cover*, pp. 68–74.

24. John S. Goff, *The Supreme Court Justices, 1863–1912* (Cave Creek, Ariz.: Black Mountain Press, 1975), p. 102; *DNM*, 17 August 1893.

25. *DNM*, 17, 22 January 1876; for session of the consolidated courts in Taos, see *DNM*, 12, 13 September 1877.

26. Ada McPherson Morley to Mary McPherson, 7 March 1877, quoted in Norman Cleaveland, with George Fitzpatrick, *The Morleys—Young Upstarts on the Southwest Frontier* (Albuquerque: Calvin Horn, 1971), pp. 129–30; *Albuquerque Review*, 23 February 1878; *WNM*, 5 October 1878, 19 April 1879.

27. Ted Raynor, *Old Timers Talk in Southwestern New Mexico* (El Paso: Texas Western, 1960), p. 65; Keleher, *The Fabulous Frontier*, pp. 268–72.

28. Andrew James Doran, "Interesting Reminiscences," *Arizona Historical Review* 1 (October 1928): 54–62; A. G. Carter, as told to C. L. Sonnichsen, "Neighborhood Talk About Pat Garrett," *Old West* 7 (Fall 1970): 20–22, 62–64.

29. *Mesilla Valley Independent*, 12, 17 May 1879; *Arizona Weekly Enterprise* (Florence), 23 August 1884, Hayden Biographical Files, Andrew J. Doran, AHS; James D. Shinkle, *Fifty Years of Roswell History—1867–1917* (Roswell, N. Mex.: Hall-Poorbaugh, 1964), pp. 110–12.

30. For county courts in Arizona, see James M. Murphy, *Laws, Courts, and Lawyers: Through the Years in Arizona* (Tucson: University of Arizona, 1970), pp. 37–39; for New Mexico's county courts, see *WNM*, 20 January 1887; *DNM*, 6 April 1893, for copy of "An Act to Provide for the Establishment of County Courts," passed 22 February 1893.

31. The New Mexico legislature raised the daily fee of jurors to two dollars (*Albuquerque*

Review, 9 February 1878); *DNM,* 4 February 1873, 28 April 1893, quoting a Silver City dispatch.

32. Poe, *Buckboard Days,* pp. 198–99; Robert E. Ladd, "Vengeance at the O.K. Corral," *Arizoniana* [now *Journal of Arizona History*] 4 (Summer 1963): 1–10, for Greene-Burnett shooting and trial.

CHAPTER 6

1. *General Laws of New Mexico,* Art. 59, Chap. 89, p. 527; Bent is quoted in Chris Emmett, *Fort Union and the Winning of the Southwest* (Norman: University of Oklahoma, 1965), pp. 50–51; Message of Acting Governor Richard C. McCormick to the Second Territorial Legislature, 6 December 1865, quoted in Kelly, comp., *Legislative History,* pp. 13–15.

2. Jo Ann Schmitt, *Fighting Editors: The Story of Editors Who Faced Six-Shooters with Pens and Won* (San Antonio, Tex.: Naylor, 1958), p. 57; for Phoenix's first "jail," see "Yavapai County—Law Enforcement to 1920," Sharlot Hall Museum, Prescott, Arizona, 1 folder; Ben W. Kemp, "Nat Straw—Squawman," *Frontier Times* 54 (September 1980): 28–30, for Chloride's "snubbing post"; Bartholomew, *Wyatt Earp: The Man and the Myth,* pp. 25–26, for Hurricaine Bill; Donna Rees, *The History, Development and Present Administration of the Mohave County Jail* (n.p.: July 1974), p. 6; Ringgold, *Frontier Days,* pp. 121–22, 126; *Arizona Republican* (Phoenix), 7 July 1904, for notice of the *Wide World Magazine* article; Carroll, ed., *Pioneering in Arizona,* p. 27; *Arizona Citizen* (Florence and later Tucson), 2 August 1878.

3. See Appendix A for list of Lincoln County sheriffs; *Las Vegas Gazette,* 24 November 1877, quoted in Keleher, *Violence in New Mexico,* p. 88; Pat F. Garrett, *The Authentic Life of Billy, the Kid: The Noted Desperado of the Southwest,* ed. Maurice Garland Fulton (New York: Macmillan, 1927; orig. pub. 1882), p. 85; Governor Samuel B. Axtell apologized for Lincoln County's jail as all "a new county is able to have" (Executive Record 2, Governors Papers, pp. 318–35, NMSRCA).

4. *Weekly Arizona Miner* (Prescott), 25 April 1866, 29 June, 23, 30 November 1867; for various New Mexico jails, see *DNM,* 2 August, 13 September 1872, 17 February 1873; for the Sierra County jail, see *WNM,* 15 May 1884.

5. *DNM,* 7 January, 23 September 1874.

6. The fact that the sheriff, and not the county, employed the jailer emerged in an investigation of a jailbreak in Tucson in 1882 (*Arizona Weekly Star,* 2 November 1882).

7. Roy O'Dell, "Joseph Casey—Arizona Escape Artist," *Quarterly of the National Association and Center for Outlaw and Lawman History* (NOLA) 13 (Fall 1988): 22–24, with a diagram of the Pima County jail; *Arizona Weekly Star,* 3 May 1883.

8. *Acts of the Legislative Assembly of the Territory of New Mexico, Thirty-Second Session, 18 January 1897–18 March 1897* (Santa Fe: New Mexican, 1897), pp. 129–33; while the salaries of Arizona jailers are less clear, the Navajo County jail attendant earned $900 annually (*Argus* [Holbrook], 2 January 1897).

9. *General Laws of New Mexico,* pp. 358–62; For the 1899 law, see *New Mexico Statutes Annotated,* p. 449.

10. Sheriff C. A. Robinson, Socorro, to editor, 21 January 1891 (*DNM,* 22 January 1891).

11. Ibid., 25 February 1891.

12. *Acts of the Legislative Assembly of the Territory of New Mexico, 1866,* pp. 129–33.

13. Hughes, *Give Me Room!,* p. 157; J. Neugass, Restaurant Owner, to Board of Supervisors, 4 December 1870, D. A. Bennett to Board, 6 January 1871, Pima County Original Documents, Special Collections Dept., University of Arizona, Tucson.

14. Frank W. Clancy Scrapbooks, New Mexico State Library and Archives, Book #1,

p. 89; Philip L. Hefley, jail inmate, to Paul, 20 January 1893, General Correspondence of the United States Marshals of Arizona, AHS.

15. *Arizona Weekly Star,* 9 September 1886.

16. *DNM,* 31 July 1877; Haley, *Jeff Milton,* pp. 126–27; Breakenridge, *Helldorado,* pp. 84–85; clipping, *Weekly Arizona Star,* 17 August 1877, Hayden Biographical Files, AHS.

17. Truman to Griffith, 1 July 1901, Dan Armstrong to Daniels, 16 December 1906, General Correspondence of the United States Marshals of Arizona, AHS; J. C. Handy, M.D., to board of supervisors, 21 August 1871, Pima County Original Documents, Special Collections Dept., University of Arizona, Tucson.

18. *WNM,* 24 May 1880; *Weekly J-M,* 21 July, 8 December 1897, 21 September, 7 December 1898; Interview, Mrs. J. P. (Amelia) Church, 9 August 1952, New Mexico Pioneers Foundation, Special Collections Dept., University of New Mexico, Albuquerque.

19. *Laws of the Territory of New Mexico, 1866,* pp. 82–84.

20. *DNM,* 21 May 1886, 5 February 1891; Victor Westphall, *Thomas Benton Catron and His Era* (Tucson: University of Arizona, 1973), p. 218.

21. Ball, *United States Marshals,* p. 24; Moorman, "Holm O. Bursum," 333–44; the City of Santa Fe opened a city jail on 17 February 1892 (*DNM,* 17 February 1892); the village of Yuma, Arizona, opened its own lockup in September 1893 (Bernts Rube, "The Yuma County Sheriff's Department," Law Enforcement Collection, AHS).

22. *Arizona Daily Star,* 10 July 1891; *Albuquerque Morning Journal,* 25 March 1908, *Daily Epitaph,* 4, 6, 26, 29 January, 18, 20 February 1886; *Arizona Daily Citizen,* 17 March 1885, for pregnancy in jail; for abuse of females in Las Vegas jail, see *DNM,* 11 August 1893; for children of female prisoners, see *DNM,* 21 December 1892, 14 August 1893; for women's quarters in jails, see *DNM,* 26 August 1893, *Weekly J-M,* 15 September 1897; *Rio Grande Republican* (Las Cruces), 25 August 1893; James Emmitt McCauley, *A Stove-Up Cowboy's Story* (Austin, Tex.: Texas Folklore Society, 1943), pp. 36–37.

23. Clippings, *Rio Grande Republican,* 20 March, 15 May 1886, C. L. Sonnichsen Collection, University of Texas, El Paso, box 2; Woody and Schwartz, *Globe, Arizona,* pp. 224–32; Elizabeth Toohey, "No Sissies Here in Old Days," *Arizona Peace Officers' Magazine* 1 (April 1937): 11–28.

24. *Laws of the Territory of New Mexico, 1866,* pp. 84–86; for Arizona's work law, see John C. Waite, Jr., "An Annotated Subject Bibliography of the Acts, Resolutions, and Memorials of the Arizona Territorial Legislature, from 1864 to 1899" (Master's thesis, University of Arizona, 1970), p. 69; clipping, *Arizona Weekly Enterprise* (Florence), 24 November 1883, Hayden Biographical Files, A. J. Doran, AHS; *Arizona Citizen,* 13 July 1879; E. W. Fish, Chairman of Board of Supervisors, Pima County, to W. S. Oury, Sheriff, 15 June 1875, Pima County Original Documents, Special Collections Dept., University of Arizona; Walker, *Death Was the Black Horse,* p. 68.

25. Schmitt, *Fighting Editors,* p. 130; *Weekly Arizona Miner,* 25 October 1873; Clipping, *Arizona Weekly Enterprise,* 11 August 1883, Hayden Biographical Files, A. J. Doran, AHS; Rees, *Mohave County Jail,* pp. 24–26; Joseph "Mack" Axford, *Around Western Campfires,* pp. 107–108.

26. Ibid., 100–101; for the mock court, see *DNM,* 12 May 1903; see letter from "Sierra County Prisoners" in the Santa Fe County Jail to Editor, 10 November 1884, in *WNM,* 20 November 1884; see letter, S. H. Drachman to Sheriff Eugene O. Shaw, 24 December 1886, and reply of prisoners, in *Arizona Weekly Star,* 30 December 1886.

27. Bernts Johnny Rube, "The Killing of Sheriff Dana," *Real West* (August 1983): 16–18; Joe Pearce, "The Killing of Arizona Rangers at the 'Battle Ground,'" *Arizona Stockman* (April 1947): 7–9, copy in Law Enforcement Collection, AHS; Robert M. Utley, *Billy the Kid: A Short and Violent Life* (Lincoln: University of Nebraska, 1989), pp. 8–9; for interview with former Sheriff Harvey Whitehill about Bonney's escape, see *Silver City Enterprise,* 1905, reprinted in "Mail Bag," *New Mexico Magazine* 26 (December 1948): 5, 51; *DNM,* 1 November 1876, 8 March 1881, 13 January, 10 March 1892; William B. Ridgway, "Climax Jim, Outlaw Houdini," *The Sheriff* (Arizona) 13 (December 1959-January 1960): 44.

28. *Message of Lionel A. Sheldon, Governor of New Mexico, Delivered to the Twenty-Sixth Legislative Assembly, February 19, 1884* (Santa Fe: New Mexican), pp. 4–5.

29. *WNM*, 5 April 1880; Lorenzo D. Walters, *Tombstone's Yesterdays* (Tucson: Acme, 1928), pp. 263–65; clipping, *Arizona Weekly Citizen*, 5 May 1883, Law Enforcement Collection, folder "Deaths and Injuries," AHS.

30. *DNM*, 6 January 1873; *Daily Arizona Miner*, 4 January 1875; Reminiscences of George J. Roskruge, as told to Mrs. George F. Kitt, Hayden Biographical Files, AHS; William Sanders Oury, "In the Matter of the Escape of Certain Prisoners," meeting of the Pima County Board of Supervisors, 11 January 1875, Pima County Original Documents, vol. 36, Special Collections Dept., University of Arizona, Tucson.

31. Joseph Miller, *Arizona: The Last Frontier* (New York: Hastings, 1956), pp. 235–38; *RMN*, 11 June 1897.

32. Axford, *Around Western Campfires*, pp. 98–99.

33. Gilberto Crespo y Martinez, Mexican Ambassador, to Philander C. Knox, Secretary of State, 31 August 1911, enc. in Acting Secretary of State to Walter L. Fisher, Secretary of the Interior, 7 September 1911, Int. Dept. Terr. Pap., Arizona, 1868–1896, Record Group 48, National Archives Microcopy M-429, roll 7; R. M. Tafel to Hayden, 18 September 1911, Carl Hayden Collection, Special Collections Dept., Arizona State University; *Weekly Arizona Miner*, 24 March 1876; *RMN*, 19 May 1902; *Arizona Weekly Star*, 4 October 1883.

34. Hochderffer, *Flagstaff Whoa!*, pp. 120–21; *Daily Epitaph* (Tombstone), 19 February 1884, reported fire in Prescott; *Weekly J-M*, 11 May 1898, 4 April 1900; *Albuquerque Morning Journal*, 17 January 1907; Ringgold, *Frontier Days*, pp. 123–24.

35. *Mineral Park Miner*, 16 November 1884, quoted in Rees, *Mohave County Jail*, p. 17; the *Tombstone Epitaph*, 26 December 1881, cited a Mohave County report that the county jail had had no occupants for a year; clipping, *Weekly Arizona Miner*, 14 June 1878, Hayden Biographical Files, Edward F. Bowers, AHS; *Arizona Citizen*, 14 January 1890, quoting the *Silver City Enterprise*.

36. Quarterly Jail Report, Pima County, 6 October 1873, Pima County Original Documents, vol. 38, Special Collections Dept., University of Arizona.

37. Report for the Year Ended 31 December 1887, vol. 36, ibid.; *Arizona Republican*, 19 July 1906.

38. *Silver City Enterprise*, 22 February 1883; Rees, *Mohave County Jail*, pp. 13–14; for promotionals of the Pauly Jail Bldg. and Mfg. Co., see letter to County Clerk, Pima County, Arizona, 18 September 1891, Pima County Original Documents, Special Collections Dept., University of Arizona; Henley R. Price, former sheriff of Pueblo, Colorado, made a proposal to Santa Fe County officials for the Pauly Company (*DNM*, 8 March 1883).

39. Santa Fe Grand Jury Reports, December 1897, September 1906, Santa Fe County District Court Records, NMSRCA; *Albuquerque Morning Journal*, 1 June 1907.

40. Message of Acting Governor Richard C. McCormick to the Arizona Legislature, 8 October 1864, State Dept. Terr. Pap., Arizona, 1864–1872, Record Group 59, National Archives Microcopy M-342, 1 roll; in this address, McCormick pointed out the law that required county jails to serve as territorial prisons until a penitentiary was built. In 1873, a district judge sentenced a murderer to serve his term in the Yuma County jail, which the bench "designated as the Territorial prison" (clipping, *Weekly Arizona Citizen*, 5 April 1873, Crime and Criminals, 1 box, folder "Manuel Fernandez," AHS).

CHAPTER 7

1. For background on vigilantism, see Richard Maxwell Brown, *Strain of Violence: Historical Studies of American Violence and Vigilantism* (New York: Oxford, 1975); *idem, The South Carolina Regulators* (Cambridge, Mass.: Harvard, 1963); Hubert Howe Bancroft, *Popular Tribunals*, vols. 31 and 32 of *Works of Hubert Howe Bancroft*; for an example of ban-

ishment from Prescott, Arizona, see *Weekly Arizona Miner,* 26 January 1867; for a lashing, see Otero, *My Life on the Frontier,* 1: 253–54.

2. *New Orleans Picayune* (Louisiana), 11 April 1851, for lynchings in Socorro, Texas; *Santa Fe Weekly Gazette,* 18 December 1852, 1 January, 10 December 1853; Doña Anans lynched four men (ibid., 28 April 1855).

3. Obituary of Abe Spiegelberg, "Necrology," *New Mexico Historical Review* 3 (January 1928): 116–19; *Santa Fe Weekly Gazette,* 14 March 1857; *Weekly Arizonian* (Tubac and Tucson), 1 July 1859.

4. Erna Fergusson, *Murder and Mystery in New Mexico* (Albuquerque: Merle Armitage, 1948), pp. 18–23; Howard Bryan, *Wildest of the Wild West: True Tales of a Frontier Town on the Santa Fe Trail* (Santa Fe: Clear Light, 1988), pp. 97–99. The railroad caused similar dislocations in Arizona; see McWilliams, *North from Mexico,* pp. 126–27.

5. Gustafson, ed., *John Spring's Arizona,* pp. 267–75; clipping, "Pioneer of West Says Hunt Is Getting Squeamish About Hangings in His Old Age," James H. McClintock Collection, Phoenix Public Library; Lake, ed., *Under Cover,* p. 55; Shaughnessy was later suggested as a possible nominee for Cochise County sheriff (*Arizona Weekly Star,* 29 May 1884); Henry F. Hoyt, *A Frontier Doctor,* ed. Doyce B. Nunis, Jr. (Chicago: R. R. Donnelley & Sons, Lakeside Press, 1979), chaps. 17–18, pp. 205–42, for the author's vigilante experiences; clipping, *Sheriff's Magazine* (Arizona), June 1946, Law Enforcement Collection, AHS; for an example of Hispano mobs, in Cuchilla Negra (*Daily Optic,* 26 November 1881), in Raton (*WNM* 14 August 1884); see *Raton Weekly Independent,* 13 September 1884, for the lynching of the suspected witch.

6. *WNM,* 31 December 1885, 16, 29 April 1886.

7. Ibid., 15 January 1885; *Gringo and Greaser* (Manzano), 1 February 1884, rept. in *Press of the Territorian* (Santa Fe) 1 (September 1961).

8. *DNM,* 1, 4, 6, 8, 11, 15, 16 May 1893.

9. Ibid., 13 November 1880.

10. Hoyt, *Frontier Doctor,* pp. 221–22; Prince to R. B. Hayes, 10 March 1880, copy in Maurice Garland Fulton Collection, Special Collections Dept., University of Arizona, Tucson.

11. Milton W. Callon, *Las Vegas, New Mexico—The Town That Wouldn't Gamble* (Las Vegas: Daily Optic, 1962), pp. 123–25.

12. Clipping, *Sheriff's Magazine,* June 1946, Law Enforcement Collection, Folder "Apache County," AHS; Smith, Jr., *William Sanders Oury,* p. 207; clipping, *Arizona Weekly Enterprise* (Tucson), 28 January 1892, Hayden Biographical Files, AHS, recalls the excuses of Sheriff Oury and Judge Titus.

13. Breakenridge, *Helldorado,* pp. 85–86; Earl Zarbin, "'The Whole Thing Was Done So Quietly': The Phoenix Lynchings of 1879," *Journal of Arizona History* 21 (Winter 1980): 353–62; John R. Winslowe, "The Making of a Renegade [Navajo Frank]," *Old West* 5 (Spring 1969): 10–12, 52–55.

14. Woody and Schwartz, *Globe, Arizona,* pp. 77–78; Lake, ed., *Under Cover,* pp. 54–55; Letter, Edward Tuttle to James H. McClintock, n.d., Edward Tuttle Papers, Special Collections Dept., University of Arizona; Joe Chisholm, *Brewery Gulch: Frontier Days of Old Arizona—Last Outpost of the Great Southwest* (San Antonio, Tex.: Naylor, 1949), pp. 16–19; John A. Rockfellow, *Log of an Arizona Trail Blazer* (Tucson: Arizona Silhouettes, 1955), pp. 96–97.

15. Woody and Schwartz, *Globe,* pp. 38–39, 65–82.

16. Hoyt, *Frontier Doctor,* pp. 208–211; Bryan, *Wildest of the Wild West,* pp. 90–92.

17. Michael M. Rice, "Pete Gabriel Was Fearless," *The Sheriff* (Arizona), 29 (February 1975): 50; Jess G. Hayes, *Sheriff Thompson's Day: Turbulence in Arizona Territory* (Tucson: University of Arizona, 1968), pp. 75–79; Rockfellow, *Trail Blazer,* pp. 46–48; *Arizona Weekly Citizen,* 5 May 1883.

18. Jim Berry Pearson, *The Maxwell Land Grant* (Norman: University of Oklahoma, 1961), pp. 32–33; *DNM,* 5 November 1874; James Steven Peters, "Postmortem of an As-

sassination: Parson Tolby and the Maxwell Land Grant Fight," *Texana* 11, no. 4 (1973): 328–61; *Albuquerque Morning Journal*, 3 October 1907; *WNM*, 21 August 1884; Simmons, *Albuquerque*, pp. 288–89; the *Weekly Epitaph* (Tombstone, Arizona), 13 November 1882, reported Sheriff Armijo's deputization of former vigilantes.

19. Rice, "Pete Gabriel," AHS; Rice, "Pete Gabriel Was Fearless," p. 50.

20. *DNM*, 13, 14, 15, 18 July 1882, 16, 18 March 1883; Callon, *Las Vegas*, pp. 125–26; Otero, *My Life*, 2: 17–20.

21. *Arizona Daily Star* (Tucson), 26 August 1879, Hayden Biographical Files, AHS.

22. Hayes, *Boots and Bullets*, pp. 124–27.

23. *WNM*, 17 August 1878, 15 November 1879; Zarbin, "'The Whole Thing Was Done So Quietly,'" pp. 353–62; *Territorial Expositor* (Phoenix), 17 October 1879, reprinted in Schmitt, *Fighting Editors*, pp. 138–39; *DNM*, 25, 26 May, 31 July 1876, 2, 18, 20 April, 12 June 1877; *Albuquerque Daily Democrat*, 16, 17 April 1883.

24. Stanley, *Desperadoes*, pp. 261–73; French, *Some Recollections*, pp. 26–34; *Weekly New Mexican Review*, 17, 25, 26 January 1884.

25. Ibid., 22, 23 January 1884; French, *Some Recollections*, pp. 26–34; for Hardy's account, see Allen A. Carter, "Joe Fowler, Notorious Bad Man, Socorro County, New Mexico. Lynched at Socorro, 1884," 20 March 1937, Works Projects Files (WPA), Folder #88, NMSRCA.

26. *Weekly New Mexican Review*, 25 January 1884; *Socorro Advertiser*, 23 January, in *Silver City Enterprise*, 25 January 1884; *Weekly New Mexican Review*, 26 January 1884.

27. *Weekly New Mexican Review*, 23 January 1884; for Hardcastle's recollections, see Kyle S. Crichton, *Law and Order, Ltd.: The Rousing Life of Elfego Baca of New Mexico* (Glorieta, N. Mex.: Rio Grande, 1970), pp. 69–73.

28. *Weekly New Mexican Review*, 25 January 1884.

29. *DNM*, 16 February 1881, 30 January 1883.

30. Hochderffer, *Flagstaff Whoa!*, p. 36; Woody and Schwartz, *Globe*, p. 172; *Weekly J-M*, 10 November 1879; Hayes, *Sheriff Thompson's Day*, pp. 92–100; *Rio Grande Republican* (Las Cruces), 2 June 1893, for lynching in Las Vegas, New Mexico.

31. Brown, *Strain of Violence*, App. 3, pp. 305–306; Robert L. Spude, "Mineral Frontiers in Transition: Copper Mining in Arizona, 1880–1885," *New Mexico Historical Review* 51 (January 1976): 19–34; see Appendix C this volume.

32. Brown, *Strain of Violence*, App. 3, p. 315; see Appendix C this volume.

33. *Daily Optic*, quoted in *Rio Grande Republican*, 2 June 1893; *Arizona Republican*, 18 November 1901, 16 January 1902; Fornoff to J. J. Brophy, City Marshal, Clayton, New Mexico, 16 July 1906, Letters Sent, New Mexico Mounted Police, Territorial Archives of New Mexico, roll 92; *Arizona Republican*, 20 December 1906; see Appendix C this volume.

34. See Sheldon's remarks, *Albuquerque Evening Review*, 21 February 1882.

35. Philip J. Ethington, "Vigilantes and the Police: The Creation of a Professional Police Bureaucracy in San Francisco, 1847–1900," *Journal of Social History* 21 (Winter 1987): 197–227; for a distinction between "minor cases," which vigilantes left to lawmen, and "black" crimes, see *Globe Chronicle*, quoted in *Weekly Epitaph*, 2 September 1882.

CHAPTER 8

1. *Compiled Laws of the Territory of Arizona*, pp. 145–46, secs. 435–49; *Laws of the Territory of New Mexico*, p. 74, sec. 6; *DNM*, 24 April 1890, noted the $100 fee for hangings; for some background, see John Laurence, *The History of Capital Punishment* (Secaucus, N.J.: Citadel Press, 1960), pp. 41–62.

2. *Weekly J-M*, 6 December 1899; *Arizona Weekly Star* (Tucson), 10 April 1884; Drais to E. E. Ellinwood, United States District Attorney, 6 July 1893, General Correspondence, United States Marshals Records, AHS.

3. *Tombstone Republican*, [?] March 1884, quoted in Miller, ed., *Last Frontier*, pp. 232–33.

4. Simmons, *Albuquerque*, p. 289; Robert K. DeArment, "The Blood-Spattered Trail of Milton J. Yarberry," *Old West* 22 (Fall 1985): 8–14; Jess G. Hayes, *Apache Vengeance: The True Story of Apache Kid* (Albuquerque: University of New Mexico Press, 1954), pp. 124–30; unidentified clipping, Globe, Arizona, 10 December [?], James H. McClintock Collection, Phoenix Public Library.

5. DeArment, "The Blood-Spattered Trail," pp. 8–14; Robert C. Stevens, ed., *Echoes of the Past: Tales of Old Yavapai*, 2 vols. (Prescott, Ariz.: Yavapai Cowbelles, Inc., 1964), 2:287; Jack Potter, "Riding with Blackjack [sic]," *Sheriff and Police Journal* (pub. quarterly by the National Co-Operative Sheriffs' and Police Association, Taos, N. Mex., n.d.), pp. 9, 17, 19, 25, 29; *Tombstone Epitaph*, 28 July 1960, reprinting 1910 items.

6. John (Jack) H. Culley, *Cattle, Horses and Men of the Western Range* (Tucson: University of Arizona, 1967), p. 48; *Arizona Sentinel* (Yuma), 3 May 1873, in Joseph C. Miller, *Arizona Cavalcade: The Turbulent Times* (New York: Hastings House, 1962), pp. 139–40; DeArment, "The Blood-Spattered Trail," pp. 8–14; *Weekly Epitaph*, 17 February 1884, for Dan Dowd; *DNM*, 20 March 1893, noted a Santa Fe lady donating a Bible to a condemned man, while Christian women gave Zach Booth much attention (*Arizona Republican*, 20 July 1905).

7. *Epitaph*, 28 March 1884, in Douglas D. Martin, ed., *Tombstone's Epitaph* (Albuquerque: University of New Mexico Press, 1963), pp. 240–42; Haley, *Jeff Milton*, p. 181; Toni and Robert McInnes, "George C. Ruffner: Frontier Sheriff," *The Sheriff* [Arizona] 9 (August 1950): 17, 19–20; French, *Further Recollections*, 2:511–12.

8. Cecil Bonney, *Looking Over My Shoulder: Seventy-Five Years in the Pecos Valley* (Roswell, N. Mex.: Hall-Poorbaugh, 1971), p. 22; *Roswell Record* (New Mexico), 11, 25 September 1896; *DNM*, 15 September 1896; Peter Hertzog, *Legal Hangings, New Mexico, 1861–1923*, Western Americana Series, No. 10 (Santa Fe: Press of the Territorian, 1966), pp. 29–34, for hanging of Conley; *Arizona Daily Citizen*, 17 October, 7 December 1889; unidentified clipping, McClintock Collection, Phoenix Public Library; Hayes, *Boots and Bullets*, pp. 111–14.

9. Ringgold, *Frontier Days*, pp. 143–44; see exhibit, with photo of Sheriff Jake Owens's scaffold, Tunstall Store Museum, Lincoln, New Mexico; Keleher, *Violence in Lincoln County*, pp. 333–37, for Billy the Kid's escape.

10. *Tombstone Epitaph*, 28 March 1884, in Martin, *Tombstone's Epitaph*, pp. 240–42; clipping, *Lincoln County Leader* (White Oaks), 26 June 1886, Philip J. Rasch Collection, "More Killings in Lincoln County," 1 folder, Lincoln County Court House Museum, copy courtesy of John P. Wilson, Las Cruces, New Mexico.

11. Ringgold, *Frontier Days*, pp. 143–44; Axford, *Around Western Campfires*, p. 109; McInnes, "George C. Ruffner," pp. 17, 19–20; Rice, "Pete Gabriel"; B. Johnny Rube, "The Yuma County Sheriff's Department," in Law Enforcement Collection, folder "Yuma County," AHS.

12. See n. 1; for Sheriff Murphy, see clipping, *Arizona Star*, 1 March 1935, Law Enforcement Collection, AHS.

13. See the correspondence and medical report, Crime and Criminals, folder "Teodoro Elias," AHS; Executive Record of the Governors of New Mexico, Book #2, pp. 497, 500, NMSRCA; *DNM*, 23 February 1881, 15 June 1882, 16, 17, 22, 23 September 1896.

14. Breakenridge, *Helldorado*, p. 197; Walker, *Death Was the Black Horse*, pp. 42–46, inc. quote from *San Francisco Chronicle*.

15. Martin, *Tombstone's Epitaph*, pp. 247–49; Robert E. Ladd, *Eight Ropes to Eternity* (Tombstone: The Epitaph, n.d.), pp. 21–31, copy in Law Enforcement Collection, AHS; Westphall, *Thomas Benton Catron*, Chap. 12, "The Borrego Murder Case," pp. 108–29 and 263–68.

16. *DNM*, 31 January, 1, 3, 7, 8, 13, 30 March 24, 25 May 1883; Simmons, *Albuquerque*, p. 289; DeArment, "The Blood-Spattered Trail," pp. 8–14.

17. Ibid.; Simmons, *Albuquerque*, p. 289.

18. Clipping, *Weekly Arizona Citizen*, 10 May 1873, Crime and Criminals, folder "Man-

uel Fernandez," AHS; James H. McClintock, *Arizona, Prehistoric—Aboriginal—Pioneer—Modern: The Nation's Youngest Commonwealth Within a Land of Ancient Culture*, 2 vols. (Chicago: S. J. Clarke, 1916), 2:479; Larry D. Ball, "Militia Posses: The Territorial Militia in Civil Law Enforcement in New Mexico Territory, 1877–1883," *New Mexico Historical Review* 55 (January 1980): 47–70.

19. Clinton E. Brooks and Frank D. Reeve, eds., "James A. Bennett: A Dragoon in New Mexico, 1850–1856," *New Mexico Historical Review* 22 (April 1947): 140–76.

20. Hunt, *Kirby Benedict*, pp. 78–81; Rees, *Mohave County Jail*, pp. 31–32; *Roswell Record*, 25 September 1896; James M. Barney, "The Story of the First Legal Hanging in Prescott, Yavapai County," *Sheriff Magazine* (Arizona), March 1956, copy in Sharlot Hall Museum, Prescott, Arizona; *WNM*, 21 April, 12 May 1887.

21. *Weekly J-M*, 14 July 1897; unidentified clipping, 10 December [?], McClintock Collection, Phoenix Public Library; two clippings, *Los Angeles Examiner*, 15 August 1908, *Arizona Daily Star Roundup*, 24 January 1954, Crime and Criminals, folder "Edwin Hawkins," AHS.

22. See n. 1; for examination of female prisoners for pregnancy, see p. 146, secs. 444–45 of *Compiled Laws of the Territory of Arizona*; *Weekly Arizona Miner*, 24 October 1868, 16 January, 10 April, 1869; *RMN*, 26 February 1897; *Albuquerque Morning Journal*, 7, 16, 25 May, 10 June 1907.

23. Hunt, *Kirby Benedict*, pp. 76–77; William A. Keleher, *Turmoil in New Mexico, 1846–1868* (Santa Fe: Rydal, 1952), pp. 397–99, 504 n. 117.

24. *DNM*, 19 August 1892; *WNM*, 28 December 1875; Jeff Burton, *Dynamite and Six-Shooter* (Santa Fe: Palomino Press, 1970), Chap. 17, pp. 145–57; Trancito Romero, "I Saw Black Jack Hanged," *True West* 6 (October 1958): 27–28.

25. Clipping, *Silver Belt* (Globe), 9 March 1884, Special Collections Dept., Arizona State University, Tempe; *Tombstone Epitaph*, 29 March 1884, quoted in C. W. Goodale, "Reminiscences of Early Days in Tombstone," *The Mining Journal: An Industrial Review of the West and Southwest* 10 (April 30, 1927): 4, 60–62, copy in Walter Noble Burns Papers, box 3, Special Collections Department, University of Arizona, Tucson; *Epitaph*, 18 November 1900, in Martin, *Tombstone's Epitaph*, pp. 247–49; Simmons, *Albuquerque*, p. 289; French, *Further Recollections*, pp. 511–13; Romero, "I Saw Black Jack Hanged," 27–28.

26. Keleher, *New Mexicans I Knew*, pp. 41–44; Schmitt, *Fighting Editors*, pp. 90–91.

27. *New Mexico Statutes Annotated*, p. 496, sec. 1474. For Ward's invitation, see Martin, *Tombstone's Epitaph*, p. 242.

28. *Arizona Weekly Citizen*, 22 March 1884; for a copy of Wattron's invitation, see Wattron to J. M. Pratt, 1 December 1899, Subject Files, "Sheriffs," AHS; Henning, "Sheriff, Scholar."

29. *Arizona Republican* (Phoenix), 8 December 1899, and Murphy's proclamation, both quoted in Henning, "Sheriff, Scholar."

30. *Holbrook Argus*, 11 November, 16 December 1899, quoted in Henning, "Sheriff, Scholar"; *Weekly J-M*, 22 November, 13, 20 December 1899, 3, 10 January 1900; *Prescott Morning Courier*, cited in *Weekly J-M*, 13 December 1899; for copy of the second invitation, see Wattron to J. M. Pratt, 1 January 1900, "Sheriffs," AHS; *Weekly J-M*, 10 January 1900.

31. *Coconino Sun* (Flagstaff, Arizona), quoted in *Albuquerque Morning Journal*, 30 August 1908; *Tombstone Epitaph*, 28 July 1960, quoting a 1910 issue; Charles C. Colley, "Carl T. Hayden: Phoenician," *Journal of Arizona History* 18 (Autumn 1977): 247–58; unidentified clipping, McClintock Collection, folder "Hangings," Phoenix Public Library.

32. *DNM*, 27 January 1897; see *DNM* of 16, 17, 19 February 1897 for debate in the New Mexico Assembly; *Acts of the Legislative Assembly of the Territory of New Mexico, Thirty-Fifth Session, 1903* (Santa Fe: New Mexican, 1903), p. 141.

33. *DNM*, 21 March 1873; Message of Governor George Curry to the Territorial Assembly of New Mexico, 18 January 1909, Dept. of Int. Terr. Pap., NM, National Archives Microcopy M-364, roll 15.

34. See Appendices B and C.

35. Louis P. Masur, *Rites of Execution: Capital Punishment and the Transformation of American Culture, 1776–1865* (New York: Oxford University, 1989), pp. 26–27, 96–97.

36. Clipping, *Lincoln County Leader*, 26 June 1886, Rasch Collection, Lincoln County Courthouse Museum, Lincoln, New Mexico.

CHAPTER 9

1. *The Kearny Code [Laws of the Territory of New Mexico]*, p. 106; *New Mexico Sessions Laws, 1852–53* (Santa Fe: n. pub., 1853), p. 51.

2. McClintock, *Arizona*, 2:465–66; clipping, *The Lever*, 14 November 1895, Louis C. Hughes Scrapbooks, Special Collections Dept., University of Arizona, Tucson; Wagoner, *Arizona Territory*, pp. 320–21; *New York Times*, 20 June 1880.

3. *Texas Live Stock Journal*, quoted in *WNM*, 6 March 1884.

4. William Blackstone, *Commentaries on the Laws of England*, ed. and abr. J. W. Ehrlich (San Carlos, Calif.: Nourse, 1959), p. 450; W. Haskell to [President of the United States], Washington, D.C., 13 May 1878, Robert N. Mullin Collection, Nita Stewart Haley Library, Midland, Texas; Edmund G. Ross to Augustus Garland, Attorney General, 3 June 1887, Letterbook of Edmund G. Ross, 1 January–19 September 1887, Governors Papers, NMSRCA.

5. *Santa Fe Weekly Gazette*, 23 February 1856, 12 January 1861; *DNM*, 4, 8 July 1882.

6. *Weekly Arizona Miner*, 6 March, 11 December 1869; *Weekly J-M*, 18 April 1897; *Arizona Daily Star*, 16 October 1921, for Shaw's recollections. The writer is indebted to John P. Wilson, Las Cruces, New Mexico, for this item.

7. *Weekly Epitaph* (Tombstone), 2 September 1882; *Weekly J-M*, 22 September 1897.

8. Philip J. Rasch, "Sudden Death in Cimarron," *Quarterly of the National Association for Outlaw and Lawman History* 10 (Spring 1986): 6–8; *DNM*, 26 January, 2 February 1875.

9. Ibid.

10. Ibid.; Parsons, *Clay Allison;* Sheriff Burleson arrested Hefferon and John Allison for carrying arms, in March 1879 (Sheriff's Journal, Colfax County, 1870–1884, pp. 78–79, 454–57, resp., NMSRCA); *DNM*, 4, 10 October 1876; C. J. Hixon, mineralogist in Cimarron at this time, recalled the sheriff's ambush of David Crockett (*Weekly J-M*, 6 October 1897; *WNM*, 19 April 1879, 4 May 1878).

11. Frank Collinson, *Life in the Saddle*, ed. Mary Whatley Clarke (Norman: University of Oklahoma, 1963), pp. 215–18; *DNM*, 27 January 1883; Simpson was noted in the arrest of another drunken reveler (*DNM*, 25 March 1883) and another man for inciting to riot, in San Marcial (*DNM*, 20 April 1883).

12. Charles Eastman, Sr., "Fighters of the Old West," 1931, xerox copy, Sharlot Hall Museum, Prescott, Arizona.

13. Smalley, *My Adventures in Arizona*, p. 131.

14. New Mexico Pioneers Foundation interview, Robert Bell, 27 October 1953, Special Collections Dept., University of New Mexico, Albuquerque; see a Phoenix dispatch, reprinted in *DNM*, 29 October 1895.

15. *New Mexico Sessions Laws, 1852–53*, pp. 67–68.

16. *Weekly New Mexican Review*, 2 August 1883.

17. Sonnichsen, *Billy King's Tombstone*, p. 153, for the velocipede race; King, *Wranglin' the Past*, pp. 187–90.

18. Ringgold, *Frontier Days*, pp. 126–27.

19. Woody and Schwartz, *Globe, Arizona*, pp. 65–78; Hayes, *Boots and Bullets*, pp. 82–83.

20. Lake, ed., *Under Cover*, pp. 45–55; *Weekly Epitaph*, 10, 12 February 1884; Martin, *Tombstone's Epitaph*, p. 239.

21. Lake, *Under Cover*, pp. 83–94; Breakenridge, *Helldorado*, pp. 227–29; New Mexico Pioneers Foundation interview, Robert and Ollie Bell, Santa Rita, New Mexico, 27 March

1954, Special Collections Dept., University of New Mexico, Albuquerque. Ollie Bell was a daughter of Sheriff Harvey Whitehill.

22. Philip J. Rasch, "The Las Cruces Bank Robbery," *Frontier Times*, new series 55 (January 1981): 48–50.

23. Maurice Kildaire, "The Fastest Gun in Phoenix," *Frontier Times*, new series 42 (January 1968): 16–19, 57–59.

24. *Mesilla Times*, 17 May 1861.

25. *Silver City Enterprise*, 22 February 1889; Axford, *Around Western Campfires*, pp. 137–40; *DNM*, 10 June 1883.

26. Frank C. Lockwood, "John Lorenzo Hubbell, Navajo Indian Trader," University of Arizona Bulletin, No. 6, 8 (1 July 1942): 64–66; Toni and Robert McInnes, "George C. Ruffner: Frontier Sheriff," *The Sheriff* (Arizona) 9 (August 1950): 17, 19–20; Charles C. Colley, "Carl T. Hayden—Phoenician," *Journal of Arizona History* 18 (Autumn 1977): 247–58.

27. W. H. Ryus, *The Second William Penn: A True Account of Incidents That Happened Along the Old Santa Fe Trail in the Sixties* (Kansas City, Mo.: Frank T. Riley, 1913), pp. 137–40.

28. C. L. Sonnichsen, *Outlaw, Bill Mitchell, Alias Baldy Russell: His Life and Times* (Denver: Sage, 1965), pp. 21–26.

29. Ibid., p. 147; Keleher, *The Fabulous Frontier*, pp. 253–55, quoting Oliver Lee's recollections in 1937 of the fight at Wildy Well.

30. Interview, Jim Brophy, 22 February 1922, Allen Erwin Collection, box 1, AHS; Harkey, *Mean as Hell*, p. 184.

31. See the inquest quoted in Erwin, *The Southwest of John H. Slaughter*, pp. 214–17.

32. *Weekly New Mexican Review*, 3 January 1884.

33. Woody and Schwartz, *Globe, Arizona*, pp. 147–50; *Arizona Journal-Miner*, 5 September 1887; Charles M. Morgan, "Sheriff Commodore Owens Shoots Straight," *The Sheriff* (Arizona) 4 (December 1945): 89, 91, quotes the coroner's inquest, copy in Law Enforcement Collection, "Apache County," AHS.

34. McClintock, *Arizona*, 2: 467; Woody and Schwartz, *Globe, Arizona*, pp. 147–50.

35. Ibid.; *Arizona Journal-Miner*, 6, 8 September 1887.

36. Garrett, *The Authentic Life of Billy, the Kid*, pp. 150–52.

37. James G. Wolf, "Story of James G. Wolf, Cochise County Guide," 4 September 1937, Small Collection, AHS.

38. Walter Noble Burns, *Tombstone: An Iliad of the Southwest* (New York: Garden City, 1937), pp. 318–19.

39. Viola Slaughter's recollections, *Daily Review* (Bisbee, Arizona), 22 April 1934, quoted in Erwin, *The Southwest of John H. Slaughter*, pp. 221–22, see also p. 253; obituary of John H. Slaughter, 17 March 1922, typescript, James McClintock Collection, Phoenix Public Library; *Arizona Journal-Miner*, 16 April 1887, 21 June 1889; *Arizona Daily Star*, 18 May 1890; *Silver City Enterprise*, 20 January, 7 September 1888, for Slaughter's arrest of felons.

40. *DNM*, 6 January 1881, for J. J. Webb.

41. *DNM*, 19 March 1881; *Newman's Semi-Weekly Thirty Four* (Las Cruces), 16 March 1881; Breakenridge, *Helldorado*, pp. 120–21.

42. *Tombstone Epitaph* [?, 1891], reprinted in *Tombstone Epitaph*, 2 March 1961; *DNM*, 4 January 1892; *Weekly J-M*, 2 February, 1 June 1898.

43. Stanley, *Desperadoes*, pp. 211–12; Philip J. Rasch, "The Pecos War," *Panhandle-Plains Historical Review* 29 (1956): 101–11.

44. See Chap. 1 for death of Stephen Lee; B. Johnny Rube, "The Killing of Sheriff Dana," *Real West* (August 1983): 16–18; Philip J. Rasch and Lee Myers, "Les Dow, Sheriff of Eddy County," *New Mexico Historical Review* 49 (July 1974): 241–52; Donald R. Lavash, *Sheriff William Brady: Tragic Hero of the Lincoln County War* (Santa Fe: Sunstone Press, 1986); Hayes, *Apache Vengeance*, Chap. 11, pp. 89–102, for death of Sheriff Glenn Reynolds. Dwight Stephens, sheriff of Luna County, New Mexico, held office under the ter-

ritory and state. Although the sources are conflicting, it appears that he was murdered while in office, possibly in 1915 (*Las Cruces Citizens,* 18 March 1916). Marcus Dobbins, sheriff of Yuma County, Arizona, was reportedly murdered by army deserters in August 1867. This has not been confirmed (*Weekly Arizona Miner,* 31 August 1867). See *Albuquerque Daily Citizen,* 14, 15, 19 December 1898, 9 January 1899. Sheriff John Elliott Walker of Maricopa County committed suicide while in office (*Arizona Republican,* 20 December 1906).

CHAPTER 10

1. *Arizona Daily Star* (Tucson), 12 July 1891; message of Governor Lionel Sheldon to the New Mexico Legislature, 3 January 1882, Executive Record #2, pp. 558–76, NMSRCA; Sheldon to Teller, 6 July 1883, Int. Dept. Terr. Pap., NM, 1851–1914, Record Group 48, 15 rolls, National Archives Microcopy M-364, roll 8; *San Angelo Standard,* 6 April 1901, quoted in John Eaton, *Will Carver, Outlaw* (San Angelo, Tex.: Anchor Pub., 1972), pp. 35–36.

2. *DNM,* 2 June 1892.

3. For Brazleton, see *Arizona Citizen* (Tucson), 30 August 1878; William F. Hogan, "John Miller: Pioneer Lawman," *Arizoniana* (now *Journal of Arizona History*) 4 (Summer 1963): 41–45; for the Kimbrell threat, see letter, "Your Friend on the Do[d]ge" to Kimbrell, 18 May 1879, Lew Wallace Papers, Indiana Historical Society, Box 8; Pedro A. Simpson, Sheriff, by R. P. Gaddis, Deputy, to Sheldon, 19 February 1883, Governors Papers, NMSRCA; *RMN,* 3 April 1902.

4. Matt Warner, as told to Murray E. King, *The Last of the Bandit Riders* (New York: Bonanza, n.d.; orig. pub. 1940), pp. 86–97; Joe Pearce and Richard Summer, "Joe Pearce—Manhunter," *Journal of Arizona History* 19 (Autumn 1978): 249–60; *Arizona Republican,* 21 June 1900; Sheldon to Teller, 6 July 1883, Interior Dept. Terr. Pap., roll 8.

5. "John Britt Montgomery," Hayden Biographical Files, see clipping, *Phoenix Daily Herald,* 4 August 1892, AHS; Larry D. Ball, "The People as Law Enforcers: The 'Posse Comitatus' in New Mexico and Arizona Territories," *Quarterly of the National Outlaw and Lawman Association* 6 (January 1981): 2–10, 22.

6. "When All Roads Led to Tombstone," unpub. ms., John Pleasant Gray Papers, 1 box, pp. 113–14, AHS; Thomas Rynning, as told to Al Cohn and Joe Chisholm, *Gun Notches: The Life Story of a Cowboy-Soldier* (New York: A. L. Burt, 1931), pp. 260–61; Lori Davisson, "Roll Call of Arizona Heroes," *Quarterly of the National Outlaw and Lawman Association* 12 (Fall 1987): 17–21.

7. Metz, *Pat Garrett,* pp. 60–61 and n. 5; Harold L. Edwards, "Barney Mason: In the Shadow of Pat Garrett and Billy the Kid," *Old West* 26 (Summer 1990): 14–19; Crime and Criminals, 1 box, folder "Geronimo, the Outlaw," and "Nathan Appel," Hayden Biographical Files, AHS; Frank M. Pool, "The Capture of the Bandit Geronimo in Arizona," *The Sheriff* (Arizona), copy of article in Arizona State University Special Collections, "Outlaws and Badmen," 1 box; New Mexico Pioneers Foundation Interviews, #106, Henry Brock, 8 October 1953, Special Collections Dept., University of New Mexico, Albuquerque, see pp. 7–8; *RMN,* 17 October 1897.

8. Montague Stevens, *Meet Mr. Grizzly: A Saga of the Passing of the Grizzly* (Albuquerque: University of New Mexico Press, 1943), pp. 83–107; clipping, *Arizona Range News* (Willcox), 31 March 1950; *El Paso Daily Times,* 1 March 1896, for Sheriff Bursum; *DNM,* 29 February, 3 March, 3 April 1896, for pursuit of Bronco Bill; *Weekly J-M,* 16 February 1898.

9. For some observations about frontier weaponry, see Joseph G. Rosa, *The Gunfighter: Man or Myth?* (Norman: University of Oklahoma, 1969), esp. pp. 167–78, 179–88; Ball, "The People As Law Enforcers," 2–10, 22; *Weekly J-M,* 19 May 1897, 22 June 1898; *WNM,* 23 August 1879. Bandits employed smokeless powder cartridges against a posse near Cimarron, in July 1899; see Burton, *Dynamite and Six-Shooter,* p. 84. *Silver City Enterprise,* 5 Sep-

tember 1884, for discussion of weapons favored by lawmen; Bonney, *Looking Over My Shoulder,* p. 24. When historian James McClintock reminded Ben Clark that as a Graham County deputy sheriff in the 1890s Clark had worn two revolvers, this peace officer replied that the times were turbulent. Clark said humorously that he carried one gun to keep the peace in Clifton and the other for Morenci (*Arizona Republican,* 4 February 1909).

10. *RMN,* 25, 27, 28 May, 2, 3 June 1898.

11. Walker, *Death Was the Black Horse,* pp. 69–73; see Dan Harvick's recollections in William Sparks, *The Apache Kid, A Bear Fight and Other True Stories of the Old West* (Los Angeles: Skelton, 1926), pp. 144–63; *Silver City Enterprise,* 18 May 1888, reprinted in William H. Mullane, ed., *This Is Silver City,* 4 vols. (Silver City: The Enterprise, 1965–67), 3:10.

12. The widespread practice of livestock theft in Arizona and New Mexico lacks scholarly attention. Many pioneer recollections devote sporadic attention to this problem. For some observations, see Will C. Barnes, *Apaches and Longhorns: The Reminiscences of Will C. Barnes,* ed. Frank C. Lockwood (Los Angeles: Ward Ritchie, 1941), pp. 132–35; Philip J. Rasch, "John Kinney: King of the Rustlers," *English Westerners' Brand Book* 4 (October 1961): 10–12; John H. Cady, *Arizona's Yesterdays,* rev. Basil Dillon Moon (Patagonia, Arizona: n. pub., 1978), pp. 113–14; Warner, *Bandit Riders,* pp. 80–97; Albert B. Fall, *The Memoirs of Albert B. Fall,* Southwestern Studies, No. 15 (El Paso: University of Texas, 1966), p. 44; for Deputy Sheriff Culberson, see *DNM,* 21 August 1891.

13. Governor Lew Wallace discussed the need for legislation to protect cattlemen in a special message to the New Mexico Assembly, 7 January 1880, Executive Record #2, p. 388, NMSRCA; For a brief introduction to cattle associations, see Joe A. Stout, "Cattle Associations," in *The Reader's Encyclopedia of the American West,* (New York: Thomas A. Crowell, 1977), pp. 172–73; for cattle legislation in Arizona, see Wagoner, *Arizona Territory, 1863–1912,* pp. 244–45, 288, 329.

14. Ball, "The People as Law Enforcers," pp. 2–10, 22; Breakenridge, *Helldorado,* p. 133; for Horn's letter, see Larry D. Ball, ed., "'No Cure, No Pay,' A Tom Horn Letter," *Journal of Arizona History* 8 (Autumn 1967): 200–202; Moorman, "Holm O. Bursum," 333–44.

15. Ball, "The People As Law Enforcers," pp. 2–10, 22; Daniel J. W. Huntington Papers, AHS; Woody and Schwartz, *Globe, Arizona,* p. 69, for the alarm bell.

16. Philip J. Rasch, "Death Comes to Saint Johns," *Quarterly of the National Association for Outlaw and Lawman History* 7 (Autumn 1982): 1–8. Sheriff Beeler arrested Bill Morris, alias Coley Morris, but the lawman evidently possessed insufficient evidence to try him. Beeler declared that he pursued this band 1500 miles and vowed to catch them. He failed, although some Apache Countians speculated that the murder of Beeler after he left office may have been connected with his ardent chase for these men; *Arizona Republican,* 7, 12 May 1900; for the death of a Silver City posseman, Joseph Laffer, see *WNM,* 20 March, 27 April 1884; *Daily Optic* (Las Vegas), 17 March 1883; for the death of posseman James Carlyle in White Oaks, see *Daily Optic* (Las Vegas) 19 January 1881: *DNM,* 8 February 1898, for the death of posseman Frank Galloway and the absence of government support for his widow.

17. Pat F. Garrett, *The Authentic Life of Billy, the Kid,* pp. 98–128; Poe, *Buckboard Days,* pp. 233–54.

18. *El Paso Daily Times,* 29 November 1896; Breakenridge, *Helldorado,* p. 238.

19. *Weekly J-M,* 11 August 1897.

20. *Silver City Enterprise,* 4 May 1883.

21. See Chapter 1.

22. Two letters, Bursum to French 15, 16 July 1897, quoted in Morrman, "Holm O. Bursum," pp. 333–44; *Arizona Republican,* 6 May 1900; "An Act for the Relief of Richard Campbell, for[mer?] Sheriff of the County of Doña Ana," 30 January 1855, "An Act for the Relief of Gregorio Maldonado," 5 February 1855, *Laws of New Mexico,* 5th Sess., 1854–55 (Santa Fe: n. pub., 1855), pp. 27, 65, resp.

23. *Weekly J-M,* 9 April, 21 November 1889; *Message of Lionel A. Sheldon, Governor of New*

Mexico, Delivered to the Twenty-Sixth Legislative Assembly, February 19, 1884 (Santa Fe: New Mexican, 1884), pp. 4–5.

24. Blackstone, *Commentaries on the Law of England,* p. 897; Leonard D. White, *The Federalists: A Study in Administrative History* (New York: Macmillan, 1956), pp. 415–17; reward for Chavez's killers, *DNM,* 31 May 1892; Arrell M. Gibson, *The Life and Death of Colonel Albert Jennings Fountain* (Norman: University of Oklahoma, 1965), p. 238.

25. Fryer to C. Meyer Zulick, 3 January 1888, Territorial Papers, Arizona State Library and Archives, Box 1D; Eugene O. Shaw to Zulick, 23 March 1887, Speedy to Matthew F. Shaw, 27 July 1889, in ibid.; Ben Williams, Superintendent, Arizona and Southeastern Railroad, Bisbee, Arizona, to Wolfley, 21 May 1890, with two clippings, in ibid., Box 1C; A. H. Barker, Deputy Sheriff, Arapahoe County, Colorado, to Axtell, 19 August 1875, Governor's Papers, NMSRCA; Lake, ed., *Under Cover,* p. 94; for Whitehill's chancery case, *WNM,* 18 September 1884; Wells, Fargo and Co. vs. Harvey Whitehill, et al., 18 July 1884, District Court Cases, Grant County, Case #1164, NMSRCA.

26. Moorman, "Holm O. Bursum," pp. 333–44; Harry E. Chrisman, *Fifty Years on the Owl Hoot Trail: Jim Herron, The First Sheriff of No Man's Land, Oklahoma Territory* (Chicago: Sage, 1969), pp. 150–51; *DNM,* 3 July 1894, 31 October 1895, 1 May 1896, and 18 May 1896, citing *Daily Optic.*

27. Otero, *My Nine Years,* p. 111; Ross to Jesus Luna, 8 April 1886, quoted in Rosenbaum, *Mexicano Resistance in the Southwest,* pp. 97–98; for extradition procedures, see Chap. 3, p. 53 this volume.

28. Cook, *Hands Up,* pp. 26–30; *DNM,* 9 November 1875, 13 September (two articles), 18 September 1876; Affidavit of John Justice, Agent of Governor of New Mexico, to John Mitchell, Governor, 11 July 1867, two telegrams, Casimero Barela, Sheriff, Conejos County, Colorado, to Samuel Axtell, Governor, 20 August 1876, Isaiah Rinehart to William Ritch, Acting Governor, 21 August 1876, and copy of requisition for Porter Stockton, dated 28 August 1876, Governors Papers, NMSRCA.

29. Bunch to Irwin, [6?] February 1891, Creaghe to Lewis Wolfley, Governor, 7 May 1890, Gutterson to C. Meyer Zulick, Governor, 5 May 1886, T. S. Bunch, District Attorney, Apache County, to John N. Irwin, Governor, 19 February 1891, Territorial Papers of Arizona, State Library and Archives, Phoenix.

30. Philip J. Rasch, "Murder in the American Valley," *English Westerners' Brand Book,* 7 (April 1965): 2–7; F. Stanley (Stanley Crocchiola), *Jim Courtright: Two Gun Marshal of Fort Worth* (Denver: World Press, 1957), Chapter 5; for some discussion of the extradition cases of Wyatt Earp and John "Doc" Holliday, see Frank Waters, *The Earp Brothers of Tombstone: The Story of Mrs. Virgil Earp* (New York: Clarkson N. Potter, 1960), pp. 207–8; Glenn G. Boyer, ed., *I Married Wyatt Earp: The Recollections of Josephine Sarah Marcus Earp* (Tucson: University of Arizona, 1976), p. 107, 111 notes 17–19; Pat Johns, *The Frontier World of Doc Holliday: Faro Dealer from Dallas to Deadwood* (New York: Hastings House, 1957), Chap. 14, pp. 238–57.

31. For some discussion of the Extradition Treaty, see Larry D. Ball, *The United States Marshals of New Mexico and Arizona Territories, 1846–1912* (Albuquerque: University of New Mexico, 1978), pp. 74–75; Robert D. Gregg, *The Influence of Border Troubles on Relations Between the United States and Mexico, 1876–1910* (New York: Da Capo, 1970), for a survey of boundary problems.

32. A. M. Gustafson, ed., *John Spring's Arizona* (Tucson: University of Arizona, 1966), p. 266; Allton Turner, "New Mexico Shoot-Out," *Frontier Times* 43 (February-March 1969): 36–37.

33. *Arizona Weekly Republican,* 27 March, 3 April 1902, 29 October 1903, for Sheriff Munds and the plea for the help of Emilio Kosteritzky; see Cornelius C. Smith, Jr., *Emilio Kosterlitzky: Eagle of Sonora and the Southwest Border* (Glendale, Calif.: Arthur H. Clark, 1970), for a biography of this noted *rurales* commander.

34. James J. Crittenden, Sheriff, Grant County (by Deputy John Long), to Marsh Gid-

dings, Governor, 11 February 1873, Richard Hudson, Probate Judge, Grant County, to Giddings, 12 February 1873, Governors Papers, NMSRCA; *DNM*, 14 April 1873, for Crittenden, and 11, 19, 23, 24 September, 23 October 1874, for McIntosh; Larry D. Ball, "'This High-Handed Outrage': Marshal William Kidder Meade in a Mexican Jail," *Journal of Arizona History* 17 (Summer 1976): 219–32.

35. For efforts at cooperation, see open letter of Ignacio Pesquiera, Hermosillo, Sonora, 21 January 1871, unidentified newspaper clipping, in Anson P. K. Safford, Governor, Arizona, to Hamilton Fish, Secretary of State, 14 February 1871, State Department Territorial Papers, Arizona, National Archives Microcopy #M-342, 1 roll; Journal of Edward D. Tuttle, Tuttle Papers, Special Collections Department, University of Arizona, recalls an instance of Mexican soldiers helping an Arizona posse in 1878; for Governor Fremont's honoring a Mexican requisition, see two proclamations, 22 December 1879, and 8 March 1880, Terr. Pap., Ariz., 1 roll; for the pursuit of the outlaws who participated in the Bisbee Massacre, see Douglas D. Martin, ed., *Tombstone's Epitaph* (Albuquerque: University of New Mexico, 1963), pp. 236–47.

36. Smith, *Emilio Kosterlitzky*, Chap. 5, pp. 95–126, for Kosterlitzky's border police activities; also, see Paul Joseph Vanderwood, "The Rurales: Mexico's Rural Police Force, 1861–1914," (Ph.D. diss., University of Texas, Austin, 1970); James G. Wolf Papers, AHS; Interview, Harry Saxon, transcript in Nita Stewart Haley Library, Midland, Texas.

37. Ibid.; Frazier Hunt, *Cap Mossman: Last of the Great Cowmen* (New York: Hastings House, 1951), Chap. 8, pp. 193–207, Chap. 9, pp. 208–17, for the capture of Chacon.

38. For Deputy James Speedy, see unidentified newspaper clippings, Hayden Biographical Files, AHS; for Deputy Roberts, see John M. Dobson, "Desperadoes and Diplomacy: The Territory of Arizona v. Jesus Garcia, 1893," *Journal of Arizona History* 17 (Summer 1976): 137–60.

39. Ball, *United States Marshals*, p. 28, for Crabb; for the Yaqui uprising, see *Arizona Republican*, 9 August 1906; "Smuggling of Arms to Yaqui Indians," File 9-2-3, Interior Department Territorial Papers, Arizona, National Archives Microcopy #M-429, roll 7, includes much correspondence about this episode, but see James E. McGee, Sheriff, to Kibbey, 31 March, and John F. White, Sheriff, to Kibbey, 3 April 1907.

40. Walker, *Death Was the Black Horse*, pp. 67–76; Sally Munds Williams, *History of Valuable Pioneers of the State of Arizona* ([Prescott, Ariz.?]: the author, 1979), pp. 60–71, for Sheriff Munds; Thomas E. Way, *The Parker Story* (Prescott, Ariz.: Prescott Graphics, 1981), Chapter 4, for pursuit of Jim Parker.

CHAPTER 11

1. We lack a comprehensive scholarly treatment of the many emergencies that beset New Mexico and Arizona territories, but see Ball, *United States Marshals*, Chaps. 7–8; for works devoted to special subjects, see Dedera, *A Little War of Our Own;* Frank Waters, *The Earp Brothers of Tombstone: The Story of Mrs. Virgil Earp* (New York: Clarkson N. Potter, 1960); Bartholomew, *Wyatt Earp: The Man and the Myth;* Pearson, *The Maxwell Land Grant;* F. Stanley (Stanley Crocchiola), *The Private War of Ike Stockton* (Denver: World Press, 1959); Philip J. Rasch, "the Horrell War," *New Mexico Historical Review* 31 (August 1956): 223–32; Wilson, *Merchants, Guns and Money;* Robert M. Utley, *High Noon in Lincoln: Violence on the Western Frontier* (Albuquerque: University of New Mexico Press, 1987).

2. For some discussion of post-Civil War politics, see Lamar, *Far Southwest; Albuquerque Weekly Democrat*, 24 May 1883; "Ranchero" to editor, 1 May 1883, *Silver City Enterprise*, 4 May 1883.

3. For the political rings, see Lamar, *Far Southwest*, pp. 136–70 for New Mexico, and pp. 422–57 for Arizona; Robert W. Larson, *New Mexico Populism: A Study of Radical Protest in a Western Territory* (Boulder: Colorado Associated University Press, 1974).

4. The subject of county building in the territories deserves more attention. A convenient place to begin is the historical atlas; see Walker and Bufkin, *Historical Atlas of Arizona;* Beck and Haase, *Historical Atlas of New Mexico.*

5. Wilson, *Merchants, Guns and Money,* Part 2, pp. 27–76, provides an insightful and searching study of the House of Murphy.

6. Lew Wallace to Juan M. Garcia, Sheriff, Socorro County, 5 June 1879, Lew Wallace Papers, box 8, Indiana State Historical Society, Indianapolis (copies to sheriffs of counties of Doña Ana, Colfax, Grant, San Miguel, and Valencia); for the "foolish virgins" allusion, see Matthew 25 : 1–13 in the New Testament.

7. *Tombstone Daily Epitaph,* 19 December 1881.

8. Blacker to William Steele, Adjutant General of Texas, [October?] 1878, *Report of the Adjutant General of the State of Texas for the Fiscal Year Ending 31 August 1878* (Galveston: Galveston News, 1878), pp. 52–54, copy in Jack Shipman Papers, El Paso Public Library; see also G. M. Frazer to Steele, 25 October 1878, and related correspondence in ibid.

9. "S. Z." to "Miss," Dark Canyon, Warloupe Mountains [sic], New Mexico, 1 September 1878, ibid.; Pat Dolan to John B. Jones, Major, Texas Rangers, 5 February 1879, in "Memoirs of Pat Dolan," Chap. 21, unpub. ms., El Paso Public Library; for the rampages of various outlaw bands connected with the Lincoln County War, see Grady McCright and James H. Powell, *Jessie Evans: Lincoln County Badman* (College Station, Tex.: Creative Publishing, 1983); Leon Claire Metz, *John Selman: Texas Gunfighter* (New York: Hastings House, 1966).

10. For the murder of Conklin, see Leon C. Metz, "An Incident at Christmas," *Quarterly of the National Association for Outlaw and Lawman History* 14 (Spring 1990): 1, 9, 15–16; Stanley, *Desperadoes,* pp. 221–36; Fergusson, *Murder and Mystery in New Mexico,* pp. 15–32; *Daily Optic,* 27 December 1880.

11. Telegram, Juan Jose Baca to Governor Lew Wallace, 28 December 1880, William G. Ritch Papers, 1539–1890, Special Collections Dept., University of New Mexico, Albuquerque, roll 6 (originals in Huntington Library, San Marino, Calif.); *Albuquerque Daily Journal,* 30 December 1880, quoted in Stanley, *Desperadoes,* p. 232.

12. For the military's constabulary duties on the early frontier, see Francis Paul Prucha, *Broadax and Bayonet: The Role of the United States Army in the Development of the Northwest, 1815–1860* (Lincoln: University of Nebraska, 1967), Chap. 5; for the long history of military participation in civil law enforcement, see Frederick T. Wilson, *Federal Aid in Domestic Disturbances, 1787–1903* (Washington: GPO, 1903); for the "Cushing device," see Edward S. Corwin, *The President, Office and Powers: History and Analysis of Practice and Opinion,* 3d ed. rev. (New York: New York University, 1948), pp. 129, 169, 174–75; for Attorney General Caleb Cushing's decision that placed the army in the civilian *posse comitatus,* see his handwritten version of the opinion of 27 May 1854 (Caleb Cushing Papers, Library of Congress, box 235) and the final version, *Official Opinions of the Attorneys General* (Washington: GPO), 6 : 466–74, and 16 : 466 for Attorney General Charles Devens's opinion conforming to the Posse Comitatus Act, 10 October 1878; S. E. Whitman, *The Troopers: An Informal History of the Plains Cavalry* (New York: Hastings House, 1962), Chap. 15, provides a general treatment of the army's constabulary duties on the frontier; United States, *Statutes at Large* (Washington: GPO), 20 : 145–52 (18 June 1878). The Posse Comitatus Act was actually a rider, Section 15, of the annual Army Appropriation Act.

13. Telegram, Bristol to John Sherman, Jr., United States Marshal, 4 October 1878, Lew Wallace Papers, box 7, Indiana State Historical Society, Indianapolis (hereafter cited as Wallace Pap.).

14. Some examples of constabulary duties include Clinton E. Brooks and Frank D. Reeve, eds., "James A. Bennett: A Dragoon in New Mexico, 1850–1856," *New Mexico Historical Review* 22 (January 1947): 51–97, pt. 1, (April): 140–76, pt. 2, for patrolling a hanging; Norman Cleaveland, comp., *An Introduction to the Colfax County War, 1875–78* (pvt. ptd., ca. 1975), for army in Cimarron; troops at San Carlos Apache Reservation assisted a deputy sheriff in pursuit of white rustlers (Personal Reminiscences of Dan R. Williamson, ms.,

AHS); Fort Marcy garrison assisted Sheriff Carlos Conklin in search for murderer (*DNM*, 4 May 1872); cavalry pursued white horsethieves in Doña Ana County (*DNM*, 18 February 1876); troops assist United States marshal in pursuit of mail robbers (*DNM*, 21 November, 27 December 1876); Fort Stanton guardhouse opened to civilian murderer (*WNM*, 10 August, 7 September 1875); army keeps peace during elections in Valencia County (*Santa Fe Weekly Gazette*, 16 September 1865); they patrol roads against Mexican bandits (ibid., 4, 11 November 1865).

15. Wallace to Schurz, 14 December 1880, Wallace Pap., box 9; clippings, *Washington Star*, [January 1881?], Wallace Pap., Scrapbook #7, p. 34 (see also unidentified clippings, pp. 28–32); Wallace to Schurz, 7 December 1880, Int. Dept. Terr. Pap., NM, National Archives Microcopy M-364, Record Group 48, roll 8; *Daily Optic*, 17 January 1881; Oakah L. Jones, "Lew Wallace: Hoosier Governor of Territorial New Mexico, 1787–81," *New Mexico Historical Review* 60 (April 1985): 129–58; *Evening Star* (Washington, D.C.), 27 September, 5 October 1878; for Arizona, see Fremont to Schurz, 26 January 1881, Gosper to Kirkwood, 5 May, 29 November, 19 December 1881, Int. Dept. Terr. Papers, Arizona, National Archives Microcopy M-429, Record Group 48, roll 3; see also *Tombstone Daily Epitaph*, [?] February 1882, quoted in Martin, ed., *Tombstone's Epitaph*, pp. 159–61; *Arizona Citizen* (Tucson), 6 September 1878.

16. Wallace to Schurz, 31 March 1879, clipping *Daily Graphic*, 7 January 1881, Wallace Pap., box 32, Scrapbook #7, p. 33; Philip J. Rasch, "The Trials of Lieutenant-Colonel Dudley," *English Westerners' Brand Book* 7 (January 1965): 1–7.

17. *Weekly Epitaph*, 1 May 1882; Anonymous to John Sherman, Jr., 20 March 1878, William G. Ritch Collection, 10 microfilm rolls, Special Collections Department, Zimmerman Library, University of New Mexico, Albuquerque, roll 5. Wallace to Edward Hatch, Commander, Department of New Mexico, 15 February 1879, Wallace Pap., box 8; see also Hatch to Wallace, 21 February 1879, ibid.; Utley, *High Noon in Lincoln*, pp. 92–111.

18. Larry D. Ball, "Militia Posses: The Territorial Militia in Civil Law Enforcement in New Mexico Territory, 1877–1883," *New Mexico Historical Review* 55 (January 1980): 47–69; John Pershing Jolly, *History, National Guard of New Mexico, 1606–1963*, comp. Russell C. Charleston and William A. Poe (Santa Fe: Adjutant-General's Department, State of New Mexico, 1964), pp. 1–18, Append. III, pp. 154–56; Philip J. Rasch, "The Rustler War," *New Mexico Historical Review* 39 (October 1964): 257–73; *Daily Epitaph*, 27 April 1882; *Weekly Epitaph*, 19 December 1881; Wagoner, *Arizona Territory*, pp. 194–96; L. Vernon Briggs, *Arizona and New Mexico, 1882, California, 1886, Mexico, 1891* (Boston: pvt. ptd., 1932), pp. 33–34; Frederick Tritle to Chester Arthur, 13 May 1882, Int. Dept. Terr. Pap., Arizona, roll 3.

19. General Order No. 14, 8 June 1882, in *Report of Edward L. Bartlett, Adjutant General of the Territory of New Mexico, from March 1, 1882 to January 1, 1884*, pp. 127–28, copy in Governor's Papers, NMSRCA; *Daily Epitaph*, 27 April 1882.

20. *WNM*, 10 April 1884; *Silver City Enterprise*, 27 July 1883; Ball, "Militia Posses," 47–69; *Message of Lionel A. Sheldon, Governor of New Mexico, Delivered to the Twenty-Sixth Legislative Assembly, February 19, 1884* (Santa Fe: New Mexican, 1884), pp. 6–7.

21. See n. 1; The connection between lawlessness in New Mexico and Arizona has been implied but not demonstrated in secondary works. Both contemporary newspapers and territorial officials noted a westward drift of outlaws from Texas and neighboring states. Residents of Silver City, New Mexico, held a town meeting to discuss ways to suppress Cowboy raiders from neighboring Cochise and Graham counties, in Arizona. For Fremont's less than glorious governorship, see Bert M. Fireman, "Fremont's Arizona Adventure," *American West* 1 (Winter 1963): 8–19; see Chap. 4 for political maneuvering to create Cochise County and events that led to the appointment of John Behan as sheriff.

22. Wyatt Earp divulged this plan to use Ike Clanton in his testimony before a justice of the peace about the OK Corral gunfight; see Ball, *United States Marshals*, Chap. 7, pp. 107–33, for this episode.

23. Henry P. Walker, "'Retire Peaceably to Your Homes': Arizona Faces Martial Law, 1882," *Journal of Arizona History* 10 (Spring 1969): 1–18.

24. Glenn G. Boyer, "Johnny Behan: Assistant Folk Hero," *Real West* (Spring 1983): 6, 8, 10–17, 70, 72–73; Gary L. Roberts, "Gunfight at OK Corral: the Wells Spicer Decision, 1881," *Montana, the Magazine of the Western History* 20 (January 1970): 62–74.

25. *Silver Belt* (Globe, Arizona), [September?] 1887, quoted in Earle R. Forrest, *Arizona's Dark and Bloody Ground*, rev. ed. (Caldwell, Idaho: Caxton, 1952), pp. 104–5.

26. *Arizona Journal-Miner* (Prescott), 29 August, 1, 2, 3, 5 September 1887, reported this conference and activities of the posse; for firsthand accounts of the posse, see Osmer D. Flake, "Some Reminiscences of the Pleasant Valley War and Causes That Led Up to It," Levi S. Udall Collection, AHS; McKinney, "Reminescences," 5 (April 1932): 33–54, (October 1932): 195–204.

27. Posseman Joe T. McKinney may have exaggerated when he asserted that the death of John Graham and Charles Blevins at the hands of the Mulvenon posse "ended the war proper," but their deaths robbed the participants of some elan (McKinney, "Reminiscences," ibid.); for C. P. Owens's battle in Holbrook, see Woody and Schwartz, *Globe*, Chap. 4; for the Committee of Fifty, see Dedera, *A Little War of Our Own*, pp. 184–90.

28. Wilson, *Merchants, Guns and Money*, Chaps. 6–7, pp. 49–76; for the assassination of Sheriff Brady, see Lavash, *Sheriff William Brady*.

29. See "Conduct of John N. Copeland, Sheriff of Lincoln, Lincoln County, New Mexico," Thomas Dale, Corporal, Co. H, 9th Cavalry, to Nathan A. M. Dudley, Commanding Officer, Fort Stanton, 1 May 1878, Department of the Missouri, Letters Received, 1878, National Archives, Washington, D.C., box 71, file 2471–1–D, Mo. 1878. This entire file is devoted to Copeland's aberrant conduct.

30. Utley, *High Noon in Lincoln*, Chap. 8, pp. 92–111.

31. Ibid., Chap. 10, pp. 118–24.

32. Ibid., pp. 131–34; Wallace to Schurz, 27 February 1879, Schurz to Wallace, 1 March 1879, Wallace Pap., box 8.

33. Metz, *Pat Garrett*, pp. 54–57, and Chaps. 8–9 for the death of Billy the Kid.

34. See copy of Sheldon's report to Secretary of Interior, 8 September 1883, in *Weekly New Mexican Review*, 13 September 1883.

CHAPTER 12

1. *The Kearny Code* [Laws of the Territory of New Mexico], ed. Noley Mumey (Denver, Colorado: no. pub., 1970; orig. pub. 1846); For medieval sheriffs, see William Alfred Morris, *The Medieval English Sheriff to 1300* (New York: Barnes & Noble, 1968; orig. pub. 1927), Chapter 9, "The Fiscal Function," pp. 241–73.

2. See Chapter 2, pp. 34–35, this volume; On 25 October 1884, the Las Vegas *Daily Optic* editorialized on the need to separate the assessorship from the county clerkship in New Mexico.

3. *Daily New Mexican*, 18 September 1873, 5 July 1876 (hereafter cited as DNM); *Weekly Arizona Miner* (Prescott), 4 April, 25 July 1868 (hereafter cited as WAM); *Albuquerque Journal*, [?] June 1885, cited in *Silver City Enterprise*, 6 June 1885.

4. Sophie Poe, *Buckboard Days* (Caldwell, Idaho: Caxton, 1936); clipping, *Prescott Courier*, William (Buckey) O'Neill Scrapbooks, Sharlot Hall Museum, Prescott, Arizona.

5. H. B. Wharfield, *Corydon Cooley: Army Scout, Arizona Pioneer, Wayside Host, Apache Friend* (El Cajon, California: the author, 1966), p. 61; *The Argus* (Holbrook), 2 April 1898, 10 March 1900, quoted in Lloyd C. Hening, *Sheriff, Scholar and Gentleman* [Frank Wattron] (Holbrook, n. pub., 1941), 30 pp., copy in Special Collections Department, University of Arizona, Tucson; Charles A. Hollister, "The Organization and Administration of the Sher-

iff's Office in Arizona," (M.A. thesis, University of Arizona, 1946), pp. 18–19, for bicycle cases.

6. For collecting difficulties along the New Mexico-Arizona border, see *Silver City Enterprise,* 5 March 1886.

7. Stinson to Bowers, 10 December 1875, 16 June 1876, quoted in clippings, WAM, 16 June 1876, Arizona Historical Society, Hayden Biographical Files, Edward Franklin Bowers; for problems on the New Mexico-Texas border, see J. F. Newman, Sweetwater, Texas, to Sheriff of Lincoln County, [1870s?], Maurice Garland Fulton Papers, Special Collections Department, University of Arizona, box 11.

8. William M. Breakenridge, *Helldorado: Bringing the Law to the Mesquite* (Boston: Houghton Mifflin, 1928), pp. 130–33.

9. Morris F. Taylor, *O. P. McMains and the Maxwell Land Grant Conflict* (Tucson: University of Arizona, 1979); even Arizona collectors encountered problems arising from disputed Spanish land grants, and Pima County Sheriff Hyler Ott failed to collect $860 delinquent taxes on such a grant (WAM, 6 January 1872); for the Populists' anti-corporate sentiments, see Robert W. Larson, *New Mexico Populism: A Study of Radical Protest in a Western Territory* (Boulder: Colorado Associated University Press, 1974).

10. *Alta Arizona* (Mohave County), cited in *Tombstone Epitaph,* 26 December 1881; *Daily Optic* (Las Vegas), 16 November 1884, for amounts of corporate tax payments in Colfax County, New Mexico; *Albuquerque Citizen,* cited in *DNM,* 27 November 1891.

11. AWS, 17, 23 February 1882; *Weekly Epitaph,* 27 February 1882.

12. *Weekly New Mexican,* 9 December 1886.

13. For Buckey O'Neill's crusade against the railroad, see Dale L. Walker, *Death Was the Black Horse: The Story of Rough Rider Buckey O'Neill* (Austin, Texas: Madrona, 1975), pp. 82–85.

14. Ibid.

15. *Weekly New Mexican,* 14 January 1886.

16. *Arizona Weekly Journal-Miner,* 20 September 1899, reported a compromise between the Navajo County Board of Supervisors and the Santa Fe Pacific Railroad.

17. See n. 1 this chapter.

18. *Roswell Register,* 18 July 1896.

19. *Arizona Daily Citizen,* 16 January 1885.

20. Alexander McSween to Joseph Blazer, 13 January 1876, "Notice For Taxes," Sheriff Mariano Barela to Blazer, 21 December 1891, Joseph Blazer Papers, Special Collections Department, University of Arizona, box 1; postcard, Sheriff George Curry to John Y. Hewitt, 13 June 1894, John J. Cockrell Letters, in Philip J. Rasch Papers, Lincoln County Historic Trust, Lincoln, New Mexico (copy courtesy of John P. Wilson, Las Cruces, New Mexico).

21. For Sheriff Kemp's notice, see *DNM,* 11 February 1893; *Proceedings of the New Mexico Bar Association,* 3d Annual Session, 3 January 1888 (Santa Fe: New Mexican, 1888), pp. 3–10.

22. See photocopy of excerpt from the diary of Benjamin Brown, Law Enforcement Collection, Arizona Historical Society, Tucson, Apache County folder, entry for 10 December 1883.

23. DNM, 19, 23 May 1883, 13 January 1885.

24. *Daily Tombstone Epitaph,* 27 February 1886; J. H. Sayre to John L. B. Alexander, Attorney, 19 January 1903, Alexander Papers, Hayden Library, Arizona State University, Tempe. "Joe" is apparently John Alexander.

25. Jay J. Wagoner, *Arizona Territory, 1863–1912: A Political History* (Tucson: University of Arizona, 1970), pp. 171–72, 287–88; John H. Cady, *Arizona's Yesterdays,* rev. Basil Dillon Moon (Patagonia, Arizona: n. pub., 1978), pp. 81–82.

26. Charles C. Colley, "Carl T. Hayden: Phoenician," *Journal of Arizona History* 18 (Autumn 1977): 247–58; Billy McGinty, *The Old West, As Written in the Words of Billy McGinty, As Told to Glenn L. Eyler* (Stillwater, Oklahoma: Redlands Press, 1958; orig. pub. 1937), pp. 77–78.

27. DNM, 11 May 1891, for quote from a *Denver News* editorial about New Mexico's high license law; Herbert V. Young, *They Came to Jerome* (Jerome, Arizona: n. pub., 1972), pp. 100–102.

28. WAM, 16 January 1869, 14 September 1872.

29. DNM, 16 February, 5, 11 March 1892, 20 July 1893; *Weekly New Mexican,* 28 February, 6, 20 March, 3, 24 April, 1, 8, 22, 29 May, 19 June 1884.

30. DNM, 22 March, 20 May 1875.

31. Ibid.; Philip J. Rasch, "Prelude to War: the Murder of John Henry Tunstall," *English Westerners' Brand Book* 12 (January 1970): 1–10.

32. *Roswell Record,* 24 April 1896.

33. Ibid.: Larry D. Ball, "Lawman in Disgrace: Sheriff Charles C. Perry of Chaves County, New Mexico," *New Mexico Historical Review* 61 (April 1986): 125–36.

34. Second Annual Message of R. B. Mitchell, December 1868, State Department Territorial Papers, New Mexico, National Archives Microcopy T-17, roll 3; see the proclamation of Governor William A. Pile, "Crisis in the affairs of the Territory," also in roll 3.

35. Governor William A. Pile to Hamilton Fish, Secretary of State, 5 October 1869, ibid., roll 3.

36. Ibid.

37. Message of Governor Samuel Axtell, 8 January 1878, Executive Record of the Governors of New Mexico, State Records and Archives Center, Record #2, pp. 218–35.

38. Ibid.

39. *Albuquerque Daily Democrat,* 9 January 1884, for the proposed conference with district attorneys; *Message of Governor L. Bradford Prince to the Twenty-Ninth Legislative Assembly, December 30, 1890* (Santa Fe: New Mexican, 1891), pp. 20–21; *Message of Governor William T. Thornton to the Thirty-First Legislative Assembly of New Mexico, December 31, 1894* (Santa Fe: New Mexican, 1895), pp. 20–21.

40. *Special Message of Governor L. Bradford Prince to the Twenty-Ninth Legislative Assembly, January 10, 1891* (Santa Fe: New Mexican, 1891), pp. 37–42; *Message of Governor L. Bradford Prince to the Thirtieth Legislative Assembly of New Mexico, December 28, 1892* (Santa Fe: New Mexican, 1892), pp. 22–23.

41. Ibid.; See, Ball, "Lawman in Disgrace," pp. 125–36, for more discussion of this subject; an Arizona law provided for the election of separate assessors in first and second class counties under the new categorization of such local governments (*Arizona Weekly Journal-Miner,* 17 March 1897).

CHAPTER 13

1. *Santa Fe Weekly Gazette,* 2 February 1856; DNM, 13 November 1896; *Acts of the Legislative Assembly of the Territory of New Mexico, Thirty-Fourth Session, 21 January 1901–21 March 1901* (n.p.: n. pub., 1901), pp. 34–41; Kelly, comp., *Legislative History,* p. 213.

2. James Speedy to Chairman of the Board, Pima County, 20 October 1887, Pima County Original Documents, Special Collections Dept., University of Arizona, Tucson; *Arizona Weekly Star,* 2 May 1895; clipping, *Arizonian* (Tucson), 23 February 1899, Edward D. Tuttle Papers, Special Collections Department, University of Arizona, Tucson; Frank C. Lockwood, "John Lorenzo Hubbell, Navajo Indian Trader," *University of Arizona Bulletin,* No. 6, 8 (1 July 1942): 66.

3. Jesse James Benton, *Cow By the Tail,* ed. Richard Summers (New York: Houghton Mifflin, 1943), reprinted, *Frontier Times* 38 (October-November 1964), 39 (December-January, February-March 1965).

4. *DNM,* 19 January 1877, 25 July 1899; *Daily Optic,* 29 August 1884.

5. *Albuquerque Morning Journal,* 16 August 1908, for the Tombstone leper colony; *DNM,* 13 November 1896.

6. *DNM,* 7 August 1896; *Weekly J-M,* 25 August 1897, 2 May 1900.

7. Whitlock, *Cowboy Life,* p. 190.

8. *DNM,* 3 February 1901; *WNM,* 19 November 1885; Rees, *Mohave County Jail,* pp. 25–26; *Journal-Miner,* 21 December 1898; *Arizona Weekly Star,* 10, 17 April 1884; Maricopa County Sheriff Noah Broadway received $375 for transporting one patient from Phoenix to Stockton, California [Richard Miller, "Noah M. Broadway," (Master's thesis, Arizona State University, Tempe, 1975?), p. 13].

9. *DNM,* 13 May 1893; clipping, *Arizona Weekly Enterprise* (Florence), 29 March 1884, Hayden Biographical Files, "Andrew J. Doran," AHS; *DNM,* 6 January 1892.

10. *DNM,* 7 January, 20 May, 13, 15 June 1882; *Arizona Weekly Star,* 28 February 1884.

11. Ibid., 22 November 1883; *Journal-Miner,* 16 February 1898; Grace McCool, *So Said the Coroner: How They Died in Old Cochise* (Tombstone: Epitaph, 1968).

12. *DNM,* 8, 9, 15 June, 16 July 1891, 30 December 1892; *Journal-Miner,* 14 November 1900.

13. *Laws of the Territory of New Mexico,* pp. 30–33.

14. Quoted in Zarbin, "'The Whole Thing Was Done So Quietly,'" 353–62.

15. Lake to Paul, 8 June 1892, General Correspondence of the United States Marshals of Arizona, AHS.

16. Miller, "Noah M. Broadway," p. 13; *Journal-Miner,* 28 April, 23 June 1897, 24 May, 20 September 1899.

17. A. Blake Brophy, *Foundlings on the Frontier: Racial and Religious Conflicts in Arizona Territory, 1904–1905* (Tucson: University of Arizona, 1972); Raymond A. Mulligan, "New York Foundlings at Clifton-Morenci: Social Justice in Arizona Territory, 1904–1905," *Arizona and the West* 6 (Summer 1964): 104–18.

18. *DNM,* 17 May 1883; Irene Cornwall Cofer, *The Lunch Tree* (Brooklyn, N.Y.: Gaus, 1969), p. 14.

19. Dan Genung, "Reminescences: Genung Family," Dan Genung Collection, AHS, xerox copy in Sharlot Hall Museum, Prescott; *Tombstone Daily Epitaph,* 19 January 1886.

20. *Arizona Weekly Citizen* (Tucson), 29 March 1884.

21. *Daily Epitaph,* 17 March 1876; *DNM,* [?] April 1882, reprinted in *Press of the Territorian* (Santa Fe), 2 (September 1962); Sharman Apt Russell, "Russian Bill: The True Story of an Outlaw," *Journal of the West* 23 (April 1984): 91–93.

22. Augustin Pina, Mexican Consul, Phoenix, to Carl Hayden, Sheriff, 20 August 1907, Carl Hayden Papers, Special Collections Dept., Hayden Library, Arizona State University, Tempe.

23. Walker, *Death Was the Black Horse,* pp. 77–80; *Arizona Citizen,* 14 March 1890.

24. Melissa Ruffner Weiner, *Prescott Yesteryears: Life in Arizona's First Territorial Capital* (Prescott: Primrose, 1976), p. 35. The author apparently confuses George Ruffner, sheriff in 1895–98, with his successor, John Munds; Ella Joliver, "Prescott's Big Fire," *Echoes of the Past* (Yavapai Cow Belles), 1955, pp. 25–31, copy in Sharlot Hall Museum, Prescott.

25. *Daily Optic,* 20 September 1880; Hayes, *Sheriff Thompson's Day,* p. 40; *Weekly Epitaph,* 10 April, 27 May 1882.

26. *Journal-Miner,* 10 March 1897; *DNM,* 31 December 1895, 11 September 1896.

27. *Arizona Republican* (Phoenix), 19 January 1905; see issue of 30 May 1901 for rabid dog.

28. *Socorro Chieftain,* cited in *DNM,* 14 September 1896; *Journal-Miner,* 2 March, 24 August 1898, 12 April 1899; Wagoner, *Early Arizona,* p. 406.

29. Poe, *Buckboard Days,* p. 206; *Arizona Daily Star,* 2 January 1912, cited in Charles A. Hollister, "The Organization and Administration of the Sheriff's Office in Arizona," (Master's thesis, 1946), pp. 53–54.

30. Sonnichsen, *Outlaw: Bill Mitchell,* pp. 137–40; Poe, *Buckboard Days,* p. 193.

CHAPTER 14

1. Beck and Haase, *Historical Atlas of New Mexico*, maps 45–50.

2. Walker and Bufkin, *Historical Atlas of Arizona*, maps 32–33.

3. Veto Messages of Governor Edmund Ross, 18, 21 February 1887, Int. Dept. Terr. Papers, Arizona, Record Group 48, National Archives Microcopy M-429, Washington, D.C., roll 8; *DNM*, 15 May 1893, reported that San Miguel County had liabilities of $400,000; *Message of Miguel A. Otero, Governor of New Mexico, to the 36th Legislative Assembly, January 16, 1905* (Santa Fe: New Mexican, 1905), p. 19; *Message of Herbert J. Hagerman, Governor of New Mexico, to the 37th Legislative Assembly, January 21, 1907* (Santa Fe: New Mexican, 1907), p. 46.

4. See Chap. 10.

5. *Albuquerque Daily Democrat*, 16 February 1884.

6. *WNM*, 30 July, 5, 12 August 1885; *Silver City Enterprise*, 28 August 1885; *Daily Optic*, 11 August 1885; *DNM*, 10, 14, 29, 31 January, 20 February 1891, 7, 26, 31 January, 3, 9, 13, 17 February 1893.

7. *Arizona Republican* (Phoenix), 22 February 1899, 2 October 1902, 9 March 1905; *RMN*, 6, 11 July 1900.

8. Louis C. Hughes to Board of Territorial Prison Commissioners, 2 April 1894, Louis C. Hughes Letterbook, p. 376, Special Collections Dept., University of Arizona, Tucson.

9. See Chap. 1.

10. Ball, *United States Marshals*, pp. 192–93; *El Paso Daily Times* (Texas), 19 March 1896, commenting on an article in *Galveston Times*.

11. *Message of Samuel B. Axtell to the Legislative Assembly of New Mexico, Twenty-second Session* (Santa Fe: Manderfield and Tucker, [1876?]), pp. 12–13; *Daily Optic*, quoted in *RMN*, 22 September 1890.

12. *Laws of the Territory of Arizona, Thirteenth Legislative Assembly* (San Francisco: H. S. Crocker, 1885), pp. 117–28, 281–84, 293–304, for specific salary laws for each county; for newspaper coverage of debates on the salary bill, see *Arizona Weekly Star*, 5, 19, 26 February, 5, 12, 19, 26 March 1885.

13. Larry D. Ball, "Lawman in Disgrace: Sheriff Charles C. Perry of Chaves County, New Mexico," *New Mexico Historical Review* 61 (April 1986): 125–36.

14. *Message of Miguel A. Otero, 1905*, p. 7; Biennial Report of the Public Examiner, 1 December 1906, N. V. Foster, Public Examiner, to Governor Joseph Kibbey, Int. Dept. Terr. Papers, roll 2.

15. Ibid.

16. Ibid.; Wagoner, *Arizona Territory*, p. 448. The position of Public Examiner was abolished in 1909.

17. *Acts of the Legislative Assembly of the Territory of New Mexico, Thirty-second Session.*

18. The removal of Thomas Hubbell created much controversy; see Miguel A. Otero, *My Nine Years as Governor of the Territory of New Mexico* (Albuquerque: University of New Mexico Press, 1940), pp. 227–28, 233, 240–48; Executive Record, Governor of New Mexico, book #6, pp. 232–33, 259, NMSRCA; "Testimony Given at the Hearing in the Case of Thomas S. Hubbell, of Bernalillo County . . . , June 28th 1905," Miguel A. Otero Papers, box 4, Special Collections Department, University of New Mexico, Albuquerque.

19. Ibid.

20. Ibid.; Thomas Hubbell carried his case to the territorial supreme court, see Poldervaart, *Black-Robed Justice*, pp. 190–91. The ousted former sheriff physically obstructed his successor, Perfecto Armijo, from occupying the lawman's office, see John Fullerton, Captain, New Mexico Mounted Police, to Cipriano Baca, Lieutenant, 12 September 1905, Letters Sent, Mounted Police, Territorial Archives of New Mexico, roll 92, NMSRCA. The Hubbell family did not forget this assault upon their political machine and regarded the removal as a gross injustice. See the letter of Frank A. Hubbell, Albuquerque, to Harlan Thurman, Carls-

bad, New Mexico, 23 October 1916, Frank A. Hubbell Papers, Rio Grande Collection, New Mexico State University, Las Cruces.

21. Hayes, *Sheriff Thompson's Day,* p. 71; Rees, *Mohave County Jail,* p. 31; "To the Voters and Taxpayers of Lincoln County," printed flyer signed by John Y. Hewitt, John A. Brothers, G. R. Young, Committee, 1891, Maurice Garland Fulton Collection, Special Collections Department, University of Arizona, Tucson; Harkey, *Mean As Hell,* p. 69.

22. *Albuquerque Morning Journal,* 27 July 1907, 7 October 1908; Axford, *Around Western Campfires,* pp. 100–101.

23. Chloe Owings, *Women Police: A Study of the Development and Status of the Women Police Movement* (Montclair, N.J.: Patterson Smith, 1969), pp. 97–104; for Mrs. Mel Greenleaf, see clipping, *Who's Who in Arizona* (n.d.), pp. 774–75, clipping, *Apache County Courier,* 13 October 1896, "Women in Law Enforcement," Law Enforcement Collection, AHS.

24. Clippings, *Tombstone Epitaph,* 10 October 1915, *Arizona Gazette,* 10 June 1914, *Arizona Star,* 26 September 1947, recalling Villman's appointment, in ibid.; see also unidentified clippings, 9, 14 December 1914, 24 July, 24 October 1915, in ibid.; Lori Davisson, "Arizona Law Enforcement: A Survey from the Collections of the Arizona Historical Society," *Journal of Arizona History* 27 (Autumn 1986): 315–48; Richard Emery Roberts, *Star in the West* (New York: Random House, 1951); this writer has not seen the novel.

25. Weiner, *Prescott Yesteryears,* p. 92; *Arizona Republican,* 7 March 1900; Callon, *Las Vegas,* p. 118; *WNM,* 30 June 1883; *DNM,* 29 August 1896; *Albuquerque Morning Journal,* 14 August 1907.

26. Bartholomew, *Wyatt Earp: The Man and the Myth,* p. 195; Grace McCool, "Tombstone Sheriffs," *The Sheriff* (magazine), 23 (25th Anniversary Issue): 19–29; Petitioners to Board of Pima County Supervisors, 7 December 1891, Pima County Original Documents, Special Collections Dept., University of Arizona, Tucson; *Weekly J-M,* 7 November, 26 December 1900; *Arizona Republican,* 30 March, 2 April, 17 November 1901.

27. *Weekly J-M,* 31 May, 19 July 1899; *Arizona Republican,* 20 March, 17 December, 1902, 19 November 1903; *DNM,* 6 May 1903; Clipping, *Roswell Record,* 28 April 1905, Maurice Garland Fulton Collection, box 9, Special Collections Dept., University of Arizona; *Albuquerque Morning Journal,* 3 July 1907.

28. E. Dana Johnson, "New Mexico's First State Automobile," *New Mexico Historical Review* 11 (January 1936): 1–8; *Albuquerque Morning Journal,* 25 March 1907, 2 February, 21 April 1910; for Arizona sheriffs, see issue of 12 May 1910; Hayes, *Sheriff Thompson's Day,* pp. 101–26; clipping, *Arizona Daily Star,* 21 September 1910, courtesy of John P. Wilson, Las Cruces, New Mexico.

29. Clipping, *Arizona Daily Star,* 17 August 1910; *Albuquerque Morning Journal,* 13 August 1907; Bill O'Neal, "Captain Harry Wheeler, Arizona Lawman," *Journal of Arizona History* 27 (Autumn: 1986): 297–314; Harkey, *Mean as Hell,* pp. 64–66.

30. Executive Proceedings of the Governor of New Mexico, 29 December 1911, Int. Dept. Terr. Pap. NM, Record Group 48, National Archives Microcopy M-364, roll 10; *Tucson Citizen,* 4 October, 14 December 1911; Charles A. Hollister, "The Organization and Administration of the Sheriff's Office in Arizona" (Master's thesis, University of Arizona, 1946), pp. 45–46; "Notebook of Reward Posters, Strayed or Stolen Stock, 'Wanted Men' and Related Correspondence, 1906–1912," New Mexico Mounted Police, Territorial Archives of New Mexico, roll 93.

31. *Harpers Weekly,* quoted in *Arizona Weekly Republican,* 22 May 1902; the horseback outlaw continued to flourish after the turn of the century. For some instances, see Ben W. Kemp, *Cow Dust and Saddle Leather,* ed. Jeff C. Dykes (Norman: University of Oklahoma, 1968), pp. 257–63, for exploits of the Greer band; Ball, *United States Marshals,* Chaps. 10–11, discusses some outlawry. George and Vern Gates, two lawless brothers, were as hardened a pair as any the sheriffs faced in the Southwest; see John Boessenecker, *Badge and Buckshot: Lawlessness in Old California* (Norman: University of Oklahoma, 1988), Chap. 10; Dep-

uty Sheriff (and later Sheriff) Herbert McGrath killed them in Separ, Grant County, New Mexico, in March 1905.

32. *Youth's Companion*, quoted in *Arizona Daily Star*, 11 June 1890; H. Parliman, Manager, Identification Department, Yawman and Erbe Manufacturing Company, Rochester, New York, to Carl Hayden, Sheriff, 3 August 1909, Carl Hayden Papers, Box 502–4, Hayden Library, Arizona State University, Tempe; in 1857, the San Francisco Police Department began a mug book, see William B. Secrest "Rogue's Gallery Helped Lawmen," *Quarterly of the National Association of Outlaw and Lawman History* 4 (Summer 1978): 1, 7–10.

33. C. L. Sonnichsen, *Tularosa: Last of the Frontier West* (New York: Devin-Adair, 1961), pp. 42–44; Moorman, "Holm O. Bursum," 333–44; *Weekly J-M*, 18 October 1899; *Tucson Citizen*, 1 July 1907; Miller, ed., *Arizona Rangers*, pp. 156–61.

34. For the latest work, which uses official sources, see Bill O'Neal, *The Arizona Rangers* (Austin, Tex.: Eakin, 1987); Richard D. Myer, "The New Mexico Territorial Mounted Police," *Cochise Quarterly* 1 (December 1971): 3–8; the records of the Mounted Police, which are conveniently on microfilm, provide the fullest account, see Records of the Mounted Police, 1905–1911, Territorial Archives of New Mexico, NMSRCA, rolls 91–93; Chuck Hornung, *The Thin Grey Line—The New Mexico Mounted Police* (Fort Worth: Western Heritage, 1971), reprints some pertinent documents and contains helpful biographical data about the mounted policemen; Frazier Hunt, *Cap Mossman: Last of the Great Cowmen* (New York: Hastings, 1951), Pt. 4, for his ranger experiences; Message of Governor Joseph H. Kibbey to the Arizona Legislature, 21 January 1907, Int. Dept. Terr. Pap., Arizona, roll 2; *Solomonville Bulletin*, [?] 1903, quoted in Miller, *Arizona Rangers*, pp. 65–66.

35. Rynning, *Gun Notches*, pp. 231, 252, 271–74, for quarrels with sheriffs. This book should be used cautiously. For critical reviews, see Sidney Kartus and Joe Chisholm, *Arizona Historical Review* 4 (October 1931): 75–78.

36. Ringgold, *Frontier Days*, pp. 138–44; Report of Captain Harry Wheeler for Fiscal Year Ending 30 June 1908, to Governor Joseph Kibbey, 13 July 1908, Int. Dept. Terr. Pap., Arizona, roll 6; clipping, unidentified Los Angeles newspaper, 8 July 1907, James H. McClintock Collection, Phoenix Public Library; John Fullerton to H. J. Hagerman, Governor, 9 February, Fullerton to Will C. Barnes, 12 April 1906, Letters Sent, Records of the Mounted Police, 1905–1911, Roll 92, Territorial Archives of New Mexico, State Records Center and Archives, Santa Fe; James A. Street, Sheriff, to George W. Prichard, Attorney General, New Mexico, 14 February 1906, Letters Received, 1905–1911, roll 91; for the investigation of Sheriff Sanchez, see "Complaint Against Torrance County Sheriff, Manuel S. Sanchez, for Extortion, 1906–1907," roll 93; Chuck Hornung, *The Thin Gray Line*, pp. 35–36.

37. *Arizona Republican*, 19 October 1905, 1 February, 26 April, 22 November 1906; Wagoner, *Arizona Territory*, pp. 440–41; *Albuquerque Morning Journal*, 21 March, 6 May, 17 October 1907, 3 January 1908.

38. For Sheriff Don Johnson's report, dated 1 July 1907, see Luna County Records, file 07–1908, NMSRCA; *Albuquerque Morning Journal*, 3 January 1907; Report of Captain Harry Wheeler to Governor Joseph Kibbey, 13 July 1908, Int. Dept. Terr. Pap., Arizona, roll 6; Hannett, *Sagebrush Lawyer*, p. 6; Keleher, *New Mexicans I Knew*, p. 54, recalls how Albuquerque police looked the other way and neglected to enforce these early anti-gambling and prostitution laws.

39. Hollister, "The Sheriff's Office in Arizona," (Master's thesis), pp. 59–60; Ball, *United States Marshals*, pp. 236–37.

CHAPTER 15

1. *Carrizozo Outlook*, quoted in *Albuquerque Morning Journal*, 10 March 1908.

2. Populations statistics are taken from Beck and Haase, *Historical Atlas of New Mexico*;

Walker and Bufkin, *Historical Atlas of Arizona*; Sigurd Johansen, *The People of New Mexico,* Agricultural Experiment Station Bulletin 606 (Las Cruces: New Mexico State University, [1970?]), p. 34. Communities of 2,500 or more population are classified as urban.

3. See Appendix A.

4. For William Wiley Berry, see unid. clipping, 11 March 1948, obituary of Rachel E. Berry, wife of the former sheriff, folder "Apache County Law," Law Enforcement Collection, AHS.

5. These statistical data are compiled from a wide range of sources, all of which are listed in the bibliography.

6. Frank Richard Prassel, *The Western Peace Officer: A Legacy of Law and Order* (Norman: University of Oklahoma, 1972), pp. 244–56.

7. R. E. Heiges, "Goodbye to the Sheriff," *Social Science* 11 (April 1936): 137–41.

Appendix A
List of Sheriffs

Two procedures were employed in Arizona and New Mexico territories to select sheriffs—the appointive and the elective systems. The governors normally appointed the first lawman for a new county. When an incumbent died or departed office for any reason, the territorial executive usually selected a temporary replacement. The county boards often nominated or recommended this person. The provisional military regime in New Mexico Territory was an exception. From 1846 to 1851, the governors appointed all sheriffs. With the advent of civilian government in 1851, the people elected their county officers. Since Arizona Territory began with a civilian regime, the governor appointed the first battery of sheriffs in 1864.

The length of terms and times of elections varied. New Mexico began general elections in September 1851. The sheriffs filed their bonds and took the oath as soon as possible, but did so on no particular designated date. Therefore, the terms of these early sheriffs varied in length; most probably assumed their duties in late September or in October. New Mexico sheriffs served a two-year term, with one exception. In 1875, lawmakers in Santa Fe changed election day to November, to take effect with the first general elections in November 1876. The newly chosen sheriffs assumed office formally on 1 January 1877. This new measure created some temporary confusion by shortening the term of the sheriff in this interregnum—elected in September 1875—to about fifteen months. The terms of office remained two years for the rest of the territorial era.

Arizonans also varied their election practices for the shrievalty. Rather than set up counties with the initiation of the new territory, the first governor divided Arizona into three judicial districts in 1864. He appointed a sheriff for each district in the spring of that year. The first session of the Assembly, which met in the fall, established counties and authorized general elections for September 1865. Newly elected sheriffs entered office on 1 December, but only for one-year terms. The lawmakers then changed the time of elections, and the first balloting under this new law took place in June 1867. Newly elected lawmen took office on 1 July. Some confusion arose when the governor neglected to issue a proclamation announcing the date of elections in June 1868. Some counties refused to hold elections. They feared that elections held without the executive sanction would be invalid. These counties followed the practice traditional in republics—that the incumbent retains his office until regularly mandated elections take place. Yuma County persisted in holding elections and thus raised doubts about the legitimacy of its new sheriff. In 1870, Arizona Territory held elections in November, with the sheriff entering office on the following 1 January 1871. Terms were also lengthened to two years. When New Mexico adopted this procedure on 1 January 1877, the two territories followed uniform practice for the remainder of the territorial period. Elections for sheriffs under statehood took place on 7 November 1911. These men entered office with the inauguration of this new status on 15 January 1912.

The following is a tentative catalog of the names and terms of sheriffs for both territories from September 1846 to 1912. In the absence of official lists, many sources have been consulted. Although the governors were required to keep an official register of all officials, neither Arizona nor New Mexico kept complete records. Newspapers often reported election results and occasionally printed a complete table of all new officials for each county. When losing candidates contested elections, much confusion occurred and the name of the sheriff finally chosen was not reported. Considerable turnover took place in some shrievalties, and the interim official is often difficult to identify. Officeholders sometimes departed the shrievalty with no regard to the legal nicety of formal resignations. Where information is available, the footnotes provide some explanation.

ARIZONA TERRITORY

Apache County (1879, Snowflake; 1879, St. Johns; 1880, Springerville; 1881, St. Johns)

[1] 1879 – Alejandro Peralta
[2]   – Luther Martin
1880 –   "   "
1881 – Ephram S. Stover
1882 –   "   "
1883 – Thomas Perez
1884 –   "   "
[3] 1885 – John Lorenzo Hubbell
1886 –   "   "   "
1887 – Commodore Perry Owens
1888 –   "   "   "
1889 – St. George Creaghe
1890 –   "   "   "
1891 – O. B. Little
1892 –   "   "   "
1893 – W. R. Campbell
1894 –   "   "   "
1895 – James Scott
[4] 1896 –   "   "
     – William Wiley Berry

1897 – St. George Creaghe
[5] 1898 –   "   "   "
     – William Wiley Berry
1899 – Edward Beeler
1900 –   "   "
1901 – Leandro Ortega
1902 –   "   "
1903 – Sylvestre Peralta
1904 –   "   "
1905 –   "   "
1906 –   "   "
1907 –   "   "
1908 –   "   "
1909 –   "   "
1910 –   "   "
1911 –   "   "
1912 –   "   "
1913 –   "   "
1914 –   "   "

1. Appointed 20 February 1879.
2. Elected 2 June 1879.
3. Certificate of election dated 17 November 1884.
4. Scott resigned in letter of 23 September 1896. Board accepted 6 October 1896. Berry filled out term.
5. Creaghe resigned July 1898. Berry filled out term.

Cochise County (1881, Tombstone)

[1]1881–John H. Behan
1882– " " "
1883–Jerome L. Ward
1884– " " "
1885–Robert S. Hatch
1886– " " "
1887–John H. Slaughter
1888– " " "
1889– " " "
1890– " " "
1891–Carlton B. Kelton
1892– " " "
1893–Scott White
1894– " "
1895–Camillus Sidney Fly
1896– " " "
1897–Scott White

1898– " "
1899– " "
1900– " "
1901–Adelbert (Del) Lewis
1902– " " "
1903– " " "
1904– " " "
1905–Stewart Hunt
1906– " "
[2]1907–John (Jack) F. White
1908– " " " "
1909– " " " "
1910– " " " "
1911– " " " "
1912–Harry Wheeler
1913– " "

1. Appointed 10 February and assumed duties 25 February 1881.
2. No relation to Scott White.

Coconino County (1891, Flagstaff)

[1]1891–Ralph Henry Cameron
–John W. Francis
1892– " " "
1892– " " "
1893–Jerome J. (Sandy) Donahue
1894– " " " "
1894– " " " "
1895–Ralph Henry Cameron
1896– " " "
1897– " " "
1898– " " "
[2]1899–Fletcher Fairchild
–James A. Johnson

1900– " " "
1901– " " "
1902– " " "
1903– " " "
1904– " " "
1905–Harry Henderson
1906– " "
1907–John W. Francis
1908– " " "
1909– " " "
1910– " " "
1911– " " "
[3]1912–T. E. Pulliam

1. Cameron appointed March 1891; Francis elected 13 May 1891.
2. Fairchild elected November 1898, but forced to resign in August 1899 due to illness; Johnson served out Fairchild's term.
3. Elected 11 December 1911.

Gila County (1881, Globe)

[1] 1881 – William (Bert) Murphy
   – W. W. (Tip) Lowther
1882 – "   "   "
1883 – Benjamin F. Pascoe
1884 –   "   "   "
1885 –   "   "   "
1886 –   "   "   "
[2] 1887 – E. E. Hodgson
   – George E. Shute
1888 –   "   "   "
[3] 1889 – Glen Reynolds
   – Jerry Ryan
1890 –   "   "
   – John Henry Thompson
1891 –   "   "   "
1892 –   "   "   "
1893 –   "   "   "
1894 –   "   "   "
1895 –   "   "   "

1896 –   "   "   "
1897 – Dan H. Williamson
1898 –   "   "   "
1899 – W. T. Armstrong
1900 –   "   "   "
1901 – John Henry Thompson
1902 –   "   "   "
1903 – C. R. Rogers
1904 –   "   "   "
1905 – Edward P. Shanley
[4] 1906 –   "   "   "
   – W. G. Shanley
1907 – John Henry Thompson
1908 –   "   "   "
1909 –   "   "   "
1910 –   "   "   "
[5] 1911 –   "   "   "
   – Frank Haynes
1912 –   "   "

1. Appointed 23 February 1881; Lowther elected first Monday in April 1881.

2. Hodgson died in the fall of 1887; Shute filled out the term.

3. Reynolds was killed in the line of duty, 2 November 1889; Jerry Ryan appointed to fill out Reynold's term; Ryan drowned accidentally, 1 June 1890; Thompson took oath of office, 9 June 1890, and filled out the term.

4. Edward P. Shanley died accidentally in October 1906; a brother, W. G. Shanley, filled out the term.

5. Thompson was indicted for murder and resigned in 1911; Haynes filled out the term.

Graham County (1881, Safford; 1883, Solomonville)

[1] 1881 – C. B. Rose
1882 – George H. Stevens
1883 –   "   "   "
1884 –   "   "   "
1885 – Ben M. Crawford
1886 –   "   "   "
1887 –   "   "   "
1888 –   "   "   "
1889 – William Baird Whelan
1890 –   "   "   "
1891 – George A. Olney
1892 –   "   "   "
1893 –   "   "   "
1894 –   "   "   "
1895 – Arthur A. Wight

1896 –   "   "   "
1897 – William P. Birchfield
1898 –   "   "   "
1899 – Ben R. Clark
1900 –   "   "   "
1901 – James V. Parks
1902 –   "   "   "
1903 –   "   "   "
1904 –   "   "   "
1905 –   "   "   "
1906 –   "   "   "
1907 – Alphie A. (Pap) Anderson
1908 –   "   "   "   "
1909 –   "   "   "   "
1910 –   "   "   "   "

1. Appointed 16 March 1881.

Greenlee County (1909, Clifton)

[1] 1911 – I. B. English
1912 – James Cash(?)

1. Elected November 1910; county formally organized, 1 January 1910.

Maricopa County (1871, Phoenix)

[1] 1871 – William A. Hancock
    – Thomas Barnum
    – T. C. Worden (Warden)
1872 – " " " "
1873 – Thomas C. Hayes
1874 – " " "
1875 – George E. Mowry
1876 – " " "
1877 – " " "
1878 – " " "
1879 – Reuben S. Thomas
1880 – " " "
1881 – Lindley H. Orme
1882 – " " "
1883 – " " "
1884 – " " "
1885 – Noah M. Broadway
1886 – " " "
1887 – Andrew J. Halbert
1888 – " " "
1889 – William T. (Bud) Gray
1890 – " " "

1891 – John Britt Montgomery
1892 – " " "
1893 – James K. Murphy
1894 – " " "
1895 – Lindley H. Orme
1896 – " " "
1897 – " " "
1898 – " " "
1899 – David L. Murphy
1900 – " " "
1901 – Samuel S. Stout
1902 – " " "
1903 – William W. (Billy) Cook
1904 – " " " "
[2] 1905 – John Elliott Walker
1906 – " " "
1907 – Carl F. Hayden
1908 – " " "
1909 – " " "
1910 – " " "
1911 – " " "
[3] 1912 – " " "

1. Hancock appointed 21 February 1871, but resigned; Barnum appointed to fill out the term, but also resigned; Worden served out the term.
2. Walker committed suicide, 19 December 1906; although uncertain, William W. Cunningham may have filled out the last few days of the term.
3. Hayden turned over his office in February 1912 to become United States congressman.

Mohave County (1864, Mohave City: 1864, Hardyville; 1873, Cerbat; 1877, Mineral Park; 1887, Kingman)

[1] 1864 – Milton G. Moore
[2] 1865 – " " "
    – Thomas J. Mathews
1866 – " " "
[3] 1867 – Milton G. Moore
[4] 1868 – Edward H. Smith
1869 – " " "
    – A. P. Prather

[5] 1870 – " " "
    – Thomas Wicks
[6] 1871 – Paul Breon
1872 – L. C. Welbourn
1873 – Edward L. Smith
1874 – " " "
1875 – A. Comstock
1876 – " "

1877– " "	1896– " " "
1878– " "	1897– " " "
1879– " "	1898– " " "
1880– " "	1899–Harvey Hubbs
1881–John C. Potts	1900– " "
1882– " " "	1900–Henry Lovin
1883–Robert Stein (Steen)	1901– " "
1884– " "	1902– " "
1885– " "	1903– " "
1886– " "	1904– " "
1887– " "	1905–Walter Brown
1888– " "	1906– " "
1889–William H. Lake	1907– " "
1890– " " "	1908– " "
1891– " " "	1909– " "
1892– " " "	1910– " "
1893–James Rosborough	1911– " "
1894– " "	1912– " "
1895–John C. Potts	

1. Moore appointed 15 December 1864, to take office 1 January 1865.

2. Mathews appointed in December 1865, to take office 1 January 1866; he was then elected in June 1866(?)

3. Moore's term in 1867 is unexplained; Mohave County sheriff held over from 1 July through 1 December 1867; new law provided for elections in November 1867, with term to begin 1 December 1867.

4. Smith was appointed 6 January 1868 and elected in June 1868, but departed the territory in February 1869; Prather may have been appointed to fill out the unexpired term; Prather was then elected 2 June 1869.

5. Wicks was appointed 10 June 1870.

6. Breon elected in November 1870, to take office 1 December 1870.

Navajo County (1895, Holbrook)

[1]1895–Commodore Perry Owens	1905– " " "
1896– " " "	1906– " " "
1897–Frank J. Wattron	1907–Joseph F. Woods
1898– " " "	1908– " " "
1899– " " "	1909– " " "
1900– " " "	1910– " " "
1901–F. P. Secrist	1911– " " "
1902– " " "	1912– " " "
1903–Chester I. Houck	1913– " " "
1904– " " "	1914– " " "

1. Appointed 25 March 1895; Owens was former sheriff of Apache County.

Pima County (1864, Tucson)

[1]1864–Hill Barry DeArmitt	1867–Peter Rainsford Brady, Sr.
1865– " " "	1868– " " " "
1866– " " "	1869– " " " "

1870– "   "   "   "   1890– "   "   "
1871–Charles Hyler Ott   1891–J. R. Brown
1872– "   "   "   1892–" "   "
1873–William Sanders Oury   1893–Joseph B. Scott
1874– "   "   "   1894– "   "   "
1875– "   "   "   1895–Robert N. Leatherwood
1876– "   "   "   1896– "   "   "
1877–Charles A. Shibell   1897– "   "   "
1878– "   "   "   1898– "   "   "
1879– "   "   "   1899–Lyman W. Wakefield
1880– "   "   "   1900– "   "   "
²1881– "   "   "   1901–Frank E. Murphy
   –Robert A. Paul   1902– "   "   "
1882– "   "   "   1903– "   "   "
1883– "   "   "   1904– "   "   "
³1884– "   "   "   1905–Nabor Pacheco
1885– "   "   "   1906– "   "
1886– "   "   "   1907– "   "
   –Eugene O. Shaw   1908– "   "
⁴1887– "   "   "   ⁵1909–John Nelson
1887–Matthew Fasion Shaw   1910– "   "
1888– "   "   "   1911– "   "
1889– "   "   "   1912– "   "

1. Appointed sheriff of First Judicial District, 9 April 1864; appointed sheriff of Pima County, 15 December 1864; and, presumably, elected September 1865.

2. Certificate of election awarded to Shibell in November 1880 election; Paul contested; court awarded Paul shrievalty; he took possession of office, 25 April 1881; Paul reelected November 1882.

3. Certificate of election awarded to Paul in November 1884 election; Eugene O. Shaw contested successfully; court awarded Shaw the office in July 1886; Shaw was reelected in November 1886.

4. Eugene O. Shaw resigned 6 September 1887 because of ill health; the county board accepted the resignation on 7 September and appointed Matthew Fasion Shaw (brother of Eugene) on 8 October 1887; Shaw was elected in November 1888.

5. Nelson was reelected in November 1911.

Pinal County (1875, Florence)

¹1875–Michael Rogers   1887–Jere Fryer
1876– "   "   1888– "   "
1877–Peter Rainsford Brady, Sr.   1889– "   "
1878– "   "   "   "   1890– "   "
1879–John Peter Gabriel   ²1891–William C. Truman
1880– "   "   "   –William Barry(?)
1881– "   "   "   1892– "   "
1882– "   "   "   ³1893–L. K. Drais
1883–Andrew James Doran   1893–William C. Truman
1884– "   "   "   1894– "   "   "
1885–John Peter Gabriel   1895– "   "   "
1886– "   "   "   1896– "   "   "

1897– " " "	1905– " " "
1898– " " "	1906– " " "
1899– " " "	1907–James E. McGee
1900– " " "	1908– " " "
1901– " " "	1909– " " "
1902– " " "	1910– " " "
1903–Thomas N. Wills	1911– " " "
1904– " " "	1912– " " "

1. Rogers appointed 9 February 1875.
2. Uncertain as to William Barry.
3. L. K. Drais also called Samuel K. Drais; he possibly contested the November 1892 elections; Truman reportedly served five consecutive terms.

Santa Cruz County (1899, Nogales)

[1] 1899–W. A. Barnett	1906– " " "
1900–Thomas F. Broderick	1907–Harry J. Saxon
1901–Thomas J. Turner	1908– " " "
1902– " " "	1909– " " "
1903– " " "	1910– " " "
1904– " " "	1911– " " "
1905–Charles L. Fowler	1912– " " "

1. Appointed.

Yavapai County (1864, Prescott)

[1] 1864–Van Ness C. Smith	1882– " " "
–Jerome B. Calkins	1883–Jacob Henkle
[2] 1865– " " "	1884– " "
–John P. Bourke	1885–William J. Mulvenon
1866– " " "	1886– " " "
[3] 1867– " " "	1887– " " "
–Andrew J. Moore	1888– " " "
1868– " " "	1889–William (Buckey) O'Neill
[4] 1869– " " "	1890– " " "
–John Langford Taylor	1891–James R. Lowry
1870– " " "	1892– " " "
1871–John H. Behan	1893– " " "
1872– " " "	1894– " " "
[5] 1873–James S. Thomas	1895–George C. Ruffner
1874– " " "	1896– " " "
–Henry M. Herbert	1897– " " "
1875–Edward Franklin Bowers	1898– " " "
1876– " " "	1899–John L. Munds
1877– " " "	1900– " " "
1878– " " "	1901– " " "
[6] 1879–Joseph Rutherford Walker	1902– " " "
1880– " " "	1903–Joseph I. Roberts
1881– " " "	1904– " " "

1905 – James R. Lowry	1909 – James W. Smith
1906 – " " "	1910 – " " "
1907 – " " "	1911 – " " "
1908 – " " "	1912 – " " "

1. Smith appointed 15 June 1864.

2. Calkins appointed 21 December 1864.

3. Bourke elected September 1865, entered office 1 December 1865, and was apparently elected; he remained in office until 1 December 1867.

4. Moore was elected 5 June 1867 and took office 1 December 1867; Yavapai County did not hold elections in June 1868; Moore continued in office; Moore resigned 21 April 1869; Taylor completed the term.

5. Thomas absconded in January 1874; Herbert served out the term.

6. Walker was nephew of Joseph Reddeford Walker.

Yuma County (1864, La Paz; 1871, Arizona City (Yuma))

[1]1864 – Isaac C. Bradshaw	1883 – " "
– William C. Werninger	1884 – " "
– Cornelius Sage	1885 – " "
[2]1865 – " "	1886 – " "
– Alexander McKey	1887 – Michael J. Nugent
[3]1866 – " "	1888 – " " "
– William T. Flower	1889 – " " "
– Marcus D. Dobbins	1890 – " " "
[4]1867 – " " "	1891 – " " "
– David King	1892 – " " "
[5]1868 – " "	1893 – Mel Greenleaf
1868 – James T. Dana	1894 – " "
1870 – " " "	1895 – " "
1871 – " " "	1896 – " "
– Oscar Frank Townsend	1897 – " "
[6]1872 – " " "	1898 – " "
– George Tyng	1899 – John M. Spees
1873 – " "	1900 – " " "
– Francis Henri Goodwin	1901 – Gus M. Livingston
1874 – " " "	1902 – " "
1875 – William A. Werninger	1903 – " "
1876 – " " "	1904 – " "
1877 – " " "	1905 – " "
1878 – " " "	1906 – " "
1878 – F. M. Hodges	1907 – " "
1879 – " " "	1908 – " "
1880 – " " "	1909 – " "
1881 – " " "	1910 – " "
– Andrew Tyner	1911 – " "
1882 – " "	1912 – " "

1. Bradshaw appointed sheriff of Second Judicial District on 1 June 1864 and resigned 10 September 1864; Werninger appointed sheriff of Yuma County on 26 September 1864

and departed office 9 November 1864; Sage appointed 21 December 1864, to take effect 1 January 1865, but resigned(?) in May 1865.

2. McKey appointed 22 May 1865.

3. Flower elected by county board 16 March 1866; Flower resigned 10 December 1866; Dobbins appointed; King elected in June 1867.

4. King resigned 6 January 1869 and Dana appointed.

5. Dobbins's term is unclear, but may have been from January to June 1868. Dana elected 3 June 1868; killed in line of duty, 20 September 1871; Townsend served out the term.

6. Tyng elected 6 November 1872, but resigned 12 April 1873 to become United States marshal of Arizona; Goodwin filled out the term and was defeated in the shrievalty race in November 1874.

NEW MEXICO TERRITORY

Bernalillo County (1846, Albuquerque)

[1] 1846—Juan Antonio Aragon
1847— "   "   "
1848— "   "   "
1849— "   "   "
1850— "   "   "
[2] 1851— "   "   "
    —Ignacio Gallegos
    —Fernando Aragon
1852—   "   "
1853—   "   "
    —Ignacio Gallegos
1854—   "   "
1855—   "   "
[3] 1856—   "   "
    —Blas Lucero
1857— "   "
1858— "   "
[4] 1859— "   "
    —Andres Analla
    —Blas Lucero
1860— "   "
1861— "   "
    —Lorenzo Montano
1862—   "   "
1863—   "   "
1863—Melquiades Chavez
1864—   "   "
1865—   "   "
1866—   "   "

[5] 1867—   "   "
    —Martin Quintana
    —Manuel Garcia
1868— "   "
1869— "   "
    —Atonacio Montoya
1870—   "   "
1871—   "   "
    —Manuel Garcia
1872— "   "
1873— "   "
    —Juan E. Barela
1874— "   "   "
1875— "   "   "
    —Atonacio Montoya
1876—   "   "
1877—Manuel Sanchez y Valencia
1878—   "   "   "   "
    —Perfecto Armijo
1879— "   "
1880— "   "
1881— "   "
1882— "   "
1883— "   "
1884— "   "
    —Santiago Baca
1885— "   "
[6] 1886— "   "
    —Jose Leandro Perea

1887–Charles W. Kennedy	1900–	" " "
1888– " " "	1901–	" " "
1889–Jose Leandro Perea	1902–	" " "
1890– " " "	1903–	" " "
1891– " " "	1904–	" " "
1892– " " "	[8]1905–	" " "
1893–Jacobo Yrissari	–Perfecto Armijo	
1894– " "	1906–	" "
[7]1895–Charles F. Hunt	1907–	" "
–Thomas S. Hubbell	1908–	" "
1896– " " "	1909–Jesus M. Romero	
1897– " " "	1910–	" " "
1898– " " "	1911–	" " "
1899– " " "	1912–	" " "

1. Aragon mentioned in office, 20 July 1847, 12 June 1849, 11 December 1850, and 28 January 1851.

2. Gallegos commissioned 27 April 1851, and apparently served until elections in September.

3. Lucero apparently filled out Gallegos's term; Lucero's bond is dated 29 February 1856; Lucero was elected for a full term 7 September 1857.

4. Analla elected 5 September 1859, but Lucero evidently successfully contested; Lucero is mentioned in office in 1860 and 1861.

5. Special election for sheriff held, 22 February 1867, and Quintana elected; his commission is dated 2 March 1867; he apparently served until regular election in September.

6. Perea's commission is dated 10 December 1886; the reason for such a short term is unclear.

7. Hunt resigned in July 1895; Hubbell filled out the term.

8. Governor Miguel A. Otero removed Hubbell on 31 August 1905 and appointed Armijo to fill out the term.

Chaves County (1891, Roswell)

[1]1891–Campbell C. Fountain	1902–	" "
1892– " " "	1903–	" "
1893–William Marshall Atkinson	1905–	" "
1894– " " "	1905–K. S. Woodruff	
[2]1895–Charles C. Perry	1906– " " "	
1896– " " "	1907–Charles L. Ballard	
–Charles W. Haynes	1908–	" " "
1897– " " "	1909–	" " "
1898– " " "	1910–	" " "
1899–Fred Higgins	1911–	" " "
1900– " "	1912–	" " "
1901– " "		

1. First sheriff, entered office 1 January 1891.

2. Perry absconded; office declared vacant 23 July 1896; Haynes appointed to fill out term.

Colfax County (1869, Elizabethtown; 1872, Cimarron; 1882, Springer)

[1] 1869–Andrew J. Calhoun
1870– "   "   "
1871– "   "   "
   –Orson K. Chittenden
1872– "   "   "
1873– "   "   "
   –John C. Turner
1874– "   "   "
[2] 1875– "   "   "
   –Orson K. Chittenden
1876– "   "   "
   –Isaiah Rinehart
1877–Peter Burleson
1878– "   "
1879– "   "
1880– "   "
1881–Allen C. Wallace
1882– "   "   "
[3] 1883–Mason Timothy Bowman
   –Matthias B. Stockton
1884– "   "   "
[4] 1885–John Thomas Hixenbaugh
   –William J. Parker
1886– "   "   "
[5] 1887–Abraham P. Sever
1888– "   "   "

1889– "   "   "
1890– "   "   "
1891–Matthias B. Stockton
1892– "   "   "
1893–Oscar W. McCuiston
1894– "   "   "
1895–S. Marion Littrell
1896–"   "   "
1897–"   "   "
1898–"   "   "
1899–Robert S. Campbell
1900– "   "   "
1901–S. Marion Littrell
1902–"   "   "
1903–"   "   "
1904–"   "   "
1905–"   "   "
1906–"   "   "
[6] 1907–"   "   "
   –Jay C. Gale
1908–"   "   "
1909–Abraham Hixenbaugh
1910–   "   "
1911–   "   "
1912–   "   "

1. Calhoun elected March 1869 and bond filed 20 May 1870.
2. Chittenden elected September 1875; Governor Samuel Axtell removed him 21 February 1876 and appointed Rinehart; Rinehart's oath dated 8 March 1876.
3. Bowman elected November 1882 but died from natural causes, 6 June 1883; Stockton appointed to fill out the term.
4. John T. Hixenbaugh wounded and permanently disabled in line of duty; he resigned 17 April 1885; Parker appointed to fill out the term.
5. Election commissioners counted into office Charles F. Hunt, a Republican, on the first count, but declared Sever the winner on a second count.
6. Littrell resigned February 1907 to become superintendent of the territorial penitentiary (appointment dated 28 June 1907); Gale, brother-in-law of Littrell, appointed to fill out term as sheriff.

Curry County (1909, Clovis)

[1] 1909–C. H. Hannum
   –W. W. Odum
1910–"   "   "

1911–C. H. Hannum
1912–"   "   "

1. Hannum appointed 10 March 1909; Odum appointed September 1909.

Doña Ana County (1852, Doña Ana; 1853, Las Cruces; 1856, Mesilla; 1882, Las Cruces)

[1] 1852–John Jones
1853– "   "
1854– "   "
  –Thomas Chunton
  –Samuel G. Bean
1855– "   "   "
  –Benjamin H. Read
  –Jesus Lucero
1856–Samuel G. Bean
1857– "   "   "
1858– "   "   "
[2] 1859– "   "   "
  –Marcial Padilla
1860– "   "
[3] 1861– "   "
  –John A. Roberts
1862– "   "   "
[4] 1863–Frederick Burkner (Beckner)
  –Apolonio Barela
1864– "   "
[5] 1865– "   "
  –Reyes Escontraras
  –Mariano Barela
1866– "   "
1867– "   "
1868– "   "
1869– "   "
  –Fabian Gonzales
1870– "   "
[6] 1871– "   "
  –Mariano Barela
1872– "   "
1873– "   "
1874– "   "
1875– "   "
1876– "   "
1877– "   "
1878– "   "

1879–Henry J. Cuniffe
1880– "   "   "
[7] 1881–James W. Southwick
  –Thomas J. Bull
1882– "   "   "
1883–Guadalupe Ascarate
1884– "   "
1885–Eugene Van Patten
1886– "   "   "
1887–Santiago P. Ascarate
1888– "   "   "
1889–Mariano Barela
1890– "   "
1891– "   "
[8] 1892– "   "
  –Martin Lohman
1893– "   "
1894– "   "
1895–Guadalupe Ascarate
[9] 1896– "   "
  –Numa Edward Reymond
  –Patrick Floyd Garrett
1897– "   "   "
1898– "   "   "
1899– "   "   "
1900– "   "   "
1901–Jose R. Lucero
1902– "   "   "
1903– "   "   "
1904– "   "   "
1905– "   "   "
1906– "   "   "
1907– "   "   "
1908– "   "   "
[10] 1909–Felipe Lucero
1910– "   "
1911– "   "
1912– "   "

1. John Jones reportedly the first sheriff of Doña Ana County; first election for sheriff scheduled for 25 July 1852; however, Jones is also reported to have been appointed 20 September 1853 and removed 4 May 1854; Chunton made acting sheriff; Richard Campbell listed as tax collector on 17 December 1853; Bean was elected 4 September 1854, with commission issued on 23 September. He submitted tax revenues to the territorial auditor as collector for the period, 8 March–15 July 1855. Bean appears to have challenged the election of Jesus Romero in September 1856 and probably won the case; one source says Bean served three terms.

2. Padilla elected 5 September 1859; a commission (or appointment) for him is dated 27 February 1861; some confusion exists about the sheriff of Doña Ana County in this period, since one source lists Alfredo H. Garcia for 1859–62; a rival sheriff, J. Peter Deus, was selected by the separatist Arizona Territory, on 5 September 1859; Padilla was possibly elected in May 1860 in elections of the extralegal territory of "Arizona" and took office in August; Samuel Bean departed the shrievalty at that time and became marshal of the "territory."

3. Confederate Colonel John R. Baylor appointed Roberts on 11 May 1861; Roberts's tenure evidently ended with the retreat of the Rebel forces in spring 1862.

4. Acting Governor W. F. M. Arny reorganized Doña Ana County on 26 March 1863; he appointed Burkner on that day; Apolonio Barela was elected at first general election, 7 September 1863, and commissioned 15 October; he was under investigation on unspecified charges, 20 April 1864.

5. Commission issued to Contreras on 13 January 1865; Mariano Barela elected(?) in September 1865 and commission issued 21 September 1865; reelected September 1867.

6. Gonzales departed the county after the Mesilla Riots, which occurred on 27 August 1871; Mariano Barela possibly filled out the term. Barela was elected sheriff in a special(?) election, in November 1871.

7. Election commission evidently counted Southwick into shrievalty after November 1879 elections; Southwick served as acting sheriff January-April 1880, which Thomas J. Bull contested; Bull won and served out the term.

8. Barela died 26 September 1892; Lohman appointed 30 September 1892; Lohman won election in November 1892; Guadalupe Ascarate unsuccessfully contested.

9. November 1894 election contested; Guadalupe Ascarate served as acting sheriff until March 1896; Reymond declared winner and qualified 21 March 1896, but resigned; Governor William T. Thornton appointed Patrick Garrett in August 1896; Garrett was elected November 1896 and November 1898.

10. Felipe Lucero was brother of Jose R. Lucero.

Eddy County (1891, Carlsbad)

[1] 1891–David L. Kemp	1901– " " "
1892– " " "	1902– " " "
1893– " " "	1903– " " "
1894– " " "	1904– " " "
1895–John D. Walker	1905– " " "
1896– " " "	1906– " " "
1897–James Leslie Dow	1907–James D. Cristopher
–Miles Cicero Stewart	1908– " " "
1898– " " "	1909–Miles Cicero Stewart
1899– " " "	1910– " " "
1899– " " "	1911– " " "
1900– " " "	1912– " " "

1. Former Sheriff David L. Kemp shot Dow on 18 February 1897; Dow died next day; Stewart was appointed to fill out the term.

Grant County (1868, Central City; 1869, Pinos Altos; 1874, Silver City)

[1] 1868–Richard Hudson	1870– " " "
[2] 1869– " "	1871– " " "
–James G. Crittenden	1872– " " "

[3]1873–   ″   ″   ″
    –Charles McIntosh
1874–   ″   ″
1875–   ″   ″
    –Harvey Howard Whitehill
1876–   ″   ″   ″
1877–   ″   ″   ″
1878–   ″   ″   ″
1879–   ″   ″   ″
1880–   ″   ″   ″
1881–   ″   ″   ″
1882–   ″   ″   ″
1883–James B. Woods
1884–   ″   ″   ″
1885–   ″   ″   ″
1886–   ″   ″   ″
1887–Andrew B. Laird
1888–   ″   ″   ″
1889–Harvey Howard Whitehill
1890–   ″   ″   ″
1891–James A. Lockhart

1892–   ″   ″   ″
1893–Andrew B. Laird
1894–   ″   ″   ″
1895–Baylor Shannon
1896–   ″   ″
1897–William G. McAfee
1898–   ″   ″   ″
1899–James K. Blair
1900–   ″   ″   ″
1901–Arthur S. Goodell
1902–   ″   ″   ″
1903–James K. Blair
1904–   ″   ″   ″
1905–Charles A. Farnesworth
1906–   ″   ″   ″
1907–Charles D. Nelson
1908–   ″   ″   ″
1909–Herbert J. McGrath
1910–   ″   ″   ″
1911–   ″   ″   ″
1912–   ″   ″   ″

1. Hudson elected 28 April 1868.
2. Crittenden elected September 1869 and reelected September 1871.
3. McIntosh absconded April 1875; Whitehill appointed to fill out the term.

Leonard Wood County [Guadalupe] (1903, Santa Rosa)

[1]1903–Leandro Casaus
1904–   ″   ″
1905–Felipe Sanchez y Baca
1906–   ″   ″   ″   ″
1907–Martin Serrano

1908–   ″   ″
1909–Jesus Maria Casaus
1910–   ″   ″   ″
1911–   ″   ″   ″
1912–   ″   ″   ″

1. Guadalupe County created in 1891 with Carlos Casaus as sheriff; evidently the county government did not function; name changed to Leonard Wood County in 1903 and back to Guadalupe in 1905; Leandro Casaus elected first effective sheriff in November 1902 and commissioned 25 April 1903.

Lincoln County (1869, Lincoln)

[1]1869–Jesus Sandoval y Sena
    –Mauricio Sanchez
    –William Brady
1870–   ″   ″
1871–   ″   ″
    –Lewis G. (Jack) Gylam
1872–   ″   ″   ″   ″
[2]1873–   ″   ″   ″   ″
    –Alexander Hamilton Mills

1874–   ″   ″   ″
1875–   ″   ″   ″
    –Florencio Gonzales
    –Saturnino Baca
1876–   ″   ″
1877–William Brady
[3]1878–   ″   ″
    –John N. Copeland
    –George Warden Peppin

[4] 1879–George Kimbrell
1880–   "   "
1881–Patrick Floyd Garrett
1882–   "   "   "
1883–John W. Poe
1884–   "   "   "
1885–   "   "   "
[5] 1886–   "   "   "
    –James R. Brent
1887–   "   "   "
1888–   "   "   "
1889–Dan C. Nowlin
1890–   "   "   "
1891–Dan W. Roberts
1892–   "   "   "
1893–George Curry
1894–   "   "
1895–George Sena
[6] 1896–   "   "

    –Emil Fritz [II?]
1897–   "   "
1898–   "   "
1899–Demetrio Perea
1900–   "   "
1901–Alfredo Gonzales
1902–   "   "
[7] 1903–John W. "Jake" Owen
    –Robert D. Armstrong
1904–   "   "   "
1905–John W. "Jake" Owen
1906–   "   "   "   "
1907–   "   "   "   "
1908–   "   "   "   "
1909–Charles A. Stevens
1910–   "   "   "
1911–   "   "   "
[8] 1912–Porfirio Chavez

1. Jesus Sandoval y Sena appointed (or elected?) 19 April 1869, but resigned in May 1869; Mauricio Sanchez appointed (or elected?) in May 1869; Brady elected at regular elections on 6 September 1869, to serve two-year term.

2. Mills elected in September 1873, but apparently resigned or was removed and indicted for murder in April 1875; Florencio Gonzales appointed 12 May 1875 to fill out the term; Baca elected 6 September, certificate of election issued 25 September and bond filed 16 October 1875; Baca's term was shortened by the election law which provided that general elections should occur in November 1876 and future sheriffs should enter office on 1 January.

3. Brady elected November 1876 to take office 1 January 1877; he was assassinated 1 April 1878; Copeland was appointed 8 April 1878 and removed 28 May 1878; Peppin appointed 30 May 1878 and served out the term.

4. Kimbrell elected November 1878.

5. Poe resigned January 1886; Brent appointed to serve out term.

6. Sena was removed March 1896; Fritz appointed to fill out term; Emil Fritz was the son of Charles Fritz, who was a brother of Emil Fritz I; the latter's insurance policy helped to set off the Lincoln County War.

7. Owen elected 4 November 1902, but Armstrong successfully contested and entered office in August 1903.

8. Chavez was elected 7 November 1911.

Luna County (1901, Deming)

[1] 1901–Cipriano Baca
1902–   "   "
1903–William H. Foster
1904–   "   "   "
1905–Dwight B. Stephens
1906–   "   "   "

1907–Don Johnson
1908–   "   "
[2] 1909–Dwight B. Stephens
1910–   "   "   "
1911–   "   "   "
1912–   "   "   "

1. Appointed 1 April 1901; Arthur S. Goodell possibly served as a temporary sheriff prior to Baca.

2. Some confusion exists about Stephens. One report says he was killed by outlaws 17

November 1911, but another says he was murdered in office in 1916 by Jesse O. Starr; Starr was sentenced to hang on 21 April 1916.

McKinley County (1899, Gallup)

1901 – William A. Smith	1907 – " " " "
1902 – " " "	1908 – " " " "
1903 – " " "	1909 – Tom P. Talle
1904 – " " "	1910 – " " "
1905 – J. H. (Harry) Coddington	1911 – " " "
1906 – " " " "	1912 – " " "

Mora County (1859, Mora)

[1] 1860 – William A. Bransford	1883 – " "
[2] 1861 – " " "	1884 – " "
– William Gandert	1885 – John Doherty
1862 – " "	1886 – " "
1863 – " "	1887 – Macario Gallegos
– Trinidad Lopez	1888 – " "
1864 – " "	1889 – Juan Navarro (Navarre)
1865 – " "	1890 – " " "
– Marcelino Rebera	1891 – Agapito Abeytia [Jr.?]
1866 – " "	1892 – " " "
1867 – " "	1893 – " " "
– Dolores Romero	[3] 1894 – " " "
1868 – " "	– Vicente Mares
1869 – " "	1895 – J. R. Aguilar
– Fernando Nolan	1896 – " " "
1870 – " "	1897 – Eusebio Chavez
1871 – " "	1898 – " "
– Dolores Romero	1899 – Rafael Romero y Lopez
1872 – " "	1900 – " " " "
1873 – " "	1901 – Teodoro Roybal
– Henry Robison	1902 – " "
1874 – " "	1903 – Tito Melendez
1875 – " "	1904 – " "
– Pablo Valdez	1905 – J. Demetrio Medina
1876 – " "	1906 – " " " "
1877 – Henry Robison	1907 – Juan B. Martinez
1878 – " "	1908 – " " "
1879 – Alejandro Branch	1909 – Andres Gandert
1880 – " "	1910 – " "
1881 – Henry Robison	1911 – " "
1882 – " "	[4] 1912 – Patricio Sanchez

1. Commissioned 13 March 1860.
2. Gandert elected 5 September 1861.
3. Abeytia removed 17 March 1894 and Mares appointed 21 March; J. R. Aguilar reportedly served part of 1894, but oath is dated 3 January 1895.
4. Sanchez elected 7 November 1911.

Otero County (1899—Alamogordo)

[1] 1899—George Curry
    —W. Riley Baker
1900— "   "   "
[2] 1901—James F. Hunter
1902— "   "   "
1903— "   "   "
1904— "   "   "
1905—A. B. Phillips

1906— "   "   "
1907—Henry M. Denney
1908— "   "   "
1909— "   "   "
1910— "   "   "
1911— "   "   "
1912— "   "   "

1. Appointed 28 March 1899 and resigned August 1899; Baker appointed in the same month; Baker's name also given as Riley H. Baker.
2. Hunter was first elected sheriff and took office 7 January 1901; Hunter was a brother-in-law of James Gilliland.

Quay County (1903, Tucumcari)

[1] 1903—James Alexander Street
1904— "   "   "
1905— "   "   "
1906— "   "   "
1907— "   "   "

1908— "   "   "
1909—J. F. Ward
1910— "   "   "
1911— "   "   "
1912— "   "   "

1. Appointed 31 March 1903.

Rio Arriba County (1846, Chamita; 1855, Los Luceros; 1860, Plaza Alcalde; 1880, Tierra Amarilla)

[1] 1846—Salvador Lopez
1847— "   "
1848— "   " (?)
1849— "   " (?)
1850—Juan [Simon?]
[2] 1851—Pedro Salazar
[3] 1852—Lafayette Head
1853— "   "
    —Pedro A. Garcia
1854— "   "   "
1855— "   "   "
    —Francisco Antonio Mestas
1856— "   "   "
1857— "   "   "
    —Francisco Martinez y Velarde
1858— "   "   "   "
1859— "   "   "   "
    —Juan Bautista Lopez
1860— "   "   "
1861— "   "   "
1862— "   "   "
1863— "   "   "

1864— "   "   "
1865— "   "   "
    —Saracino de Herrera
1866— "   "   "
1867— "   "   "
    —Luciano de Herrera
1868— "   "   "
1869— "   "   "
1870— "   "   "
1871— "   "   "
1872— "   "   "
1873— "   "   "
    —Juan B. Lopez
1874— "   "   "
1875— "   "   "
    —Jose Nemecio Lucero
1876— "   "   "
1877— "   "   "
1878— "   "   "
1879—Vicenti Archuleta
1880— "   "
1881—Jose Nemecio Lucero

1882– "   "   "   1898– "   "
1883– "   "   "   1899–Amado Ortiz
1884– "   "   "   1900– "   "
1885–Perfecto Esquibel   1901–Alexander Read
1886–   "   "   1902–   "   "
1887–Luis M. Ortiz   1903–   "   "
1888– "   "   "   1904–   "   "
1889–Perfecto Esquibel   1905–B. C. Hernandez
1890–   "   "   1906– " "   "
⁴1891–William F. Burns   1907–Narcisco Sanchez
1892–   "   "   "   1908–   "   "
1893–Francisco C. Chavez   1909–Silviano Roybal
1894–   "   "   "   1910–   "   "
1895–Felix Garcia   1911–   "   "
1896–   "   "   1912–   "   "
1897–Perfecto Esquibel

1. Lopez performing official duties in January and June 1847; Simon listed as sheriff in 1850 census.

2. Pedro Salazar elected September and commissioned 2 October 1851.

3. Head commissioned 20 February 1852; possibly contested election.

4. William F. Burns died in office 13 December 1891; his brother, John F. Burns, was appointed in January 1892 to fill out the term.

Roosevelt County (1903, Portales)

¹1903–William W. Odom   1908–   "   "
1904–   "   "   "   1909–R. A. Bain
1905–Joseph Lang   1910– " "   "
1906–   "   "   1911– " "   "
1907–   "   "   1912– " "   "

1. Odom appointed 31 March 1903.

Sandoval County (1903, Sandoval)

¹1903–Alfredo M. Sandoval   1908– " "   "
    –F. J. Otero   1909–Candido G. Gonzales
1904– " "   "   1910–   "   "   "
1905–Emiliano Sandoval   1911–   "   "   "
1906–   "   "   1912–   "   "   "
1907–C. M. Sandoval

1. County commissioners appointed Alfredo M. Sandoval about 30 March 1903, but the governor removed him through court action in April 1903 and appointed F. J. Otero.

San Juan County (1887, Aztec)

¹1887–Dan Sullivan   1891–   "   "   "
1888–   "   "   1892–   "   "   "
²1889–John C. Carson   1893–A. E. Dustin
1890–   "   "   "   1894– " "   "

1895 – A. H. Dunning
1896 – " "
1897 – John W. Brown
1898 – " " "
1899 – J. C. Dodson
1900 – " " "
1901 – John W. Brown
1902 – " " "
1903 – J. E. Elmer

1904 – " " "
1905 – Boone C. Vaughan
1906 – " " "
1907 – " " "
1908 – " " "
1909 – William T. (Al) Dufur
1910 – " " " "
1911 – " " " "
1912 – " " " "

1. Sullivan appointed 25 February 1887.
2. Carson was the son of Christopher (Kit) Carson, the famous scout.

San Miguel County (1846, San Miguel; 1864, Las Vegas)

[1] 1846 – Santiago Trujillo
1847 – " "
1848 – " "
1849 – " "
1850 – A. T. Donaldson
[2] 1851 – " " "
    – Jesus Lucero
    – Jose Guadalupe Gallegos
1852 – " " "
1853 – " " "
    – Antonio Baca y Baca
[3] 1854 – " " " "
    – Prudencio Lopez
1855 – " "
1856 – " "
1857 – " "
1858 – " "
1859 – " "
    – Jose Guadalupe Romero
[4] 1860 – " " "
    – Antonio Gallegos y Baca
    – Jose Sena
[5] 1861 – Antonio Abad Herrera
    – Juan Bernal
[6] 1862 – " "
    – Benigno Ulibarri
1863 – " "
    – Desiderio Romero
[7] 1864 – " "
    – Juan Romero
    – Redusindo Chaves
[8] 1865 – Pascual Baca
[9] 1866 – " "
    – Victorino Baca

1867 – " "
    – Juan Romero
1868 – " "
1869 – " "
1870 – " "
1871 – " "
    – Leon Pinard
1872 – " "
1873 – " "
    – Lorenzo Labadie
1874 – " "
1875 – " "
    – Benigno Jaramillo
1876 – " "
1877 – " "
1878 – " "
1879 – Desiderio Romero
1880 – " "
1881 – Hilario Romero
1882 – " "
1883 – Jose Santos Esquivel
1884 – " " "
1885 – Hilario Romero
1886 – " "
1887 – Eugenio Romero
1888 – " "
1889 – Lorenzo Lopez
1890 – " "
1891 – Jose L. Lopez
1892 – " " "
[10] 1893 – Eugenio Romero
    – Lorenzo Lopez
1894 – " "
1895 – Hilario Romero

1896–	"	"	1905–	"	"
1897–	"	"	1906–	"	"
1898–	"	"	1907–	"	"
1899–Cleofes Romero			1908–	"	"
1900–	"	"	1909–	"	"
1901–	"	"	[11]1910–	"	"
1902–	"	"	–Secundino Romero		
1903–	"	"	1911–	"	"
1904–	"	"	1912–	"	"

1. Evidence for Santiago Trujillo's tenure is inconclusive; court records reveal him serving the October 1848 term of district court. Donaldson is listed as sheriff in the 1850 census.

2. Lucero appointed 9 May 1851; Gallegos was elected September 1851.

3. Antonio Baca y Baca elected 5 September 1853, but resigned; Prudencio Lopez appointed 20 March 1854 to fill out the term; Lopez departed office for unknown reason and Romero was appointed 26 February 1859; Romero then elected 5 September 1859.

4. Evidence for term of Antonio Gallegos y Baca is unclear; Jose Sena was appointed 4 December 1860; Antonio Abad Herrera reported in office April 1861.

5. Bernal elected 5 September 1861.

6. Ulibarri commissioned 11 September 1862.

7. Juan Romero commissioned 15 September 1864; Redusindo Chaves commissioned 25 November 1864, possibly after contested election.

8. Pascual Baca commissioned 25 September 1865.

9. Victorino Baca commissioned 29 January 1866.

10. Lorenzo Lopez successfully challenged the election of Eugenio Romero and took office April 1893.

11. Cleofes Romero resigned office to become superintendent of the penitentiary in March 1910; Secundino Romero, brother of Cleofes, was appointed to fill out sheriff's term.

Santa Ana County (1846, Santa Ana; later Pena Blanca)

[1]1846–Romualdo Archiveques				–Simon Sandoval		
1847–	"	"		1859–	"	"
1848–	"	"		1859–Manuel Viscarra		
1849–	"	"		1860–	"	"
1850–	"	"		1861–	"	"
[2]1851–	"	"		1862–	"	"
–Manuel Viscarra				1863–	"	"
–Patricio Silva				1864–	"	"
1852–	"	"		1865–	"	"
[3]1853–	"	"		1866–	"	"
1854–	"	"		1867–Antonio Ortiz		
1855–	"	"		1868–	"	"
–Jesus Maria Silva				1869–	"	"
1856–	"	"	"	1870–Juan Antonio Duran		
1857–	"	"	"	1871–	"	"	"
–Meliton Vigil				–Manuel Hurtados y Gallegos		
[4]1858–	"	"		1872–	"	"	"	"

1873– "   "   "   "   ⁵1875– "   "   "   "   "
   –Jesus Maria Silva y Baca   –Juan Antonio Duran
1874– "   "   "   "   "   1876– "   "   "

1. Archiveques's exact term unknown; however, he corresponded with Acting Governor Donaciano Vigil in an official capacity, 1847 and 1848; documents exist for his shrieval activities in 1849; on 26 January 1851, he deposited tax collections, probably for the previous year, 1850.

2. Viscarra appointed 20 March 1851; Patricio Silva elected September 1851.

3. Ambrocio Gonzales was apparently declared the winner in the September 1853 elections; Patricio Silva challenged successfully and was declared the winner 18 October 1853.

4. Meliton Vigil elected 7 September 1857, but left office for unexplained reason; Simon Sandoval appointed 19 March 1858.

5. Juan Antonio Duran elected September 1875; his term ended with merger of Santa Ana with Bernalillo County in 1876.

Santa Fe County (1846, Santa Fe)

¹1846–Francis (Frank) Redman
1847– "   "   "
   –Ennis J. Vaughn
²1848– "   "   "
   –Richard Campbell
³1849– "   "
   –Charles H. Merritt
1850– "   "   "
⁴1851–John G. Jones
   –Nicholas Quintana Rosas
   –Richard M. Stephens
1852– "   "   "
⁵1853– "   "   "
   –Lorenzo Labadie
1854– "   "
   –Jesus Maria Baca y Salazar
1855– "   "   "   "   "
1856– "   "   "   "   "
1857– "   "   "   "   "
   –Jesus Maria Sena y Baca
1857– "   "   "   "   "
1858– "   "   "   "   "
1859– "   "   "   "   "
   –Jesus Maria Baca y Salazar
1860– "   "   "   "   "
1861– "   "   "   "   "
   –Antonio Ortiz y Salazar
⁶1862– "   "   "
   –Juan Moya
1863– "   "
1864– "   "
1865–Jose E. Duran
   –Jose D. Sena

1866– "   "   "
1867– "   "   "
1868– "   "   "
1869– "   "   "
1870– "   "   "
   –Charles (Carlos) M. Conklin
1871– "   "   "   "
1872– "   "   "   "
1873– "   "   "   "
1874– "   "   "   "
1875– "   "   "   "
1876– "   "   "   "
1877–Martin Quintana
1878– "   "
1879–Jose D. Sena
1880– "   "   "
1881–Romulo Martinez
1882– "   "
1883– "   "
1884– "   "
⁷1885– "   "
   –Francisco (Frank) Chavez
1886– "   "   "
1887– "   "   "
1888– "   "   "
1889– "   "   "
1890– "   "   "
⁸1891– "   "   "   "
   –Charles (Carlos) M. Conklin
1892– "   "   "   "
1893– "   "   "   "
   –William P. Cunningham
1894– "   "   "

1895 – " " "	1904 – " " "
1896 – " " "	1905 – Antonio J. Ortiz
[9] 1897 – Harry D. Kinsell	1906 – " " "
1898 – " " "	1907 – Charles C. Closson
1899 – " " "	1908 – " " "
1900 – " " "	1909 – " " "
1901 – Marcelino Garcia	1910 – " " "
1902 – " "	1911 – " " "
1903 – Harry D. Kinsell	1912 – " " "

1. Redman probably the first sheriff; mentioned in office as early as 12 November 1846; Redman's departure from office not explained; Vaughn reported in office as early as March 1847 term of district court and in September 1848 at a coroner's inquest; he resigned 24 March 1849; Vaughn is also reported as sheriff in service to the November 1848 district court in San Miguel County. This may have been temporary duty.

2. Campbell's dates are uncertain since they conflict with the term of Ennis J. Vaughn.

3. Merritt's dates uncertain, but reported in office on 5 August, 1 December 1849, and 5 April 1850; Merritt listed as chief of police of Santa Fe, 15 April–1 July 1849.

4. John G. Jones appointed 8 March 1851, but resigned to become United States marshal (appointed 15 August 1851); Rosas appointed sheriff on 15 August 1851; Stephens elected September 1851.

5. Labadie elected 5 September 1853 and resigned 16 October 1854; Jesus Maria Sena y Salazar appointed on same day.

6. Antonio Ortiz y Salazar elected September 1861, but departed office for unknown reason; Moya elected September 1862 and reelected September 1863; Moya's departure from office and entry of Jose E. Duran unexplained; Jose D. Sena elected 5 September 1865.

7. Romulo Martinez resigned to become United States marshal (appointed 8 June 1885); Francisco Chavez appointed to fill out the term.

8. Francisco Chavez resigned 4 September 1891; Conklin appointed to fill out term; Conklin elected November 1892, but governor removed him 27 June 1893; Cunningham appointed 27 June 1892 to fill out the term and elected November 1894.

9. Kinsell elected November 1896; Cunningham contested unsuccessfully.

Sierra County (1884, Hillsboro)

[1] 1884 – Thomas Murphy	1899 – Max L. Kahler
1885 – " "	1900 – " " "
1886 – " "	1901 – J. D. Chandler(?)
1887 – Alexander M. Story	1902 – " " "
1888 – " " "	1903 – Max L. Kahler
1889 – " " "	1904 – " " "
1890 – " " "	1905 – William C. Kendall
1891 – S. W. Sanders	1906 – " " "
1892 – " " "	1907 – Eduardo Tafoya
1893 – " " "	1908 – " "
1894 – " " "	1909 – William C. Kendall
1895 – Max L. Kahler	1910 – " " "
1896 – " " "	1911 – " " "
1897 – August Reingardt	1912 – " " "
1898 – " "	

1. Murphy appointed 18 April 1884.

Socorro County (1851, Socorro; 1854, Limitar; 1867, Socorro)

[1]1851 – Esquipula Vigil
 – Antonio N. Ruiz
 – Jose Antonio Torres
[2]1852 – " " "
 – Jose Apodaca
1853 – " "
 – Celso Cuellar Medina
1854 – " " "
1855 – " " "
 – Jose Apodaca
1856 – " "
1857 – " "
 – Luis Tafoya
1858 – " "
1859 – " "
1860 – " "
1861 – " "
 – Jose Miguel de Luna
1862 – " " " "
1863 – " " " "
 – Marcos Baca
1864 – " "
1865 – " "
 – J. Alvino Gonzales
1866 –" " "
1867 –" " "
1867 – Andres Montoya
1868 – " "
1869 – " "
1870 – " "
1871 – " "
1872 – " "
1873 – " "
 – Juan Pino
1874 – " "
 – Vivian Baca
1875 – " "
 – Luis Tafoya
1876 – " "

 – Jesus Maria Baca
1877 – " " "
1878 – " " "
1879 – " " "
1880 – " " "
1881 – Andres Montoya
1882 – " "
1883 – Peter (Pedro) A. Simpson
1884 – " " " "
1885 – Charles T. Russell
1886 – " " "
1887 – " " "
1888 – " " "
1889 – Clarence A. Robinson
1890 – " " "
1891 – " " "
1892 – " " "
1893 – Leopoldo Contreras
1894 – " "
1895 – Holm Olaf Bursum
1896 – " " "
1897 – " " "
1898 – " " "
1899 – Charles F. Blackington
1900 – " " "
1901 – " " "
1902 – " " "
1903 – Leandro Baca
1904 – " "
1905 – " "
[3]1906 – " "
 – Misais Baca
1907 – Aniceto C. Abeytia
1908 – " " "
1909 – Geronimo E. Sanchez
1910 – " " "
1911 – " " "
1912 – " " "

1. Esquipula Vigil appointed 21 April 1851, but resigned to enter assembly; Antonio N. Ruiz appointed 28 May 1851 to serve until elections; Jose Antonio Torres elected September 1851, but resigned 1 December 1851.

2. Jose Apodaca appointed 12 January 1852.

3. Governor removed Leandro Baca 6 October 1906 and appointed Misais Baca. Leandro Baca was brother of Cipriano Baca, sheriff of Luna County, 1901–1902. Leandro Baca became first sheriff of Catron County in 1921.

Taos County (1846, Taos)

1846 – Stephen Louis Lee
[1] 1847 –   "   "   "
     – Archibald C. Metcalf
     – James Barry (temporary)
1848 – Julian Jones
     –   "   "
     – Richens S. Wootton
1849 –   "   "   "
     – A. Trigg
1850 – "   "
     – Julian Duran
[2] 1851 –   "   "
     – Julian Ledoux
1852 –   "   "
1853 – Marcelino Vigil
1854 –   "   "
     – Nestor Martinez
     – Ezra N. DePew
1855 –   "   "   "
1856 –   "   "   "
1857 –   "   "   "
     – Gabriel Vigil
1858 –   "   "
1859 –   "   "
     – Henry James
[3] 1860 –   "   "
1860 – Gabriel Lucero
1861 –   "   "
     – Francisco Sanchez
1862 --   "   "
1863 –   "   "
     – Aniceto Valdez
1864 –   "   "
1865 –   "   "
1866 –   "   "
1867 –   "   "
1868 –   "   "
1869 –   "   "
     – Julian Ledoux
1870 –   "   "
1871 –   "   "
     – Jose Quiniel
1872 –   "   "

1873 –   "   "
1874 –   "   "
1875 –   "   "
     – Guillermo Trujillo
1876 –   "   "
     – Gabriel Lucero
1877 –   "   "
1878 –   "   "
1879 – Santiago J. Valdez
1880 –   "   "   "
1881 – Leandro Martinez
1882 –   "   "
1883 – Guillermo Trujillo
1884 –   "   "
1885 – Bonifacio Barron
1886 –   "   "
1887 – Lorenzo Lovato
1888 –   "   "
1889 – Guillermo Trujillo
1890 –   "   "
1891 – Caesario Garcia
1892 –   "   "
1893 –   "   "
1894 –   "   "
1895 – Francisco Martinez y Martinez
1896 –   "   "   "   "
1897 – Luciano Trujillo
1898 –   "   "
1899 – Higinio Romero
     – Faustin Trujillo
1900 –   "   "
1901 –   "   "
1902 –   "   "
1903 –   "   "
1904 –   "   "
1905 – Silviano Lucero
1906 –   "   "
1907 – Donaciano Graham
1908 –   "   "
1909 – Elizardo Quintana
1910 –   "   "
1911 –   "   "
1912 –   "   "

1. Date of Lee's appointment is unknown, although Taos County Prefect Robert Cary reported (11 January 1848) that the sheriff began to collect taxes on 28 October 1846; Taos Rebels assassinated him on 19 January 1847; Metcalf appointed 1 March 1847, but the circuit court judge appointed James Barry as sheriff "during the temporary absence" of Metcalf for the July 1847 session of court; Metcalf collected taxes through 1 October 1847;

Judge Carlos Beaubien recommended Greenwood as replacement in letter 19 September 1847; nothing is known about Aragon, who probably also served as temporary sheriff; date of Julian Jones's appointment is not known; In January 1848, Judge Carlos Beaubien informed the governor that a replacement was needed. In a letter of 8 February, Beaubien confirmed the death of Julian Jones (cause not specified) and requested the appointment of Childs. Apparently the governor refused, since Richens S. "Uncle Dick" Wootton collected taxes from 13 March–1 December 1848 and made a trip to Santa Fe to settle his accounts on 14 March 1849; A. Trigg began collecting taxes on 6 March and was performing law enforcement duties as late as October 1849; Julian Duran reported as alguacil mayor and collector in December 1850 and on 1 May 1851; Santiago Valdez collected taxes from 7 July to 18 August 1851 and Jose Antonio Romero performed these services from 19 August to 8 September 1851

2. Julian Ledoux elected September 1851; Marcelino Vigil collected taxes from 12 September to 8 November 1853, but was killed in 1854; Nestor Martinez succeeded Vigil; Ezra N. DePew was reported as collector on 10 November 1854.

3. Reason for James's short tenure is not known; Gabriel Lucero's commission is dated 9 July 1860; Francisco Sanchez elected 5 September 1861.

Torrance County (1903, Progresso; 1909, Estancia)

[1] 1903–?	1908– " "
1904–?	1909–Julius Meyers
1905–Manuel C. y Sanchez y Valdez	1910– " "
1906– " " " " " "	1911– " "
[2] 1907– " " " " " "	1912– " "
—Pedro Schubert	

1. First sheriff not known.
2. Valdez removed 19 February 1907; Schubert appointed 21 February 1907; Meyers elected November 1908.

Union County (1894, Clayton)

[1] 1894–Saturnino Pinard	1903–P. Baca y Sanchez
1895–Vattell L. (Bat) Overbay	1904– " " " "
– " " " "	1905–Tranquilino Garcia
1896– " " " "	1906– " "
1897–Luciano B. Gallegos	1907–Leandro M. Gallegos
1898– " " "	1908– " " "
1899–Saturnino Pinard	1909–D. W. Snyder
1900– " "	1910– " " "
1901–Salome Garcia	1911– " " "
1902– " "	1912– " " "

1. Pinard appointed first sheriff: Overbay elected November 1894.

Valencia County (1846, Valencia; 1852, Tome; 1872, Belen; 1874, Tome; 1876, Los Lunas)

[1] 1846–James L. Hubbell	1849– " "
1847– " " "	1850– " "
1848– " " "	1851– " "
—Lorenzo Labadie	1852– " "

[2] 1853–   "   "
          –Anastacio Garcia
1854–   "   "
1855–   "   "
          –Jesus Aragon y Chavez
[3] 1856–   "   "   "   "
          –Francisco Chavez y Armijo
1857–   "   "   "   "
1858–   "   "   "   "
1859–   "   "   "   "
          –Clemente Chavez
1860–   "   "
1861–   "   "
          –Dionicio Chavez
1862–   "   "
1863–   "   "
1864–   "   "
1865–   "   "
1866–   "   "
1867–   "   "
          –Antonio y Luna
1868–   "   "   "
1869–   "   "   "
          –Matias Baca
1870–   "   "
1871–   "   "
          –Jesus Maria Sena y Baca
1872–   "   "   "   "   "
1873–   "   "   "   "   "
          –Jesus Maria Luna y Baca
1874–   "   "   "   "   "
1875–   "   "   "   "   "
          –Patrocinio Luna
1876–   "   "
1877–   "   "
1878–   "   "
1879–   "   "

1880–   "   "
1881–Henry Connelly
1882–   "   "
1883–Patrocinio Luna
1884–   "   "
[4] 1885–   "   "
          –Jesus M. Luna
1886–   "   "   "
1887–   "   "   "
[5] 1888–   "   "   "
          –Tranquilino Luna
1889–   "   "
1890–   "   "
1891–   "   "
[6] 1892–   "   "
          –Solomon Luna
1893–   "   "
1894–   "   "
          –Maximiliano Luna
1895–   "   "
1896–   "   "
1897–Jesus Sanchez
1898–Carlos Baca
1899–   "   "
1900–   "   "
1901–   "   "
1902–   "   "
1903–   "   "
1904–   "   "
1905–   "   "
1906–   "   "
1907–   "   "
1908–   "   "
1909–Ruperto Jaramillo
1910–   "   "
1911–   "   "
1912–   "   "

1. Hubbell reported (*Santa Fe Weekly Gazette*, 23 July 1853) that he was appointed sheriff in September 1846 and resigned September 1848 to become county prefect; however, Manuel Antonio Otero performed some duties of sheriff, in June 1847, and P. R. Pratt did similar service in the following month, with Hubbell returning thereafter; Labadie evidently succeeded Hubbell, since he reportedly served about seven years; he was in office in February 1851 and was elected in September 1851.

2. Some uncertainty exists about the election of 5 September 1853; Anastacio Garcia was declared elected, but a subsequent grand jury report lists Aragon as sheriff from October 1853; Aragon was in office in April 1856.

3. The abrupt end of Aragon's term is unexplained; Armijo completed the term (commissioned 17 April 1857); he was then elected 18 September 1857.

4. Patriciano Luna was elected November 1884, but resigned in January 1885; Jesus M. Luna was appointed 10 January 1885 to fill out the term.

5. Jesus M. Luna was elected November 1888, but died soon after; Tranquilino Luna was appointed to fill out the term and was then elected in November 1890.

6. Tranquilino Luna died 10 November 1892; Solomon Luna, sheriff-elect, was appointed to fill out the last few weeks of the term; he took the oath of his elective term, 31 December 1892, to begin the following day.

Appendix B
Legal Hangings

The following list of legal executions in New Mexico and Arizona territories is only tentative. While the governors' registers note the issue of a death warrant, they often lack an official "return" or final action of the sheriff or United States marshal. This omission indicates that the victim's attorney had filed an appeal or taken some other action and the governor had granted a stay of execution. Some condemned men escaped jail before execution, and they eluded pursuit. Newspapers supplement the official record. Not only did they cover specific hangings, but they occasionally provided historical summaries of previous executions. When a Denver newspaper opined that the recent hanging of Nestor Lopez represented the first such legal event in New Mexico, the *Daily New Mexican* of 28 November 1863 took offense. The Santa Fe writer pointed out that nine men and one woman had died on the gallows. The sheriffs did not preside over all hangings. The United States marshals administered such sentences in federal cases. The executions of the Taos rebels took place under military auspices in 1847, although some attempt was made to clothe them in civilian law enforcement garb.

NEW MEXICO

Bernalillo County

Unidentified Hispano	28 July 1855
Milton Yarberry	9 February 1883
Dionicio Sandoval	24 September 1896
Jose P. Ruiz	1 June 1900

Chaves County

Antonio Gonzales	24 September 1896

Colfax County

William Breakenridge	8 May 1876
Damion Romero	2 February 1883
David Arguello	25 May 1906
John Medlock	25 May 1906

Doña Ana County

Santos Barela	20 May 1881
F. C. Clark	13 May 1881
Ruperto Lara	30 April 1885
Jesus Garcia	6 November 1896
Toribion Huerta	26 April 1901

Eddy County

James Barrett	15 September 1894

Grant County

Charles Williams	21 August 1880
Lewis P. Gaines	21 August 1880
Richard Remine	14 March 1881
William Young	25 March 1881
Pilar Perez	6 July 1888
Goldensen	14 September 1888

Lincoln County

William Wilson	10 December 1875
John James	18 June 1886
Bolt	June 1886(?)
Howe	19 November 1886(?)
Dewitt C. Johnson	19 November 1886

Rio Arriba County

Perfecto Padilla	24 September 1896
Rosario Ring	24 September 1896

San Miguel County

Robert Stanfield	27 July 1849
Paula Angel (female)	26 April 1861
(Pablita Martin?)	
Unidentified	17 April 1863
Theodore Baker	11 May 1887
Frederick Falkner	19 August 1892
Herman (German) Maestas	25 May 1894

Santa Fe County

Andrew Jackson Simms	30 November 1849
Thadeus M. Rogers	14 September 1860
Jesus Vialpondo	19 November 1895
Feliciano Chavez	19 November 1895
Francisco Gonzales y Borrego	2 April 1897
Antonio Gonzales y Borrego	2 April 1897
Lauriano Alarid	2 April 1897
Patricio Valencia	2 April 1897
Alejandro Duran (Jose Telles)	3 April 1903

Socorro County

John Henry Anderson	11 May 1887
Carlos Sais	12 January 1907

Taos County

James B. Sumner	17 July 1857
Julian Trujillo	13 May 1864
Jesus Maria Martinez	13 May 1864
Juan Conley	28 February 1906

Union County

Thomas E. Ketchum	26 April 1901

Valencia County

Felipe Garcia	25 May 1852
Unidentified	28 July 1855

ARIZONA

Cochise County

Dan Delaney	28 March 1884
Dan Dowd	28 March 1884
Tex Howard	28 March 1884
York Kelley	28 March 1884
Omer W. Sample	28 March 1884
Thomas Haldiman	16 November 1900
William Haldiman	16 November 1900
Frank Spence	5 August 1910

Gila County

Nah-deiz-az (Carlyle Kid)	27 December 1889
Zack Booth	15 September 1905
William Baldwin (black)	12 July 1907

Graham County

El-chus-choose	11 July 1890
Antonio Granado	June 1891
Frank Nelson (black)	30 June 1891
Ramon Peineida	1 June 1900
Augustino Chacon	14 November 1902

Maricopa County

Demetrio Dominguez	November 1880
William Price	1 February 1895(?)

Mohave County

Michael DeHay	14 January 1876
Clement Leigh	19 January 1907

Navajo County

George Smiley	8 January 1900

Pima County

Thomas Harper	13 July 1881
Joseph Casey	15 April 1884
Firminino (Papago)	1889
Manuel Verdugo	1891(?)
Philip Lashley	9 July 1897
Teodoro Elias	26 July 1904
Edwin W. Hawkins	14 August 1908

Pinal County

Nacon-qui (Apache)	6 December 1889
Kah-dos-la	6 December 1889

Yavapai County

Manuel Aviles	1875
James Malone	15 March 1878
John Berry	February 1882
Henry H. Hall	10 February 1882
Dennis Dilda	5 February 1886

Frank Wilson   12 August 1887
James Sherley   [1895?]
Fleming (Jim) Parker   3 June 1898
Hilario Hidalgo   31 July 1903
Francisco Rentino (Rentario)   31 July 1903

Yuma County

Manuel Fernandez   3 May 1873
Santiago Ortiz   16 November 1900
Martin Ubillos   16 June 1905

Arizona Penitentiary (Florence)

Cesario Sanchez   2 December 1910
Alejandro Gallego   28 July 1911

Military Executions (Fort Grant)

Dandy Jim (Apache)   6 March 1882
Skippy (Apache)   6 March 1882
Dead Shot (Apache)   6 March 1882

George Woods   Date and location uncertain

Appendix C
Lynchings

The following list of lynching victims is merely preliminary. Many newspaper reports were based upon rumor or misinformation. Other vigilante acts were not reported at all. Still, the frontier press remains the best source and sometimes provides helpful statistical data. The *Santa Fe Weekly Gazette* in 1853 (1 January) reported five lynchings in less than a year, and in 1855 (28 April) that five men had been so victimized within the last eighteen months. The *Albuquerque Review* of 23 August 1879 remarked that six men had been lynched in that community.

NEW MEXICO

Name	Place	Date
1 man (Texan)	Santa Fe	14 June 1851
Jose de la Cruz (Navajo)	Mora	Sept. 1852
Gabriel Luhan (Mexican)	"	" "
1 man (American)	Doña Ana	[Dec.?] 1852
Giddion Scallion	Santa Fe	12 Nov. 1853
2 men (Indians)	Nambe Pueblo	[March?] 1854
4 men (Mexicans)	Doña Ana (village)	10 March 1855
Matias Ribera	Santa Fe	March 1857
John Miller	Albuquerque	4 July 1857
Carlos Martinez	"	April 1858
1 man (Mexican)	Mora	May 1858
Joseph Cummings	Placita (Lincoln)	Nov. 1859
1 man (Mexican)	" "	" "
"Colonel" Sterten	Mesilla	30 Dec. 1860
Charles Hampton (Hampden)	"	"

1 man (Mexican)	Mesilla	[22?] March 1861
1 man (Mexican)	Mesilla	10 April 1861
William Watts	Puerto de Magdalena (near Mesilla)	19 April 1861
J. W. Hagar	" "	" " "
2 women (Hispanic)	" "	" " "
James Adams	Sapello	[1864?]
Thomas Means	Taos	2 Jan. 1867
Dan Dimon (Ben Dimond)	Pinos Altos	28 July 1867
"Pony" O'Neil	Elizabethtown	[1869?]
1 man (Mexican)	"	13 Sept. 1869
Charles Kennedy	"	7 Oct. 1870
[2?] men	Los Lunas	Feb. 1871
Jesus Pino		
Diego Lucero	Albuquerque	14 April 1871
Pablo Padilla	near Peralta	30 Dec. 1871
Juan Sandobal	near Peralta	[5?] Jan. 1872
4 men (stock thieves)	Loma Parda	July/Aug. 1872
Wiley	Fort Union	13/16 Nov. 1872
Hill	" "	" " "
John Cowley	Cimarron	28/30 Dec. 1873
Zachariah Compton	Lincoln County	Feb. 1874
Still	" "	" "
1 man	Cimarron	Spring 1874
Pas Mes	Doña Ana County	Aug. 1875
Thomas Madrid	" " "	" "
Jermin Aguirre	" " "	" "
Cruz Vega	Cimarron	30 Oct. 1875
Manuel Cardenas	"	10 Nov. 1875
Charles von Kohler, alias Alex. C. Collier	Abiquiu	27 Dec. 1875
Juan Miera	Albuquerque	23 June 1876
Jose Miera	"	" " "
Meliton Cordova	"	" " "
Jose Segura	Lincoln	18 July 1876
Jesus Largo	near Lincoln	Aug. 1876
1 man	Albuquerque	[18?] Jan. 1878
George Washington (black)	Lincoln	[28 June?] 1879
Manuel Barela	Las Vegas	4/5 June 1879
Louis Torbillo (Giovanni Dugi)	" "	" " "
Beckwith	" "	[June?] 1879
Romulo Baca	Los Lunas	12 June 1879
J. P. Fish	Albuquerque	12 Nov. 1879
Dick (Tom) Hardeman, alias Dick Turpin	Lincoln	23 Nov. 1879
Thomas Jefferson House, alias Dutchy, Tom Henry	Las Vegas	7/8 Feb. 1880
John Dorsey (Jim Dawson)	" "	" " "

Anthony Lowe, alias Jim West	" "	" " "
3 men	Albuquerque	[20?] Feb. 1880
Paz Chaves	Lincoln	March 1880
Juanito Mes	Seven Rivers	March 1880
Joseph Murphy, alias One Armed Joe	Lincoln	July 1880
Harriman (Harrison)	Lincoln	3 July 1880
1 man (deputy sheriff)	Lincoln	4 July 1880
1 man	Lincoln	5 July 1880
Jim Dunnigan	Santa Fe	18 July 1880
Washington (quack doctor)	Raton	[1 Dec.?] 1880
Pantaleon Miera	Bernalillo	28 Dec. 1880
Santos Bernavides	"	" " "
Sandy King	Shakespeare	1 Jan. 1881
William Tattenbaum, alias Russian Bill	"	"
Porter Stockton	Farmington	10 Jan. 1881
California Joe	Albuquerque	31 Jan. 1881
Escolastico Perea	"	" " "
Miguel Barrera	"	" " "
Faustino Gutierres	"	24 Feb. 1881
Jose Lopez	Rio Arriba Co.	Feb. 1881
Juan Chaves	"	" "
2 men (Hispanos)	Otero	1 March 1881
Tom Gordon	Socorro	10 March 1881
Enofre Baca	Socorro	31 March 1881
Santos Barela	Mesilla	[23?] May 1881
Jim Flynn	Mogollon	April 1881
J. F. Jennings	Tierra Amarilla	24 July 1881
2 men (Hispanos)	Los Lunas	Oct. 1881
Del Lockhart	Tierra Amarilla	26 Oct. 1881
"Kid" Coulter	" "	" " "
"Slim Kid"	" "	" " "
Ike Hazelitt	Eureka	[15?] June 1881
Bill Hazelitt	"	" " "
Francisco Jordan	Cuchillo Negro	25 Nov. 1881
Dan Swany (black)	Cerrillos	Feb. 1882
Charles Shelton	Los Lunas	7 March 1882
Henry French, alias Simpson	" "	" " "
Johnnie Redmond	" "	" " "
Gus Mentzer	Raton	22 June 1882
Frank McHand	Las Vegas	[1882?]
Jose Mares, alias Frank Tafoya, alias Navajo Frank	Las Vegas	25/26 June 1882
1 man (Italian)	Deming	27 Aug. 1882
Guadalupe Archuleta	Bloomfield	31 Oct. 1882
1 man (Hispano)	Loma Parda	Nov. 1882

William Pearl	Lincoln	23 Jan. 1883
John Welch	Lordsburg	April 1883
Hank Andrews	Socorro County	[1883?]
Gilmore	Bernalillo County	[1883?]
Joe Fowler	Socorro	22/23 Jan. 1884
Mitch Lee	Silver City	13 March 1884
Frank Taggart	" "	" " "
1 man (horse thief)	Tularosa	7/13 April 1884
Juan Castillo	Raton	Aug. 1884
1 woman (suspected witch)	Chimayo	Sept. 1884
Henry Thomas (black)	Las Vegas	Jan. 1885
Joseph Chaca	Wallace	26 Aug. 1889
Leandro Gonzales	Cebolleto	5 Feb. 1893
3 men	Los Lunas	[5?] May 1893
Cecilio Lucero	Las Vegas	29 May 1893

ARIZONA

Name	Place	Date
Rafael Polacio (Polano)	Tucson	Oct. 1859
Mateo (Hispano)	Arizona City (Yuma)	Jan. 1861
Jack Hewing	" " "	27 March 1866
3 men (Mexican)	Florence [or Ft. Thomas]	[1870s?]
2 men (Mexican)	Maricopa Wells	29 Aug. 1871
Gandara	Sandford	March 1872
Manuel Reyes	"	" "
Aguilar	"	" "
1 man (Mexican)	Stanwix Sta.	8 Aug. 1872
Ramon Cordovo	[Phoenix?]	[1872?]
Mariano Tisado	Phoenix	3 July 1873
Manuel Subiato(?) and 3 others	Yuma	8 Aug. 1873
Leonardo Cordoba	Tucson	8 Aug. 1873
Clemente Lopez	"	" " "
Jesus Saguaripa	"	" " "
John Willis	"	" " "
Lucas Lugas	Kenyon Station	31 Aug. 1873
1 man (Mexican)	[Yuma?]	Sept. 1873
Ventura Nunez	Burke Station	11 Dec. 1874
George Young		[1876?]
Oliver McCoy	Safford	3 Aug. 1877
William Snyder, alias Bill Caveness	Springerville	Dec. 1877
E. M. Overstreet	"	" "

Charlie Rice	Hackberry	18 Dec. 1877
Bob White	"	"
1 man (Pima)	Florence	15 July 1878
William McCloskey	Phoenix	22 Aug. 1879
John Keller	"	" " "
Edward Fales	Silver King (camp near Pinal)	[1880s]
William Campbell	St. Johns	1881
Joseph Walters	" "	"
3 men (Mexican)	San Simon Valley	14 July 1881
Jose Ordina (Mexican)	Graham County	[Aug.?] 1881
4 men (Mexican)	San Xavier (near Tucson)	Aug. 1881
1 youth (Mexican, whipped to death)	Charleston	[1?] Sept. 1881
2 men (Mexican)	Tres Alamos	[5?] Oct. 1881
William Lewis, alias Arizona Bill (deputy sheriff)	Pittman Valley	Jan. 1882
Jack Winn	(?)	Jan. 1882
J. O. Weldon	Hackberry	21 Feb. 1882
Lafayette (Fate) Grimes	Globe	24 Aug. 1882
Curtis E. Hawley	"	" " "
1 man (Mexican)	Bisbee (near Castle Rock)	[11 Sept.?] 1882
Thomas Kerr	Pioneer Camp (near Globe)	24 Dec. 1882
Len Redfield	Florence	3 Sept. 1883
Joe Tuttle	"	" " "
John Heith	Tombstone	22 Feb. 1884
Antonio Quinones	San Pedro Valley, Cochise County	Nov. 1884
2 men	Holbrook	1885
George Hawks	Flagstaff	19 Jan. 1887
William Hawks	"	" " "
Albert Rose	Pleasant Valley	1 Nov. 1887
James Stott	Tonto Basin, Apache County	Aug. 1888
James Scott	" "	" "
Jeff Wilson	" "	" "
Peter Burke	Yuma	[1897?]
1 man	Clifton	[Nov.?] 1897
Kingsley Olds	Globe	3 July 1910

Bibliography

PUBLISHED DOCUMENTS

Arizona

The Compiled Laws of the Territory of Arizona, Including the Howell Code and the Session Laws, From 1864 to 1871, Inclusive. comp. Coles Bashford. Albany, N.Y.: Weed, Parsons, 1871.
Laws of the Territory of Arizona (containing acts, resolutions, and memorials. Also called *Session Laws*). First through Twenty-Fifth Sessions. 1864–1909.
Revised Statutes of Arizona. Prescott: Prescott Courier, 1887.
Revised Statutes, Arizona, 1913, Civil Code. Comp. Samuel L. Pattee. Phoenix: McNeil, 1913.

New Mexico

The General Laws of New Mexico: Including All the Unrepealed General Laws, from the Promulgation of the 'Kearny Code' in 1846, to the End of the Legislative Session of 1880, with Supplement, including the Session of 1882. comp. L. Bradford Prince. Albany, N.Y.: W. C. Little, 1882.
The Kearny Code [Laws of the Territory of New Mexico]. ed. Nolie Mumey. Denver, Colo.: n. pub., 1970. Orig. pub. Santa Fe: October 7, 1846.
Laws of New Mexico Territory (containing acts, resolutions and memorials. Also called *Session laws*). First through Thirty-First Sessions. 1852–1912.
Message of Governor L. Bradford Prince to the Twenty-Ninth Legislative Assembly, December 30, 1890. Santa Fe: New Mexican, 1891.
Special Message of Governor L. Bradford Prince to the Twenty-Ninth Legislative Assembly, January 10, 1891. Santa Fe: New Mexican, 1891.
Message of Governor L. Bradford Prince to the Thirtieth Legislative Assembly of New Mexico, December 18, 1892. Santa Fe: New Mexican, 1892.
Message of Governor William T. Thornton to the Thirty-First Legislative Assembly of New Mexico, December 31, 1894. Santa Fe: New Mexican, 1895.
New Mexico Statutes Annotated: Containing the Codification Passed at the Second Session of the Legislature of the State of New Mexico. comps. Stephen B. Davis, Jr., & Merritt C. Mechem. Denver: W. H. Courtright, 1915.
New Mexico Bar Association. *Minutes and Proceedings of the New Mexico Bar Association, 1886–1919.* Santa Fe: New Mexican, 1886–1919.

Town Ordinances of Albuquerque, New Mexico, 1863. Albuquerque: Vinegar Tom Press, facsimile, 1970.

United States

Congress. *Statutes at Large.* 32 vols. (1789–1912). Washington: GPO, 1789–1912.
Department of Justice. *Official Opinions of Attorneys-General.* 27 vols. (1789–1909). Washington: GPO, 1844–1909.
House of Representatives. *Occupation of Mexican Territory.* 29th Cong., 2d sess., 1848, Exec. Doc. 19.

UNPUBLISHED DOCUMENTS AND MANUSCRIPTS

Albuquerque, New Mexico

University of New Mexico. Special Collections.
    Holm O. Bursum Papers.
    Miguel A. Otero Papers.
    New Mexico Pioneers Foundation Interviews.
    William G. Ritch Collection. Microfilmed. (Original collection in Huntington Library, San Marino, California).

El Paso, Texas

University of Texas. Special Collections.
    Charles Leland Sonnichsen Papers.
——, Public Library.
    Pat Dolan Papers.
    Jack Shipman Papers.

Indianapolis, Indiana

Indiana Historical Society.
    Lew Wallace Papers.

Las Cruces, New Mexico

New Mexico State University. Rio Grande Collection.
    Katherine Stoes, et al. "Dona Ana County History." Las Cruces, New Mexico: Aztec Lodge No. 3, n.d.

Lincoln, New Mexico

Courthouse Museum.
    Philip Rasch Papers.
    Tunstall Store Museum Exhibits.

Midland, Texas

Nita Stewart Haley Library.
   Jim East Collection.
   J. Evetts Haley Interviews.
   Robert N. Mullin Collection.

Phoenix, Arizona

Phoenix Public Library.
   James H. McClintock Collection.
   ———. State Library and Archives.
   Arizona Territorial Papers.

Prescott, Arizona

Sharlot Hall Museum.
   Dan Genung Collection (photocopy of original in Arizona Historical Society).
   Angie Mitchell (Brown) Notebook, 1880–81.
   William [Buckey] O'Neill Scrapbooks.
   Yavapai County Law Enforcement to 1920. 1 folder.

Santa Fe, New Mexico

State Records Center and Archives.
   Bernalillo County District Court Records.
   Executive Record No. 2.
   First Judicial District, Criminal Cases, Santa Fe County, 1846–51.
   Frank W. Clancy Scrapbooks.
   Colfax County Sheriff's Journal, 1870–1884.
   Dona Ana County Records, 1844.
   Governor's Papers, 1852–94.
   Grant County District Court Records.
   Napoleon Laughlin Papers.
   Santa Fe County District Court Records.
   Sierra County District Court Records.
   Works Projects Administration Interviews.
   ———. Territorial Archives of New Mexico. 189 rolls
   Records of the Mounted Police. 1905–1911. 3 rolls.
   Donaciano Vigil Papers. 1 roll.
   ———. Museum of New Mexico History Library
   Lincoln County Collection

Tempe, Arizona

Arizona State University. Hayden Library.
   John L. B. Alexander Collection
   William Eugene Brooks Collection
   Carl Hayden Collection.
   "Outlaws and Badmen," 1 box.
   B[enjamin] Sacks Collection.

Tucson, Arizona

University of Arizona. Special Collections.
  Walter Noble Burns Papers.
  Crime and Criminals. 1 box.
  Maurice Garland Fulton Collection.
  Lloyd C. Hening. "Sheriff, Scholar and Gentleman [Frank J. Wattron]. Holbrook,
    Arizona, 1941. 30 pp.
  Louis C. Hughes Collection.
  William D. Monmonier Papers.
  Pima County. Original Documents.
  Edward D. Tuttle Collection. Originals in Huntington Library, San Marino California.
————. Arizona Historical Society.
  Crime and Criminals. 1 box.
  Allen A. Erwin Collection.
  John Pleasant Gray Papers.
  J. C. Hancock Papers.
  Hayden Biographical Files.
  Law Enforcement Collection.
  Michael M. Rice Papers.
  George Herbert Smalley Collection.
  Dan R. Williamson Papers.
  Reminiscences of Leonard Alverson.
  United States Marshals' Records, 1882–1927.
  Levi S. Udall Collection.
  James Wolf Papers.

Washington, D.C.

Library of Congress
  Caleb Cushing Papers.
————. National Archives
  Record Group 48, Interior Department.
    Territorial Papers of New Mexico, 1851–1914. Microcopy M-364. 15 rolls.
    Territorial Papers of Arizona, 1868–1913. Microcopy 429. 8 rolls.
  Record Group 59, State Department.
    Territorial Papers of New Mexico, 1851–1872. Microcopy T-17. 4 rolls.
    Territorial Papers of Arizona, 1864–1872. Microcopy M-342. 1 roll.
  Record Group 60, Justice Department.
    Letters Received, New Mexico, 1 box.
    Letters Sent to Judges and Clerks, 1874–1885. Microcopy 703. 2 rolls.

PRIMARY PUBLISHED SOURCES

Axford, Joseph (Mack). *Around Western Campfires*. Tucson: University of Arizona, 1969.
Barnes, Will C. *Apaches & Longhorns: The Reminiscences of Will C. Barnes*. Ed. Frank C. Lock-
  wood. Los Angeles: Ward Ritchie, 1941.
Bennett, James A. *Forts and Forays: A Dragoon in New Mexico, 1850–1856*. Eds. Clinton E.
  Brooks and Frank D. Reeve. Albuquerque: University of New Mexico Press, 1948.

Benton, Jesse James. *Cow by the Tail*. Ed. Richard Summers. New York: Houghton Mifflin, 1943.

Bonney, Cecil. *Looking Over My Shoulder: Seventy-Five Years in the Pecos Valley*. Roswell, New Mexico: Hall-Poorbaugh, 1971.

Bourke, John Gregory. *On the Border with Crook*. Lincoln: University of Nebraska, 1971. Orig. pub. 1891.

Boyer, Glenn G. Ed. *I Married Wyatt Earp: The Recollections of Josephine Sarah Marcus Earp*. Tucson: University of Arizona, 1976.

Breakenridge, William M. *Helldorado: Bringing the Law to the Mesquite*. Boston: Houghton Mifflin, 1928.

Briggs, L. Vernon. *Arizona and New Mexico, 1882, California, 1886, Mexico, 1891*. Boston: Privately printed, 1932.

Cady, John H. *Arizona's Yesterdays*. Rev. Basil Dillon Moon. Patagonia, Ariz.: n. pub., 1978.

Carroll, John Alexander, ed. *Pioneering in Arizona: The Reminiscences of Emerson Oliver Stratton & Edith Stratton Kitt*. Tucson: Arizona Pioneers Historical Society, 1964.

Chesley, Hervey E. *Adventuring with the Old-Timers: Trails Traveled-Tales Told*. Ed. B. Byron Price. Midland, Tex.: Nita Stewart Haley Memorial Library, 1979.

Chisholm, Joe. *Brewery Gulch: Frontier Days of Old Arizona—Last Outpost of the Great Southwest*. San Antonio, Tex.: Naylor, 1949.

Chrisman, Harry E. *Fifty Years on the Owl Hoot Trail: Jim Herron, The First Sheriff of No Man's Land*. Chicago: Sage, 1969.

Cofer, Irene Cornwall. *The Lunch Tree*. Brooklyn, New York: Gaus, 1969.

Collinson, Frank. *Life in the Saddle*. Ed. Mary Whatley Clarke. Norman: University of Oklahoma, 1963.

Cook, D. J. *Hands Up: Or, Twenty Years of Detective Life in the Mountains and on the Plains*. Norman: University of Oklahoma, 1958. Orig. Pub. 1882.

Culley, John H. (Jack). *Cattle, Horses & Men of the Western Range*. Tucson: University of Arizona, 1967.

Curry, George. *George Curry, 1861–1947: An Autobiography*. Ed. H. B. Hening. Albuquerque: University of New Mexico Press, 1958.

Davis, William Watts Hart. *El Gringo: Or, New Mexico and Her People*. Santa Fe: Rydal, 1938. Orig. pub. 1856.

Fall, Albert B. *The Memoirs of Albert B. Fall*. Southwestern Studies, No. 15, El Paso, Texas: University of Tex., 1966.

French, William. *Some Recollections of a Western Ranchman: New Mexico, 1883–1899*. London: Methuen, 1927, vol. 1. *Further Recollections of a Western Ranchman, New Mexico, 1883–1899*, vol. 2, Ed. Jeff C. Dykes. New York: Argosy-Antiquarian, 1965.

Garrett, Pat F. *The Authentic Life of Billy, The Kid: The Noted Desperado of the Southwest, Whose Deeds of Daring and Blood Made His Name a Terror in New Mexico, Arizona and Northern Mexico*. Intro. J. C. Dykes. Norman: University of Oklahoma, 1954. Orig. Pub. 1882.

———. *Authentic Life of Billy the Kid*. Ed. and annotated Maurice Garland Fulton. New York: Macmillan, 1927.

Gustafson, A. M., ed. *John Spring's Arizona*. Tucson: University of Arizona, 1966.

Hannett, Arthur Thomas. *Sagebrush Lawyer*. New York: Pageant, 1964.

Harkey, Dee R. *Mean as Hell*. Albuquerque: University of New Mexico Press, 1948.

Hilzinger, George. *Treasure Land: A Story*. Tucson: Arizona Advancement Co., 1897. Rpt. ed., Rio Grande Press, 1969.

Hochderffer, George. *Flagstaff Whoa! The Autobiography of a Western Pioneer*. Flagstaff, Ariz.: Museum of Northern Arizona, 1965.

Horn, Tom. *Life of Tom Horn: Government Scout and Interpreter, Written By Himself: A Vindication*. Norman: University of Oklahoma, 1964. Orig. pub. 1904.

Hoyt, Henry F. *A Frontier Doctor*. New York: Houghton Mifflin, 1969.

Huning, Franz. *Trader on the Santa Fe Trail*. Notes by Lina Fergusson Browne. Albuquerque: University of Albuquerque, in collab. with Calvin Horn, 1973.

King, Frank M. *Wranglin' the Past: The Reminiscences of Frank M. King.* Pasadena, Calif.: Trail's End, 1946.

Klasner, Lily. *My Girlhood Among Outlaws.* Tucson: University of Arizona, 1972.

Lake, Carolyn, ed. *Under Cover for Wells Fargo: The Unvarnished Recollections of Fred Dodge.* Boston: Houghton Mifflin, 1969.

McCauley, James Emmitt. *A Stove-Up Cowboy's Story.* Austin: Texas Folklore Society, 1943.

McGinty, Billy. *The Old West, As Written in the Words of Billy McGinty, As Told to Glenn L. Eyler.* Stillwater, Oklahoma, Redlands Press. 1958. Orig. pub. 1937.

McIntire, Jim. *Early Days in Texas; [and] A Trip to Hell and Heaven.* Kansas City, Mo.: McIntire Pub., 1902.

Martin, Douglas D., ed. *Tombstone's Epitaph.* Albuquerque: University of New Mexico Press, 1951.

Miller, Joseph C., ed. *Arizona Cavalcade: The Turbulent Times.* New York: Hastings House, 1962.

———. *The Arizona Rangers.* New York: Hastings House, 1972.

———. *Arizona: The Last Frontier.* New York: Hastings House. 1956.

Mullane, William H., ed. *This is Silver City,* 4 vols. Silver City: The Enterprise, 1965–67.

Nicolson, John, ed. *The Arizona of Joseph Pratt Allyn, Letters from a Pioneer Judge: Observations and Travels, 1863–1866.* Tucson: University of Arizona, 1974.

Otero, Miguel A. *My Life on the Frontier, 1864–1882.* 2 vols. Albuquerque: University of New Mexico Press, 1939.

Poe, Sophie. *Buckboard Days.* Ed. Eugene Cunningham. Caldwell, Idaho: Caxton, 1936.

Reeve, Frank D., ed. *Albert Franklin Banta: Arizona Pioneer.* Historical Society of New Mexico Publications in History, vol. 24. Santa Fe: Historical Society of New Mexico, 1953.

Ringgold, Jennie Parks. *Frontier Days in the Southwest: Pioneer Days in Old Arizona.* San Antonio, Tex.: Naylor, 1952.

Rockfellow, John A. *Log of an Arizona Trail Blazer.* Tucson: Arizona Silhouettes, 1955.

Rynning, Tom. As told to Al Cohn and Jose Chisholm. *Gun Notches: The Life Story of a Cowboy-Soldier.* New York: A. L. Burt, 1931.

Ryus, W. H. *The Second William Penn: A True Account of Incidents That Happened Along the Old Santa Fe Trail in the Sixties.* Kansas City, Mo.: Frank T. Riley, 1913.

Siringo, Charles A. *Riata and Spurs: The Story of a Lifetime Spent in the Saddle as Cowboy and Detective.* Boston: Houghton Mifflin, 1927.

———. *A Texas Cowboy: Or Fifteen Years on the Hurricane Deck of a Spanish Pony.* New York: New American Library, Signet Paperback, 1950. Orig. pub. 1885.

———. *Two Evil Isms: Pinkertonism and Anarchism.* Facs. Ed. Austin, Texas: Steck-Vaughn, 1967. Orig. Pub. 1915.

Sloan, Richard E. *Memories of an Arizona Judge.* Stanford: Stanford University, 1932.

Smalley, George Herbert. *My Adventures in Arizona: Leaves from a Reporter's Notebook.* Ed. Yndia Smalley Moore. Tucson: Arizona Pioneers Historical Society, 1966.

Sonnichsen, C. L. *Billy King's Tombstone: The Private Life of an Arizona Boom Town.* Tucson: University of Arizona, 1972.

Stevens, Montague. *Meet Mr. Grizzly: A Saga of the Passing of the Grizzly.* Albuquerque: University of New Mexico Press, 1943.

Taylor, Benjamin F. *Short Ravelings from a Long Yarn, or Camp March Sketches.* From notes of Richard L. Wilson. Santa Rosa, Calif.: Fine Arts Press, 1936. Orig. pub. 1847.

Turner, Alford E. ed. *The O. K. Corral Inquest.* College Station, Tex.: Creative Pub., 1981.

Wallace, William Swilling, intro. & ed. *A Journey Through New Mexico's First Judicial District in 1864: Letters to the Editor of the Santa Fe Weekly New Mexican.* Los Angeles: Westernlore Press, 1956.

Warfield, H. B. *Corydon Cooley: Army Scout, Arizona Pioneer, Wayside Host, Apache Friend.* El Cajon, Calif.: the author, 1966.

Warner, Matt. As told to Murray E. King. *The Last of the Bandit Riders.* New York: Bonanza, n.d. Orig. pub. 1940.

Whitlock, V. H. (Ol' Waddy). *Cowboy Life on the Llano Estacado.* Norman: University of Oklahoma, 1970.

Wilson, Frederick T. *Federal Aid in Domestic Disturbances, 1787–1903.* Washington: GPO, 1903.

NEWSPAPERS

Arizona

Phoenix *Arizona Republican* (weekly and daily), 23 December 1898–31 December 1906, 1 May–31 August 1909.

Prescott *Arizona Miner* and *Arizona Weekly Journal-Miner* (Semi-monthly, Weekly & Daily), 1864–89, 1897–1900. Various Names.

St. Johns Herald, 1885–1898.

Scottsdale Progress, 8 August 1987.

Tombstone *Daily Nugget,* 8 June–4 December 1881, 2–5 May 1882.

Tombstone Epitaph (Weekly and Daily), 1880–82, 1885–86.

Tucson *Arizona Daily Citizen,* 25 January–31 March 1885, 1 October 1889–15 March 1890, 23 December 1901, 10–22 November 1910, 4 October–23 December 1911.

Tucson *Arizona Daily Star,* 14 January 1882, 15 April–14 August 1884, 17 April–16 August 1890, 4 April–31 August 1891.

Tucson (and Florence) *Arizona Weekly Citizen,* 29 March 1878–28 August 1879, 19 November–10 December 1882.

Tucson *Arizona Weekly Star,* 1 January–14 August 1879, 27 January–17 February 1881, 15 January–26 March 1891, 25 April–6 June 1895.

Weekly Arizonian (Tubac & Tucson), 3 March 1859–12 April 1860.

New Mexico

Albuquerque Daily Democrat, 3 April–7 May 1883, 5 January–29 February 1884.

Albuquerque Evening Democrat, 20–26 October 1884, 14 April–13 May 1885.

Albuquerque Evening Review, 20 February–4 March 1882.

Albuquerque Morning Journal, 1907–1908, 1910.

Albuquerque Review, 19 January–14 December 1878, 28 April–26 May 1883.

Albuquerque *Rio Abajo Weekly Press,* 3 February–4 October 1863.

Albuquerque Weekly Democrat, 17 May–7 June 1883.

Capitan Press, 26 June 1903.

Cimarron News and Press, 29 November 1879–7 January 1882.

Las Cruces *Newman's Thirty-Four,* 20 August–3 September 1879, 23 February 1881.

Las Cruces *Rio Grande Republican,* 8 January–31 December 1897.

Las Vegas *Daily Optic,* 5 November 1879–26 November 1881, 17 March, 19 December 1883–31 January 1884, 28 October 1884–13 May 1885, 12, 17 November 1886, 29 August–2 September 1889.

Lincoln County Leader, 21 October 1882.

Manzano *Gringo & Greaser,* 1 February 1884.

Mesilla Valley Independent, 12, 17 May 1879.

Roswell Record, 11, 25 September 1896.

Roswell Register, 18 July 1896.

Santa Fe *Daily New Mexican,* 22 August 1863–4 March 1898, 3 March–12 May 1903.

Santa Fe Republican, 1 January 1847–23 September 1848.
Santa Fe Weekly Gazette, 6 November 1852–18 September 1869.
Santa Fe *Weekly New Mexican*, 3 August–14 September 1875, 31 October 1876, 1 January 1878–8 March 1879, 12 July 1879–16 August 1880, 9 June 1883–16 June 1887.
Silver City Enterprise, 16 November 1882–26 June 1891.
White Oaks *Lincoln County Leader*, 21 October 1882.

Other Newspapers

Washington *Daily National Intelligencer*, 2 July 1849–27 August 1850, 18 February–26 April 1851, 29 May–7 August 1854.
El Paso Daily Times, 1895–96.
Washington *Evening Star*, 27 September, 5 October 1878.
New Orleans Picayune, 11 April 1851.
New York Times, 20 June 1880.
Denver *Rocky Mountain News*, 1896–1903.

SECONDARY PUBLISHED SOURCES

Ball, Larry D. *The United States Marshals of New Mexico and Arizona Territories, 1846–1912.* Albuquerque: University of New Mexico, 1978.
Bancroft, Hubert Howe. *Works of Hubert Howe Bancroft.* 39 vols. New York: Arno, n.d. Orig. Pub. 1889. vol. 17, *History of Arizona and New Mexico, 1530–1888*, vols. 31 & 32, *Popular Tribunals.*
Bartholomew, Ed. *Wyatt Earp: The Man & the Myth.* Toyahvale, Texas: Frontier Book Company, 1964.
———. *Wyatt Earp, 1848 to 1880: The Untold Story.* Toyahvale, Texas: Frontier Book Company, 1964.
Baylor, George Wythe. *John Robert Baylor: Confederate Governor of Arizona.* Ed. Odie B. Faulk. Tucson: Arizona Pioneers Historical Society, 1966.
Blackstone, William. *Commentaries on the Laws of England.* Ed. and abr. J. W. Ehrlich. San Carlos, California: Nourse, 1959.
Brent, William. *The Complete and Factual Life of Billy the Kid.* New York: Frederick Fell, 1964.
Brophy, A. Blake. *Foundlings on the Frontier: Racial and Religious Conflicts in Arizona Territory, 1904–1905.* Tucson: University of Ariz., 1972.
Brothers, Mary Hudson. *Billy the Kid: The Most Hated, the Most Loved Outlaw New Mexico Ever Produced.* Story by Bell Hudson. Farmington, N.M.: Hustler Press, 1949.
Brown, Richard Maxwell. *The South Carolina Regulators.* Cambridge: Harvard University Press, 1963.
———. *Strain of Violence: Historical Studies of American Violence and Vigilantism.* New York: Oxford University, 1977.
Burns, Walter Noble. *Tombstone: An Iliad of the Southwest.* New York: Garden City, 1937.
Burroughs, Jean M., ed. *On the Trail: The Life and Tales of 'Lead Steer' Potter.* Santa Fe: Museum of New Mexico, 1980.
Burton, Jeff. *Dynamite and Six-Shooter.* Santa Fe: Palomino, 1970.
Callon, Milton W. *Las Vegas, New Mexico—The Town That Wouldn't Gamble.* Las Vegas: Daily Optic, 1962.

Cleaveland, Norman, comp. and anno. *An Introduction to the Colfax County War, 1875–78*. N. p.: Privately printed, [1975?].

———, and George Fitzpatrick. *The Morleys—Young Upstarts on the Southwest Frontier*. Albuquerque: Calvin Horn, 1971.

Cline, Donald. *Alias Billy the Kid: The Man Behind the Legend*. Santa Fe: Sunstone, 1986.

Collier, William Ross, and Edwin Victor Westrate. *Dave Cook of the Rockies: Frontier General, Fighting Sheriff and Leader of Men*. New York: Rufus Rockwell Wilson, 1936.

Corwin, Edward S. *The President, Office and Powers: History and Analysis of Practice and Opinion*. 3d ed. New York: New York University, 1948.

Crichton, Kyle S. *Law and Order, Ltd.: The Rousing Life of Elfego Baca of New Mexico*. Glorieta, N.M.: Rio Grande, 1970.

Cummings, Homer, and Carl McFarland. *Federal Justice: Chapters in the History of Justice and the Federal Executive*. New York: Macmillan, 1937.

Cutts, James Madison. *The Conquest of California and New Mexico by the Forces of the United States in the Years 1846 & 1847*. Philadelphia: Carey & Hart, 1847.

Dedera, Don. *A Little War of Our Own: The Pleasant Valley Feud Revisited*. Flagstaff, Ariz.: Northland, 1988.

Dozier, Edward P. *The Pueblo Indians of North America*. New York: Holt, Rinehart and Winston, 1970.

Dykes, Jeff C. *Law on a Wild Frontier: Four Sheriffs of Lincoln County*. Washington, D.C.: Potomac Corral of Westerners, n.d.

Emmet, Chris. *Fort Union and the Winning of the Southwest*. Norman: University of Oklahoma, 1965.

Erwin, Allen A. *The Southwest of John H. Slaughter, 1841–1922: Pioneer Cattleman and Trail-Driver of Texas, the Pecos, and Arizona and Sheriff of Tombstone*. Glendale, Calif.: Arthur H. Clark, 1965.

Fergusson, Erna. *Murder & Mystery in New Mexico*. Albuquerque: Merle Armitage, 1948.

Forrest, Earl R. *Arizona's Dark and Bloody Ground*. Rev. ed. Caldwell, Idaho: Caxton, 1952.

Ganaway, Loomis Morton. *New Mexico and the Sectional Controversy, 1846–1861*. Philadelphia: Porcupine, 1976.

Goebel, Julius, Jr., and T. Raymond Naughton. *Law Enforcement in Colonial New York: A Study in Criminal Procedure. (1664–1776)*. Montclair, New Jersey: Patterson Smith, 1970.

Goff, John S. *The Supreme Court Justices, 1863–1912*. Cave Creek, Ariz.: Black Mountain Press, 1975.

Gregg, Robert D. *The Influence of Border Troubles on Relations Between the United States and Mexico, 1876–1910*. New York: Da Capo, 1970.

Griggs, George. *History of Mesilla Valley, or the Gadsden Purchase, Known in Mexico as the Treaty of Mesilla*. Mesilla, N.M.: n. pub., 1930.

Haley, J. Evetts. *Jeff Milton: A Good Man With a Gun*. Norman: University of Oklahoma, 1948.

Hayes, Jess G. *Apache Vengeance: The True Story of Apache Kid*. Albuquerque: University of New Mexico, 1954.

———. *Boots and Bullets: The Life and Times of John W. Wentworth*. Tucson: University of Arizona Press, 1967.

———. *Sheriff Thompson's Day: Turbulence in Arizona Territory*. Tucson: University of Arizona, 1968.

Hertzog, Peter. *Legal Hangings, New Mexico, 1861–1923*. Western Americana Series, No. 10. Santa Fe: Press of the Territorian, 1966.

Horn, Calvin. *New Mexico's Troubled Years: The Story of the Early Territorial Governors*. Albuquerque: Horn & Wallace, 1963.

Hornung, Chuck. *The Thin Gray Line—The New Mexico Mounted Police*. Fort Worth, Tex.: Western Heritage, 1971.

Hughes, Delbert Littrell. *Give Me Room! [Marion Littrell]*, *1855–1910*. El Paso, Tex.: Hughes Pub., 1971.

Hunt, Aurora. *Kirby Benedict, Frontier Federal Judge, An Account of Legal and Judicial Development in the Southwest, 1853–1874*. Glendale, Calif.: Arthur H. Clark, 1961.

———. *Major General James Henry Carleton, 1814–1873: Western Frontier Dragoon*. Glendale, Calif.: Arthur H. Clark, 1958.

Hunt, Frazier. *Cap Mossman: Last of the Great Cowmen*. New York: Hastings House, 1951.

———. *The Tragic Days of Billy the Kid*. New York: Hastings House, 1956.

Ireland, Robert M. *The County Courts in Antebellum Kentucky*. Lexington: University of Kentucky, 1972.

Jolly, John Pershing. *History, National Guard of New Mexico, 1606–1963*. Comps. Russell C. Charleston and William A. Poe. Santa Fe: Adjutant-General's Department, State of New Mexico, 1964.

Karraker, Cyrus Harreld. *The Seventeenth-Century Sheriff: A Comparative Study of the Sheriff in England and the Chesapeake Colonies, 1607–1689*. Chapel Hill: University of North Carolina, 1930.

Keleher, William A. *The Fabulous Frontier: Twelve New Mexico Items*, rev. ed. Albuquerque: University of New Mexico, 1962.

———. *New Mexicans I Knew: Memoirs, 1892–1969*. Intro. Lawrence R. Murphy. Albuquerque: University of New Mexico Press, 1983.

———. *Turmoil in New Mexico, 1846–1868*. Santa Fe: Rydal, 1952.

———. *Violence in Lincoln County, 1869–1881: A New Mexico Item*. Albuquerque: University of New Mexico Press, 1957.

Kelly, George H., comp. *Legislative History: Arizona, 1864–1912*. Phoenix: Manufacturing Stationers, 1926.

Lamar, Howard Roberts. *The Far Southwest, 1846–1912: A Territorial History*. New York: W. W. Norton, 1970.

Larson, Robert W. *New Mexico Populism: A Study of Radical Protest in a Western Territory*. Boulder: Colorado Associated University Press, 1974.

Lavash, Donald R. *Sheriff William Brady: Tragic Hero of the Lincoln County War*. Santa Fe: Sunstone, 1986.

Lockwood, Frank C. *Pioneer Days in Arizona: From Spanish Occupation to Statehood*. New York: Macmillan, 1932.

McClintock, James H. *Arizona: Prehistoric—Aboriginal—Pioneer—Modern: The Nation's Youngest Commonwealth Within a Land of Ancient Culture*. 2 vols. Chicago: S. J. Clarke, 1916.

McCool, Grace. *So Said the Coroner: How They Died in Old Cochise*. Tombstone: Epitaph, 1968.

McCright, Grady and James H. Powell. *Jessie Evans: Lincoln County Badman*. College Station, Tex.: Creative Publishers, 1983.

McWilliams, Carey. *North from Mexico: The Spanish-Speaking People of the United States*. New York: Greenwood, 1968.

Masur, Louis P. *Rites of Execution: Capital Punishment and the Transformation of American Culture, 1776–1865*. New York: Oxford University, 1989.

Mayer, Brantz. *Mexico: Aztec, Spanish and Republican*. 2 vols. in 1. Hartford, Conn.: S. Drake, 1851.

Metz, Leon C. *Pat Garrett: The Story of a Western Lawman*. Norman: University of Oklahoma, 1974.

———. *John Selman: Texas Gunfighter*. New York: Hastings House, 1966.

Monkonnen, Eric H. *Police in Urban America, 1860–1920*. Cambridge: Cambridge University, 1981.

Morn, Frank. *'The Eye That Never Sleeps': A History of the Pinkerton National Detective Agency*. Bloomington: Indiana University, 1982.

Morris, William Alfred. *The Medieval Sheriff to 1300*. New York: Barnes and Noble, 1968.

Murphy, James M. *Laws, Courts, & Lawyers: Through the Years in Arizona*. Tucson: University of Arizona, 1970.

Myers, John Myers. *I. Jack Swilling: Founder of Phoenix, Arizona*. New York: Hastings House, 1961.

Parsons, Chuck. *Clay Allison: Portrait of a Shootist*. Seagraves, Tex.: Pioneer Book Pub., 1983.

Patterson, Richard. *Train Robbery, The Birth, Flowering, and Decline of a Notorious Western Enterprise*. Boulder, Colo.: Johnson, 1981.

Pearson, Jim Berry. *The Maxwell Land Grant*. Norman: University of Oklahoma, 1961.

Poldervaart, Arie W. *Black-Robed Justice: A History of Justice in New Mexico from the American Occupation in 1846 until Statehood in 1912*. Historical Society of New Mexico Publications in History, vol. 13. Santa Fe: Historical Society of New Mexico, 1948.

Prassel, Frank Richard. *The Western Peace Officer: A Legacy of Law and Order*. Norman: University of Oklahoma, 1972.

Prucha, Francis Paul. *Broadax and Bayonet: The Role of the United States Army in the Development of the Northwest, 1815–1860*. Lincoln: University of Nebraska, 1967.

Raynor, Ted. *Old Timers Talk in Southwestern New Mexico*. El Paso: Texas Western, 1960.

Rees, Donna. *The History, Development and Present Administration of the Mohave County Jail*. N. p.: July 1974.

Rosa, Joseph G. *The Gunfighter: Man or Myth?* Norman: University of Oklahoma, 1969.

Rosenbaum, Robert J. *Mexicano Resistance in the Southwest: 'The Sacred Right of Self-Protection.'* Austin: University of Tex., 1981.

Sacks, B[enjamin]. *Arizona's Angry Man: United States Marshal Milton B. Duffield*. Arizona Monographs, No. 1. Tempe: Arizona Historical Foundation, 1970.

Savage, Pat. *One Last Frontier: A Story of Indians, Early Settlers and Old Ranches of Northern Arizona*. New York: Exposition, 1964.

Schmitt, Jo Ann. *Fighting Editors: The Story of Editors Who Faced Six-Shooters with Pens and Won*. San Antonio, Tex.: Naylor, 1958.

Shelton, Wilma Loy, comp. *Checklist of New Mexico Publications, 1850–1953*. Albuquerque: University of New Mexico Press, 1954.

Shinkle, James D. *Fifty Years of Roswell History—1867–1917*. Roswell, N. Mex.: Hall-Poorbaugh, 1964.

Simmons, Marc. *Albuquerque: A Narrative History*. Albuquerque: University of New Mexico, 1982.

———. *Spanish Government in New Mexico*. Albuquerque: University of New Mexico, 1968.

Smith, Cornelius C., Jr. *Emilio Kosterlitzky: Eagle of Sonora and the Southwest Border*. Glendale, Calif.: Arthur H. Clark, 1970.

———. *William Sanders Oury: History-Maker of the Southwest*. Tucson: University of Arizona, 1967.

Snowflake Centennial Committee. *The Life and Times of Snowflake, 1878–1978: A History in Stories*. Snowflake, Ariz.: 1978.

Sonnichsen, Charles Leland. *Billy King's Tombstone: The Private Life of an Arizona Boom Town*. Tucson: University of Arizona, 1972.

———. *Outlaw, Bill Mitchell, Alias Baldy Russell: His Life and Times*. Denver: Sage, 1965.

———. *Roy Bean: Law West of the Pecos*. New York: Macmillan, 1944.

———. *Tularosa: Last of the Frontier West*. New York: Devin-Adair, 1963.

Sparks, William. *The Apache Kid, A Bear Fight and Other True Stories from the Old West*. Los Angeles: Skelton, 1926.

Stanley, F. (Stanley Crocchiola). *Dave Rudabaugh: Border Ruffian*. Denver: World Press, 1961.

———. *Desperadoes of New Mexico*. Denver: World Press, 1953.

———. *Giant in Lilliput: The Story of Donaciano Vigil*. Pampa, Tex.: Pampa Print Shop, 1963.

———. *Jim Courtright: Two Gun Marshal of Fort Worth*. Denver: World Press, 1957.

——. *No Tears for Black Jack Ketchum.* Denver: World Press, 1958.

Stevens, Robert C., ed. *Echoes of the Past: Tales of Old Yavapai.* 2 vols. Prescott, Ariz.: Yavapai Cowbelles, Inc., 1964.

Taylor, Morris F. *O. P. McMains and the Maxwell Land Grant Conflict.* Tucson: University of Arizona, 1979.

Trover, Ellen Lloyd. *Chronology and Documentary Handbook of the State of Arizona.* New York: Oceana Pub., 1972.

Twitchell, Ralph Emerson. *Leading Facts of New Mexican History.* 2 vols. Albuquerque, New Mexico: Horn & Wallace, 1963. Orig. pub. 1917.

——. *Old Santa Fe: The Story of New Mexico's Ancient Capital.* Chicago: Rio Grande Press, 1963. Orig. pub. 1925.

——. *The History of the Military Occupation of the Territory of New Mexico.* New York: Arno, 1976. Orig. pub. 1909.

Utley, Robert M. *High Noon in Lincoln: Violence on the Western Frontier.* Albuquerque: University of New Mexico Press, 1987.

Wagoner, Jay J. *Arizona Territory, 1863–1912: A Political History.* Tucson: University of Arizona, 1970.

——. *Early Arizona: Prehistory to the Civil War.* Tucson: University of Arizona, 1975.

Walker, Dale L. *Death Was the Black Horse: The Story of Rough Rider Buckey O'Neill.* Austin, Tex.: Madrona Press, 1975.

Walters, Lorenzo. *Tombstone's Yesterdays.* Tucson: Acme, 1928.

Waters, Frank. *The Earp Brothers of Tombstone: The Story of Mrs. Virgil Earp.* New York: Clarkson N. Potter, 1960.

Way, Thomas E. *The Parker Story.* Prescott, Ariz.: Prescott Graphics, 1981.

Webb, Walter Prescott, ed.-in-chief. *The Handbook of Texas.* 3 vols. Austin: Texas State Historical Association, 1952. Vol. 3, ed. Eldon Stephen Branda, 1976.

Weiner, Melissa Ruffner. *Prescott Yesteryears: Life in Arizona's First Territorial Capital.* Prescott, Primrose, 1976.

Westphall, Victor. *Thomas Benton Catron and His Era.* Tucson: University of Arizona, 1973.

White, Leonard D. *The Federalists: A Study in Administrative History.* New York: Macmillan, 1956.

Whitman, S. E. *The Troopers: An Informal History of the Plains Cavalry.* New York: Hastings House, 1962.

Williams, Sally Munds. *History of Valuable Pioneers of the State of Arizona.* N. p.: 1979.

Wilson, John P. *Merchants, Guns & Money: The Story of Lincoln County and Its Wars.* Santa Fe: Museum of New Mexico, 1987.

Woody, Clara T., and Milton L. Schwartz. *Globe, Arizona.* Tucson: Arizona Historical Society, 1977.

Wunder, John R. *Inferior Courts, Superior Justice: A History of the Justice of the Peace on the Northwest Frontier, 1853–1889.* Westport, Conn.: Greenwood, 1979.

Young, Herbert. V. *They Came to Jerome.* Jerome, Arizona: n. pub., 1972.

PERIODICALS

Anderson, Mike. "Posses and Politics in Pima County: The Administration of Sheriff Charles Shibell." *Journal of Arizona History* 27: 253–82.

Baker, A. C. "Interview with Hon. A. C. Baker at Phoenix, Arizona, March 23, 1917." *Arizona Historical Review* 2: 73–87.

Ball, Larry D. "Frontier Sheriffs at Work." *Journal of Arizona History* 27: 286–96.

———. "The Frontier Sheriff's Role in Law and Order." *Western Legal History* 4: 13–25.

———. "Lawman in Disgrace: Sheriff Charles C. Perry of Chaves County, New Mexico." *New Mexico Historical Review*. 61: 125–36.

———. "Militia Posses: The Territorial Militia in Civil Law Enforcement in New Mexico Territory, 1877–1883." *New Mexico Historical Review*. 55: 47–70.

———. "'No Cure, No Pay,' A Tom Horn Letter." *Journal of Arizona History*. 8: 200–202.

———. "Outlaws of the Southwest, 1895–1905." *Denver Westerners' Brand Book*. 20: 281–99.

———. "The People As Law Enforcers: The 'Posse Comitatus' in New Mexico and Arizona Territories." *Quarterly of the National Association for Outlaw and Lawman History*. 6: 2–10, 22.

———. "'This High-Handed Outrage': Marshal William Kidder Meade in a Mexican Jail." *Journal of Arizona History* 17 (Summer 1976): 219–232.

Blair, Bob D. "The Murder of William Joe Giles, 1905." *Journal of Arizona History* 7: 27–34.

Bloom, Lansing B. "Beginnings of Representational Government in New Mexico." *El Palacio* 12: 74–78.

Boyer, Glenn G. "Johnny Behan: Assistant Folk Hero." *Real West* Spring 1983.

Brooks, Clinton E. and Frank D. Reeve, eds. "James A. Bennett: A Dragoon in New Mexico, 1850–56." *New Mexico Historical Review*. 22: 140–76.

Carter, A. G., as told to C. L. Sonnichsen. "Neighborhood Talk About Pat Garrett." *Old West* 7: 20–22, 62–64.

Coleman, Evans. "The Jury Strike at Solomonville." *Journal of Arizona History*. 16: 323–34.

Colley, Charles C. "Carl T. Hayden: Phoenician." *Journal of Arizona History*. 18: 247–58.

DeArment, Robert K. "The Blood-Spattered Trail of Milton J. Yarberry." *Old West* 22: 8–14.

Dobson, John M. "Desperadoes and Diplomacy: The Territory of Arizona v. Jesus Garcia, 1893." *Journal of Arizona History*. 17: 137–60.

Donoho, Ron. "Lore of the 'Tin Star.'" *Collector's World* (July–August 1970): 6–9.

Doran, Andrew James. "Interesting Reminiscences." *Arizona Historical Review* 1: 54–62.

Edwards, Harold L. "Barney Mason: In the Shadow of Pat Garrett and Billy the Kid." *Old West* 26: 14–19.

Ethington, Philip J. "Vigilantes and the Police: The Creation of a Professional Police Bureaucracy in San Francisco, 1847–1900." *Journal of Social History* 21: 197–227.

Fireman, Bert M. "Fremont's Arizona Adventure." *American West* 1: 8–19.

"The First Election in Maricopa County." *The Sheriff* [Arizona]. 7: 5–11.

"From Whence It Came: Title and Badge." *The Sheriff* [Arizona]. 25: 25–28.

Heiges, R. E. "Goodbye to the Sheriff." *Social Science* 11: 137–41.

Hogan, William F. "John Miller: Pioneer Lawman." *Arizoniana* [now *Journal of Arizona History*] 4: 41–45.

Hornung, Chuck. "The Lynching of Gus Mentzer." *Real West* Special ed. Spring 1986: 31–37.

Jones, Oakah L. "Lew Wallace: Hoosier Governor of Territorial New Mexico, 1878–81." *New Mexico Historical Review* 60: 129–58.

Jordan, Philip D. "The Town Marshal: Local Arm of the Law." *Arizona and the West* 16: 321–42.

Kelly, George H. "First Term District Court Held in Graham County." *Arizona Historical Review*. 1: 63–67.

Kemp, Ben W. "Nat Straw—Squawman." *Frontier Times* 54: 28–30.

Kildaire, Maurice. "The Fastest Gun in Phoenix." *Frontier Times,* n. s. 42: 16–19, 57–59.

Ladd, Robert E. "Vengeance at the O. K. Corral." *Arizoniana* [now *Journal of Arizona History*] 4: 1–10.

Lockwood, Frank C. "John Lorenzo Hubbell, Navajo Indian Trader." University of Arizona Bulletin, No. 6. July 1942.

Loyola, Sister Mary. "The American Occupation of New Mexico, 1821–1852." *New Mexico Historical Review* 14: 34–75.

McInnes, Toni and Robert. "George C. Ruffner: Frontier Sheriff." *The Sheriff* [Arizona] 9: 17.

McKinney, Joe T. "Reminiscences of J. T. McKinney." *Arizona Historical Review* 5:33–54.

Metz, Leon C. "An Incident at Christmas." *Quarterly of the National Association for Outlaw and Lawman History* 14: 1, 9, 15–16.

Moorman, Donald R. "Holm O. Bursum, Sheriff, 1894." *New Mexico Historical Review* 39: 333–44.

Morgan, Charles M. "Sheriff Commodore Owens Shoots Straight." *The Sheriff* [Arizona] 4: 89, 91.

Mulligan, Raymond A. "New York Foundlings at Clifton-Morenci: Social Justice in Arizona, 1904–1905." *Arizona and the West*, 6: 104–18.

Mullin, R. N. "An Item from Old Mesilla." *Password* 15: 128–29.

"Necrology" [Abe Spiegelberg]. *New Mexico Historical Review* 3: 116–19.

O'Dell, Roy. "Joseph Casey—Arizona Escape Artist." *Quarterly of the National Outlaw and Lawman Association* 13: 22–24.

Pearce, Joe, and Richard Summer. "Joe Pearce—Manhunter." *Journal of Arizona History* 19: 249–60.

Peters, James Steven. "Postmortem of an Assassination: Parson Tolby and the Maxwell Land Grant Fight." *Texana* 11: 328–61.

Pinkerton, William. "Highwaymen." *North American Review* 157: 530–40.

Potter, Jack. "Riding with Black Jack [sic]." *Sheriff and Police Journal* [Taos, N. M.]. n.d., pp. 9, 17, 19, 25, 29.

Rasch, Philip J. "A. Ham Mills—Sheriff of Lincoln County." *English Westerners' Brand Book* 4: 11–12.

———. "Death Comes to Saint Johns." *Quarterly of the National Association for Outlaw and Lawman History* 7: 1–8.

———. "The Horrell War." *New Mexico Historical Review* 31: 223–31.

———. "John Kinney: King of the Rustlers." *English Westerners' Brand Book* 4: 10–12.

———. "The Las Cruces Bank Robbery." *Frontier Times*, n. s. 55: 48–50.

———. "Murder in the American Valley." *English Westerners' Brand Book* 7: 2–7.

———. "The Pecos War." *Panhandle-Plains Historical Review* 29: 101–111.

———. "Prelude to War: The Murder of John Henry Tunstall." *English Westerners' Brand Book* 12: 1–10.

———. "The Rustler War." *New Mexico Historical Review* 39: 257–73.

———. "Sudden Death in Cimarron." *Quarterly of the National Association for Outlaw and Lawman History* 10: 6–8.

———. "The Trials of Lieutenant-Colonel Dudley." *English Westerners' Brand Book* 7: 1–7.

———, and Lee Myers. "Les Dow, Sheriff of Eddy County." *New Mexico Historical Review* 49: 241–52.

Rice, Michael M. "Pete Gabriel Was Fearless." *The Sheriff* [Arizona] 29: 50.

Ridgway, William B. "Climax Jim, Outlaw Houdini." *The Sheriff* [Arizona] 13: 44.

Roberts, Gary L. "Gunfight at OK Corral: The Wells Spicer Decision: 1881." *Montana, the Magazine of Western History* 20: 62–74.

Romero, Trancito. "I Saw Black Jack Hanged." *True West* 6: 27–28.

Rube, Bernts. "A Yuma Tragedy." *Quarterly of the National Association of Outlaw and Lawman History* 5: 16–18.

Russell, Sharman Apt. "Russian Bill: The True Story of an Outlaw." *Journal of the West* 23: 91–93.

Schmidt, Mrs. Kurt. "Vignettes of Arizona Pioneers: Commodore Perry Owens." *Arizoniana* 1: 6–8.

Spude, Robert L. "Mineral Frontiers in Transition: Copper Mining in Arizona, 1880–1885." *New Mexico Historical Review* 51: 19–34.

Tittmann, Edward D. "By Order of Richard Campbell." *New Mexico Historical Review* 3: 390–98.

———. "The Last Legal Frontier." *New Mexico Historical Review* 2: 219–27.

Toohey, Elizabeth. "No Sissies Here in Old Days." *Arizona Peace Officers' Magazine* 1: 11–28.

Traub, Stuart H. "Rewards, Bounty Hunting, and Criminal Justice in the West, 1865– 1900." *Western Historical Quarterly* 19: 287–302.

Turner, Allton. "New Mexico Shoot-Out." *Frontier Times* 43: 36–37.

Walker, Henry P. "'Retire Peaceably to Your Homes': Arizona Faces Martial Law, 1882." *Journal of Arizona History* 10: 1–18.

Winslowe, John R. "The Making of a Renegade [Navajo Frank]." *Old West* 5: 52–55.

Zarbin, Earl. "'The Whole Thing Was Done So Quietly': The Phoenix Lynchings of 1879." *Journal of Arizona History* 21: 353–62.

THESES AND DISSERTATIONS

Bloom, Maude Elizabeth. "History of the Mesilla Valley." Master's thesis, New Mexico College of Agriculture and Mechanic Arts, 1903.

Donlon, Walter John. "Lebaron Bradford Prince: Chief Justice and Governor of New Mexico Territory, 1879–1893." Ph.D. diss., University of New Mexico, 1967.

Hollister, Charles A. "The Organization and Administration of the Sheriff's Office in Arizona." Master's thesis, University of Arizona, 1946.

Miller, Richard. "Noah M. Broadway." Master's thesis, Arizona State University, [1975?].

Peterson, Charles Sharon. "Settlement on the Little Colorado, 1873–1900: A Study of the Processes and Institutions of Mormon Expansion." Ph.D. diss., University of Utah, August 1967.

Waite, John C., Jr. "An Annotated Subject Bibliography of the Acts, Resolutions, and Memorials of the Arizona Territorial Legislature, from 1864 to 1899." Master's thesis, University of Arizona, 1970.

Vanderwood, Paul Joseph. "The Rurales: Mexico's Rural Police Force, 1861–1914." Ph.D. diss., University of Texas, Austin, 1970.

AUTHOR INTERVIEWS

Mary Foraker, Albuquerque, N.M., 12 August 1976.

ATLASES

Beck, Warren A., and Ynez D. Haase. *Historical Atlas of New Mexico.* Norman: University of Oklahoma, 1969.

Walker, Henry P., and Don Bufkin. *Historical Atlas of Arizona*. Norman: University of Oklahoma, 1979.

REFERENCE WORKS

Encyclopedia of the Social Sciences. Edwin R. A. Seligman, editor-in-chief. 15 vols. New York: Macmillan, 1930–34.

Index